CW00823547

Nietzsche and Political Thought

Studies in Contemporary German Social Thought
Thomas McCarthy, General Editor

Theodor W. Adorno, *Against Epistemology: A Metacritique*

Theodor W. Adorno, *Prisms*

Karl-Otto Apel, *Understanding and Explanation: A Transcendental-Pragmatic Perspective*

Richard J. Bernstein, editor, *Habermas and Modernity*

Ernst Bloch, *Natural Law and Human Dignity*

Ernst Bloch, *The Principle of Hope*

Ernst Bloch, *The Utopian Function of Art and Literature: Selected Essays*

Hans Blumenberg, *The Genesis of the Copernican World*

Hans Blumenberg, *The Legitimacy of the Modern Age*

Hans Blumenberg, *Work on Myth*

Helmut Dubiel, *Theory and Politics: Studies in the Development of Critical Theory*

John Forester, editor, *Critical Theory and Public Life*

David Frisby, *Fragments of Modernity: Theories of Modernity in the Work of Simmel, Kracauer and Benjamin*

Hans-Georg Gadamer, *Philosophical Apprenticeships*

Hans-Georg Gadamer, *Reason in the Age of Science*

Jürgen Habermas, *The Philosophical Discourse of Modernity: Twelve Lectures*

Jürgen Habermas, *Philosophical-Political Profiles*

Jürgen Habermas, editor, *Observations on "The Spiritual Situation of the Age"*

Hans Joas, *G. H. Mead: A Contemporary Re-examination of His Thought*

Reinhart Koselleck, *Critique and Crisis: Enlightenment and the Pathogenesis of Modern Society*

Reinhart Koselleck, *Futures Past: On the Semantics of Historical Time*

Harry Liebersohn, *Fate and Utopia in German Sociology, 1870–1923*

Herbert Marcuse, *Hegel's Ontology and the Theory of Historicity*

Claus Offe, *Contradictions of the Welfare State*

Claus Offe, *Disorganized Capitalism: Contemporary Transformations of Work and Politics*

Helmut Peukert, *Science, Action, and Fundamental Theology: Toward a Theology of Communicative Action*

Joachim Ritter, *Hegel and the French Revolution: Essays on the* Philosophy of Right

Alfred Schmidt, *History and Structure: An Essay on Hegelian-Marxist and Structuralist Theories of History*

Dennis Schmidt, *The Ubiquity of the Finite: Hegel, Heidegger, and the Entitlements of Philosophy*

Carl Schmitt, *The Crisis of Parliamentary Democracy*

Carl Schmitt, *Political Romanticism*

Carl Schmitt, *Political Theology: Four Chapters on the Concept of Sovereignty*

Gary Smith, editor, *On Walter Benjamin: Critical Essays and Recollections*

Michael Theunissen, *The Other: Studies in the Social Ontology of Husserl, Heidegger, Sartre, and Buber*

Ernst Tugendhat, *Self-Consciousness and Self-Determination*

Mark Warren, *Nietzsche and Political Thought*

Nietzsche and Political Thought

Mark Warren

The MIT Press, Cambridge, Massachusetts, and London, England

© 1988 Massachusetts Institute of Technology

All rights reserved. No part of this book may be reproduced in any form by any electronic or mechanical means (including photocopying, recording, or information storage and retrieval) without permission in writing from the publisher.

This book was set in Baskerville by Asco Trade Typesetting Ltd., Hong Kong, and printed and bound by Halliday Lithograph in the United States of America.

Library of Congress Cataloging-in-Publication Data

Warren, Mark (Mark E.)
 Nietzsche and political thought/Mark Warren.

       p.   cm. — (Studies in contemporary German social thought)
 Bibliography: p.
 Includes index.
 ISBN 0-262-23135-2
 1. Nietzsche, Friedrich Wilhelm, 1844–1900 — Political and social views. I. Title. II. Series.
 JC233.N52W37 1988   320'.01 — dc19   87-21274

Contents

Contents

Preface

My aim in this study is to look at Nietzsche in light of critical and postmodern political thought. This means that the study is not primarily about Nietzsche's own political theory, but rather about what his philosophy as a whole implies for political thought today. My interests here are less scholastic than theoretical: I am especially interested in Nietzsche's pivotal role in the transition from modern to postmodern approaches to philosophical issues, and in what this transition implies for political thought. By "modern" I generally mean to characterize rationalist approaches that, roughly since the Enlightenment, have relied on metaphysical (that is, real but nonempirical) characterizations of human agency as a knowing subject and rational actor. By "postmodern," I simply mean those approaches that try to do without metaphysical characterizations of human agency—attempts that begin, at least self-consciously, with Nietzsche.

My own sympathies lie halfway between modernism and postmodernism. On the one hand, I accept a number of the ideals of modern rationalism, including the notion that humans ought to be able to use their reason to decide on courses of action, control their futures, enter into reciprocal agreements, and be responsible for what they do and who they are. My suggestion throughout this book, however, is that these ideals are possible only within a postmodern view of the world: modernism lacks an account of how its ideals are possible. We ought not to presume that the individual capacities we usually think of as defining one's agency, subjectivity, or self (terms I use more or less interchangeably) are metaphysically given. Rather, it seems to me that we must find ways of thinking about how these capacities emerge within a contingent, historical universe.

It is with this concern that I return to Nietzsche, whom I take to be the first thoroughgoing postmodern, and who has in many ways become the symbol of postmodernism. But it is also important for my concerns that Nietzsche is not simply postmodern, if by "postmodern" one means only to identify ways of thinking that break with modernist categories and ideals. In important ways he reconceives central ideals of modern rationalism, especially the ideal of humans as agents with capacities for freedom, sovereignty, reciprocity, and responsibility. If I am right, Nietzsche reinterprets these ideals as immanent possibilities of human practices, and at the same time uses these possibilities to distinguish between better and worse practices. The result is what I shall sometimes refer to as a "critical postmodernism." As I suggest throughout this book, the bulk of contemporary literature has missed this critically postmodern Nietzsche, much of it consisting either in traditional or modernist rejections, or in postmodern celebrations. This polarity of interpretations has made it difficult to engage those aspects of Nietzsche from which we might learn.

The interpretation I offer is, of course, contestable. Nietzsche's texts move in very many directions, and which of these one deems most important is as much a function of current concerns as of the texts themselves. In looking at Nietzsche through questions of postmodern transitions, I take the liberty of developing and exploring these suggestions in ways that I see as consistent with Nietzsche's philosophy. In certain cases—mostly those involving his political thought—I suggest that developing some aspect of Nietzsche's thought would violate another, and I conclude that the conflict itself is important for assessing his limits. What I am interested in here are the problems themselves, and the manner of Nietzsche's approach. I leave it to the reader to decide the extent to which my ways of dealing with these problems are in Nietzsche or are my own extrapolations based on what I take to be fruitful suggestions. The line between these possibilities is not always clear in an interpretive project, and this one is no exception. I do not mean to imply that Nietzsche's texts place no limits on possible interpretations. To the contrary, it seems to me that making sense of postmodern transitions in political thought especially requires making sense of those texts that seem contradictory, enigmatic, or incomprehensible, as well as attending to those many texts that are usually ignored.

Yet even methods of textual reading and selection are controversial, including those I use here. Perhaps most controversial will be my approach to the question of the continuity between Nietzsche's philosophical concerns (about ontology, epistemology, and ethics) and his political visions (about what is a possible and desirable political life). Typically, one makes the methodological assumption that a thinker's positions are cut from the same cloth, that they are consistent pieces of a more comprehensive whole. I assume that this unity exists in Nietzsche, but I do not assume, as do many commentators, that his philosophical positions uniquely determine his political judgments and conclusions. Rather, I argue that his philosophical concerns are narrowed by a number of assumptions about social and political life. These assumptions are both insupportable and extraneous to his postmodern concerns, as is evident once they are identified. By isolating these assumptions, I aim to show both the continuity within Nietzsche's thought and how—once one removes the insupportable assumptions—the political possibilities of his philosophy are much broader than he himself imagined or desired. My interpretive goal is to liberate the possibilities of Nietzsche's postmodern transitions from the distortions of his politics, but without ignoring his politics, and without eclecticism. I make this argument at length in the last chapter of this book, and presuppose it in the first part, where I am mostly concerned with the possibilities of Nietzsche's thoughts about human agency.

Another controversial point of method will be the way I use Nietzsche's texts to support my interpretation. I assume that his texts are consistent with one another, and I draw textual support from all his works, often to support a single point. I do so respecting only the differences between published and unpublished materials, as well as differences between early, middle, and late works. One objection to this approach will be that it ignores the importance of style in Nietzsche because it fractures the unity of each work. This unity of style and substance is not accidental, but reflects Nietzsche's concern with overcoming the metaphysical implications of language when used in propositional form. The substance of what Nietzsche has to say can only be appreciated by interpreting the movement and continuity of single texts.

That Nietzsche's style is a form of argument is beyond dispute, and no one who has enjoyed the beauty, wit, and force of his writing could wish to dispute it. Much of what Nietzsche has to say can only be appreciated through careful attention to the movement of his texts, and many contemporary interpretations are exemplary in this respect. Yet this is never enough, nor for that matter is it even a good way of entering Nietzsche's thought. When one infers meaning from style, one presupposes a specific account of how this is possible, in terms of relations between rules and meanings, between author and audience, and between interpretation and practice. This means that one ought to be able to reconstruct an *explicit* account of the kind of world in which some kinds of truths or insights cannot be formulated in direct propositions. Indeed, failure to articulate these assumptions can lead to conclusions that are bizarre, as well as being quite uncharacteristic of Nietzsche. It is common in literary interpretations of Nietzsche, for example, to confuse the world with a text by mistaking reality with discursive reality, points I explore in chapters 2 and 5. Moreover, there is a general tendency in readings that emphasize style to fall back on metaphor and style too quickly, often as a way of explaining apparent contradictions or other points that seem inexplicable. Thus, Nietzsche's straightforward propositions are ignored, and he is made to seem inarticulate and fuzzy—something he almost never is. This in turn is often used as an excuse to provide preferred readings of Nietzsche, or simply to make the point, after which nothing more can be said. What I am suggesting is simply that a critical reconstruction of Nietzsche's philosophy needs to coexist with readings of style and metaphor. I intend to provide such a reconstruction here.

Another point of controversy will be my reliance on portions of Nietzsche's *Nachlass*—his unpublished notes, manuscripts, fragments, plans and the like, many of which were collected by at the behest of his sister, Elizabeth Förster-Nietzsche, under the title *Der Wille zur Macht* (*The Will to Power*). There are two schools of thought on the use of the *Nachlass*. At one extreme is Heidegger, who argues that the *Nachlass*, especially *The Will to Power*, contains the philosophy that Nietzsche intended to and would have written, had he not lost his mental capacities.[1] Nietzsche did in fact leave dozens of plans for a *magnum opus* to be entitled *The Will to Power*. At the other extreme is Bernd Magnus, who argues that the *Nachlass* ought not to be used at all since Nietzsche rejected his plan to write a book entitled *The Will to Power* in 1888, several months before his insanity.[2] Moreover, what was eventually published as *The Will to Power* was based on an outline and included a number of notes that he rejected in February 1888. Thus what we have today as *The Will to Power* is nothing more than a random collection of notes written between 1883 and 1888, whose philological status is ambiguous at best. Magnus suggests that the primary motivation of those who use *The Will to Power* in their interpretations of Nietzsche is to find notes that portray a "metaphysical" Nietzsche, a Nietzsche that is less postmodern than the image that comes from his published texts alone. Heidegger is a case in point. In contrast, most of the *Nachlass* that does not rely on metaphysical language was incorporated into published work in one way or another. For these reasons, Magnus argues that there are no good reasons for referring to the *Nachlass* at all.

I take the position of a moderate on this issue: Heidegger clearly uses the *Nachlass* to give a "metaphysical" reading of Nietzsche, something I shall comment on in appropriate places. Yet the fact that the *Nachlass* can be abused, that *The Will to Power* can be confused with one of Nietzsche's books, and that the notes are often tentative and sketchy, does not mean that they ought to be avoided altogether. The issue is rather one of knowing when referring to the *Nachlass* is appropriate. It is clearly inappropriate when there is a conflict between notes and published works, as there sometimes is. In these cases, one must simply note the conflict and opt for the published material. But in other cases, the notes are extremely useful. Sometimes they throw light on terse and unelaborated comments in the published texts. Often, they give insight into the ways in which Nietzsche thought, again making the task of understanding his published work less formidable. Finally, there is material in the *Nachlass* that is clearly implied in the published work, but not spelled out. It is especially in these latter cases that we must speculate on Nietzsche's motives for not publishing these notes. Certainly, he may have simply decided to reject them. But we also know that he did not have time to finish his work before his insanity, notwithstanding his immense productivity in the few years preceding. Plans for a major work, for example, were not dropped when Nietzsche finally rejected the plan for a book called *The Will to Power*. He replaced *The Will to Power* with plans for a new *magnum opus* in four parts, to have been entitled *Umwertung aller Werte* (*Revaluation of All Values*), of which *The Antichrist* was to have been the first part. Thus we might quite reasonably expect to find anticipations of future work in the *Nachlass* that never appeared in published work. What these considerations suggest is that while one must be cautious in using the *Nachlass*, it would be foolish to reject them out of hand. In my use of the *Nachlass* here, I follow a few simple rules. Where there are conflicts between the *Nachlass* and published texts, I opt for the published texts. Where the texts are similar, I favor the published versions. Where I use material that can only be found in the *Nachlass*, in many cases I provide references from published texts that would support my interpretation.

A final point of methodological controversy has to do with the division of Nietzsche's texts into early, middle, and late periods. Most commentators agree that there are differences between these texts, but differ as to their significance. I see the divisions as significant for problems of postmodern transitions, and divide Nietzsche's published texts accordingly. *The Birth of Tragedy* (1872) is the only purely "early" work, and is distinguished by Nietzsche's metaphysical use of categories (see chapter 2 on this point). The four essays that comprise the *Untimely Meditations* (1873–1876) are transitional: residual uses of metaphysical explanations remain, but the burden of argument does not depend on them. *Human, All-Too-Human* (1878–1880) and *Daybreak* (1881) are middle period works, characterized by criticisms of prevailing values. One finds no metaphysical residuals here, but also little philosophic reconstruction. *The Gay Science* (1882) is transitional to Nietzsche's mature works: here one finds a systematic concern with how interpretations relate to forms of life, power, and historical evolution. *Thus Spoke Zarathustra* (1883–1885) is the first fully mature work, in which one can find most of the central themes and arguments of the mature period. This is followed by *Beyond Good and Evil* (1886), which contains the most comprehensive of Nietzsche's philosophical analyses, and is in turn followed in rapid succession by *On the Genealogy of Morals* (1887), *The Case of Wagner* (1888), *Twilight of the Idols* (1888), *Nietzsche contra Wagner* (1888), *The Antichrist* (1888), and *Ecce Homo* (1888). Since these texts contain most of Nietzsche's philosophic reconstruction, I rely most heavily on them, and read earlier texts as anticipations of mature conclusions.

A comment on gender biased language is no doubt in order as well, especially in light of Nietzsche's well-known misogyny. Where Nietzsche's own language is gender biased, I replicate it in order to avoid anachronistic usage. In my own usage, I have tried to reconcile neutrality with style, except in those very few cases where gender specificity actually makes a difference to Nietzsche's points. Regrettably, there are a few cases in which neutral alternatives would seem clumsy, forced, or distracting; in these cases I have opted for compromises in which gender biased language wins out. For this I apologize in advance.

I have incurred many debts in the process of writing and rewriting this book. A number of people have been generous with their comments, discussion, criticism, skills, time, and encouragement. Edward Andrew, Christian Bay, William Connolly, Thomas Dumm, Robert Fenn, Eugene Gendlin, Gad Horowitz, Alkis Kontos, David Levin, Thomas McCarthy, David Savan, Tracy Strong, and Charles Warren each read the manuscript in various stages of preparation. Keith Ansell-Pearson, Steven Crowell, Mary Devereaux, Nancy Hartsock, Thomas Haskell, Gene Holland, Asher Horowitz, and Rod Olsen each read portions of the manuscript. Sevin Hirschbein introduced me to Nietzsche as an undergraduate in a way that compelled me to continue. Margaret Warren, Donna Ahrens, and Theresa Parker helped with typing. I developed several of the main themes of this book as a doctoral dissertation at the University of Toronto, during which time I was supported by a University of Toronto Doctoral Fellowship. A Mellon Post-Doctoral Fellowship at Rice University provided the time and secretarial support that enabled me to produce a first draft. Northwestern University subsequently provided secretarial support for successive drafts. Earlier versions of several arguments were published as articles in *Theory and Society*, *Political Theory*, and *Political Studies*. Larry Cohen of MIT Press facilitated publication with patience and competence. My parents, Charles Warren and Margaret Warren, encouraged me to pursue my chosen endeavors at every step of the way. Finally, my wife and friend, Janet Joy, has built with me the kind of life that makes these things possible.

Evanston, Illinois
June 1987

Introduction: Subjectivity and Power

This is a study of what Nietzsche can tell us about humans as subjects, agents, or selves. The concepts "subject, agent, and self" are intrinsic to political thinking, simply because they identify humans as the bearers of politically significant capacities. Examples would be capacities for decision-making, for initiating projects, for determining futures, for entering into reciprocal obligations, and for taking responsibility for actions. Politics—and much else as well—would be quite inconceivable should humans not have capacities such as these. This is no doubt why, until very recently, most political thinkers relied on metaphysical postulates that, in effect, endowed humans with the capacities for rationality, free will, and moral choice—in short, capacities that universally and transcendentally distinguished humans from nature and history, and in so doing seemed to endow them with capacities for a political life. At the same time, much contemporary political thinking suggests that these capacities are not metaphysical in nature, but rather social and historical achievements predicated upon biological capacities. They are one kind of effect of social relations rather than their foundation, and they are historically situated rather than universally and transcendentally existent. To the extent that the metaphysical assumptions of modern political thought obscure the socially and historically situated qualities of subjectivity, it remains unable to conceive of how politics is possible at all.

The Nietzsche I develop in this book is central to the transition from metaphysical to situated—from modern to postmodern—ways of thinking about humans as agents. My thesis is that Nietzsche's transition is marked by his reconception of certain modernist ideals—especially those that identify politically relevant capacities—within

a postmodern view of the world. His most pressing problems have to
do with the nature of subjectivity, especially how subjective capacities
relate to historically situated practices, relations of power, culture,
and language. He views modern forms of subjectivity as ambiguous
achievements: valuable in their capacities, but uncertain in their
identities. I want to suggest here that Nietzsche not only draws into
question modern assumptions about humans as subjects, but also—
and equally importantly—shows how subjects are possible as historical achievements. He shows us how capacities of the self evolved
together with domination, and how they might be reconceived to go
beyond their origins. In other words, his texts are both critical and
reconstructive. The point of this book is to suggest that Nietzsche
helps us think about how the politically significant capacities of
subjectivity are possible in a world without metaphysical entities or
the guarantees they are supposed to offer. To the extent that he does
so, his philosophy provides a transitional preface to a critically postmodern political thought.

Reading Nietzsche in this way is not, however, an entirely straightforward enterprise. With respect to issues of postmodern transitions,
his writings are both troubling and compelling. They have the qualities of transitional texts, looking both backward and forward, implicated in problems of the past, and ambiguously suggestive of new
ones. Many different kinds of positions on this ambiguity are possible,
and Nietzsche's commentators have taken most of them at one time
or another. One might write Nietzsche off as confused, although
he is more likely to be taken seriously today than just a few decades
ago. More interestingly, one might try to show how Nietzsche fails
to break with the very ways of thinking he implicates. One might
point to the many strains that lead to self-refuting positions or bizarre
conclusions. Or, finally, one might celebrate Nietzsche's ambiguity
as itself a statement about the fundamental ambiguity of the world.
Nietzsche leaves us with more than enough material for any of these
approaches. I take none of them here; my attitude is cautiously
optimistic and reconstructive. I want to know what Nietzsche has to
offer, while also explaining why he held many of the seemingly
contradictory positions that he did.

Nor are all substantive approaches to Nietzsche useful to the kind
of enterprise I pursue here. One approach, the most obvious and also
the most troubling, looks at the totality of Nietzsche's thinking in

light of his political visions—that is, his views on what kinds of human associations are possible and desirable.[1] It is well known that many of Nietzsche's writings seem to glorify domination in human relations, especially in its class and gender forms. His view that domination is both necessary and desirable in society is part of a more general ideology I characterize as a "neoaristocratic conservatism" in the final chapter. I do not, however, see Nietzsche's political ideology as a worthwhile way of relating his philosophy to political thought. His insights into the *nature* of domination are invaluable to critical, post-modern political thought, but his judgments about its *necessity* and *desirability* are not—a point I argue at length in the final chapter. This is why this book is not mainly, or even importantly, about Nietzsche's own political ideas.

Still, unlike many other commentators, I do not think that Nietzsche's political visions can be ignored, or treated as merely metaphorical. While showing how Nietzsche could have arrived at his political conclusions, I also argue that they were inessential to the progressive aspects of his philosophy. They stem primarily from erroneous assumptions about the nature and limits of modern institutions, assumptions that impoverished his thinking about social structures, and caused him to mistake their historical limitations for ontological ones. These assumptions in turn required Nietzsche to read domination back into his philosophy of power in ways that violated the internal integrity of his critical, postmodern insights. For these reasons, Nietzsche does not offer a complete, or even entirely coherent, political philosophy. This is unfortunate not only for historical reasons (it meant, for example, that the Nazis could easily abuse his writings), but also because the political commentary on Nietzsche usually assumes that what explains Nietzsche's political ideology is his philosophy of power. The results have tended to range from dismissal to caricature of his philosophy, stunting possibilities for fruitful engagement. Part of what I offer here, mostly in the final chapter, is an explanation of Nietzsche's politics that does not ignore their brutality, but also does not truncate his philosophy—specifically, his thinking about how capacities of agency are possible. This is what makes it possible to write about how Nietzsche's philosophical concerns with human agency relate to the most pressing issues of postmodern political thought, while not writing a study that is mainly about Nietzsche's politics.

If the political commentators have tended to lose Nietzsche's philosophy in explaining his politics, the philosophical commentators—those concerned with his views of morality, truth, personal identity, and the like—often lose the political significance of his thoughts about human agency in attempting to save Nietzsche from himself. Those who are interested in Nietzsche's philosophical concerns are understandably reluctant to see them in political terms: it seems impossible to reconcile his philosophy with his politics without trivializing his philosophy. There are at least two ways of dealing with this kind of tension in the philosophical literature I wish to avoid here. First, commentators often treat Nietzsche's political remarks as metaphorical embellishments of what they take to be essentially philosophical points.[2] While this approach in some sense resolves conflicts between Nietzsche's philosophy and his politics, it does so only by denying any political consequences of his philosophy, making it uninteresting for problems of postmodern political thought. Second, and more seriously, commentators often depoliticize Nietzsche's philosophy by asking narrowly philosophical questions, questions that presuppose answers to the broader, or at least prior, ones that are of interest for postmodern issues.[3] They do so by collapsing social and political perspectives (those having to do with questions of subjectivity, agency, and power) into more specific questions of epistemology (which presuppose knowing subjects), and ethics (which presuppose moral agents). A key claim of this study is that for Nietzsche questions of agency, or power organized as subjective capacity, have a priority over epistemological and ethical ones. Questions about man's active being in the world take precedence over questions of certainty and ethical standards. The reason is that the latter questions already presuppose some understanding about the nature of the self as a knowing subject or moral agent. It is not that Nietzsche does not address questions of certainty and morality. To the contrary, he is constantly engaging them. But he engages them as a consequence of asking questions about worldly practices, both because these practices irreducibly involve claims of truth and morality and also because he asks questions about the possible truth value of his own power/agency perspective. Because much of the philosophical literature overlooks this point, it also misses Nietzsche's congeniality to postmodern transitions in political thought.

There are, of course, philosophical approaches that do ask the right

questions of Nietzsche. Heidegger, for example, carefully and systematically interrogates Nietzsche's texts for answers to questions
about the nature of subjectivity, power, and historicity.[4] But the results are disappointing. On the one hand, Heidegger is insensitive to
Nietzsche's emphasis on the concrete and materially situated nature
of subjectivity, a topic I investigate in chapter 1. On the other hand,
Heidegger tries to fit Nietzsche into a "metahistory" of philosophy,
one in which Nietzsche is made to play the role of the last metaphysical philosopher. Heidegger's agenda produces a Nietzsche with a
dehistoricized and essentialist notion of the subject, one that completes rather than breaking with metaphysics, a point I examine in
chapter 4.

A third approach that has tended to lead to dead ends for postmodern transitions comes, perhaps surprisingly, from within postmodernism itself. These approaches are best described as literary or
textual.[5] What they have in common is an analogy between the world
and a text. These commentators are attracted to Nietzsche by his
claim that the world is radically indeterminate with respect to its
meaning. Like a text, world and self are constantly reinterpreted
according to new needs and circumstaces; like a text, one cannot
determine ultimate meanings by referring to either the intentions of
its author or essential attributes of the world. If there is no essence to
world or author, neither is there any intelligible sense in which we
might speak of subjects of actions, selves with capacities to determine
the future, or morally responsible agents.

These approaches have much to offer in the proper context, but
the proper context is ultimately literary, and not political. The
fundamental problem is the analogy between text and world. The
text (or, more accurately, the work of art) is a model of meaningful
practices for Nietzsche, and not a model of the world. Textual models
fail to capture the contingencies and open-endedness of actions, nor
do they capture the otherness of the world that partly constitutes
experience or the material forces embedded in relations of domination. For these reasons, textual models produce an impoverished
conception of the political world. The problem is not so much that
they are wrong as that they are incomplete: they presuppose some
other, more comprehensive, account of what the world is, such that
humans might experience the world and self as a meaningful place.
The ramifications of this point are numerous, and I expand on them

in different ways in chapters 2–5. We require such an account for any critical and lasting postmodern transitions, because it is only in such terms that we can see how postmodern, politically capable selves are possible. Because they lack such accounts, postmodern literary approaches are apolitical, uncritical, and often nihilistic in their implications.

The Problem for Postmodern Political Thought

My thesis in this book is that the intrinsic interest of Nietzsche's philosophy for political thought lies in the possibilities for such an account. I presuppose the validity of the various critiques of metaphysics of subjectivity that one finds in different ways in Marx, Freud, Heidegger, poststructuralism, and critical theory, and that are implicit in much contemporary social science. But, as I have suggested, I also presuppose that no political theory, postmodern or otherwise, can do without concepts that in one way or another identify capacities of subjectivity. The reason is that concepts of subjectivity unavoidably define what it means to view humans "politically." Politics is about many things, but it is partly about the abilities of people to choose and make a difference, about people as *political agents*. It is not by accident that the language of political theory reflects this: all political theory presupposes that people have, at least potentially, the capacity to reflect on and evaluate the world and themselves, to communicate, and to act with an eye to the future. Terms like rationality and responsibility, good and bad, interest and ideology, right and duty, authority, legitimacy, and obligation presuppose that humans are potentially subjects of social action; that they are beings capable of intentional behavior in social situations. It is hard to imagine a genuinely political subject matter without such assumptions, however badly they may be realized in practice. This is why modern political thinkers have always tacitly defined politics as the category of social actions that are oriented toward rational collective decision-making. Not coincidentally, progressive political thinkers from Rousseau to Marx and J. S. Mill also assume that political knowledge has value because it allows people to relate their own actions to social and political outcomes in a considered manner, in this way securing their humanity.

It is difficult to think of any desirable postmodern political theory that would not, somehow, show how these modernist assumptions are possibilities of the political universe. And yet we know little about how such an account would be possible. Postmodern thinkers have so far told us much more about what is not possible, about the deteriorating conceptual support structures of modern ideals. We know that metaphysics of subjectivity are philosophically, sociologically, and psychologically naive, however desirable from a moral perspective. This has produced an extended crisis in contemporary political thought: on the one hand, because the metaphysical hopes of political theory cannot be related to realities, they are marginalized as naive and utopian; on the other hand, there are even worse results when these hopes are mistaken for realities, when they are posited as real because of the nihilistic consequences of not doing so. Mistaking the desirability of subjects for their reality leads to expectations for social performances that are misplaced, and often politically pernicious. For example, as Foucault has pointed out, the self in part develops through enforced distinctions that tie a set of expectations for a normal selfhood to mechanisms of social control.[6] This means that the kind of subjectivity achieved in many Western societies may be closely related to domination—a point originally developed by Nietzsche, as I shall suggest in chapter 1. Thus we are seemingly left with a dilemma: the concepts of subjectivity that are available to contemporary political thought tend to vacillate between the utopian and the ideological.

It seems to me that this dilemma presents the foremost challenge to critical, postmodern political thought, and this is where I think Nietzsche's philosophy turns out to be important. The point is to see that Nietzsche's philosophy is in many ways an extended answer to a pivotal question: How can humans be subjects of actions, historically effective and free individuals, in a world in which subjectivity is unsupported by transcendent phenomena or metaphysical essences? Or, put in slightly different terms, supposing that human subjectivity (selfhood, agency) is intrinsically valuable, how can we conceive of it as a *worldly* (social and historical) phenomenon? In this question we find Nietzsche's relevant postmodernism.

But Nietzsche's approach to this question is also *critical* in two respects. First, it is critical in the Kantian sense: Nietzsche constantly reminds his audience of the limits of the claims of reason. He criticizes universalistic claims by showing how they relate to historically specific and contextual interests in subjectivity. Nietzsche is critical in a second sense as well: in showing how universalistic claims are limited by context, he provides an account of the qualities of practices that make subjectivity a possible historical achievement. In so doing, he judges the relative merits of claims in terms of their contributions to constituting humans as agents. This is how Nietzsche retains good reasons for his criticisms, and avoids undermining his own critique. As I shall argue in chapters 3 and 4, Nietzsche's concept of will to power, combined with his genealogical method, performs these critical functions within his thinking as a whole. My suggestion is that interpreting Nietzsche in light of the problems of *critical* political thought provides a missing methodological point of convergence between Nietzsche and modern rationalism on the one hand, and postmodern problems on the other. This particular point of convergence will, I argue, produce the rigorous and fruitful engagement of Nietzsche that is currently lacking within political thought.

Eight Theses on Subjectivity and Power

Much of the first part of this book, especially the first three chapters, consists of preliminaries. They cannot be skipped without losing a sense for the problem of human agency/subjectivity/selfhood as Nietzsche develops it. However, the preliminaries may be somewhat more palpable if I summarize some of the novel aspects of Nietzsche's thinking about what subjectivity is, and about how it relates to power, history, and knowledge.

1. *Subjectivity involves power.* For Nietzsche, power and subjectivity are intrinsically related: his most fundamental assumption about subjectivity is that it is intimately involved with attributes of the human condition that enable us to experience ourselves as causes of effects, as agents with capacities to do things—as centers of power. Power is primarily an existential concept for Nietzsche, referring to practices that cause changes in the world. Subjectivity is a reflexive interpretation of those intentional and goal-directed practices through which individuals project their biographies into the future. As I shall suggest in chapter 1 (on nihilism) and chapter 4 (on the will to power), subjectivity is a reflexive residue of worldly practices. This is one reason why Nietzsche pairs the terms "power" and "will"

in the term will to power (*Wille zur Macht*), and distinguishes this concept from force (*Kraft*). In this sense, power is prior to subjectivity; subjectivity is a practical achievement. Power is Nietzsche's most important category of meaningful behavior because it is intrinsically related to reflexive processes of self-constitution. For these reasons, power is neither the effect of a metaphysical subject nor reducible to observable physical dimensions and conditions. It is also important to emphasize, however, that Nietzsche has no theoretically articulated concept of power beyond the actions of individuals. His strength in the analysis of subjectivity becomes his weakness in relating his thoughts to social structure and politics, a point with important ramifications for how one extends his analysis of power to politics.

2. *Humans are motivated by power as subjectivity.* Humans strive to experience themselves as agents, as the cause of effects, and therefore as beings who determine their futures. One's experience of the world as a valuable place depends in part on a continuous identification of oneself as an agent in the stream of historical changes, and on experiencing the self as transforming the past into the future. On Nietzsche's account, nihilism results from the loss of this identity. Experiences of subjectivity and personal identity are therefore closely related to power and powerlessness in historically specific situations. What Nietzsche means by his famous claim that humans are "will to power" is that they desire subjectivity, the experience of being an effective subject in the world, the experience of transforming what one was into what one will be. In more classical terms, humans are motivated by positive freedom. Thus power has *value* when it attains a self-reflective identity experienced as subjectivity, when it is an individuated capacity for free agency. Like Durkheim, Nietzsche is a moral individualist without being an ontological individualist, and this provides the basis for his critical, postmodern evaluations.

3. *Power as subjectivity is relational and has no ontological correlates or identities, only ontological conditions of possibility.* The organization of power as subjectivity/agency/selfhood is intrinsically problematic rather than foundational. The capacities that make subjectivity possible (intentionality and reflexive monitoring of action) are given to the human condition, but subjectivity is not. Nietzsche's refusal to use metaphysical categories of agency, such as "will," "self," "soul," or "subject," distinguishes his approach from his precursors in the

German tradition from Kant through Schopenhauer. Power is organized as subjectivity through constant interaction with the world.
In contrast, metaphysical stipulations of subjectivity remove self-
identities from the otherness of internal and external nature, and
thus cannot show how subjects as empirical entities could exist in
spite of historical contingency and change. For Nietzsche, the identity of human agents depends not on metaphysical certainties, but
on the continuity of practices, practices that are enabled by a complex of interpretations of the world and self together with a personal
biography of experiences.

4. *Power as subjectivity depends on individuals' evaluations of both the world
and of their own intentions.* While practices have worldly conditions of
existence, human capacities to organize and experience these practices as subjectivity stem in part from their abilities to evaluate their
worlds in terms of their intentions, and at the same time to evaluate
these intentions. Self-identities depend on valuative processes, and
this is why Nietzsche so closely connects power and judgments about
values, including moral ones. An interesting consequence of his position is that power as agency and moral evaluation are neither opposites nor reducible to one another. Rather, moral judgments are
one way of organizing power as subjectivity. This insight is behind
Nietzsche's move toward a postmodern morality that draws on certain modernist innovations, especially Kantian ones, as I shall argue
in chapters 4 and 5. For Nietzsche, the posibility of positively moral
action is part of power organized and experienced as agency.

5. *Interpretive organization of power into subjectivity depends on worldly
resources.* The organization of power as agency through evaluation is
not *sui generis*, but depends on a background of culture, language,
and experience. Culture and language structure and limit consciousness, and therefore provide a definite range of possibilities for self-
identity (chapters 1 and 2). Practices are structured and limited by
material possibilities as well as by social power relations. This means
that power as subjectivity is relational and conditional. Nor are the
resources of subjectivity ever fully transparent at any point in time.
In part, this means that subjectivity is constantly being constructed
out of otherness, and that a denial of this otherness is the same as
denying the world within which subjectivity is possible. Nietzsche's
analysis of nihilism is essentially about this denial, about the social

and cultural conditions that produce it, and about its historical consequences. When one denies the otherness of the world, its separate existence and one's dependence on this separate existence for one's own being, then one not only undermines oneself by masking the world that makes the self possible, but also produces a conception of the world as something that can be fully mastered, and hence fully dominated. This is why metaphysics of subjectivity are closely related to domination, and why Nietzsche's analysis of nihilism is, in ways I shall draw out, an implicit critique of domination. At the same time, Nietzsche prefigures Foucault's insights into how the dependence of the self on otherness can lead to self-identities organized in ways that sustain political domination. But unlike Foucault, Nietzsche does not dispense with the category of the subject; instead he asks about the kinds of relations that would make individuated power possible. Nietzsche intends his work to locate these potentials, although, for reasons I detail in chapter 7, he fails to identify them politically.

6. *Power as subjectivity is historically specific.* Because of the relational nature of power as subjectivity, it can only be studied in historically specific terms. For Nietzsche, this means that power should be studied by "genealogically" reconstructing the experiential and cultural-linguistic conditions that make specific forms of subjectivity possible in any given time and place. Human potentials for agency will be differently realized according to different experiences and different cultural conceptions of the self. For this reason, Nietzsche rejects historical philosophies based on lineages of ideas, laws, or logics that require privileged standpoints or suprahistorical agents. In chapter 3, I shall show how Nietzsche's historicism stems from his understanding of the situated nature of practices, including his own.

7. *Knowledge about the human world anticipates power as subjectivity.* That is, knowledge about human practices is defined by interests in constituting the self as a subject. This is why Nietzsche argues that all knowledge is "perspectival." This does not mean that knowledge is arbitrary, however. I shall argue in chapters 3 and 4 that Nietzsche relies on criteria that are immanent to practices, and that are appropriate to the worldly, interpretive, and reflexive conditions of practice identified by his concept of will to power. I shall also argue that Nietzsche's theory of knowledge is consistently "critical." It requires constant reflection on background interests in subjectivity that, in

Nietzsche's view, motivate knowledge, serve as conditions of possibility, and provide criteria of adequacy. The aim of Nietzsche's philosophy is self-clarification in the service of subjectivity. It thus involves the assumption that humans have a general interest (whether or not they are aware of it) in reflecting on their motivations and interests as subjects, and in developing an understanding of the interdependence of self and world. For this reason, a Nietzschean knowledge of power would be cumulative not so much as a body of knowledge, but as an increasing ability of humans to use knowledge as a means to self-constitution.

8. *Nietzsche's philosophy of power is politically relevant, but also politically indeterminate.* Nietzsche's thinking about power as a subjective capacity is not fully political because he is unable to extend his concept to most modern institutions, notwithstanding his penetrating critiques of the modern nation-state and aspects of liberal-democratic ideology. I shall argue in chapter 7 that Nietzsche lacked the concepts necessary to modern power relations—especially those of markets and bureaucracies. Instead, he accounts for institutional power in terms of an underlying will to domination. In these cases, he uses the concept of power metaphysically, as if it denoted an underlying essence, an essence manifesting itself in domination. Thus when Nietzsche extends his critical, postmodern account of human agency to modern, institutional life, we find that he often violates his own critique of modernist metaphysics. This means, in effect, that his postmodern conception of power lacks a political theory. While Nietzsche's philosophy of power is invaluable as a preface to critical, postmodern political theory, it is a mistake to see it as more than a preface.

1

Nihilism and Power: Identifying the Problematic

When texts long outlive their author, it is often because they formulate a problematic, a set of interrelated questions that capture the movement of an epoch, or cause us to think about ongoing human concerns in ways we had not done so before. Knowing a thinker's problematic is perhaps the most important thing we can know about this person's thinking as a whole. Without knowing a thinker's questions, of course, we can make little sense of his answers. Less obviously, the way a thinker formulates his questions often anticipates a way of thinking that transcends his own. Both considerations apply to Nietzsche: knowing what he meant by the problematic of "nihilism" is the most important thing we can know about the nature and implications of his thought.

Nihilism is usually understood as a philosophical doctrine (there exist no objective grounds for truth) from which follows an ethical doctrine (there exist no objective grounds for moral judgment). It follows from these doctrines that the world offers no guidance or limits to human activity. Accordingly, a nihilist usually is taken to be one living a life without intellectual grounds of conduct, a life in which "everything is permitted." For these reasons, those who are concerned about nihilism generally also concern themselves with questions about the presence or absence of metaphysical standards of truth and right conduct.

These understandings of nihilism miss Nietzsche's problematic. Theodor Adorno once noted that Nietzsche was the first to use the term "nihilism" in such a way that he questioned the question itself—namely, the problem of metaphysical standards to which nihilism seemed linked.[1] Rather than understanding the root cause of nihilism to be the loss of a metaphysically grounded realm of truth, Nietzsche saw it as a symptom of dissolving subjectivity, of disintegrating power, and of a failing mode of living and acting. The failure of metaphysical truth expresses this deeper problem: nihilism is a symptom of an increasingly untenable relation between basic tenets of Western culture and modern experience. Nietzsche did not see the doctrine of nihilism as a necessary or even possible "truth." Indeed, he did not view nihilism as something that could be discussed on its own terms. The philosophic position of nihilism defies the possibility of rational discourse. For these reasons, he approached nihilism not as a doctrine, but as an attitude, as a symptom of a deeper pathology in Western ways of living and acting. For Nietzsche, we shall see, the nihilist's psychology and conduct point to more fundamental issues that eclipse the nihilist's intellectual polarity of truth and nothingness, however acutely conceived it may be. These oppositions of thought in nihilistic doctrine raise the problem of the totality of practical and intellectual relations that make up a form of life.

With the exception of Adorno, commentators have failed to notice what is distinctively original about Nietzsche's approach to nihilism, namely, his deconstruction of nihilistic doctrines into questions about how subjectivity is organized. Stanley Rosen argues, for example, that nihilism is an intellectual position that fails to recognize moral laws discernible by reason, a position he ascribes to Nietzsche.[2] But Rosen fails to see that Nietzsche's problem is not about whether or not moral laws exist, but what subjects are like so that they could act in accordance with moral laws. Nor could nihilism be primarily a crisis of the correspondence theory of truth, as in Arthur Danto's reading of Nietzsche.[3] While Danto raises philosophical questions that are important in their own right, he sees Nietzsche's primary concern as an epistemological one. Because Nietzsche rejects what is often called the "correspondence theory of truth" (the doctrine that truth consists in a correspondence between beliefs and facts), Danto concludes that at the core of his philosophy is the doctrine of nihilism. In arriving at this conclusion, however, Danto relies on a problematic that Nietzsche sought to repudiate, namely, the question of how a pregiven, knowing subject conceptually maps a world of objects. It is only if one sees this problematic as fundamental that rejecting the correspondence theory of truth leaves no good reasons for any claims whatsoever.[4] The reason it makes little sense to see Nietzsche as addressing questions of truth and right conduct is that he is interested in a prior question of what knowing subjects and moral agents are like, such that these could be problems.

Perhaps ironically, the seemingly more radical interpretations of Nietzsche by deconstructionists such a Jacques Derrida and Paul de Man revolve in this same universe.[5] They rightly assert that Nietzsche is beyond the polarity of a metaphysics of subjectivity and nihilism: questions such as Danto's and Rosen's can only be asked from standpoints Nietzsche rejects. But Derrida and de Man do little to tell us why Nietzsche's deconstructions of metaphysical questions are not precisely the kind of nihilism that more traditional philosophers deplore. They accept the popular notion that Nietzsche lacked a theory of truth, that Nietzsche believed all truth claims to be interpretations without foundation. Thus while more traditional philosophers view Nietzsche's supposed nihilism with apprehension, Derrida and de Man celebrate it. In their concern to deconstruct metaphysical questions, they take us only halfway to Nietzsche's positive, postmodern offerings. What they miss is that although Nietzsche rejected the correspondence theory of truth, his philosophy does include criteria that suggest good reasons why we might want to accept one interpretation of the world rather than another.

Nihilism and the Human Condition

Nietzsche's positive offerings (which I discuss in subsequent chapters) will make little sense, however, without a precise account of what his problematic of nihilism does involve. His problematic is complex and multifaceted, ultimately drawing a picture of how acting, knowing, culture, language, experiences of power, and historicity are intertwined with subjectivity. The existential predicament and historical movement Nietzsche identifies as "nihilism" requires him to go behind modern conceptions of the knowing subject and moral agent, *since it is the very possibility of goal-directed, meaningful action that nihilism draws into question.*

For Nietzsche, the classical symptoms of nihilism—the "feeling of nothingness," the "pathos of 'in vain,'" and meaninglessness[6]—express a failure to relate interpretations of self and world to possibilities of practice. This view of what nihilism is presupposes a view of humans as beings who produce and reproduce both their conditions of existence and themselves by means of the constraints and resources of history. If one experiences nihilism first as a failure of meaning, Nietzsche understands this failure in terms of an underlying failure of those capabilities by means of which human beings constitute their surroundings, social relations, and selves. In our highest potential, writes Nietzsche, we are creatures possessed of both *vis contemplativa* and *vis creativa*: "We who think and feel at the same time are those who effectively and at all times *fashion* something that had not been there before."[7] As I shall detail in chapter 4, for Nietzsche our reflexive sense of subjectivity emerges out of practices that are enabled and constrained by experiences and interpretations. Experiencing the world as a meaningful and valuable place unfolds within this engagement. "We are neither as proud nor as happy as we might be," he argues, because we have failed to understand the nature of our self-constituting activities and their worldly conditions of possibility.[8]

Nietzsche suggests a structural formulation of the problem in a note defining nihilism as "the opposition of the world we revere and the world we live and are."[9] The "nihilist" is "one who judges the world as it is that it ought not to be, and of the world as it ought to be that it does not exist. According to this view, our existence [*Dasein*] (acting, suffering, willing, feeling) has no meaning: the *pathos* of 'in vain' is the nihilist's *pathos*."[10] Nihilism, Nietzsche is saying here, signifies a situation in which our *Dasein*—our "being there" in the world through acting, suffering, willing, and feeling—appears so unrelated to anything we know, think, or value that an orientation toward existence becomes impossible. Hence "radical nihilism is the conviction of the absolute untenability of existence [*Dasein*] when it comes to the highest values one recognizes."[11] The most "extreme" nihilism "places the value of things precisely in the lack of any reality corresponding to these values and in their being merely a symptom of strength on the part of the value-positers."[12]

The fundamental structural contradiction in nihilism, then, is between humans as sensuous, worldly beings who suffer, feel, and act, and humans as conscious, cultural beings who constantly interpret and evaluate the world and themselves. Individuals lose their orientation and become nihilistic when they cannot fit experience and interpretation together to form a "will" to act: that is, when they fail to organize their powers as agency. Nietzsche is suggesting that this practical dislocation causes existence *as such* to seem to lack value, solidity, and truth. It is precisely the fact that nihilism denotes an untenable relation between culture, experience, and self-reflection that highlights the peculiar—and in Nietzsche's view as yet unconceptualized—nature of human agency.

Nietzsche's concept of nihilism can be structurally defined, then, as referring to *situations in which an individual's material and interpretive practices fail to provide grounds for a reflexive interpretation of agency*.[13] Many of Nietzsche's descriptions of nihilism bear out such a definition; most others presuppose it in one way or another. "The most universal sign of the modern age," he writes in a note, is that "man has lost dignity in his own eyes to an incredible extent." Man no longer sees himself as "the center [*Mittelpunkt*] and tragic hero of existence [*Dasein*] in general."[14] He writes in another that "we are losing the center of gravity [*Schwergewicht*] that allowed us to live."[15] Viewed in light of the above definition, these comments suggest that nihilism expresses a failure of the powers of human agency.

The above definition, we shall see, provides a systematic sense to Nietzsche's many apparently unsystematic comments on nihilism. These include his claims that nihilism is

a. an *experience* of lost meaning;

b. a condition or *situation* that one is in, regardless of what one thinks about that condition;

c. an attribute of certain *values* or cultures that provides an illusory sense of power as agency; and

d. an attribute of the *historical development* of Western culture, regardless of whether those who orient themselves by means of that culture experience the loss of meaning.

For Nietzsche these are not different understandings of nihilism, but different facets of the same crisis of human agency as it has developed in Western history.

The Genealogy of Nihilism

The possibility of nihilism exists wherever human practices have come to depend on evaluations of both the world and the self's place within it. But only certain historical configurations of experience and culture cause this possibility to become a problem. Moreover, it is in Nietzsche's genealogical detailing of these conditions that we find that the story of nihilism is also a political story about the relation between oppression, culture, and the constitution of subjects. Nietzsche was particularly interested in two historical outbreaks of nihilism, dividing Western history into three grand epochs. The first instances of nihilism occurred during the transition from premoral to moral culture (c. 500 BC–200 AD), while the modern occurrences mark the end of the period of what Nietzsche broadly refers to as "Christian-moral" culture and the beginning of some new—as yet unknown—"extramoral" period.[16] Nihilism not only marks the transition points between these epochs but also characterizes in latent form the entire Christian-moral period.

The causes of emergence of nihilism at each transition, Nietzsche's analysis suggests, are to be found in the characteristics of the preceding epoch. Consistent with this, Nietzsche makes a little noticed yet politically consequential distinction between the ancient *original* outbreak of nihilism (*die erste nihilismus*) and the specifically modern *European* occurrence.[17] The distinction provides a further elaboration of Nietzsche's structural definition of nihilism as something that results from disjunctions between experiential and interpretive conditions of acting. Theoretically, a disjunction might be caused by changes in experience. Or it might result from failures of an interpretive schema. Or it might be caused by some combination of the two. On Nietzsche's account, original nihilism stems from the first possibility, resulting from rapid changes of experience, while European nihilism stems from the second and third possibilities, that is, from an internal crisis of interpretation such that it becomes inappropriate to experience. Original nihilism is "original" in the sense that European nihilism could only have developed because of its prior occurrence. This structural sequence underlies Nietzsche's genealogical hypothesis about the history of nihilism, a hypothesis most fully developed in *On the Genealogy of Morals*.

The political and cultural content of Nietzsche's distinction shows up in the kinds of experiences and interpretations related to each kind of nihilism. He traces the causes of original nihilism directly to the slave's experiences of oppression in ancient class society. Original nihilism would have been the result of an increase in politically perpetrated suffering. Thus Nietzsche claims that "it is the experience of being powerless against men, *not* against nature, that leads to the most desperate embitterment against existence."[18]

Nietzsche finds the modern, European case of nihilism in an entirely different source. Here, the cause is not any radical alteration of experience by political oppression, but rather the evolution of Christian culture up to the point at which it finally becomes quite inappropriate to the world of which it is a part: "Nihilism now appears *not* because the displeasure with existence has become greater than before, but rather because one has come to distrust any 'meaning' in suffering, indeed, even in existence. One interpretation has collapsed; but because it was considered *the* interpretation it now seems as if there were no meaning at all in existence, as if everything were in vain."[19] European nihilism results from a divorce between those intellectual demands created and legitimized by Christian culture and modern experience. Any account of European nihilism, Nietzsche argues, must look for the causes of this divorce in a dynamic peculiar to the interpretive dimension of human agency, a dynamic borne historically by Christian culture.

Nietzsche structurally interrelates the two kinds of nihilism, and finds the key to the dynamics and necessity of European nihilism in original nihilism.[20] The relation results from the refraction of original nihilism—the nihilism of political experience—into the interpretive structures of Christian-moral culture. On Nietzsche's account, this could occur because Christian-moral culture interpretively suppressed original nihilism by lending a vicarious meaning to suffering. He writes that the great advantage of the "Christian-moral hypothesis" was its provision of "the great *antidote* against practical and theoretical *nihilism*."[21] In the Christian "revaluation of values," Nietzsche writes elsewhere, the will was "saved," the dignity of man reasserted, and "the door was closed to any kind of suicidal nihilism."[22] The Christian-moral world view solved the problem of original nihilism—the nihilism of political experience. But it did so at the price of recasting the identities of subjects "beyond" the realm of suffering, in what Nietzsche thought of as the purely imaginary "backworld" of Christian ideals.

For reasons of the conditions under which it was born, then, Christian-moral culture retained within itself the structure of original nihilism, but sublimated into culture. Owing to its interpretive structure, Christian-moral culture in turn produced the crisis of European nihilism. Because Nietzsche finds the source of European nihilism in this inverted image of original nihilism, he is able to relate the ancient and modern instances of nihilism dialectically through the epoch of Christian-moral culture. During this epoch the individual stood in a contemplative relationship to his own practice, taking guidance from a God and nature created out of political duress.

Original Nihilism and Ancient Class Society

The reason that the structural relation between original and European nihilism warrants special attention, then, is that it provides Nietzsche with his genealogical hypothesis about contemporary crises of subjectivity. His account traces a myriad of relations between political experience, culture, and subjectivity, and it turns out to be a story about how culture can refract oppression and perpetuate domination. His argument in the *Genealogy* suggests that original experiences of meaninglessness—with their correlative bad conscience and *ressentiment*—can only be explained as psychological residues of political oppression. His critique of Christian-moral culture in terms of the situation of the slave presupposes a background understanding of how power permeates culture, and how both affect the constitution of subjects.

Indeed, only in terms of this background can we see how Nietzsche develops his own peculiar brand of materialism regarding culture. New interpretations, he suggests, become a part of culture because there is a need for them, often a need that is a result of political experience. New interpretations are "practical" in the sense that they speak to the "human, all-too-human" motive to understand oneself as the subject of one's present and future. Thus Nietzsche looks upon the psychological residues of violence with great interest: they provide the soil that gives rise to moments of great interpretive creativity under pressures of the need for a "will"—that is, for a reflexive interpretation of agency.[23]

Still, the constraints of political experience dictate that cultural creativity cannot assume just any form. Nietzsche finds this particularly significant for explaining why Christian-moral culture developed the kinds of interpretations it did. Experience acts as a constraint on possible interpretations, and violent experience so constrains the possibilities of meaningful interpretation that the oppressed are driven to find meaning outside of experience altogether: they take flight from experiential reality into an imaginary world. As Nietzsche explains it, sometimes whole classes of people are confronted with situations in which they must "will nothingness" or not will at all.[24] Nietzsche's account of modern, European nihilism will make most sense, then, on the assumption that he construes the political experiences that generate original nihilism as the pervasive events of Western history. Like Hegel (and partly in parody), Nietzsche casts these events as a dialectic of master and slave.

Because Nietzsche's typology of master and slave has implications for his account of nihilism, it is important to notice that it is more subtle than most commentators appreciate. The concepts do not, for example, denote different kinds of natures from which different political consequences flow. Gilles Deleuze makes this mistake when he equates mastery and slavery with "active" and "reactive" types of forces, from which he then deduces Nietzsche's critique of slave morality.[25] But for Nietzsche, positing originating principles from which empirical consequences might be deduced is a kind of uncritical metaphysics, and Deleuze's "types" of forces are no different in this respect than any other kind of originating idea.[26] Nor does Nietzsche's use of the typology of mastery and slavery signify sociological classes, at least not in the first instance. Rather, Nietzsche is interested in the typical *experiences* attaching to the class situations of master and slave, since these experiences are the raw material of emergent interpretive schemas. By structuring experience, social situations also structure a range of possibilities for interpretive schemas. We find this assumption, for example, in Nietzsche's general claim that cruelty became progressively inverted and embedded in Western culture: The "ever-increasing spiritualization and 'deification' of cruelty . . . permeates the entire history of higher culture (and in a significant sense actually constitutes it)."[27]

Out of such relations between culture and cruelty Nietzsche understands certain "types" of human psychologies to emerge, and this is what forms the psychological context of original nihilism. The psychological configuration emerging from the slave's situation he termed "bad conscience." As Nietzsche considered mastery and slavery to be the primal social relations of Western society, he considered bad conscience to be Western man's most primal psychology. His anthropological hypothesis—one intended more as a theoretical claim than as a historically accurate account—is that bad conscience is the psychological moment of the first society. This first society Nietzsche took to be identical with the first *class* society and with the first *state*, both created by a "master" class capable of forging and maintaining these political relations. All of these moments— as Nietzsche's hypothesis runs—appeared suddenly and simultaneously, as different moments of the birth of civilization: "The welding together of a hitherto unchecked and shapeless populace into a firm form was not only instituted by an act of violence, but also carried to its conclusion by nothing but acts of violence .... The oldest 'state' thus appeared as a fearful tyranny, as an oppressive and remorseful machinery, working until this raw material of people and semi-animals was at last not only thoroughly kneaded and pliant but also *formed.*" [28] The origins of the first state, Nietzsche argues—contrasting his view to historically literal contract theories of the state—were not in a "contract," but rather in the dominion of warrior peoples over peaceful ones. The word "state" once signified a situation where "some pack of blond beasts of prey, a conqueror and master race that, organized for war and with the ability to organize, unhesitatingly lays its terrible claws upon a populace perhaps tremendously superior in number, but still formless and nomad." [29] Moreover, all legal and contractual relations that came to be a part of civil society Nietzsche understands to have originated in violence and to have been enforced by threat of punishment. Behind all institutions of state and economy —at least in their origins—were classes of "masters" capable of imposing them by force. [30]

The historical accuracy of Nietzsche's genealogical hypothesis— that societies and states emerged from warrior peoples conquering peaceful ones—is probably quite limited. But historical accuracy is not really the point. Rather, Nietzsche's narrative makes a theoretical claim about the *psychological* and ultimately *cultural* effect of class society, an effect that he sees as coextensive with civilization, at least through the modern period. The theoretical point has to do with the interrelations between the experiences of oppression and the formation of particular kinds of agents. His claim is about what is presupposed *socially* and *politically* in those several psychological attributes that make society in general and class-society in particular possible, attributes like memory, guilt, conscience, and the senses of duty and obligation. [31] Thus, "Perhaps there is nothing more fearful and uncanny in the whole prehistory of man than his *mnemotechnics*. 'If something is to stay in the memory it must be burned in: only that which never ceases to hurt stays in the memory'—this is the main clause of the oldest (unhappily also the most enduring)—psychology on earth." [32] Bad conscience is the pervasive psychological effect of violent social existence. These effects, Nietzsche carefully points out, originated *only* among the oppressed. It was not in masters that bad conscience developed, "but it would not have developed *without them*. This ugly growth would be lacking if a tremendous quantity of freedom had not been expelled from the world, or at least the visible world, and made latent, as it were, under their hammer blows and artist's violence." [33]

Bad conscience, then, is the psychology of class society that comes to pervade Western culture. In terms of the problem of nihilism, we might say that bad conscience is psychological evidence of a *de facto* inability to will, indicating the loss of the natural ground of meaning in practice. On Nietzsche's account, the shattering of the will can be seen, symptomatically, in the ideals of Christian-moral culture that come to value selflessness, self-denial, and self-sacrifice.[34] Such ideals can be found coexisting with bad conscience wherever the "instinct for freedom" has been "pushed back and repressed, incarcerated within and finally able to discharge itself and vent itself only on itself." [35] The will of the oppressed must become a "will to self-denial" and a "will to nothingness" simply because the worldly avenues for experiencing oneself as an agent are blocked.

Bad conscience is intimately related to, although not identical with, original nihilism in the structure of Nietzsche's argument. Original nihilism grows out of bad conscience, and all bad conscience is potentially nihilistic, since it indicates that the ground of meaning in self-constituting practices is absent. But original nihilism is a unique moment of bad conscience. It is not suffering, Nietzsche points out, but the "meaninglessness" of suffering that engenders the tendency toward "suicidal nihilism." [36] The movement from a nihilistic situation where purposeful willing is impossible (signified by bad conscience) to a self-awareness of this situation (signified by the nihilistic attitude) has ramifications for the origins of cultural change beyond anything that could come of bad conscience itself. In the case of original nihilism, Nietzsche directs our attention to a moment of self-awareness that oppression leads to a life lived in vain, a moment when suffering is senseless and has yet to be given meaning.[37]

Bad conscience produces original nihilism, then, only where it cannot be integrated into some interpretive schema. For original nihilism to emerge out of bad conscience, some existing culture would have had to fail, unable to make coherent existing levels of suffering. One should note here—lest Nietzsche seem to be an egalitarian political thinker—that he did not think it possible to abolish socially engendered suffering. He saw domination as natural and inevitable (see chapter 7). Nonetheless, in his early *Birth of Tragedy*, Nietzsche did hold that suffering could be given a vicarious meaning through tragic drama, so that a class society might also attain cultural unity in spite of the powerlessness of the lower classes. As Tracy Strong has noted, the early Nietzsche's ideal culture would be strong enough, and of the right type, to conceal ideologically the foundations of the state in oppression (see chapter 2).[38]

But Nietzsche's early assessments of the ideological possibilities of tragic culture fell victim to his later analyses of the effects of suffering on the structure of culture. To be sure, he would have liked to see these possibilities realized, since he had a conservative's view of the desirability and necessity of class hierarchies in society. But he later became less optimistic that a cathartic identity of classes could be achieved in the way he had once thought possible. He pointed out in the *Genealogy* that dominant cultures generally follow dominant power relations, excluding precisely those classes that experience the ill-effects of these power relations. Master cultures tend to be class-exclusive in nature and to interpretively affirm what is already true in practice. "It is a rule," writes Nietzsche, "that a concept denoting political superiority always resolves itself into a concept denoting superiority of the soul."[39] Nietzsche's analysis of this resolution of power into culture is perhaps the best-known aspect of the *Genealogy*: master classes tend to affirm actions emanating from themselves as "good" and "noble," while they designate enslaved or lower classes as "bad," "impure," and "immoral."[40]

In such situations the process of oppression is twofold, for a *de facto* oppression is buttressed by cultural exclusion. It is exactly this situation, suggests Nietzsche, that would bring one who is oppressed face to face with the meaninglessness of life, by exposing to consciousness his lack of selfhood, power, and recognition by others. According to

Nietzsche's analysis, a master culture is rarely capable of endowing experiences of oppression with meaning. It is this lack that turns bad conscience into original nihilism.

While Nietzsche's portrayal of the slave in ancient class society is his paradigmatic example of original nihilism, it leads to a more general claim. One can conclude that original nihilism will manifest itself wherever political oppression is coupled with cultural exclusion. Or, more abstractly, original nihilism will result wherever a dominant class imposes its power without a cross-class rationalization of its power.[41] Within the structure of Nietzsche's world view, one can further conclude that original nihilism is a transhistorical possibility for humans *just insofar* as one understands the social and political relations that generate experiences of oppression to be transhistorical. Thus it is incorrect to assert, as Michel Haar does, that Nietzsche understands the first expressions of nihilism to have been caused by an impotent will as such recoiling against "life." Rather, individuals recoiled against particular kinds of social relations, in terms of which they were relatively impotent. In chapter 7, I shall suggest that the political significance one ascribes to original nihilism will to a large extent depend on this specificity.

Original Nihilism and Cultural Creativity

Nietzsche's own interest in original nihilism is even more specific. His construction of the problem clearly suggests a link between original experiences of nihilism and cultural creativity. He wishes us to notice that precisely such experiences give rise to creative alterations of interpretation, since this is an option that can be exercised when goal-oriented actions cannot. Thus explaining the refraction of polit-ical experience into culture requires that we consider those moments of original nihilism that Nietzsche thought to be rife among the oppressed during certain periods of history. These moments some-times led to suicide, but more often to new ways of giving "meaning" to suffering, and finally to the deification of cruelty in Christian-moral culture.[42]

Before looking more closely at original nihilism and the creativity it engendered, however, let us step back to speculate on what kind of link must exist between the two. Nietzsche hints that it is not only in the ancient situation that nihilism is linked to cultural creativity.

Contemporary revaluation of values, he writes, presupposes "perfect nihilism ... logically and psychologically, and certainly can come only after and out of it."[43] This claim makes sense if we recall that manifest nihilism occurs whenever there is a disjunction between one's experience of the world and one's culturally available interpretation of it. Similar disjunctions are at work in any thought process oriented toward making sense of experience. Nietzsche's constructions suggest that these creative processes of disjunction and intellectual adjustment include nihilism because they include the moments of disorientation when previous interpretations lose their meaning. These experiences, Nietzsche seems to suggest, can be powerful stimuli toward creative thought and/or action, according to circumstances. Such reasoning is probably behind his claim that European nihilism could be seen as a good thing—even a "divine way of thinking."[44] Commentators often argue that this kind of text shows that Nietzsche affirms the doctrine of nihilism, and that he thought of himself as a nihilist.[45] But such claims miss Nietzsche's point: he is arguing that nihilism as an *experience* is an inevitable aspect of any creative *process* of thinking, simply because these processes include moments of interpretive disorientation. In comments such as these, Nietzsche is more interested in how thought and experience relate to action and selfhood than he is in the truth status of nihilism as a doctrine.

These general considerations help to make sense of Nietzsche's explanation of the birth of the Christian-moral world view out of original nihilism. What is decisive for his explanation is the occurrence of political violence coupled with the victims' attempts to make sense of their suffering. Specific interpretations of suffering are, of course, the acts of individuals, such as religious prophets and ascetic priests. But for a prophecy to become a *cultural* phenomenon, it must speak to a field of needs that have heretofore gone unsatisfied.[46] Thus, in the *Genealogy* Nietzsche explains why one such field of needs should have come into existence by looking at the political experiences of "slaves." In so doing, he can account for both the motivation and the content of the slave's cultural creativity. He can make sense of the motive because original nihilism had to signify an intolerable situation for the slave's self-identity. Because of its intolerability, the situation was also unstable, dynamic, and potentially creative. The slave, having experienced powerlessness, would have been left with only two paths of action: "suicidal nihilism" or "revaluation" of the experience of suffering. This is why Nietzsche thought that the psychological residues of violence—bad conscience generally, and the nihilism and *ressentiment* of the slave particularly—must eventually become creative elements in Western culture. Nietzsche can account for the content of the slave's creativity in the same way. Constrained by violent experience, only some kinds of interpretations will accomplish the illusory resolution of the slave's need for meaning, namely, those that reject experience and reconstitute self-identity in some nonworldly sphere.

Although Heidegger and others have carefully examined Nietzsche's conception of the structure of nihilistic values, they consistently miss his explanation of why this structure came to be, and thus its political content. They trace nihilistic values to a "mistaken turn" in philosophical and religious interpretation, without seeing how this "mistake" addressed the kinds of needs generated by oppression. Stated somewhat cryptically, they do not see that Nietzsche's claim that "man would rather will *nothingness* than not will" presupposes a politically significant background of limited options. In this sense, the "philosophical errors" that produce the nihilism of Christian-moral culture are a residue of political oppression.[47] Nietzsche, in other words, focuses on the interpretive activities of the victims. It is worth noting in this regard that Nietzsche's understanding of the relation between political oppression and cultural creativity is not without consequences for theories of ideology (see chapter 2). His formulations suggest that an ideology is as likely to be produced by victims attempting to make sense of their actual social situation as by a dominant class attempting hegemony. Power is decisive for the origins of ideologies, but often only indirectly, through an experiential structuring of the interpretative options of the oppressed.

Nietzsche's analysis of the psychology of *ressentiment* in the *Genealogy* underscores the pivotal nature of the relationship between violence and interpretation in explaining the origins of the Christian-moral world view. The slave's *ressentiment* was precisely the species of original nihilism that could become creative rather than suicidal. Nietzsche says that *ressentiment* develops in those "natures who are denied true reactions, those of deeds."[48] *Ressentiment* psychology is thus a species of bad conscience. But Nietzsche's descriptions of *ressentiment* suggest that it is distinguished by a consciousness of loss, the loss of the relationship between goals and actions necessary to a sense of agency.

Thus one who experiences *ressentiment* also directly confronts his predicament, places the blame on the oppressor, and finally asserts the evil nature of life under these conditions while projecting a situation in which life is better.

It is in this sense that *ressentiment* is a special and uniquely creative case of original nihilism. While it signifies a movement toward self-awareness of a nihilistic situation, and while it signifies a loss of self-constituting practice, it nonetheless rests on a retention of self-identity sufficient to recast interpretively the meaning of one's situation. The difference between an outwardly directed nihilism of *ressentiment* and outright despair—a self-destructive, suicidal nihilism —is the degree to which some cultural avenue exists for understanding and identifying oneself outside the culture of the dominant class. This can be inferred from Nietzsche's comments on the situation of the ancient Jews. The ancient Jews were the one group, in his estimation, who experienced slavery and nonetheless deepened their culture over and against that of their oppressors.[49] This is why among the Jews original nihilism became creative, deepening the Jewish sense of selfhood in the face of oppression and the cultural imperialism of the "master" class. For Nietzsche, the ancient Jews' struggle was the most important event leading to the Christian-moral world view: they introduced into history a cultural horizon that retained the structure of the original nihilistic situation.

But the Jewish "revaluation of values" remained nihilistic because *ressentiment* creativity was only an interpretive solution to a practical problem. Any resolution to suffering that is solely interpretive must move away from experience if it is to solve in the imagination the problems presented by experience. As Weber was later to note, Nietzsche saw in this sort of confrontation with suffering the root of all other-worldly religion and philosophy.[50] "Who alone has good reason to lie his way out of reality?" asks Nietzsche. "He who suffers from it. But to suffer from reality is to be a piece of the reality that has come to grief."[51] Any interpretive resolution to suffering without a practical resolution retains the mark of suffering in its movement away from the world. The "price" paid by the ancient Jews for their survival "was the radical falsification of all nature, all naturalness, all reality, of the inner worlds as well as the outer."[52] Yet Nietzsche clearly admired their creativity: "placed in the impossible circumstances," they could survive only through a revaluation of values.

Because the inversion stemmed from a struggle for life, the ancient Jews were "the antithesis of all decadents." The Jewish inversion of values, as a cultural logic taken over by Christianity, *became* decadent when wedded to new conditions and new people.[53] Christianity attained a structure and an internal logic that set the course of Western culture as a whole—thus achieving an importance far beyond its origins. Even so, it retained the imprint of original nihilism.

How Is Nihilistic Culture Possible?

That original nihilism *could* lead to a structurally nihilistic culture once again tells us something of Nietzsche's view of human agency— this time, something about how the fragile relation between self-interpretation and worldly practices might sustain nihilistic values. In the first aphorism of *The Gay Science*, he writes that "gradually, man has become a fantastic animal that has to fulfill one more condition of existence than any other animal: man *has* to *believe*, to know, from time to time *why* he exists...." Like Hegel, Nietzsche understands our experiences of value to flow from the confirmations of selfhood that result from worldly engagement. Our sense that the world is an ordered and meaningful place follows from our abilities to situate ourselves in relation to the world, to reproduce the continuity of ourselves in time, and to know ourselves to be doing so. Nihilistic values emerge from situations—those, for example, of a politically oppressive nature—that frustrate practices that confirm the effectiveness and continuity of the self in time. Such situations negate, but do not alter, the *need* humans have for self-confirmation, and this is why nihilism can occur. Nietzsche sees this need as a motivating force, one that leads to assertions of the identity of the will even under conditions that defy all possibilities for achieving this identity in practice. In a well known remark, Nietzsche puts it this way: "The basic fact of the human will is its *horror vacui: it needs a goal*—and it would rather will *nothingness* than not will."[54]

What Nietzsche means by "willing nothingness" is that—under conditions in which goal-directed actions are difficult—the will creates meanings that fail to relate to and even negate goal-oriented practices. In the process of endowing the life-world with meaning, the power of interpretive delusion takes over when self-constituting practices fail. The resulting ungrounded values Nietzsche calls *nihil-*

istic values, and Christian values are his most important examples. He understood Christianity to have created a nonpresent, nonexistent, "antinatural" world of meaning—what he calls "nothingness"—as a necessary condition for "saving the will" over and against its actual impotence. Christian values are "nihilistic in the most profound sense" because they exhibit the fundamental structural contradiction of nihilism.[55] "When one places life's center of gravity [*Schwergewicht*] not in life but in the 'beyond'—in *nothingness*—one deprives life of its center of gravity altogether."[56]

Nietzsche's use of the term "nihilism" to cover certain cultural values as well as overtly nihilistic attitudes suggests the importance of his implicit distinction between interpretations of the world that are directed toward the experiential world and those self-interpretations that constitute the identity of the agent. With this distinction, it becomes clear how Nietzsche can, with consistency, use the concept of nihilism to refer to both the nihilistic attitude (or sense of meaninglessness) and certain kinds of values (like Christian values). Nihilistic attitudes and nihilistic values share an incapacity of goal-oriented consciousness. Both are unable to attain self-reflective goals through an interpretive and potentially practical orientation toward the present world. But nihilistic values are distinguished from the overtly nihilistic attitude by the self-understanding one has in relation to practices. If the world can be creatively engaged, then one's sense of self-certainty flows directly from this engagement. While the Christian attains a self-identity in spite of and against the failure of engagement, the overt nihilist is in some sense conscious of this failure and experiences a corresponding lack of value.[57] The attitude of the nihilist is a reflection without delusion of the failure of power in practice. But nihilistic values such as Christian ones are self-delusions: they veil without changing situations that produce a nihilistic attitude.

Nihilistic Values and Decadence

Because they were nihilistic, Christian-moral values were a pathological antidote to the suffering of the slave. They both affirmed his condition and perpetuated the fragmentation of practice from self-constitution—a situation that Nietzsche refers to as one of "decadence," a situation of deterioration and decline. The ancient Jews, on Nietzsche's account, provided the cultural "formula" for decadence.

But it was in Christian-moral culture that these values reflected and affirmed decadence.[58]

Decadence, for Nietzsche, consists in the collapse of this-worldly willing and even this-worldly *ressentiment* itself.[59] While the Jews retained the reality of themselves as a "people," the first Christians detached themselves even from this social reality, and all new feelings of selfhood were attained only through a negative relation to reality. A central message of the *Genealogy* is that interpretive structures are closely related to social relations of power. For the powerless this relation occurs through an active process of inversion according to self-constitive needs. Thus Christian values, especially of the ascetic type, were brought about through a denial of the "natural" world of experience. And the unity of the will was gained through the projection of a "beyond." Existence was justified only to the extent that it served as a means to this projected end. But existence *as such* remained without value, reflecting the incapacity of the self in original nihilism.[60]

Christian-moral culture comes to affirm decadence because it turns this inverted reflection of violence into a valuative stance. It places a value on the lack of power of the slave and affirms passivity as a means to dignity in an afterlife. Any "feeling of power" achieved by these means is, in Nietzsche's view, only an imaginery one. The unity of the subject is vicarious, because it is gained solely by interpretation and remains ungrounded in practice. Meanings come to depend on moving away from experience, and on devaluing experiences that are "natural," sensuous, changing and transitory, and "instinctual." Hence meaning is gained at the expense of engagement of experience, driving a wedge between Christian values and the ground of meaning in practice. Mind and body become a duality in conception because they are split in everyday life. This is why Nietzsche accuses Christian-moral values of lacking any "contact with actuality [*Wirklichkeit*]" and of substituting a "world of pure fiction" for the world that presents itself in everyday life.[61]

Such values undermine the conditions for willing in the process of "saving" the will. It is not that one who lives decadently does not engage in daily activities, but rather that, at least in the limiting case, these behaviors are not properly *actions*, for they are not the result of an intentional agent possessing the resources to direct behavior toward goals. Instead, the decadent reacts adaptively to experienced powers in accordance with an interpretive orientation "outside" himself—in a God- or abstraction-centered "other world," for example. This results, in Nietzsche's language, in the kind of will that increases its "feeling of power" through obedience.[62] The Christian slave, for example, obeys the master in practice as a condition for attaining a "feeling of power" in his imagination. At the same time, this practice becomes a negative point of reference for interpretation: suffering sustains the split between the actual capacity to act and the vicarious feeling of power, which is attained through values that project consciousness away from the experienced world, and toward God with His promise of a life better than this one. For Nietzsche, then, what is definitive of Christianity in particular and nihilistic culture in general is that they institutionalize horizons of consciousness in which one condition of willing—the "natural" world of experience—is hidden from view.

Nihilism, Metaphysics, and Heidegger

Because Nietzsche extracts this deeper structural contradiction as definitive of nihilism, he can apply the term to all ways of thinking that exhibit this structure. Indeed, *any* values that negate the world of experience, appearance, sensuousness, and change and in so doing remove one essential condition of power as agency are nihilistic in this structural sense—whether these are the values of Platonism, Stoicism, categorical morality, or the Cartesian ideals of modern science.[63] Nietzsche argues that one can generally characterize nihilistic values by their polarities of appearance and essence, the "apparent" and the "true" worlds, the world of the senses in contrast to the world of Reason, the real versus the ideal worlds, and so on.[64] Through recourse to a quasi-Hegelian logic, Nietzsche argues that once such interpretive polarities occur, all categories of "being"— like the true, essential, and eternal—resolve into "nothing."[65] "Logical world denial and nihilation," he writes in a note, "follow from the fact that we have to oppose nonbeing with being and that the concept of becoming is denied."[66] Where value is understood to reside in categories of "being," we are led to judge negatively the changing, the sensuous, the differential, and appearances generally. When categories of "being" are seen as true in themselves, they do not permit the engagement of present conditions, precisely because, in contrast to presence, these truths are unconditional.[67] Where there is no way of valuing changing life-worlds, then humans cannot organize their powers as agency.

Without a doubt, the commentator who has done most to illuminate the implications of Nietzsche's claims in this regard is Heidegger.[68] Nietzsche's understanding of nihilism, he argues, points toward a general critique of metaphysical philosophy from Plato through Nietzsche's own concept of will to power. Heidegger sees "metaphysics" (or "metaphysical humanism") as any way of looking at the world that makes the human subject in one way or another the ground of its objectivity. Metaphysics endows the world with objectivity to the extent that the world fits human values and designs—hence, its "humanism." In this way, the world's objectivity comes to depend on a previously existing knowing subject or moral agent. Although this essence of metaphysics only becomes clear with modern philosophy, especially in Descartes' grounding of existence in the thinking "I," Heidegger argues that it was present even in Plato's claim that the Good is the highest truth, since this claim identifies the world's essence according to the moral values of humans. Along Nietzschean lines, Heidegger points out that the hidden logic of metaphysics is nihilism, since the world exists only to the extent that it reflects human values and designs. But this logic equally threatens human subjects: if the world is nothing in itself, humans lose their place in the world, and ultimately lose themselves.

What is missing from metaphysics, according to Heidegger, is the ability to ask questions about the *possibility* of subjectivity. As he so nicely puts it, the fact that man "becomes the executor and trustee and even owner and bearer of subjectivity in no way proves that man is the essential ground of subjectivity." [69] Or, to put the same point into a Heideggerian formula, because of the subjective presuppositions of metaphysical thinkers, they can only think about the objective "being of beings," but not about Being—the world that makes subjectivity and objectivity possible. In metaphysics, subjectivity is simply posited; it remains impossible to show how subjectivity could exist at all, and this is why metaphysics must ultimately resolve into nihilism.

The irony of Heidegger's interpretation of Nietzsche is that, although he relies heavily on Nietzsche for his account of nihilism in metaphysics, he characterizes Nietzsche himself as the last metaphysical philosopher in his own "metahistory of philosophy" from Plato to Nietzsche.[70] Nietzsche, according to Heidegger, diagnosed the nihilism of metaphysics, but failed to overcome the same nihilism in his own thinking. Nietzsche still asked his questions in metaphysical ways, and for this reason his philosophy became the ultimate expression of nihilism in metaphysics.

The root of Heidegger's assessment is his claim that Nietzsche's concept of will to power is the final (that is, self-destructive and nihilistic) expression of metaphysical humanism. He interprets the will to power as an ontological doctrine of becoming and overcoming: in order to overcome itself, the will to power posits values in the form of aesthetic illusions. In this way, it organizes and evaluates the world as a condition of its own expansion.[71] But because all that is true is man's willful activity, the world turns out to be an aesthetic fiction. In itself, it is nothing, and the doctrine of will to power must therefore collapse into nihilism.

There are three points that are significant about Heidegger's interpretation in this context. First, the difficulty with his interpretation is not so much his critique of metaphysics, at least as far as it goes, but rather his view of how Nietzsche fits into it. Nietzsche had already produced a similar critique of metaphysical humanism and nihilism. While it is not as systematically portrayed as Heidegger's, its substantive points are much closer to Heidegger's own position than Heidegger admits. Indeed, by constructing a Nietzsche that is distant and distinct from himself, Heidegger buries a much more interesting and critical Nietzsche.[72]

Second, Heidegger interprets Nietzsche's concept of will to power in a way that is alien to Nietzsche's problematic. If the will to power were a metaphysical concept in the sense that Heidegger suggests, Nietzsche's thought would indeed be essentially nihilistic—not only in Heidegger's terms, but also Nietzsche's. In chapter 4, I shall argue for what is essentially a nonmetaphysical, and critical interpretation of the concept of will to power. Nietzsche's concept of will to power includes some very Heideggerian claims about the kind of world that could produce subjectivity. Moreover, his concept is best understood as having a critical epistemological status, one based on the Kantian distinction between the use of general claims as intellectual presuppositions of explaining things about the world and dogmatic uses of general claims to denote underlying essences or attributes of the world.

Third, Nietzsche is not simply a precursor of Heidegger, but beyond him in many respects. Heidegger's own approach to the question of nihilism is idealistic in a way that misses the political content one finds in Nietzsche. In focusing on nihilism as "history," Heidegger is concerned primarily with the inner contradictions of metaphysics as they veil the existence out of which they emerge. But concrete political practices—indeed practices of any sort—rarely touch Heidegger's notion of what history is. To some extent, this is why Heidegger does not develop the facets of Nietzsche that are central to problems of critical postmodernism in political thought.

The Evolution of European Nihilism

In contrast to Heidegger, then, it is well to keep Nietzsche's account of the political background of metaphysical ideas in mind when we look at his account of how Christian-moral culture could produce its own seemingly independent historical logic. Cultures have their own cunning. The cunning of Christian-moral culture, in Nietzsche's view, was to refract the effects of political violence far beyond its actual occurrences. This is why Nietzsche does not trace the imme-diate origins of modern "European" nihilism—the second major outbreak of manifest nihilism in Western history—directly to polit-ical experience. In contrast to original nihilism, he finds European nihilism to be the effect of those interpretations bearing the imprint of original nihilism: "Nihilism stands at the door: whence comes this uncanniest of all guests? Point of departure: it is an error to consider 'social distress' or 'physiological degeneration,' or, worse, corruption, as the *cause* of nihilism. Distress, whether of the soul, body, or intellect, cannot of itself give birth to nihilism. . . . Such distress always permits a variety of interpretations. Rather: it is in one particular interpreta-tion, the Christian-moral one, that nihilism is rooted." [73] Nietzsche considered it unlikely that nihilism induced by distress would appear in the modern period. Rightly or wrongly, he viewed social life in late nineteenth-century Europe as relatively pacified compared to ancient experience. "Actually, we have no longer such a need of an antidote to the *original* nihilism [*den ersten Nihilismus*]: life in Europe is no longer that uncertain, capricious, absurd. Such a tremendous increase in the value of man, the value of trouble, etc., is not so needful now. . . . 'God' is far too extreme a hypothesis." [74]

It is important to understand that Nietzsche is making a relative claim here: he believed that violence is intrinsic to the social and political world, and that it could not be removed. His claim is simply that violence in the modern era is something less than that of the early Christian era. Since violence is decreasing, Nietzsche reasons that it could not be an *increase* in violence that has produced European nihilism, as it was in the case of original nihilism. A least this is his claim: in chapter 7, I criticize his idea that situations that would produce original nihilism (in general, those of powerlessness) tend to decline in the modern era.[75] Here, however, it is enough to note Nietzsche's view that any account of European nihilism must be in terms of the tendencies brought to self-constituting practices by their interpretative rather than experiential aspects: "One interpretation has collapsed, but because it was considered *the* interpretation it now seems as if there were no meaning at all in existence, as if everything were in vain."[76]

It is also important to understand that Nietzsche is not working with an idealistic view of historical determination when he claims that nihilism occurs when the "highest values devaluate themselves."[77] Heidegger and many others give an idealistic reading of statements such as these.[78] But Nietzsche's uniqueness stems from the way he explains the power of ideas in terms of the way in which humans produce and reproduce their lives. Nihilism could never be embodied *solely* within the structure of an interpretation. It must be something we are, in terms of the way we make our life in the world under specific material as well as cultural conditions.

That nihilism is a condition of the total organism comes through even in the fact that Nietzsche used psychological and biological language to write about nihilism.[79] Still, it is clear that in his use of psychological and biological language, Nietzsche did not mean to suggest that cultural ideas merely reflect what we are biologically or psychologically.[80] Although nihilistic values may first *express* a (politically formed) psychological need where they serve as an antidote to original nihilism, they later come to *generate* new needs, because interpretations enter into the manner in which practices constitute the self. In this way, Nietzsche understands culture to become a "second nature" and nihilistic culture to cause a nihilistic will. The cultural continuity of nihilistic values, as I shall suggest, stems from the fact that interpretations are embedded and historically transmitted within shared contexts of meaning.[81] Only by viewing cultural evolution as an aspect of "life" in this sense can we understand how original nihilism, refracted into nihilistic culture, could reappear as a crisis of culture in the modern period.

The Two Crises of European Nihilism

Consistent with his view of cultural determination, Nietzsche locates two different processes of breakdown that cause the latent nihilism of Christian-moral culture to become a manifest crisis of individual power. The first occurs within the culture as a system of ideas: for reasons unique to theoretical world views, Christian-moral culture comes to require a certain internal consistency. At some point, in Nietzsche's account, the Christian-moral world view can no longer maintain its internal consistency and becomes irrational as a system of ideas. The second process runs deeper, and consists in a disjunction between the entire system of ideas and modern experience that leads to a loss of ability to orient toward the world. The modern crisis of nihilism, then, proceeds not only from the increasing *incoherence* of the Christian-moral world view, but also from its increasing *inadequacy* to the world of everyday practice. We find Nietzsche's account of these two kinds of tensions and their interrelations in what is certainly one of his best notes on nihilism:

Among the forces cultivated by morality was *truthfulness*: this eventually turned against morality, discovered its teleology, its interested perspective— and now the recognition of this incarnate mendaciousness that one despairs of shedding becomes a stimulant. Now we discover in ourselves needs implanted by centuries of moral interpretation—needs that now appear to us as needs for untruth; on the other hand, the value for which we endure life seems to hinge on these needs. This antagonism—*not* to esteem what we know [*erkennen*], and not to be *allowed* any longer to esteem the lies we should like to tell ourselves—results in a process of dissolution [*Auflösungsprocess*].[82]

This note contains Nietzsche's best formulation of the two crises. The contemporary crisis, he is saying, occurs because of a conjunction between our being unable any longer to find a way to "esteem the lies we should like to tell ourselves" without hitting upon intolerable contradictions combined with our being unable to find a way to "esteem what we know" or recognize to be a part of experience. I shall call the first antagonism a *crisis of rationalist metaphysics*, or, more simply, a *crisis of rationality*. The second I shall call a *crisis of legitimacy*. Together they are sufficient, at least from Nietzsche's perspective, to explain the dissolution of the Christian-moral world view in particular, or *any* rationalized ideology in general.

The Crisis of Rationalist Metaphysics

On Nietzsche's account, the crisis of rationality could not happen without a simultaneous development of a specific kind of need for meaning, a kind formed within Christian-moral culture. Christian-moral meanings arise from a need to provide a self-interpretation of agency in spite of practical failures. Once detached from practice, needs for subjective identity appear as needs for meaning guaranteed by other-worldly concepts, theories, and beings; that is, meanings guaranteed *meta*physically. But since metaphysics is inherently incapable of providing meaning, this kind of demand must eventually be disappointed and result in nihilism.

The reason that metaphysics must fail is that it involves the attempt to find meaning in truths *about the world as such*—as a natural or God-given order—rather than understanding meaning as a product of processes of cultural, material, and self-reflective intercourse with the world. As I shall argue in chapters 3 and 4, for Nietzsche, interpretations of the world can be called "true" in a meaningful sense only insofar as they have the ability to serve as conditions for self-constituting practices within the context of a world with irreducibly cultural-linguistic and Dionysian qualities. The "truth" of interpretations resides in their roles in human life-activities and they cannot be divorced from this context without losing their meaning and value. This is what the metaphysical tradition misunderstood.

Still, such metaphysical needs have lasting cultural effects. Not unlike Hegel, Nietzsche understands the need for meanings that attach to metaphysical truths (what he often calls the "will to truth") to have deepened and spiritualized consciousness, to such a degree that "truth" in the Christian-Platonic sense becomes a world unto itself. While the unconditionality of Christian-Platonic truth marks its separation from practice, the same unconditionality allows this culture to attain its own logic and rationality of evolution, detached from the conditions of its genesis. A crisis of rationality occurs when conflicts develop between the various claims that the system of interpretation holds to be true. When Nietzsche refers to nihilism as a situation in which "the highest values devaluate themselves," he is referring to these conflicts.[83]

Especially in its Platonic and Judaic aspects, Nietzsche saw the Christian-moral world view to be subject to an increasing rationalization, even in Weber's sense of the term.[84] Nietzsche considered rationalization to have its own teleology of development just insofar as metaphysical "truth" is understood to coincide with "meaning"— that is, insofar as individuals attempt to satisfy needs for subjectivity in contemplation, but not in practice. The slave introduced into history a "need" for truth that had never before existed, since his experience dictated that he look for meaningful truth outside of worldly practices. When this need was exploited and institutionalized by priestly types (see chapter 7), the pursuit of truth acquired a sanctity. Indeed, it became what Weber and Husserl later referred to as a "calling" or "vocation" (*Beruf*), justifying and giving meaning to the unlimited accumulation and systematization of knowledge. Nietzsche refers to this "calling" as the "will to truth."

The peculiar passion acquired by the will to truth is fueled by another unique and remarkable characteristic of the Christian-moral world view. Because this world view has a split structure, it generates the need for a *specifically* intellectual defense of itself. In *The Antichrist* and elsewhere, Nietzsche emphasizes that the Christian-moral universe holds itself to be true in relation to experience only in a negative sense. It posits a realm of truth over and against experience, one possessing the meaning that is absent in experience. But for the same reason, the truth of this new world is not self-evident in experience. Indeed, it is—as Nietzsche puts it—ultimately imagined, unknowable, and unprovable in relation to experience.[85] Thus he suggests that one will hold the Christian-moral universe to be true only insofar as it forms, articulates, and consolidates a complete and coherent *conceptual* universe.

It is the coincidence of this drive toward intellectual coherence with the Christian-Platonic equation of truth and value that exposes the intellectual limits of the Christian-moral universe: "You see what it was that really triumphed over the Christian god: Christian morality itself, the concept of truthfulness that was understood ever more rigorously, the father confessor's refinement of the Christian conscience translated and sublimated into a scientific conscience, into intellectual cleanliness at any price."[86] For the Christian philosopher and scientist especially, Christian dogma comes to contradict the high moral evaluation that the dogma itself places on the quest for truth. By legitimating the quest for truth, Christianity endangers itself as a system of faith. Nietzsche speculates that once the linchpin of Christianity—the concept of God—is removed by truth-seeking activities, the coherence of the entire world view is irreparably damaged: "Christianity is a system, a whole view of things thought out together. By breaking one main concept out of it, the faith in God, one breaks the whole: nothing necessary remains in one's hands. Christianity presupposes that man does not know, cannot know what is good for him, what is evil: he believes in God, who alone knows. Christian morality is a command; its origin is transcendant ...— it stands and falls with faith in God."[87] Without God, the entire Christian-moral world view loses its internal coherence, engendering a crisis of rationality.[88]

The Crisis of Legitimacy

As I have suggested, it would be a mistake to read Nietzsche as saying that the occurrence of European nihilism can be explained *solely* by the crisis of rationality. To do so would be to miss the distinctive way he relates ideas and practices. Heidegger makes this mistake by emphasizing Nietzsche's claim that nihilism occurs *because* the "highest values devaluate themselves." But while the crisis of rationality is necessary to explain European nihilism, it is not sufficient. Nietzsche understands meaning to dissolve only when a world view is no longer adequate to the "facts" of experience in terms of reflexive needs for subjectivity. This is true whether the adequacy is negative (as in the slave's need to reject the harsh facts of experience to sustain his other-worldly belief) or positive (where interpretation engages the facts of experience as a means to practice). Moreover, a world view need not be "rational" to be adequate to experience. Magical and mystical world views, for example, may be adequate to experience without having a rationalized structure. And, in Nietzsche's view, even an irrational Christianity can remain adequate to the degree that it maintains its meaning through what he calls "orgies of feeling" rather than through appeals to intellectual coherence.[89] Nietzsche seems to suggest that a world view like the Christian-moral one could not fail simply owing to its internal inconsistencies. Ultimately, it fails because of an inadequacy to self-constitutive needs in relation to modern experiences. Thus nihilism can surface only where the Christian-moral world view becomes incoherent within itself *and* fails to provide plausible subjective identities in relation to everyday life.

Nietzsche formulates the crisis of *legitimacy*, then, by asserting that the Christian-moral world view does not permit us to "esteem what we know [*erkennen*]."[90] The word he uses, *erkennen*, denotes one's recognition that some essential aspects of modern existence cannot be expressed in the Christian-moral world view. Here, *erkennen* seems to refer to an awareness of the world of everyday experience. It is a kind of knowing of the "world we live and are,"[91] which is in some sense different from and even prior to rationalized interpretation.[92] Nietzsche is very likely referring to a "tacit knowledge," to borrow Michael Polanyi's term, a cognition of the Dionysian world of experience, a world always richer, deeper, and more chaotic than the interpretive system into which it is appropriated.

Nietzsche is saying that a world view is in trouble when it cannot account for most of what we *erkennen* in terms of our need to live, to act, and to situate ourselves as agents. Because it relies on negative references to what we recognize about our experience, a world view like the Christian-moral one can remain intact only so long as experience is a source of otherwise intolerable suffering. But should experiences change and no longer need to be avoided, then the "truths" of such a world view are no longer insulated from comparison with experience.[93] Hence "God" becomes "far too extreme a hypothesis" for the relatively pacified life of the nineteenth century: "Life in our Europe is no longer that uncertain, capricious, absurd."[94]

These points underscore the fact that Nietzsche's account of cultural evolution is never purely structural. Culture refracts experience, and experience is appropriated within culture. In the case of European nihilism, the link between experience and cultural structure stems from the fact that the experiential content of original nihilism was refracted into the structure of Western culture. For Nietzsche the modern crisis of legitimacy reflects the same aspect of Christian-moral culture that had accounted for its success as an antidote to original nihilism—namely, its distance from and denial of violent experience.

Its legitimacy had rested upon its ability to explain suffering in terms of guilt, sin, redemption, and the afterlife. As Nietzsche points out at length in the *Genealogy* and *The Antichrist*, otherwise senseless suffering made sense when understood as punishment for sins for which the individual was deemed ultimately responsible, while the resulting bad conscience became explicable as guilt. The same logic occurs in the Christian attempt to make such experience coherent by seeing it as a negative referent to a metaphysical world that compensates the individual with a sense of dignity. Thus Nietzsche understood the Christian-moral world view to have maintained its legitimacy on the basis of a fundamental but delicate contradiction: while it ascribed free will and responsibility to the individual as his greatest potential, it denied him the understanding of experience and selfhood necessary for free will and responsible action.[95]

The Christian-moral contradiction is stable under some experiential conditions but not under others. Practical engagement of experience is continuous in Nietzsche's understanding of life; more, it is *definitive* of life. If one interpretively hides this engagement because of its intolerability, then continuing to hide the engagement depends upon its continuing intolerability. Changes in situation can invite direct comparison of the Christian-moral world view with experience by reducing the motive to escape. Comparisons stimulated by situational changes eventually undermine the legitimacy of the Christian-moral world view and lead to European nihilism.

Nietzsche viewed the surfacing of European nihilism as a catastrophic yet not an entirely undesirable event. To the degree that the Christian-moral world view is undermined by the absence of experiences supporting the notions of sin, guilt, judgment, and God, man becomes more "natural," closer to the "basic text of *homo natura*." [96] With modern science came the modern acceptance of the "testimony of the senses." [97] Nietzsche considers the dissolution of the Christian-moral world view through recognition of the claims of experience to be the genuinely progressive aspect of European nihilism, opening the possibility of a practice-oriented culture.

The Political Consequences of Nihilism

Along with the progressive side of the crisis of legitimacy to which Nietzsche looks forward, there is also a regressive side he believes will give rise to wars and violence. These can be expected where the crisis is politicized through applications of Christian-moral ideals to political practice. While modern science tends to measure the actual world against the metaphysical one to the detriment of the latter, Nietzsche understood much of modern politics—especially liberal democratic politics—to be based on a demand that the actual world embody the Christian-moral promise—that is, on a politicization of the ideals of brotherhood, equality of rights, happiness, and peace. Nietzsche believed that nihilism would affect politics through the practical failures of these ideals. In contrast to modern politics, feudal politics maintained a strict separation of Christian promise and worldly actuality—the City of God and the City of Man in Augustine's formulation. The separation sustained Christianity as a sphere of hope precisely because it could not be acted upon. But when, as in the case of the French Revolution, the Christian-moral promises become interpretive points of reference for social change, Nietzsche believed they must contradict the nature of the political world.[98] The political world, in Nietzsche's view, was necessarily and inevitably a hierarchy of classes involving a domination of the stronger over the weaker. As I have indicated, the meaning and assumptions of these claims will be addressed in the final chapter of this book. But insofar as he believed that this was the case, it made sense to conclude that Christian ideals applied in practice would literally *demoralize* themselves. Nietzsche thought that the Terror was a case in point.[99] Modern attempts to take seriously and apply in practice aspects of the Christian-moral world view must finally expose the fundamental incompatibility of practice with the *kind* of world view founded on the annihilation of practice. European nihilism as a psychological condition occurs only after every aspect of the Christian-moral world view has been found to be illegitimate in this sense.

More generally, in Nietzsche's usage, European nihilism is ideologically significant because it expresses at the individual level a dissolution of dominant forms of social consciousness. Individuals are situated in society insofar as the dominant form of social consciousness permits a self-identity corresponding to social experience. But where the dominant culture becomes illegitimate and no longer provides a vicarious feeling of selfhood, individuals are thrown into a state of extreme and helpless isolation, losing their sense of direction and selfhood. At this point the ideological cement of a society dissolves, and nihilism once again becomes an overtly political category.[100] Through the cunning of culture, the modern politics of nihilism involves an inversion and return of the ancient politics of original nihilism.

The "great politics" of the future that Nietzsche refers to in *Beyond Good and Evil* is a shorthand for political struggles engendered by cultural transitions with their shifting definitions of selfhood.[101] Thus, for example, "great politics" occurs when issues arise that go behind the questions of interests and obligations that define much liberal politics, and challenge the very conception of a subject-citizen who has interests and obligations in the liberal sense. This is why the problematic of nihilism is ultimately about how political subjects are formed, even though Nietzsche himself only touched on these implications.

Nihilism and the Future

From this survey, I think we can see that Nietzsche's problematic of nihilism is precise in its formulation and far reaching in its implications. It is most striking, for example, that he intends to incorporate yet goes beyond epistemological and ethical problems as they are traditionally understood. Crises of "truth" are symptomatic of deeper crises—crises of entire cultures, crises of entire modes of living and acting. The moral problems commonly associated with nihilism are seen by Nietzsche as central, but in such a way that they are not bracketed from "life" or credited with independent meaning. By redefining what nihilism is about, Nietzsche could return in a radical way to the issues associated with the birth of political philosophy—issues of the relationship between knowledge, power, and living a good life.

In a broad, historical perspective, Nietzsche thought nihilism would make it possible—perhaps for the first time—to address in a new way the radical issues raised by the ancient Greeks. The surfacing of nihilism marks a cultural upheaval. But it also gives rise to the possibility that we, as the inheritors of many kinds of possibilities, could become conscious of the problem and reorder the fragments of our culture by utilizing their potentials. Many interpreters of Nietzsche have argued that he understood nihilism to mark the end of the Western world and to require, literally, something beyond what Western man is now. One commentator writes, for example, that "Nietzsche did not think, as did Marx and the liberals, that our present condition contains the conditions of its own self-transcendence."[102] As I shall argue in chapters 3 and 5, however, such views overstate the discontinuity at the expense of the continuity of past and future. Even more, they fail to understand that for Nietzsche discontinuity is an essential part of growth and development. From an individual perspective, nihilism signifies a dissolution, a loss of power, and the ultimate alienation of man from his creative capacities. From a functional perspective, this same decline signifies an intimate relationship between crisis and creativity, power and knowledge, willing and truth. This is why Nietzsche views European nihilism as a "sign" of "crucial and essential growth, of transition to new conditions of existence."[103] Western man is at a turning point in history marked by the "sickness" of nihilism, but it is a sickness linked to the development of *vis contemplativa*. Modern nihilism is an opportunity to relate *vis contemplativa* to *vis creativa*. It is only necessary for the Christian-moral world view to draw "its most striking inference, its inference *against* itself; this will happen, however, when it poses the question '*what is the meaning of all will to truth?*'"[104] This question coincides with the emergence of nihilism, but it is also an imperative for humans to know how their *vis contemplativa* and *vis creativa* produce their historical existence. In this sense, we might see Nietzsche's problematic of nihilism as a way of elaborating Marx and Engels' famous comment on the revolutionary qualities of bourgeois society in the *Communist Manifesto*: "All fixed, fast-frozen relations, with their train of ancient and venerable prejudices and opinions, are swept away, all new formed-ones become antiquated before they can ossify. All that is solid melts into air, all that is holy is profaned, and man is at last compelled to face with sober senses, his real conditions of life, and his relations with his kind."[105]

2

Culture and Power; Culture and Ideology

Politics presupposes that individuals have the capacities of agents: the ability to choose and evaluate goals, to take responsibility for actions, to enter into agreements and obligations, and to determine the future. In Nietzsche's way of thinking, where such capacities develop at all they do so within the medium of culture. Cultures mold political agents by filtering and assigning meaning to experiences, by identifying familiar points of reference in everyday life, and by providing implicit reasons for acting one way rather than another. In doing these kinds of things, cultures tell people who they are, how they relate to nature and society, and what they are capable of accomplishing.[1] But Nietzsche's problematic of nihilism suggests that we cannot take these functions of culture for granted: when cultures change and dissolve, so do identities and capacities of agency. European nihilism indicates that in Western cultures the issues are even more complicated: capacities for agency are both promised and to a large extent unrealized. It seems that if cultures can constitute people as agents, as subjects, as individuals, they can also systematically undermine capacities of agency, distort self-understandings, and become ideological.

This chapter is about why, in Nietzsche's terms, culture can have these kinds of effects. For Nietzsche, the tension between the agent-forming and ideological possibilities of culture stems from the fact that it simultaneously serves different—and often opposed—functions having to do with individuals' interests in being agents, with forming their practices, with social cohesion, and with reconciling and legitimating political power relations. Cultures mediate and reflect these conflicting demands: this is why they can be genealogically deconstructed to reveal a context of social and linguistic practices, as Nietzsche shows in the *Genealogy of Morals*. This is also why one can, in Nietzsche's terms, *judge* cultures from the perspective of how they organize subjective powers: in some cases cultures serve the conflicting demands of their context in such a way that they organize power as agency. Others may serve ideological functions, blocking, masking, or displacing potentials for agency. Nietzsche's critique of Christian-moral culture presupposes distinctions such as these, and they imply a *critical* approach to culture. But Nietzsche does not always respect these distinctions, especially in his politics. For this reason, we find conflicting models of political culture in his thinking: one affirms culture as ideology, while the other moves toward realizing potentials for agency. To a large extent, these conflicts point toward the need to elaborate a more exacting concept of subjectivity within Nietzsche, one that takes account of the noncultural contexts of practices. I take up this task in subsequent chapters.

The Cognitive Status and Relative Autonomy of Culture

Nietzsche sees culture as a medium of human activities in sensuous and intersubjective contexts. From a cognitive perspective, this means that culture is intrinsically problematic, constrained by the demands of practice in situated contexts. It will not do, for example, to see culture as made up of representations of entities. The constraints and possibilities of context mean that culture never could represent Platonic or Christian conceptions of nature even as an ideal, for such ideal realities do not exist. Rather, as we saw in the last chapter, Nietzsche sees these views of cultural referents as evidence of an other-worldly creativity in the face of adverse experience. Nor is it adequate to see cultures (say, modern scientific ones) as accumulated representations of the laws governing natural experience, as in empiricist and realist accounts. The issue for Nietzsche is not one of whether or not natural experiences are real, but rather how humans cognitively process experiences as active beings.[2] Nor is the issue one of the usefulness of much culturally accumulated knowledge that claims a representational basis. Rather, for Nietzsche the problem is that experience possesses qualities of flux, complexity, and incertitude that make it exceedingly problematic as a representational basis for the languages, symbolizations, and ideas that make up a culture. Humans are embodied within a world that is fundamentally "Dionysian," with its sensuality and flux, *pathos* and chaos. These Dionysian qualities of the world are, as Nietzsche puts it, the "foundation of all existence" and the "basic ground of the world." [3] The world is not the kind of thing that readily admits of stable cognitive and cultural representations. This is why, for example, Nietzsche is critical of the cultural ideals of the Enlightenment. It is a naive faith, in his view, that nature might reveal, through logical orderings of sense data, a universe of ordered, eternal, physical laws. It is not that "nature" has no necessities or exigencies, nor even that it is impossible to know about them, but rather that no "order, arrangement, form, beauty, wisdom," or other "aesthetic anthropomorphisms" exist in nature itself. [4]

Nonetheless, such ordering ideas are essential aspects of human life and action. If the Dionysian *pathos* of embodiment—what Nietzsche calls "nature"—is a deep and multifaceted resource and ground of human life, it is intelligible only through our interpretive and material appropriations of it. Because "nature" consists only in the flux and multiplicity of raw experience, it has no humanly intelligible qualities. This is why Nietzsche sees culture as much more than an inevitable mediation of nature. Cultural interpretations sustain and are inscribed in practices by lending familiarity, stability, and continuity to the world. They do so within the limits and possibilities of the sensuous world on the one hand, and the human interest in subjectivity on the other. Culture is, on Nietzsche's account, the intrinsically human way of transforming the phenomenal realm of experience into a universe within which agency is possible.

The conclusion Nietzsche draws from these considerations on the existential functions of culture is most striking: cultures construct cognition in a way that enables individuals to maintain an intellectual distance from experiential reality while simultaneously engaging it. It is this distance to which Nietzsche refers when he writes, famously, of the "falseness" of culture: culture does not, and cannot, directly represent the *pathos* of the life-world. Culture *must* be "false," for in itself experiential reality would steal away the humanity, self-identity, and power of anyone who would directly confront it: "Anyone who has looked deeply into the world may guess how much wisdom lies in the superficiality of men. The instinct that preserves them teaches them to be flighty, light, and false. Here and there one encounters an impassioned and exaggerated worship of 'pure forms,' among both philosophers and artists: let nobody doubt that whoever stands in that much *need* of the cult of surfaces must at some time have reached beneath them with disastrous results."[5] "Indeed, it might be a basic characteristic of existence," Nietzsche suggests in another aphorism, "that those who would know it completely would perish, in which case the strength of the spirit would be measured according to how much of the 'truth' one could still barely endure—or, to put it more clearly, to what degree one would *require* it to be thinned down, shrouded, sweetened, blunted, falsified."[6] The wisdom of the Greeks that enabled them to live was their ability to "stop courageously at the surface, the fold, the skin, to adore appearance, to believe in forms, tones, words, in the whole Olympus of appearance. Those Greeks were superficial—out of *profundity*."[7] In Nietzsche's formulation, all cultures perform a mediation of existence in the service of "life" by securing cognitive horizons.

Cultures not only mediate external nature; they also mediate internal nature. They secure subjective identities. Thus, he comments that most historically existing cultures have served self-reflective functions at the expense of "reasonable" courses of action:

What is the cause of our keen resoluteness in action? . . . The oldest and still most common answer is: God is the cause. In this way he gives us to understand that he approves of our actions. When in former ages people consulted oracles, they did so that they might return home with such a keen resoluteness. . . . [T]hey did not decide, in other words, on the basis of what is a reasonable course of action, but on the basis of that image that could fill the soul with hope and courage. A cheerful state of mind was placed on the scales as an argument, and proved to be heavier than reasonableness.[8]

The effect of such "superficiality" in culture is to carve out a horizon, making possible a mode of acting and providing an interpretive space for a feeling of power. Of course, as suggested in the last chapter, Nietzsche is critical of those cultures—like Christian-moral culture—in which the self-reflective aspects outweigh their abilities to mediate basic exigencies of life and action. Such cultures lose their worldly basis in experience and lead to nihilism. But even cultures most faithful to "life" cannot faithfully *represent* its exigencies. At best they can only relate to them in such a way that action is possible. This is why Nietzsche can claim ironically that "the falseness of a judgment is for us not necessarily an objection to a judgment. In this respect our new language may sound strangest. The question is to what extent it is life-promoting, life-preserving, species-preserving, perhaps even species-cultivating [*Art-züchtend*]." [9] Thus, although cultural interpretations may not be true in terms of representational theories of truth, neither are they arbitrary. An interpretation is likely to be a collective, even "species," product of living and acting over time. They are ways of mediating the necessities and exigencies of the life-world—a category in which Nietzsche varyingly includes exigencies of physiology, psychology, self-identity, language, society, and political power relations. Accordingly, the structure of a culture will inevitably reflect contingencies of materially practical, psychological, self-reflective, linguistic, social, and political kinds. Over time, these contingencies solidify within a culture, not because they represent any single order of contingency but rather because they mediate them in ways that are simultaneously functional for the demands embedded within a people's form of life.

In his "new language," then, Nietzsche wishes to conceive of culture as an intrinsic part of practice. His aims were clear even in an early essay where he asserted that "nature" is the goal of culture, and, conversely, the ideal culture is a "new and improved nature." [10] Accordingly, Nietzsche's desire to "translate man back into nature" should not be understood as a romantic desire to *return* man to some primitive or animal nature, nor even as a desire to reverse the traditional esteem for reason over experienced nature, but rather as an attempt to find the kind of culture that would allow the sublimation, humanization, and transformation of nature, through a unity of interpretive and material activities. [11]

Cultural Structure and Language

To look at culture in these terms is, of course, to presuppose an action frame of reference. Should we look at this same complex from the point of view of social structures, we find that Nietzsche sees the consciousness of the individual as culturally and socially constructed. Individuals orient their practices in part by relying on cultural backgrounds of meaning that also bind them into social wholes. In the *Untimely Meditations*, for example, Nietzsche defines culture as the "unity of artistic style in every life-expression of a people." [12] Insofar as a people forms a "mighty community" (*mächtige Gemeinschaft*), it is "held together not by external forms and laws, but by a fundamental idea of culture. . . ."[13]

Cultures serve this social function because they consist in common sets of rules and perspectives that individuals take for granted in their everyday practices. As Tracy Strong has put it, Nietzsche sees all societies as resting upon systems of "predicates unconditioned by consciousness."[14] These predicates permit certain questions and problems concerning life in a society to enter individual consciousness, while others remain unthinkable within that culture. While some aspects of a society will be questionable in terms of its culture, others will be unquestionable because the interpretive hegemony of the culture will make questions about them quite literally inconceivable. In this sense, culture automatically binds individuals to society. Indeed, Nietzsche even thinks of the link between individual and society as "instinctive": as cultures develop, they gradually "sink down" into individuals, forming their "second natures." These "second natures," molded and reinforced by culture, form one necessary condition for the existence of a "people." Like Hegel and Marx, Nietzsche held that humans must be social animals before they can be individuals—that is, before their powers can come to have the qualities of agency. Cultures precede and transcend individuals; they have a structural autonomy and historical continuity that is irreducible to any other dimension of existence.

But why, on Nietzsche's account, would cultures have such attributes? We have seen why they would from an existential or action perspective: the autonomy of culture stems from its cognitive functions in mediating exigencies of experience for purposes of action. At the social level, however, the problem is slightly different: the autonomy of cognition with respect to experience is maintained by the fact that it develops within the medium of *language*. Language formulates and directs human actions because it imposes a stable matrix of identities on worldly experience. One commentator summarizes the point quite nicely when he writes that "the focus on language allows Nietzsche to bring Hegel back to earth: language provides a set of plebeian *Weltgeister* which establish the recurrent and recognizable developmental patterns in the world around us."[15]

Owing to its linguistic qualities, culture forms a transindividual reality that organizes interpretations over and beyond any immediate material and individual self-reflective functions they might serve. The irreducibility of language in turn stems from the fact that it organizes practices in accordance with two intrinsic and inter-related constraints, both of which Nietzsche presupposes in one way or another. On the one hand, language structures culture because it is consists in *rules* embedded in grammars. On the other hand, the rulelike structures of language serve *social utilities of communication.* Owing to their grammatical and social nature, the linguistic qualities of culture form a level of historical reality that constrains and patterns interpretations in such a way that it is not reducible to, or derivable from, any other kind of reality.

In the broadest sense, a language is any configuration or arrange-ment of symbols and signs that is systematic and relational. A body of symbols and signs qualifies as a language if any particular symbol or sign refers to other symbols or signs by means of rules of relation, correspondence, and habits of use—in other words, by means of a grammar. Their linguistic attributes provide interpretations with a measure of distance from their material context simply because they must satisfy grammatical conditions of intelligibility in order to formulate experience. The various ensembles of philosophic and scientific logics, religious and moral systems, ritualized practices, aesthetic styles and rules of composition, and political ideologies that make up culture all possess this characteristic of linguistic "distance," as well as everyday languages like English and German.

For Nietzsche, because language is a necessary resource of interpre-tation, it has the dual quality of being both a means and limitation of possible interpretive orientations. It constitutes much of our cognitive life: "We cease to think when we refuse to do so under the compulsion of language." [16] Language is a condition of thinking, and thinking develops in the form of language. Cognitive categories of quality, causality, identity, and distinction—categories that form the bases of our thought processes and claims about the world—are supplied for us by language, as are logical operators and connectives of grammar. We take them over from our intersubjective context, and we could not think without them; they are the means by which we formulate claims about the world, claims that orient us toward our various internal impulses and external goals.

But because there is a developmental connection between thought and language, Nietzsche fears that our thoughts more often reflect their linguistic medium than exigencies of practice. Language can cast a spell over thinking, and trap it in the self-referencing world of grammar.[17] This is why Nietzsche believed that many of the "truths" of Western metaphysics were essentially indistinguishable from grammatical relations: "In its origin language belongs in the age of the most rudimentary form of psychology. We enter the realm of crude fetishism when we summon before consciousness the basic presuppositions of the metaphysics of language, or, more clearly put, *Reason*. . . . "Reason" in language—oh, what a deceptive old female she is! I am afraid we are not rid of God because we still have faith in grammar."[18] Indeed, Nietzsche sees the entire Western metaphysical tradition as to a large extent a self-contained grammar, a grammar attempting to derive meaning from itself while steadfastly avoiding the experiential condition of meaning given by the "natural" presence of the world. Because Western metaphysics has avoided this engagement, it has functioned as a self-contained grammar. This is why Nietzsche claims that what has been called "truth" and "knowledge" within this tradition is really "the posture of various errors in relation to one another." "Truth" and "knowledge" are systems of mutually supporting "errors" insofar as they evolve internally by measuring earlier or later errors against one another.[19]

But Nietzsche does not hold that language *as such* exhausts our thinking or constitutes its outer limits. If language is a prison of our thoughts, this is a historical, not an ontological, problem. Although "we cannot change our means of expression at will, it is possible to understand to what extent they are merely semiology."[20] We can understand the degree to which words depend for their intelligibility upon their position within some kind of grammar. And subsequently we can inquire into how well our grammars allow us to formulate our practices (see chapter 3 on Nietzsche's criteria for judging interpretations). Nietzsche regards thinking as a process that is not only analytic—working within the confines of a grammar—but also synthetic. As a synthetic activity, thinking as a constant attempt to relate our means of expression to our experiences. Productive and creative thought proceeds by means of tensions between our systems of symbols and signs and the Dionysian presence of the world.[21]

By itself, language only constitutes the most explicit and communicable level of thinking, always leaving a residue of unexpressed feelings and images resulting from the affective Dionysian presence of the world. Presumably—although Nietzsche does not address the

issue directly[22]—even where the subconscious and unconscious processes of the mind partake of linguistic symbols and forms, they
remain "nonsense" in terms of language. These latent processes of
"thinking continually without knowing it" have little respect for the
neat relations established by grammar, as Freud later pointed out in
his theory of dream interpretation.[23] This is why we must always
reformulate our dreams before we can communicate them. On the
other hand, the meanings of conscious formulations are parasitic on
the inexplicit, Dionysian aspects of the world. As a more or less
ordered and explicit system of signs and symbols, language depends
upon rich but implicit levels of awareness for its meaning—that level
of awareness referred to by Polanyi as "tacit knowledge."[24] Language is hollow without the constant projection of experiences and
practices that are by their very nature deeper, more powerful, and
more complex than language. Indeed, the mere presence of a multifaceted world that constantly requires articulation makes it possible
for us to experience and even conceptualize language's inadequa-
cies, even it we cannot immediately overcome them. In this sense,
Nietzsche's views on language anticipate the later Wittgenstein's:
meanings depend on context bound usages and practices of language,
and so cannot be reduced to a definitive system of rules.

Nietzsche's cure for the potential reification of language is not to
demand an (impossible) abolition of language as an independent
entity by linking it to a definitive reality (for no *definitively* intelligible
reality exists), nor is it to demand definitive and unambiguous meanings (for to do so would be to affirm this reification). Rather he
demands that we become aware of language's worldly context together with its formative role in constituting practices. This is why
on the one hand Nietzsche can praise positivism for accepting the
"testimony of the senses," while on the other hand he praises poetry
and music as kinds of languages that push the limits of our expression
closer to our tacit knowledge of experiences.[25]

When one brings these considerations to bear on questions of how
culture could constitute a relatively autonomous sphere of historical evolution, then one finds that Nietzsche looks to the linguistic
medium of cultural practices. As a grammarlike structure of rules, a
culture can evolve solely in terms of relations between its parts. The
crisis of rationality of Christian-moral culture exemplifies this dimension of the process. As orientations toward experience, action, and

self, however, cultures are practical, and their structures reflect these practicalities. In this way, culture forms a discrete but not detached level of historical reality.

The Tendency for Cultural Reification

But the fact that cultures attain a structural rigidity and continuity of their own prior to any possibilities of individuation means that, by the very nature of their embeddedness in culture, individuals often reify their own interpretive practices. That is, they confuse the limits of socially constructed consciousness with the limits of the world in which they live. They mistake their own interpretive constructs for natural ones, their own conditioned perspectives for universal ones. Nietzsche's claim is not only that this possibility is inherent in language and culture, but that the social imperatives of communication endow culture with a tendency toward reification. In his best aphorism on the subject, he explains that

consciousness is really only a net of communication between human beings; it is only as such that it had to develop; a solitary human who lived like a beast would not have needed it. . . . The development of language and the development of consciousness . . . go hand in hand. Add to this that language serves not only as a bridge between human beings, but also as a mien, a pressure, a gesture. The emergence of our sense impressions into our own consciousness, the ability to fix them and, as it were, exhibit them externally, increased proportionately with the need to communicate them to *others* by means of signs. The human being inventing signs is at the same time the human being who becomes ever more conscious of himself. It was only as a social animal that man acquired consciousness—which he is still in the process of doing, more and more.[26]

Like Marx and most contemporary anthropologists, Nietzsche understands language and consciousness as practical phenomena, arising through social intercourse. They would have been sustained in the earliest societies simply by the material needs of the collective. In their evolution as social animals, humans communicate their desires and intentions to others by means of accepted rules of expression that are practical in nature. Communication requires agreement about how to identify things, about what kinds of distinctions are important, and about how individuals identify themselves in relation to these distinctions. The resulting network of communication in turn both forces and permits the development of consciousness and self-consciousness; it both connects humans and allows them to distinguish themselves as individuals.

Nietzsche's interest in this process is quite different than Marx's, however. He is not interested in the intrinsically social nature of language and consciousness *per se*, but rather in the effect these "herd" origins come to have on the *kind* of universality that language assumes in history, especially as it relates to the reification of individual consciousness. Because language arises for reasons of utility in the struggle against nature, its standards of adequacy are, at least in origin, suited primarily to this utility. Complicated, subtle, and playful uses of language are not suited to the coarser tasks of the collective struggle against nature: language must be simple and not susceptible to misunderstanding in times of need and danger. For this reason, Nietzsche calls the history of language the "history of a process of abbreviation" under pressure of social utility.[27]

Thus it is not the grammatical quality of communication *as such* that causes language to form a world of its own, but the fact that these grammatical qualities develop out of social utilities. Beyond all requirements of grammar, these utilities require that language be greatly simplified and thus "falsified" in comparison with the natural world of experience to which it relates. As Mary Douglas points out in an anthropological context, the cultural rules of institutions impose similarity and identity on the world, and endow these particular identities with the status of "nature."[28] It is through the cultural-linguistic control of cognition that the actions of individuals are coordinated into collective ones. A more subtle and complex language, while more adequate to expression of individual needs and experiences, would also be so particular in nature as to be useless for collective survival. Moreover, a language suited to expressing unique individual experiences could not become a *historical* language, for in expressing the unique it would remain a private language. Language tends to be suited to experiences held in common, precisely because only common experiences can provide a basis for communication.

Nietzsche refers to the role of language in articulating common experiences as "the genius of the species."[29] But he does not celebrate it. To the contrary, he believes that the social character of language entails a "natural, all-too-natural *progressus in simile*."[30] Because it tends to enforce similarity, language has an intrinsic tendency for reification from the individual experiences and practices of those who use it. Simply because of the nature of language, it presses toward the reification of the entire interpretive dimension of power as agency in human evolution, one extending inward to consciousness and outward to culture. Nietzsche explains the problem in the following way:

> My idea is that consciousness does not really belong to man's individual existence but rather to his social or herd nature, that, as follows from this, it has developed subtlety only insofar as this is required by social and herd activity. Consequently, given the best will in the world to understand ourselves as individually as possible, "to know ourselves," each of us will always succeed in becoming conscious only of what is not "individual" but "average." Our thoughts themselves are continually governed by the character of consciousness—by the "genius of the species" that commands it—and translated back into the perspective of the herd. Fundamentally, all our actions are incomparably personal, unique, and infinitely individual; there is no doubt about that. But as soon as we translate them in consciousness they no longer seem to be.[31]

There is a necessary tension between the universalizing aspects of language, with its hold over consciousness, and the individualizing qualities of experience and personal biography. Unless we see that this is a problem, Nietzsche is arguing, we shall fail to understand the experiential bases of meaning and agency. He claims in the first lines of *On the Genealogy of Morals*, for example, that "we are unknown to ourselves, we men of knowledge—and with good reason. We have never sought ourselves—how could it happen that we should ever *find* ourselves? . . . Whatever else there is in life, so-called 'experiences'—which of us has sufficient earnestness for them? Or sufficient time? Present experience has, I am afraid, always found us 'absentminded' [*bei der Sache*]. . . . "[32] Nietzsche's point is not simply that we are looking in the wrong places for meaning. He is also saying something about how the mind relates to the body, about how consciousness relates to embodiment, especially insofar as consciousness develops through language. Human bodies were not designed so that human capacities for articulation necessarily correspond to the experiences that inspire expression. For this reason, there can neither be a clear duality nor a unity of mind and body. But under the "spell of language" we fail to understand this: on the one hand, we forget that language is parasitic on embodiment for its meaning; on the other, we fail to realize that what we can articulate does not exhaust experience. For these reasons, we become "absentminded" with respect to experience, and thus with respect to our own individuality and practices. This is why language presses toward a reification of experience, at the expense of individuality and in favor of social sameness and social control.

Another way of saying the same thing about language is that it has an inherent potential for *fetishism*, in the sense that totems are a fetish for Freud, and money and commodities are fetishes for Marx.[33] In each case, humans mistake products of their own practices for natural phenomena; the outcomes of humans practices, both interpretive and material, assume the appearance of a "natural" constraint on practice. This is why language *in itself* is fertile soil for ideology. It automatically, as it were, instills a "second" social or "herd" nature in the human animal, and equates the limits of the social order with that of the natural order.

The Social Origins of Individuality

Yet Nietzsche is not arguing that language *must* reify individual consciousness in such a way that individuation is impossible. Western culture, for example, develops potentialities of individual subjectivity, while simultaneously reifying them. Thus, these potentials also belong to culture, but they are rarely realized. Much of his later work is based on this insight combined with the fear that Western culture will remain a "herd" culture, one that is *merely* social. Historically, Nietzsche claims, culture did not work to develop individual powers and personalities. Rather, culture would have been a means for society as a whole to overcome the exigencies of nature and hostile powers, and must have functioned to assure the unity of the collective enterprise. Nietzsche suggests that various social moralities might be seen as means for "breeding" (*züchten*) the kind of human nature that could survive collectively under unfavorable conditions.[34] But if culture provided the animal man with a social second nature, the individual—as one who possesses self-consciousness and has the capacity to act as an agent—might be thought of as a kind of "third nature." Language can also provide a field of possibilities for self-reflective interpretation. Recall Nietzsche's comment that "the human being inventing signs is at the same time the human being who becomes ever more conscious of himself. It was only as a social animal that man acquired self-consciousness—which he is still in the process of doing, more and more."[35]

As I shall suggest in chapter 4, Nietzsche held that self-consciousness transforms power as a generalized capacity to effect things into *will to power*, that is, into power organized as subjectivity. Accordingly, the individual *qua* agent is a product of those aspects of culture that go beyond their original function of insuring survival against nature. Having come into being under the constraints of survival, cultures can grow and become more than a simple "reflex" to conditions of existence, while still continuing to fulfill their original function. This allows individuality to emerge from the womb of society—the "ripe fruit" of the second nature acquired through culture.[36] Interestingly, Nietzsche holds that individuality can only be the result of collective achievement: "Evolution of man: a. To gain power over nature and in addition a certain power over oneself. (Morality was needed that man might prevail in his struggle with nature and the 'wild animal.') b. If power has been attained over nature, one can employ this power in further free development of oneself: will to power as self-elevation and strengthening."[37] There exists no concept of an original or prehistorical individual in Nietzsche's world view. There is only the individual who is a product, indeed a "luxury," of a people who have mastered the physical exigencies of nature and who for this reason can afford individual personalities. The individual who sees himself as a center of action "is something completely new and something newly creative."[38] Nietzsche even has his Zarathustra proclaim that "first, peoples were creators; and only in later times individuals. Verily, the individual himself is still the most recent creation."[39] Georg Simmel quite rightly comments in an early study of Nietzsche that his individualism was not the abstract kind associated with classical liberalism, but was rather a "social ideal." Nietzsche's defense of the freedom of the individual against society, Simmel noted, does not contradict his view that the individual is possible only within a system of "social supports."[40]

Simmel's comments are unique among Nietzsche's interpreters, however. The common view is that Nietzsche is a "radical individualist" who has little use for society. J. P. Stern, for example, argues that Nietzsche fails to value the "sphere of associative forms," that is, the sphere of social customs, rituals, habits, and moralities that make up culture. This is simply wrong. Nietzsche not only recognizes but values this sphere of existence since he sees it as a necessary condition for individuality. Like so many others, Stern confuses Nietzsche's moral individualism with ontological individualism; he confuses Nietzsche's stated goal—the individual—for an explanation of the possibility of this goal.[41]

Nietzsche locates the possibility for individuation in those cultures that attribute freedom, responsibility, or selfhood to individuals in ways fostering their self-images as centers of activity.[42] Such attributions provide the self-reflective component of culture necessary for individuals to develop. If the individual requires cultural horizons to orient activity, he also depends upon these horizons to identify the self as a center from which actions emanate. Nietzsche points out, for example, that "the invention of gods, heroes, and overmen of all kinds, as well as near-men, undermen, dwarfs, fairies, demons, and devils was the inestimable preliminary exercise for the justification of the egoism and sovereignty of the individual: the freedom that one conceded to a god in his relation to other gods, one eventually also granted to oneself in relation to laws, customs, and neighbors."[43] Likewise, religious interpretations that assign an importance to the individual as a member of a community—Christianity is the most important—have the effect of increasing the individual's feeling of importance. In this way, "collective self-esteem is the great preparatory school for personal sovereignty."[44] Thus the individual arises within collective culture on the basis of mythologies, religions, and moralities that are internalized as horizons of self-constituting practices. For Nietzsche, the fact that most of these horizons consist in collective "falsehoods" does not decrease the reality and the value of these historical effects.

But the emergence of the self out of society produces a tension between the individual and the collective moments of action and interpretation—a tension Nietzsche would like to resolve in favor of the individual, even knowing he cannot. Cultural horizons may inform individuals of their individuality. They may even provide individuals with the ability to act by justifying individualistic orientations toward the world. But because individual consciousness operates with interpretive tools provided by society, individuals can never gain an intersubjective formulation of their unique individuality. As we saw in a passage quoted above, Nietzsche claims that actions themselves are individual, because they combine unique experiences and conditions with common interpretations. But the interpretive dimension of action remains tied to society through the common body of symbols, rituals, languages, and manners of thought employed by consciousness in defining the self. Nietzsche fully acknowledges the deep interdependence of the individual and society even while he speaks on behalf of the individual. Unlike other thinkers who try conceptually to ease or resolve the tension between society and the individual, Nietzsche understands the tension to be a necessary part of any social structure and culture that allows some measure of individuation. This is true even of the most progressive societies: the conflict stems from social existence as such. If society could be said to possess a collective consciousness, it would be interested in the individual primarily as a tool of unity—as a function of "the herd." [45] The individual, however, has an existential interest in being an individual *qua* agent. As I shall suggest later in this chapter, Nietzsche occasionally, and significantly, suggests that these might coincide. But for the most part, he remains an advocate of the individual against the "herd" tendencies of society.[46] In the end, Nietzsche is so taken with this opposition that he sees it as a permanent and tragic feature of the human condition.[47]

Culture as Ideology

Nonetheless, Nietzsche's distinctions between the individuating and "herd," or fetishizing, possibilities of culture provide the tools for interpreting another, often troublesome, aspect of his thinking—yet an aspect of key importance for political thought. Can Nietzsche be said to have a concept of ideology, and, if so, is it a *critical* one? Nietzsche rarely used the term "ideology" (*Ideologie*), but he did conceive of cultures as being made up of various ideals, idols, illusions, and falsehoods that mask various forms of power.[48] This is why many commentators group Nietzsche with Marx and Freud on questions of how cultural entities relate to interests.

A *critical* theory of ideology, however, would seem to have requirements that are missing from Nietzsche's philosophy, namely, some way of distinguishing between cultural interpretations that are ideological and those that are not.[49] Commentators often point out that Nietzsche sees all forms of consciousness as expressing specific configurations of will to power. Hence all ideas concerning universal laws, necessities, truths, and values are "masks": they hide their particular and interested relations to power. For this reason, Nietzsche seems to treat *all* ideas as ideological. According to this objection, then, Nietzsche's view of ideology is so radical and thoroughgoing that it turns out to be indiscriminate and uncritical.[50] Comparing Nietzsche to Horkheimer and Adorno in their *Dialectic of Enlightenment*, for example, Jürgen Habermas argues that Nietzsche destroys the rational ground on which critiques of ideology depend.[51] At minimum, Habermas and others suggest, a critical approach to ideology presupposes criteria that could distinguish between true and false consciousness of one's interests, between rationality and irrationality, and between knowledge and illusion. Without criteria like these, the concept of ideology loses its meaning, and at least two types of consequences follow. First, we can no longer hope for a critical understanding of our interests since we lose the ability to distinguish true interests (however abstractly conceived) from expressed preferences or any other illusions of consciousness. Second, without such distinctions, the prevailing culture would seem to determine what one's true interests are. If humans simply reflect prevailing structures of interpretation and the powers they express, and it becomes a matter of indifference as to whether one calls interpretations "ideological" or not, the concept loses its force.

But this conclusion is too quick. It fails to make sense of distinctions implicit in Nietzsche's approach to culture: for example, between the "herd" and individuating functions of cultural ideas and values. Surely such distinctions imply that revealing the "power interest" of an idea is not all that one can say about it. Where commentators go wrong is in arguing that Nietzsche understands ideas to be ideological *because* they manifest a power interest. Nietzsche does claim that all ideas are interpretative functions of will to power. Precisely the sense in which this is so will be seen in chapters 3 and 4. Here, however, it is important to note that to consider the power interests of ideas does not mean that they are all of equal status and value. The general claim is rather that all ideas bear some kind of intimate relationship (although not relations of correspondence or reflection) to specific historical realities. These relations define specific modes of power, and different forms of consciousness are appropriate to different modes. Thus all ideas are bound to modes of practice, and all ideas have power interests in the sense that they are necessary conditions of specific modes of life. But this does not mean that all ideas are "ideological": in Nietzsche's terms, only some perform the kind of concealment *within* a mode of power that would allow them to be viewed as ideology. Nietzsche judges ideas not in terms of their power interests, but in terms of the way they work to organize and individuate practices. Some ideas serve interests in subjectivity, and some do not. For this reason, some ideas are broadly rational for individuals, and others are not. This is the distinction that, should one wish to see Nietzsche's genealogies as ideology critique, constitutes its critical edge.

That Nietzsche's thinking involves some such distinction is implied in his critique of the rationalism of Christian-moral culture. As I suggested in chapter 1, Nietzsche understood rationalism in Western culture to have evolved in a way that it had become divorced from experience, thus veiling the practical bases of subjectivity. This suggests that his critique of Western rationalism is a mode of ideology critique grounded in an *Aufhebung* (an abolition, preservation, and transcendence) of Western rationalism. If so, then Nietzsche's critique implies and requires a distinction between self-reflectively rational and irrational modes of interpretation. The importance of the distinction would be, of course, that it would provide a critical dimension to Nietzsche's concept of ideology in particular, and more generally his postmodernism.

The question, then, is only whether or not the remainder of Nietzsche's philosophy makes sense in terms of such a distinction. Allow me to anticipate the answer. I argue in chapter 4 that Nietzsche's implicit distinction between self-reflectively rational and ideological interpretations follows from his concept of will to power. I argue there that the concept of will to power functions in Nietzsche's thought to relate the conditional (experiential and cultural-interpretive) nature of agency to self-interpretations of agency. On the one hand, it specifies those aspects of practice (experiential, cultural-interpretive, and self-reflective) that are necessary conditions of agency. Interpretations are rational and give rise to value insofar as they aim at illuminating conditions of practice. On the other hand, it shows that self-interpretations of agency (interpretations like "I" and "free will") are rational insofar as they express a continuity of practices.

As I argue in chapter 3, Nietzsche supports the distinction between interpretations that illuminate conditions of practice and those

that do not with a "praxis" epistemology, what he calls a "perspective theory of the affects." Specifically, our forms of consciousness
identify "true" aspects of the world insofar as they are successful
performances, in the rigorous sense Nietzsche defines success. We are
justified in regarding our ideas, statements, or beliefs as successful
if, having acted on them, experimented with them, or otherwise
used them to formulate agency, we find they do not violate the
self-reflective motive of power, the requirements of intelligibility,
or the exigencies of the social and physical world. Rational individuals will understand that they can experience the reality of their
own agency only by relating the self-reflective motives of power to
their conditions of actualization. Nietzsche's "sovereign individual,"
whom he describes in the *Genealogy*, is one model of rational self-
understanding (see chapter 5).

A Nietzschean concept of ideology, then, judges ideas in terms
of how they constitute individual agents and provide them with a
"feeling of power," that is, a subjective identity. This rules out some
ways of distinguishing ideologies from other ideas. Nietzsche would
not, for example, define ideologies in terms of their function in a
political system, or in terms of their relation to specific class interests,
or in terms of class genesis. It is not that he would deny that ideologies
have specific social functions and serve particular political power
interests: after all, these functions provide initial orientations toward
the problem. Nietzsche points out that Christian ideology served
the Machiavellian political function of teaching obedience and thus
served both the priestly and aristocratic classes.[52] And Christian
ideology served to suppress conflict in class-divided societies. It is also
true that ideological forms of consciousness often have their origins
in specific classes. Christian ideology, according to Nietzsche, was
born of the slave's interest in rationalizing suffering, and was subsequently reinterpreted by priestly classes in a way that solidified
their power.[53] Nonetheless, for Nietzsche, political interests, functions, and genesis are not *definitive* of the ideological nature of an idea.
The reason, of course, is that ideas can serve different interests in
different ways in different contexts: rational ideas can have irrational
origins, and ideas produced by slaves can reconcile them to the rule
of masters.

What Nietzsche cares about is how ideas organize or disorganize
individual powers of action. Ideologies mask one or more essential

conditions of willing. They speak only vicariously to the individual's self-reflective need for a "feeling of power," identifying subjects apart from their actual capacities of agency. This process is exemplified by Nietzsche's Christian slave, whose "feeling of power" is illusory because it is not based on actual willing, and the willing that actually occurs is not guided by ideals but rather by superior social and political forces. Christianity is ideological, on Nietzsche's account, because it suppresses the sensuous aspects of the world—one "ingredient" of willing—and projects the "feeling of power" into a world unrelated to the mundane, thus effecting a destruction of the individual *qua* agent. "When one places life's center of gravity [*Schwergewicht*] not in life but in the 'beyond'—in *nothingness*—one deprives life of its center of gravity altogether."[54] Because Christian interpretations delude the individual with regard to the basic conditions of willing, they destroy the "presupposition of knowledge" and commit the "greatest crime against humanity."[55] They are, in other words, illusions, self-deceptions, or ideological forms of consciousness.[56]

It is essential to Nietzsche's approach that ideologies are not simply "errors" or accidental forms of consciousness. Rather, they are *systematic illusions* in Freud's sense.[57] They mask conditions of willing because they serve a socially molded psychological need to mask the conditions in question. In his diatribe against Christianity in *The Antichrist*, for example, Nietzsche writes that "this *world of pure fiction* is vastly inferior to the world of dreams as the latter *mirrors* reality, whereas the former falsifies, devalues, and negates reality.... *But this explains everything*. Who alone has good reason to lie his way out of reality? He who suffers from it. But to suffer from reality is to be a piece of the reality that has come to grief. The preponderance of feelings of displeasure over feelings of pleasure is the cause of this fictitious morality and religion...."[58] Like Freud, Nietzsche is suggesting that illusions reassert what is psychologically necessary when they cannot be had in reality: in this sense, they are psychologically functional. Nietzsche, in other words, focuses on the interpretive activities of the victims: they may acquiesce in political power relations, but they are never passive in constructing self-identities. An ideology (such as that of salvation religion) is as likely to be produced by victims attempting to rationalize their social situation as by a dominant class attempting hegemony. But also like Freud, Nietzsche emphasizes that imaginary satisfactions produce an inability to act, to change one's situation and with it the cause of the problem. They are, in Nietzsche's terms, a "formula for decadence" because they destroy the individual's ability to engage reality.[59] This is why illusions like Christian ones are pathological in Freud's terms, and nihilistic in Nietzsche's. This is also why it is not trivial to call such illusions ideological: they reconcile individuals to their realities in ways that violate their interests in subjectivity.

It is worth pointing out that defining ideologies in terms of psychological functions is different than psychologizing the problem. Rather, it is to emphasize the interpenetration of psyche and society, subjectivity and power. The way that social and political contexts become relevant in Nietzsche's approach is in the fact that the realities individuals face are structured by social and political forces: psychological needs are *systematically* reproduced by concrete social situations. As I pointed out in chapter 1, for example, for Nietzsche *ressentiment* is not a natural psychological attribute but a psychological effect of the social condition of slavery. Systematic needs for illusion result from social situations in which the need to will—the need to experience the self as an agent—is systematically subverted and can find no actual expression.[60]

Two Models of Political Culture

Whatever its general usefulness, Nietzsche's implicit distinction between the ideological and self-reflectively rational possibilities of ideas does help locate alternative and even opposed models of political culture within his thought. Only one of these models ultimately finds expression in his politics. More will be said about the model expressed in Nietzsche's politics and its presuppositions in chapter 7, but its mention here will be helpful. One might describe Nietzsche's political ideal as a cultural aristocracy, an ideal varyingly inspired, it seems, by nostalgia for the Greek *polis*, the city-states of the Italian Renaissance, and the French and Prussian monarchies. As an ideal transplanted into the late-nineteenth-century social and political situation in Europe, however, it goes beyond nostalgia for a vital hierarchical community and moves toward a cultural-aesthetic fascism. The political function of culture in the contemporary world must, in Nietzsche's view, follow from the fact that society had split into two broad segments. One of these, of course, he calls the "herd." The other consists in a few "higher" individuals who by good fortune or breeding had escaped the totalizing drives of "herd" culture and politics. Nietzsche thought that any new culture would and should function for the "herd" as ideology, while serving to individuate and express the powers of the few "higher" types. In this model, culture would be a means of subordinating the "herd" to a dominant class of culturally superior individuals.

The second model of political culture in Nietzsche remained implicit, and found only limited expression in his politics. The importance of this model lies in preserving the productive political ambiguity of his considerations on culture in spite of his own politics. This latent model portrays culture as having the capacity to identify the individual and the collective on the basis of the interests individuals share in subjective identities. In this case, culture would serve as the collective means through which individuation occurs. Culture here would not assert a simple identity of interests between individual and collective, nor would it be ideological. Rather, it would consist in a collective interpretive process that would mutually cultivate individuals' interests in subjectivity.

The Dominant Model of Political Culture

We find Nietzsche's first—albeit limited—formulations of the political functions of culture in *The Birth of Tragedy*. The model of political culture that dominates *The Birth of Tragedy* comes through in Nietzsche's few comments on the political effects of tragic drama. Tragedy, according to Nietzsche, effects a balance between political individuation for the citizenry and hierarchical community for all within the context of a slave-based society. While combating the divisive effects of a politically sustained class hierarchy, the culture emerging out of tragedy permitted the Greek "political instincts" to develop by institutionalizing an arena of individual action.[61] In strictly political terms, tragedy oscillates between Apollinian representations of individuals engaged in political combat and Dionysian representations of affective unity of man and man regardless of political distinctions. While Apollinian representations bring visions of fragmented relations between peoples and classes, the Dionysian representations contain a moment of unity in which the bonds between humans are reasserted. In the Dionysian "song and dance,"

Nietzsche notes, "man expresses himself as a member of a higher community."[62] But the communal experience is only momentary because the tragedy reasserts the inevitability of class society as part of the drama, thus excluding this "higher community" as it brings to the surface the deeds of citizen-heroes.

The political successes of tragic horizons, in Nietzsche's view, stemmed precisely from their ability to evoke communal identities, identities that override actual class distinctions and oppression. The Dionysian moment of catharsis in tragedy made this identity possible, and it did so without disrupting the existing political order and without implanting unfulfillable expectations in the lower classes for social and political equality, as was the case with "Alexandrian" culture—Nietzsche's term for the culture stemming from a combination of "Socratism" and Judaism.[63] In contrast to the moral and ultimately democratic optimism of Alexandrian culture, the Dionysian moment of tragedy identifies suffering with existence as such. The fatality of existence includes the fatality of political life just as it is. Tragedy constituted a community of Greeks that rose above all other identities; it also constituted subjects in a way that made Greek political institutions possible, including those of citizenship and slavery.

The political assumptions of *The Birth of Tragedy* underwrite this model of political culture. Generalizing from the Greek case, Nietzsche assumes that an individuating culture can be maintained only on the basis of a slave class, while only a unified culture makes a "people" capable of surviving the exigencies of nature.[64] For this reason, implicit in *The Birth of Tragedy* is a distinction between those who *consume* culture as ideology and those who *live* culture, who reproduce it as a means and assertion of their individuality. Thus the effect of tragic culture, whether it subordinates or humanizes, depends upon the status of each individual in society. Its differential effects depend on differing possibilities for action. For the citizen, Greek tragic culture turns the political sphere into *vita activa*, the political thus becoming a means to individual development.[65] For the proletarian, the foreigner, the slave, and the woman, tragedy asserts a vicarious identity with society while it affirms their subordination.

Nietzsche develops this model of political culture in later works to the extent that he could be charged with advocating a culturally totalitarian model of society—one not so different from the one that

emerges from a literal reading of Plato's *Republic*. In his mature
writings, Nietzsche claims that the political condition for any great
culture is a reduction of the mass of humanity to "instruments," so
they might serve as scaffolding for a few "noble" producers of culture
to elevate themselves. Most people would, in turn, consume these
cultural productions, productions that justify their existence by assigning meaning to their rank.[66] A case in point is Nietzsche's praise
of the Hindu's Law of Manu, with its order of castes sanctioned by
God, its accumulated wisdom justifying this-worldly existence, and
its balance between the laboring many and the spiritual few. With
unsettling clarity, he analyzes and cites with approval the social
psychology of traditional political culture:

The authority of the law is founded on the thesis: God gave it, the forefathers
lived it. The higher reason in such a procedure lies in the aim, step by step
to push consciousness back from what had been recognized as the right life
(that is, *proved* right by a tremendous and rigorously filtered experience), so
as to attain the perfect automatism of instinct—that presupposition of all
mastery, of every kind of perfection in the art of life: to set up a code of laws
after the manner of Manu means to give a people the chance henceforth to
become master, to become perfect—to aspire to the highest art of life. *To
that end, it must be made unconscious*: this is the aim of every holy lie.[67]

The great mass of humanity, Nietzsche is adamant to point out, will
indeed reach the limits of their perfectibility through their culturally
sustained identification with ascribed roles in society. The kind of
"perfection" they attain, other writings make clear, is that of an
animal instinctively adjusted to its environment.[68] Why Nietzsche
defends this conception of political culture will become clear in
chapter 7.

The Latent Model of Political Culture

Nietzsche's understanding of the political function of culture could
be categorized simply as an aristocratic-conservative organic view of
society somewhat unfortunately displaced into the modern world
were it not for occasional suggestions that desirable political cultures might function differently. The most prominent aspects of this
countercurrent can be found in three parts of Nietzsche's work. First,
in *The Birth of Tragedy*, Nietzsche asserts that there exists a natural,
sympathetic identity of individuals in society. Second, in his mature

work he suggests that when communication is broadly conceived, the tension between individuality and culture disappears. And finally, in his middle years he put forth a model of political equality based on cultural development. Together, these paint an image of political culture very different from the one dominant in Nietzsche's thinking. Yet—I shall argue in subsequent chapters—this latent model is equally consistent with his philosophy of power.

The aspect of this latent model found in *The Birth of Tragedy* consists in his assertion that tragedy portrays and affirms a unifying moment grounded in the fundamental nature of the world. This is the Dionysian moment, the affective basis of a desire for community common to all humans. Indeed, the ideological effects of tragedy, as is the case for all ideological effects, are dependent upon vicarious experiences of intersubjectivity within community, and occur in spite of and against convention, class society, and war.[69] The opposition highlights a communal moment of the human condition different in kind from the communities formed negatively out of mutual weakness that Nietzsche despised. Were it not for the harshness of political and natural reality, the Dionysian moment might attain greater expression in political reality rather than existing only as an illusory "higher community." What we find is that Nietzsche must equate politics with a particular hierarchy of power in order to assert that the Dionysian moment can exist only when it is strictly separated from the political realm: "The whole opposition of prince and people—indeed the whole politico-social sphere—was excluded from the purely religious origins of tragedy.... Ancient constitutions knew of no constitutional representation of the people *in praxi*, and it is to be hoped that they did not even 'have imitations' of it in tragedy." [70] The Dionysian moment of communal identity is, in Nietzsche's view, a desirable and necessary background of politics, but only if it remains a precondition, separated from politics "*in praxi*." Formulated in these terms, his point is, of course, quite consistent with all conservative organicism, its political implications being altered neither by its ironic aspect nor by its tragic setting.

As we have already seen, however, Nietzsche's later work goes beyond his suggestion in *The Birth of Tragedy* that a natural *affective* basis for community exists, to suggest that individuation can occur only within the intersubjective fabric of culture. While Nietzsche's general considerations on culture merely point to an interdependence and (tragic) tension between the social and individual functions of culture, several of his later notes experiment with *positive* constructions of this same relationship. Communication might be something more than the "genius of the species" that continually usurps differential experiences and individuality. Convention, language, and the "aesthetic state" might coincide to produce individual creativity on the basis of communication. "The aesthetic state," Nietzsche writes,

possesses a superabundance of means of communication, together with an extreme receptivity for stimuli and signs. It constitutes the high point of communication and transmission between living creatures—it is the source of languages. This is where languages originate: the language of tone as well as the language of gestures and glances. . . . Every enhancement of life enhances man's power of communication as well as his power of understanding. Empathy with the souls of others is originally nothing moral, but a physiological susceptibility to suggestion: "sympathy," or what is called "altruism," is merely a product of that psychomotor rapport that is reckoned a part of spirituality. . . . One never communicates thoughts: one communicates movements, mimics signs, which we then trace back to thoughts.[71]

The development of a network of conventional meanings on the basis of "physiological susceptibility" (the Dionysian moment) permits not only recognition of and empathy with the "souls" of others, but also the development of creative powers. "Every mature art has a host of conventions as its basis—insofar as it is a language. Convention is the condition of great art—not an obstacle." [72] What Nietzsche is suggesting is perhaps quite obvious: language does not exhaust communication. Everyday interactions contain a wealth of nonlinguistic means of communication that are intersubjective without having the potential for reification inherent in language. The point to notice in this context, however, is that these aspects of culture might reinforce the powers of individual subjectivity, rather than inevitably conflicting with them.

The alternative political possibilities of this view of culture are explicit in the third aspect of this latent model of political culture. Several aphorisms from Nietzsche's middle period delineate a positive political equality based on a mutual recognition. Because Nietzsche is well-known for his opposition to democracy and for his radical inegalitarianism, the suggestion that his thinking contains an egalitarian strain may seem odd. Yet there is no necessary contradiction:

Nietzsche did not oppose equality on principle but rather because he viewed its modern form as a ideology devoid of content. All too often, in Nietzsche's view, the ideal of equality expressed a mutual envy of, and a revenge against, individual personalities. Moreover, notes from Nietzsche's middle period suggest that he did not believe—at least in principle—that equality is necessarily anti-individualistic. Indeed, culture under the right circumstances might serve to mediate power in ways that a community of equals could serve as a means to organizing individual power as agency.[73]

Nietzsche seemed to think that a positive political equality had existed within the ruling classes of some societies. The best example would be the political equality of the citizens of Periclean Athens, an equality that Nietzsche admired while having no illusions about its class base. Reflection on the ancient Greek situation is probably what led him to more general considerations about the conditions under which positive political equality might be possible. The crucial element of the Greek "equality of peers" was not the presence of equal rights as a legal guarantee (a Roman invention) but the presence of a culturally sustained mutual respect for others. This respect became part of the very definition of power in that society. It presupposed an actual equal ability to will, an ability that required a political culture attuned to sustaining its various conditions. Only this would permit a culture embodying an *agonistic* equality.[74] This possibility is even woven into Nietzsche's strongest diatribes against equality: "Refraining from mutual injury, violence, and exploitation, and placing one's will on par with that of someone else—this may become, in a certain rough sense, a good custom [*gute Sitte*] among individuals if the appropriate conditions are present (namely, if these individuals are actually similar in strength and value standards and belong together in *one* body)."[75] One rather radical conclusion of this comment would appear to be that equality of political rights is possible only where there is a *de facto* equality of the capacity to act. Nietzsche does not, then, oppose political cultures that include equal rights. But he does hold that rights will function ideologically if they lack a basis in a rough equality of individual capacities for action—a condition generally not met in liberal-democratic societies. "Where right *rules*," Nietzsche argues in *The Dawn*, "a certain state and degree of power is maintained, and all attempts at increasing it or decreasing it are repelled...." Conversely, "if our power shows itself to be deeply

shattered and broken, our rights cease to exist."[76] Should one alien-
ate any part of one's power to a dominant body or class, the very
possibility of substantive equal rights would disappear.

These comments imply that even in Nietzsche's terms individuality
is quite consistent with a positive equality, and perhaps even best
attained in this way. One means would be a recognition of others
as subjective beings in Kant's sense, and not simply as means or
obstacles to power (see chapter 5). This can have the effect of
originating rights and duties toward others: "The right of others,"
says Nietzsche, "is the concession granted by my feeling of power to
the feeling of power in others." Like Kant, he asserts that rights might
arise in a Hobbesian manner out of "cleverness, fear, and prudence,"
but they might also be "granted by donation and cessions" directed
toward the subjectivity of others: "In this case, the others not only
have enough power, but more than enough, allowing them to give
up a part of their power and guarantee it to the person to whom they
give it: whereby there presume an inferior feeling of power in the
person upon whom they have bestowed the gift. Thus rights emerge
as recognized and guaranteed degrees of power."[77] "Rights," then,
follow from benefaction, and benefaction is both a capacity given by
power and a means to further subjective powers through mutual
recognition. One bestows rights and accepts duties as a means to
seeing oneself through the eyes of others *as* an individual and rights
and duties come to serve as conditions for self-reflective individuation. Although one might construe this position as *noblesse oblige*,
Nietzsche quite pointedly elaborates it in an egalitarian manner:
"Our duties—these are rights that others have with regard to us.
How did they gain these rights? By considering us capable of making
agreements and contracts, by understanding us as equal to and like
themselves, and for this reason entrusting us with something, educat-
ing us, reprimanding us, supporting us."[78] Here Nietzsche defines a
cultural locus of political power in such a way that power is reflexively
formed and cultivated within and between individuals.

Significantly, Nietzsche held that individual rights could be sustained by a healthy political culture, but not by state institutions.
True rights are positive achievements rather than the institutionalized sediment of compromise between competing, atomized individuals as in classical utilitarian liberalism. In contrast to some contract
versions of liberalism, Nietzsche sees political society following not

from a renunciation but from a development of rights. Thus rather than presenting the state as a necessary external guarantor of rights, Nietzsche could foresee a self-policing community of individuals, one to which he gives a Kantian formulation: "Is a social state unimaginable in which the wrongdoer would bring a denunciation upon himself and publicly dictate his own punishment in the proud feeling that he is thus honoring a law he has made himself, and that in punishing himself he is exercising the power of a lawmaker? ... This would be a criminal of a possible future, which, of course, presupposes legislation based upon the fundamental idea: 'I bow only before laws I have given to myself in both small and great matters.'"[79] By conceiving of rights as a cultural achievement based on the development of sovereign individuality, Nietzsche suggests an alternative to statist politics, one reminiscent of the anarchism of Godwin.

Discontinuities

But Nietzsche did not believe such libertarian possibilities could ever become realities. Why? If culture might serve either as ideology or as a means to individuated equality, why does Nietzsche affirm an ideological role for culture—at least for the vast majority—and exclude its role as a medium of individuation? And even if culture has performed one political role in the past, why should it not come to perform another in the future?

Within Nietzsche's terms of discourse, the answer to these questions resides in the nature of the social, psychological, and economic exigencies to which culture is a response. Cultural possibilities for positive political equality might exist, only to be defeated—as Nietzsche thought they would be—by social, economic, or psychological limits to political organization. But these questions cannot be addressed without an adequate mode of conceptualizing the limits and exigencies of existence.

Two points help explain why Nietzsche is unable fully to conceptualize the problem. The first has to do with limitations of Nietzsche's early formulations in *The Birth of Tragedy*, formulations that carry over into political elaborations of his later work in spite of fundamental shifts in philosophical perspective. Notwithstanding its brilliance in other respects, *The Birth of Tragedy* lacked the kind of philosophical apparatus within which the problem of the exigencies of politics might be addressed. Nietzsche formulated the problem of individuation here solely in terms of interpretive and cultural adjustment to pregiven and static exigencies of existence.[80] As Nietzsche himself intimates in his mature 1886 preface to *The Birth of Tragedy*, the work is profoundly ahistorical in spite of its intentions. Here he saw culture as the only changing element of human existence—a moving interpretive medium that produces meaning within more or less fixed parameters. These parameters—the Will, the political hierarchy of power, and the exigencies of external nature—characterize the human condition *as such* to which culture must respond more or less adequately. From Schopenhauer, Nietzsche borrowed the proposition that the human condition is inevitably one of suffering and alienation dictated by the confrontation of Will and world. And like Schopenhauer, the young Nietzsche understood the Will to be an insatiable, blind, overpowering force striving toward the world in search of satisfaction. He saw the world in terms of social and natural limitations that repel the Will and determine an (ontological) alienation of man from man, man from nature, and even man from inner self. Only culture, as the sole realm open to human control, can change so as to accommodate these limitations, and mediate them so that they become livable. Thus, the polarity of the Apollinian and Dionysian moments of existence in Nietzsche's early work conceals an ontology that abstractly polarizes a formless, energistic psychology and an impenetrable social and natural order. Will and world become the two unexamined limitations that culture must reconcile.[81] Thus wherever Nietzsche seems to make assumptions about the exigencies of politics—whether social, economic, or biological—they are unspecified and unexamined; worse, they are asserted as being part of universal limits of existence. This is why the political assumptions and model of political culture in *The Birth of Tragedy* are directly related to its theoretical and philosophical failings.

For these reasons, interpretations of Nietzsche that build on *The Birth of Tragedy* and other writings of this period will be profoundly apolitical. Because Nietzsche's early writings hide their ontological commitments while emphasizing the constitutive power of culture, they seem entirely appropriate for those who are attracted to his claim that textual interpretations cannot refer to a world of objective referents to establish their meaning. The connection is that if, as in *The Birth of Tragedy*, culture establishes politics, then textuality establishes the world. The claims of many of Nietzsche's early writings suggest that the difficulties with *The Birth of Tragedy* are part of a more general model that conflates interpretation and existence, or at least could seem to do so. Truth, Nietzsche writes in a now famous fragment from the time of *The Birth of Tragedy*, is "a mobil army of metaphors, metonyms, and anthropomorphisms—in short, a sum of human relations, which have been enhanced, transposed, and embellished poetically and rhetorically, and which after long use seem firm, canonical, and obligatory to a people: truths are illusions about which one has forgotten that this is what they are. . . . "[82] There are many possible interpretations of this passage. For example, if one focused on truth being "a sum of human relations," a different account would follow than if—as is usually the case—one focused on truth being a "mobile army of metaphors." What I am interested in for the moment is the latter possibility, which leads one to conclude that the "world," or "life," is constituted by interpretation. Alexander Nehamas, for example, writes that "Nietzsche's model for the world, for objects, and for people turns out to be the literary text and its components; his model for our relations to the world turns out to be interpretation."[83] Nietzsche's early writings encourage such an account. In the above passage, for example, he inverts "truth" and "illusion" in such a way that what the world is would seem to be entirely determined by a process of interpretation, simply for the reason that interpretations cannot refer to any underlying "truth" about the world—that is, anything not exhausted by the interpretation itself.[84]

Why is this an unfortunate reading? Why does it produce a flawed conception of politics? The problem has to do with the ontology of practices that such readings presuppose. Texts are appropriate as models of discursive *meaning* for Nietzsche, and perhaps even appropriate as models of cognition. But even meanings and cognitions presuppose *nondiscursive* relations to the world: relations of sensuousness, power, limits and possibilities of the material world, and the like. These are what Nietzsche means to capture in his notion that much of life is made up of multifaceted "Dionysian" qualities. Modeling "life" after the text, however, means that we shall have no cognitive categories, such as the notion "Dionysian," with which to express those things about life that are not meaningful in themselves, but that nonetheless situate us in a world that, through our practices, becomes meaningful for us.

For similar reasons, the textual conflation also turns out to be quite apolitical. Nehamas and many others who expand Nietzsche's early emphasis on interpretation to an account of the world are only able to give a thin, textual account of what institutions are. Nehamas writes, for example, that "the institutions that guide our lives" are "the products of older interpretations." [85] Institutions are partly interpretive, of course, but also more. Politics also rests on prediscursive relations between people, those of force, control over resources, confrontation, gesture, and spectacle. It includes sensuous relations of need, embodiment, position, and relations to nature. Nietzsche's later work appreciates this point, as is clear in his account in the *Genealogy* of the close relationship between institutions of contractual obligation and the spectacle of punishment. [86] But because the textual metaphor for the world lacks concepts for such relations (even though they are, as cognitive categories, "interpretations"), it is incapable of identifying the distinctive conditions and causes of political organization.

Moreover, without categories with which to identify the nondiscursive and prediscursive, we are unable to identify the possibilities and limits of the political world. If our concepts are unrelated to the exigencies of practice, then they will become ideological. This is precisely the problem with *The Birth of Tragedy*. Because Nietzsche models the world, or at least its human, dynamic part, on the work of art—the tragedy—he simply identifies its context with what exists, using metaphysical placeholders to identify this context. That this remains a problem for Nehamas is clear from his discussion of the causes of suffering: he writes that for Nietzsche the "weak actually suffer from envy, from *ressentiment* ... the weak are suffering from themselves." [87] This would, of course, have been a plausible account in terms of the framework of *The Birth of Tragedy*, because suffering simply turns out to be intrinsic to existence as such. But it would not have been adequate for later work, as I suggested in chapter 1: for the later Nietzsche, what *instigates* suffering is meaningless social violence. Only when suffering is imprinted in a culture that subsequently comes to orient practice would it make sense, as a shorthand, to say that "the weak are suffering from themselves." But where one's model of the world does not permit categories that identify such causes (which include prediscursive, and hence non-textual, elements), the limits of existence become static and non-political attributes of internal and external nature.

Nietzsche's critique of metaphysics (see chapters 1 and 4) applies to his early work as well: naturalizing the limits of "existence" can ideologically veil experience in ways that keep it from being engaged. Indeed, he eventually discards the philosophical apparatus of *The Birth of Tragedy* for a more subtle view of the historicity of existence. In works postdating *The Birth of Tragedy*, Nietzsche comes to define the individual's existential universe in terms of practices or "power," and comes to see value and meaning as dependent upon practices. This in turn allows him to see the individual's life-world in terms of its dependence on the systematic exigencies of action—a perspective that places a relatively greater emphasis on conceptualizing historical conditions and possibilities of action. Exigencies of action that appear as assumptions in *The Birth of Tragedy* become open to investigation, for in Nietzsche's mature philosophy they no longer have an uncritically metaphysical status. This will become apparent in the next two chapters.

Yet, as I shall argue in chapter 7, Nietzsche never performed the analysis of his social and political assumptions demanded by his later critical and historical view of power. For this reason, the metaphysical assumptions of *The Birth of Tragedy* reappear in Nietzsche's later works as mere prejudices, neither justified by his mature philosophy nor subjected to the rigorous examination he characteristically gave to assumptions. But we can pursue these difficulties only after we reconstruct Nietzsche's mature approach to history and power in the next four chapters.

3

The Historicity of Power

Nietzsche introduced the first volume of *Human, All-Too-Human* (1878) with the claim that "historical philosophy is from now on necessary."[1] From this time forward he was concerned with the historicity of the human condition and its consequences for relating knowledge and action. Although implicit in earlier work, it is in *Human, All-Too-Human* and later work that questions of the historicity of the human agency begin to focus his thinking. On the one hand, Nietzsche comes to see historicity in terms of human potentials to create material, social, and cultural conditions of their existence according to the constraints and possibilities given by the past. On the other hand, he sees the knowledge that people develop within this process as conditioned by their places in the world, that is, by their "perspective." If humans are historical beings, so must their knowledge be conditioned by their historical situations.

This chapter is about the nature and implications of Nietzsche's "historical philosophy." As Nietzsche constructs it, the demands of historical philosophy are fairly specific if somewhat demanding: it is to understand both the constraints and possibilities of practices at any point in time, and to understand how history is reproduced by these practices. Any approach adequate to this view of historicity would in turn have to combine two perspectives on history, one evolutionary and the other existential. On the one hand, a conception of historical existence adequate to the dialectics of "life" would, like Hegel's, view history from the "outside" as a transindividual process of development, one that would express the contingencies and possibilities into which each new generation is born; on the other hand, it would also require a "subjective" view—one like Schopenhauer's embryonic existentialism that sees history from the "inside," one that would capture the individual's narrative perspective and sense for the meaningfulness of self, world, and action. Nietzsche locates himself in relation to these views with extraordinary clarity in one of his notes:

The two greatest philosophical points of view (devised by the Germans):
a) that of *becoming*, of *development*
b) that according to the *value of existence* (but the wretched form of German pessimism must first be overcome!)—both brought together by me in a decisive way.[2]

According to the view of history as *development*, the world is a historical process determining our being. Each of us is, as Nietzsche puts it, "a piece of *fatum* from the front and from the rear, one necessity more for all that is yet to come and be."[3] In this perspective we are products of our past; our experience, thoughts, and actions are all determined by what history has caused us to be. From this perspective, we can understand the historical limits and possibilities of action.

The view of ourselves as beings wholly determined by history is, however, quite inadequate to the way in which we actually experience, live, and reproduce history. When we are confident of the meaningfulness of self and world, we approach historical experience as active rather than passive and determined beings. As we act, we experience ourselves—at least potentially—as agents of our futures. If history determines the content of our being, it is also true that we, considered from an existential perspective, constantly appropriate these determinations interpretively and materially. We experience our historical location as a set of existential resources and possibilities for acting. Thus action—the appropriation and reproduction of historical determinations—is intrinsic to any meaningful sense of historicity.[4]

Nietzsche's twofold view of the historicity of practice is far from arbitrary in terms of his problematic: it is closely connected to how he thought it possible for humans to experience nihilism. Historical experiences are fundamentally Dionysian, and for this reason humans can conceptualize directly neither the historicity of their experience nor the determinacy of their historical situation without experiencing nihilism. And yet the imperatives of action orientation require that humans possess the kind of consciousness that makes engagement of worldly exigencies possible. Nihilism can be avoided only by appropriating historical determinations and by experiencing one's agency in the process of doing so.

While historical experience is thus a problematic feature of the human condition, Nietzsche does not see it as absolutely so. His insight is that historical experience is problematic only when action is impossible and individuals lose the basis for experiences of agency. Humans will tend to resist conceptualizing their historicity when they lack the ability to transform determinations into possibilities. A lack of power changes one's experiences of history: a field of possibilities and resources becomes limitations and determinations; history becomes a fate. Depending on its relational qualities, history can be either a meaningful realm of action or an immediate cause of nihilism.

This relational element of Nietzsche's view of historicity has not been well understood by interpreters. Heidegger, for example, holds that Nietzsche sees the "will" as something that by nature seeks a "revenge against time."[5] Bernd Magnus follows Heidegger in claiming that Nietzsche understands humans to be "chronophobes," beings that resist the comprehension of time.[6] But these approaches transform the problem from what is for Nietzsche a historical problem into an ontological one. There is no ontological "chronophobia" for Nietzsche, but only the chronophobia that results from an inability to act in such a way that the possibilities of the past are transformed into the future. What causes "chronophobia" is a lack of power organized as subjectivity: for Nietzsche, humans do not resist time as such, but rather the feeling of being unfree, of being determined by mere historical circumstance, of living a life that is not *self*-determined. When humans are able to organize their capacities of agency, they also gain the capacity to appropriate "time" through action, and in this way become more than merely determined beings. There is no intrinsic conflict between "time" and self-determination, since the self can only be built out of a field of historical possibilities. It is neither possible nor desirable to transcend history, since one can become self-determining only within a field of historical possibilities. Yet when one loses the capacity to exploit these possibilities in practice, then one experiences history as determination, and it is here that "time" becomes a problem. It is in such cases that one experiences the nihilism of being a merely determined being who is no longer a historical agent, the subject of possible futures.[7] Whether history is a realm of determination or freedom depends upon whether worldly practices provide the grounds for self-interpretations of agency.

For Nietzsche, then, without both moments of historical understanding—history as an evolutionary process of becoming and history as our practical appropriations of it—our understanding of ourselves as historical beings who can experience nihilism as well as freedom is incomplete and unintelligible. Thus to arrive at an adequate conception of *historicity*, Nietzsche understood his task as one of combining the "objective" perspective of historical *becoming* with the way we live and act history "subjectively" through cultural *being* and action.[8]

"On the Uses and Disadvantages of History for Life"

With these considerations in mind, we can understand the position Nietzsche develops in "On the Uses and Disadvantages of History for Life," a well-known essay that appeared as part of his *Untimely Meditations* in 1874, two years after *The Birth of Tragedy*. Although Nietzsche has not yet broken decisively with his early philosophical framework (he himself claims the break occurs in his succeeding *Human, All-Too-Human*[9]), the essay remains his definitive statement on historical modes of thought. Even so, it is often viewed as little more than an extension of *The Birth of Tragedy*. Hayden White, for example, has interpreted the essay primarily as an argument for "mythologizing" the past, since Nietzsche argues that history should be written to serve "life," and not the other way around.[10] But White, like so many others, misses the essay's fundamental innovation. Here, as in his later work, Nietzsche is interested in developing an approach to history that is informed by a philosophy of "life"; one that would show how knowledge is involved with structures of human practice.[11]

Nietzsche's strategy is to assemble criticisms of the several modern approaches to history: the "monumental," the "antiquarian," the "objectivistic," and the Hegelian. The "monumental" and the "antiquarian" views of the past are *narrative* approaches to history and thus lend themselves to description of the subjective horizons of action and selfhood. The Hegelian and the "objectivistic" approaches to history, on the other hand, lend themselves to knowledge of historical *determination and necessity*, knowledge Nietzsche takes to be necessary for actions to achieve their goals.[12] But if Nietzsche is careful to delineate the necessity of each of these approaches to history in their respective spheres of understanding, he is equally adamant to point out that each, taken by itself and divorced from a total conception of "life," stifles action and leads to mysticism, passivity, or meaninglessness. For this reason, Nietzsche aims to show how each relates to "life" through the partial view it provides, in this way contextualizing their limited perspectives within a broader conception of "life."

Nietzsche describes *monumental* history as an approach to the past focusing on great deeds and achievements—"monuments" to greatness and action. Monumental history is essentially the narrative of great actors in history, portraying history as the effect of individuals who create and shape historical circumstance through the sheer power of the will. Nietzsche argues that such narratives serve to relate the "action and struggle" of the living individual to an inspiring example from the past.[13] This is necessary to "life," according to Nietzsche, because in preserving the narrative context, monumental history portrays the reality of the subjective horizon that goes into making history. As a succession of examples, monumental history demonstrates the human potential for transforming history in an immediate, spectacular, and expressive manner.

But Nietzsche's acceptance of monumental history is limited to its action-oriented narrative structure. Monumental history is incomplete in that it cannot account for the historical conditions of each act, event, or work it puts forth as exemplary. It provides no conception of historical causality, necessity, contingency, or continuity, and simply links great individual to great individual. Rather than grasping the "true historical *connexus* of cause and effect," monumental history's "object is to depict effects at the expense of causes—that is, monumentally, as examples for imitation." The result, writes Nietzsche, is merely a "collection of 'effects in themselves.'"[14] Monumental history fails to view action in the context of a concrete and contingent historical reality.

If monumental history leads to mysticism regarding the contingencies of action, it also fails to develop fully the subjective realm of horizon since it has no capacity to deal with the place and contingency of self-identity. By considering *antiquarian* modes of history—history concerned with the importance of ancestry—Nietzsche's aim is to understand history as it relates to one's self-reflective sense of identity, as it is lodged in and emerges from a recognizable and stable world of human making. For the antiquarian, "The history of his town becomes the history of himself. . . . 'Here one could live,' he says, 'as one lives here now, and will go on living; for we are a tough people and will not be uprooted overnight.' With this 'we,' he looks beyond his transitory and wayward individual life, and feels himself a part of the house, generation, and city."[15] A conservative in the best Burkean sense, the antiquarian understands the contingency of self-hood on intersubjective practices. And like Hegel, Nietzsche accepts the antiquarian's intuition that the self depends, at least in part, on *recognition*. The self defines and orients itself against a background of familiar identities that locate everyday activities in terms of a culturally defined people. The antiquarian understands that contexts allowing recognition are rooted in the continuity of the present with the past, that they grow within and through traditions which in turn come to define a people's horizons of existence.

Nietzsche's affirmation of antiquarian history is significant not only because it incorporates sociocultural conditions of action, but also because it highlights the historicity of cultural formations themselves as the sedimented products of social life-histories. Considered together with the monumental mode, the antiquarian mode provides an adequate account of history from the perspective of the agent. Together the two modes grasp the dialectic of action and recognition that describes humans as makers of history.

Still, the monumental and antiquarian modes are inadequate to a view of history that would sustain practice. Although they can describe the agent's existential situation in history, they cannot describe the theoretical orientation the agent would need in order to act with rational knowledge of the contingencies of practice. These approaches do not tell individuals how to relate knowledge of the historical determination of the resources and limits of action to action itself. Monumental history by itself leads either to irrational emulation of past actions or to passive adoration of past greatness.[16] Antiquarian history cannot go beyond its fundamental conservatism: it "understands only how to preserve life, not how to generate it, and for this reason always undervalues present change."[17] Even considered together, these approaches remain incapable of relating knowledge of the contingencies of action to action itself.

But when Nietzsche considers those modes of historical knowledge that break with the narrative context to view history as a determinate, transindividual process, he also finds that they fail to relate history to the agents that produce it. If narrative approaches lead to irrational action or uncritical acceptance of tradition, transindividual views lead to detached passivity. Thus Nietzsche criticizes historiography that believes it can attain a purely *objective* approach to the past—what today we might call a positivistic or scientistic approach—for holding that history is the sort of thing that could or should be described in a purely disinterested and detached manner.[18] The objectivistic historian attempts to place himself outside of history, seeking a disinterested stance toward the facts of the past. He sees all interests as distorting his access to the past, and is therefore unable to relate the knowledge he produces to those present interests that motivate concern for the past. Thus objectivistic history "weakens the personality" by portraying history as separate from and superior to present activity. Ultimately, this approach reduces individuals to passivity and paralysis in the face of their own knowledge.

Nietzsche's critique of Hegel and the Hegelian approach to history is ultimately more interesting than his critique of objectivism, not only because of Hegel's sophistication and pervasive influence in questions concerning history, but also because Nietzsche's critique parallels Marx's. Nietzsche's opposition to Hegel stems from the manner in which he saw Hegel to have subjected both the value and rationality of present action to a determinate logic of historical process. Against Hegel and like Marx and Feuerbach, Nietzsche opts for a conception of history that would view transindividual historical processes as outcomes of the material practices generating them. Nonetheless, since Nietzsche includes interpretive activities in his conception of practice, he sides unknowingly with Marx against Feuerbach: both Marx and Nietzsche retain Hegel's emphasis on the importance of active consciousness and self-consciousness in constituting actions.[19] Unlike the positivistic historiographers, Hegel does in fact relate the existential universe and actions of individuals to transindividual historical processes. Nietzsche does not object to Hegel's phenomenology, but rather to his view that individuals can never be in a position in history to act as rational agents. According to Hegel, the difficulty of appropriating knowledge of history for present action occurs not because history cannot be known, but because of an ontologically unbridgeable time lag between an action and knowledge of the conditions of action. Knowledge can never be in a position to guide action: "Philosophy," Hegel proclaimed, "always arrives too late for preaching what the world ought to be like."[20] Hence, humans produce historical outcomes that necessarily escape them.

It is true, of course, that Hegel did not see his contemplative stance toward history as a problem: he saw himself to be thinking from the vantage point of a nearly completed process of development. The retrospective comprehension of history in philosophy would overcome the alienation of the self from its world because it would be possible from this vantage point to recognize the world as a product of the Spirit, and hence as an incarnation of the Rational in the Real. Recognizing this renders the problem of practice guided by knowledge obsolete, or at least much less urgent than it was for Nietzsche.

For Nietzsche, Hegel's claim to have a privileged stance at the end of history was a delusion with harmful consequences for "life." We can never remove ourselves from the flow of history but continue to make history from within its limits and possibilities. However truly Hegel grasped the unbridgeable gap between action and rational understanding of the conditions of action, this self-understanding has an insidious effect on the human agents who must live within the processes of historical development. Nietzsche rejects Hegel's identification of the Real and the Rational and with it the passive reverence of history of many of Hegel's followers. Hegel, claims Nietzsche,

has implanted in a generation that he has thoroughly penetrated the worship of the "power of history" that turns practically every moment into a sheer gaping at success, into an idolatry of the actual.... If each success is comprised by a "rational necessity," and every event is the victory of logic or the "Idea," then—down on your knees quickly, and let every step in the ladder of "successes" be revered! What? There are no more ruling mythologies? What? Religions are becoming extinct? Look at the religion of the power of history, and the priests of the mythology of Ideas with their scarred knees![21]

Although Hegel provided a description of the historical development of agents, he provided no way of thinking about their *continuing* development. The individual who views himself through Hegelian eyes "allows himself to be exhausted [*ausblasen*]" by turning into an "objective mirror" of all that exists, into a merely determined expression of the powers of history.[22] This is why even Hegel's approach to history reinforces nihilism.

Nietzsche's rejection of the objectivistic and Hegelian approaches is not, however, a rejection of the attempt to grasp history as an object of study. He rejects these views because they fail to relate objective processes to the self-constituting practices of individuals. In the event of a crisis of practice, as in nihilism, these modes have no way of orienting the individual toward those inheritances that are making practices impossible. The objectivistic and Hegelian modes can show the necessities of such inheritances but not how to change them.

Critical History and Nihilism

One of Nietzsche's innovations in *On the Uses and Disadvantages of History for Life* is a view of history he calls "critical" history, a precursor to his later genealogical method. Critical history is especially important in treating those moments in history when practice has failed, nihilism has emerged into consciousness, and change is needed. Nietzsche writes that "man must have and from time to time apply the power to break up and dissolve the past in order to live: he achieves this by putting the past on trial, by painstakingly investigating it, and finally condemning it. . . . The same life that needs forgetfulness sometimes needs to destroy this forgetfulness; for should it ever become clear how unjust the existence of something is, a monopoly, a caste, or a dynasty, for example, then this thing deserves to fall." [23] Nietzsche intended critical history to focus on the juncture of knowledge and practice, in such a way that existing modes of historical consciousness can be assimilated to "life." Critical history untangles inheritances, relates them to practices, in this way helping to break the hold of the past over the future.

Critical history, Nietzsche suggests in his early essay, is an *interested* perspective on the past, owing to its connections with problematic aspects of the present. If one assumes that the problematic character of the present Nietzsche describes in this early essay with terms like passivity, injustice, weakness, and consciousness of historical flux identifies a nihilistic situation, one finds that he also suggests an intimate relationship between experiences of nihilism and critical history. The experience of nihilism signifies violation of the basic human interest in being the subject of one's existence. Critical history would thus be an attempt to conceptualize the historical determinacy of nihilism at that point where one is exposed to one's impotence in the face of history. If critical history is successful, it would help make action possible, restoring the experience of power. Action guided by knowledge of this sort changes the *determinacy* of history into a *resource* for the future, thus securing conditions of human power and freedom. It also, as I shall suggest below, endows history with meaning and justification *ex post facto*.

Nihilism not only makes a critical orientation toward history *necessary* but also makes it *possible*. Nihilism signifies a problematic historical situation. For the situation to be altered and nihilism overcome, the situation itself must become an *object* of rational inquiry. Nihilism provides this possibility by forcing one to become conscious. Ideally, one becomes conscious of the way the past has undermined the present, thus—in Nietzsche's phrase—enabling one to call the past to account for itself. When present horizons are ruptured and the present appears meaningless, then "one puts the knife to its roots," in order to find what historical determinants of experience and culture have made meaning impossible.[24]

Nihilism not only forces consciousness but also *distances* one from the conditions of one's existence that are now no longer adequate. Nihilism can be viewed as a release from the cultural constraints of the past—a stepping from under the world view dissolving before one's eyes. Thus nihilism can provide a standpoint from which inheritances might be "painstakingly investigated and put on trial." Like Marx, who thought that alienation would press the consciousness of the proletariat beyond the ideology of bourgeois society, Nietzsche saw nihilism as an imperative to go beyond the dominant culture—the one defined by the Christian-moral world view.[25] This is why Nietzsche believed his historical situation placed him in a standpoint of objectivity relative to the Christian-moral world view, why he thought he could assume a "position *outside* morality, some point beyond good and evil."[26]

The Limits of Critical History

Nietzsche's comments suggest that a critical approach to history may, at some points in time, gain an objectivity relative to some preceding era. But attaining a critical perspective does not mean that one is stepping outside of history to gain a universal objectivity. Not least among the reasons why Nietzsche thinks this is not possible is the subtlety and complexity of history: "Countless things that humanity acquired in earlier stages, but so feebly and embryonically that nobody could perceive these acquisitions, suddenly emerge into the light much later—perhaps after centuries; meanwhile they have become strong and ripe. Some ages seem to lack altogether some talent or virtue, as certain individuals do, too. But just wait for their children and grandchildren, if you have time to wait that long: they bring to light what was hidden in their grandfathers and what their grandfathers themselves did not suspect." [27]

What one comes to know about history is subject not only to history's subtlety and complexity. It is also subject to the fact that we come to history with an interest in constituting ourselves as agents of history. Thus, just as judgments concerning the total value of "life" can never be more than ungrounded dogmatism (for, Nietzsche points out, we are necessarily an "interested" party[28]), we are never in a position in history to draw absolute conclusions about its course. We can only structure our understanding of history by reading back present concerns. Each new interest and problem brings to light a new way of relating history. For this reason, "there is no way of telling what may yet become a part of history. Perhaps the past is still essentially undiscovered! So many retroactive forces are still needed!" [29]

Nietzsche's epistemological skepticism about the rational reconstruction of history along Hegelian lines does not lead him to withdraw the claims of knowledge, but rather, like Kant, to reflect on its necessary limitations. Insofar as we wish to base actions on knowledge that we know will be, of necessity, imperfect, we must proceed with the modesty given by the assumption that at any point in history we are capable of more or less than we know: "We may estimate our strengths, but not our *strength*. The circumstances not only conceal or show them to us—no! They also diminish or exaggerate them. We should consider ourselves to be variable quantities, whose productive capacities under beneficial circumstances could perhaps reach the greatest possible heights: one should thus reflect upon these circumstances, and spare no diligence in the consideration of them." [30] Thus while Nietzsche is opposed to the comprehensive systems of German philosophy—of which Hegel is the greatest example—he is in favor of applying the powers of reason to human situations with an experimental attitude, guided by overarching genealogical hypotheses about history.[31] For both epistemological and practical reasons Nietzsche praises the "virtue of modesty" in questions of knowledge,[32] and suggests we ought to "value little unpretentious truths that have been found by means of method more highly than the joy-diffusing and dazzling errors that spring from metaphysical and artistic times and peoples."[33] Indeed, insofar as reason might come to move within its necessary limits, Nietzsche is optimistic about its power. "The forces of history," he writes, "are doubtless discernible if one strips off all moral and religious teleology."[34]

The Possibility of Knowledge

Nietzsche is not a skeptic or defeatist, then, regarding the possibilities of knowledge. Usable and authoritative knowledge is possible, he believes, if it is grounded in those philosophical considerations that follow from the historicity of the human condition. The fact that we are historical beings does, however, distinguish the way Nietzsche sees knowledge to be possible from traditional approaches. Any account of the possibility of knowledge would have to build upon two postulates derived from the historicity of the human condition. First, all knowledge is necessarily "perspectival"—one of several claims for which Nietzsche is best known. All knowers are historically conditioned beings, each necessarily viewing the world from within a specific set of relations. Knowledge is not something apart from, but rather consists in, a specific mode of conditioning and constituting relations. Knowledge cannot be extricated from these relations to achieve the universal truths sought by metaphysical rationalism or the general laws sought by empiricism. This does not mean that humans are doomed to irrationalism, but rather that it is necessary to understand the conditions of possibility and limits of knowledge.

Second, these conditions of possibility are in part *interests* relating to human agency. Most fundamentally, these involve interests in the material, social, and cultural worlds as means to and conditions of power organized as subjectivity. Knowledge cannot be extricated from the interest the self has in increasing its "feeling of power." The reason Nietzsche views knowledge in this way is to show how a method adequate to human interests in self-determination might be grounded in a conception of practice—in the will to power.

It is important to understand the nature of Nietzsche's position here. When he claims that knowledge is interested and perspectival, he is not saying that an otherwise objective activity is distorted or biased by the intrusion of perspectives and interests. Rather, he is arguing that the perspectives of time, place, culture, and language as well as interests in agency are intrinsic to the situation of the investigator. This means, of course, that Nietzsche is arguing for a species of historical relativism: the meanings of claims are relative to the situation that makes them meaningful in practice.

But Nietzsche's relativism is not one that challenges the possibility of knowledge as such. His rather remarkable claim is that the interested and perspectival stance of all knowledge is not an impediment, but a *necessary condition* of knowledge.[35] "Coming to know," he writes, means "to place oneself in a conditional relationship to something; to feel oneself conditioned by something and oneself to condition it—it is therefore under all circumstances an establishing, denoting, and making-conscious of conditions. . . . "[36] This is also why Nietzsche sees knowledge as increasingly likely when relations that sustain a particular form of life become problematic. Experiencing qualities of the world as problematic enables us to constitute them as objects of knowledge, and to attain a critical perspective in relation to them. Nietzsche sees the experience of strangeness and uncertainty about something to be a first condition for abstracting or "objectifying" experience as an object of study. Objects and experiences close to and continuous with the self cannot be abstracted from the observer in a way they can be taken as distinct objects of study: "What is familiar [*das Bekannte*] is what we are used to [*das Gewohnte*]; and what we are used to is most difficult to 'know' [*erkennen*]—that is, to see as a problem; that is, to see as strange, as distant, as 'outside us.' "[37] Whenever we can take for granted the familiar (*das Bekannte*) and the usual (*das Gewohnte*: literally, what is lived) we find it difficult to gain a critical, penetrating knowledge of these conditions of life and action. Most aspects of existence are unproblematic most of the time because we take them for granted whenever they function smoothly in our lives. We fail to notice them in the same way we fail to notice the most essential organs of our body until they malfunction.

In this respect, knowledge in the natural sciences is no different from any other kind of knowledge, and Nietzsche thinks this may explain something about why the human sciences seem relatively less advanced: "The great certainty of the natural sciences in comparison with psychology and critique of the elements of consciousness—one might almost say, with the *unnatural* sciences—is due precisely to the fact that they choose for their object what is strange, while it is almost contradictory and absurd even to *try* to choose for an object what is not-strange." [38] Elements of Christian-moral culture have not been fully subjected to rational scrutiny, in Nietzsche's view, because they have not yet become entirely strange. Until the surfacing of nihilism, they are inextricably linked to familiar horizons. [39] But with the death of God, Nietzsche believes this familiarity with vanish, providing the kind of historical conditioning appropriate to the study of psychology and culture.

Perspectivism and Truth

It is one thing to assert that all knowledge is perspectival, interested, and historically conditioned. But it is quite another to explain how claims of knowledge could be true, or at least nonarbitrary and reasonable, in light of Nietzsche's account. It is commonly pointed out that precisely because Nietzsche's approach to knowledge is consistently historical, it lacks a theory of truth. Without such a theory, Nietzsche can neither distinguish the relative truth of any competing claims nor defend the truth of his own. It usually is thought that Nietzsche's philosophy must founder here if anywhere.

If by "theory of truth" one means a traditional epistemology in which the question is how the beliefs of a knowing subject could correspond to reality, then Nietzsche does not have a theory of truth, but only a critique of the epistemological perspective. If, however, by "truth" one simply means that it is possible to have good reasons for accepting one interpretation rather than another in a given situation, then Nietzsche does have a theory of truth—one that is more interesting and demanding than his commentators usually suppose.

Nietzsche did not, of course, use the term "truth" in a way that would suggest that he had anything as comprehensive as a *theory* of truth. Most often, for example, he simply refers to "truth" in quotation marks, indicating that someone else's truths are in fact illusions. These kinds of references are interesting only in the sense that they imply criteria in terms of which Nietzsche is willing to judge an interpretation "false."

A second use of the term is more interesting, although ambiguous in its implications. Nietzsche often uses the term "truth" to denote the factual existence of experientially given qualities of the world. At the beginning of the *On the Genealogy of Morals*, for example, he expresses the hope that the "English psychologists" will continue their investigations of the soul, training "themselves to sacrifice all desirability to truth, *every* truth, even plain, harsh, ugly, repellent, unchristian, immoral truth.—For such truths do exist."[40] He writes elsewhere that the basic (Dionysian) aspects of existence "might be true, while being harmful and dangerous in the highest degree." They consist in truths that are possibly ugly, questionable, unordered, and chaotic.[41] Such comments suggest, as John Wilcox has convincingly argued, that Nietzsche is a "cognitivist": it is possible to refer the truth of statements to cognitions of experiential states of affairs.[42] If so, then Nietzsche is not renouncing truth as such, but simply metaphysical theories of truth. In contrast to these theories, he uses the term "true" to denote the existence of the Dionysian qualities of experience—the "fundamental ground" of the world. In this usage, "truth" for Nietzsche is neither good nor evil, neither human nor inhuman: in itself it lacks anthropomorphic qualities.

While it is clear that Nietzsche rejects metaphysical correspondence and coherence theories of truth, these few, entirely characteristic, comments also rule out other, perhaps less obvious, possibilities, namely, pragmatism and positivism. Pragmatism holds that we judge beliefs to be true because they serve our (pragmatic) purposes in one way or another. Nietzsche is clearly not a pragmatist, since he holds that "a belief, however, necessary it may be for the preservation of a species, has nothing to do with truth."[43] Against pragmatism, Nietzsche holds that truths may actually be harmful: they may pierce the veil of illusion that makes action possible at all.

What is perhaps less clear is why Nietzsche's statements are not simply a kind of positivism—that is, a version of the correspondence theory of the truth that tests statements against sense data without regard to questions of utility, value, or identity with metaphysical entities. Nietzsche does agree with the positivists that it is possible, indeed necessary, to rely on the "testimony of the senses" for knowledge.[44] But he disagrees with postivists about how this is possible. Like Kant, Nietzsche holds that our minds actively construct experience, and therefore truth and falsehood cannot be determined by direct reference to sense data.[45] But even if statements *could* directly represent sense data, this kind of knowledge would never be generally beneficial and useful: as we shall see in chapter 5, Nietzsche argued that it is only a (positivistic) faith of scientists that their senses will eventually reveal general, lawlike, logically ordered knowledge from sense data that causes them to hold to the theory of truth they do. In marked contrast, Nietzsche's point is that sensory experience is complex and multifaceted; it is "Dionysian." This is why one must "falsify" experience by imposing a more simple, ordered, harmonious view of the world, even though the best of these "falsifications" may rely heavily on cognitions of experience.

Are we to conclude, then, that Nietzsche has a theory of truth—one in which truth reflects a correspondence between statements and cognitions—but that he thinks that such truths are quite dangerous, and that we must *therefore* opt for illusion? Does it mean that, as Habermas claims, Nietzsche makes a virtue of illusion because he accepted the positivist critique of metaphysics, and yet could not go beyond the positivist account of what knowledge is?[46] Does it mean that, as Mary Warnock has argued, Nietzsche is a skeptic in the Humean tradition?[47] Or does it mean that, as Alexander Nehamas has suggested, Nietzsche has no *general* theory of truth?[48] If so, then Nietzsche's "perspectivism" would amount to the claim that people subscribe to the illusions appropriate to their circumstances—a pragmatist theory of illusion, as it were.

But these conclusions miss the point. Nietzsche does not deny that better accounts of the world have a higher cognitive content, but only that this content is actively ordered so that it is representational only in a weak sense. But even more important is that Nietzsche's approach to truth is not fundamentally epistemological: he was not providing another answer to the question of how we know that our concepts correspond to the world outside our minds.[49] He regards the question itself as disembodied from practice and therefore unintelligible.[50] The very terms of the question concerning "truth" presuppose the reality of our life, and when we understand this, such questions become altogether different. This is essentially Marx's position in the second of his "Theses on Feuerbach," where he writes that "the question whether objective truth can be attributed to human thinking is not a question of theory but is a practical question. Man must prove the truth, i.e., the reality and power, the this-worldliness of his thinking in practice. The dispute over the reality or non-reality of thinking which isolates itself from practice is a purely scholastic question."[51] In this respect, Nietzsche's project is comparable to Marx's: whereas epistemological approaches presuppose a knowing subject and then ask how knowledge of the world is possible, Nietzsche and Marx presuppose the reality of worldly practices, and then ask how knowing subjects and worldly objects become categories of consciousness.[52] This is why if either Marx or Nietzsche can be said to have an epistemology, their approaches do not fit the pattern of traditional epistemology. The reason that Alexander Nehamas cannot find such a theory in Nietzsche, why Habermas sees him as an inverted positivist, and why Mary Warnock sees him as a Humean skeptic is that Nietzsche's approach is not couched in the traditional form. Like Marx, Nietzsche's problematic has to do with how activities of knowing are part of the totality of relations that make up human practices.

For this reason, we need to look for Nietzsche's conception of truth in his account of how experiential truths are assimilated to practices, self-experience, and value. We know, of course, that Nietzsche is quite willing to judge interpretations. What is less obvious is that in doing so, he presupposes criteria that are immanent to practices, criteria that follow from his more general conception of what human practices are like. His theory of truth is a part of his ontology of practices, his "perspective theory of the affects."[53] More specifically, the concept of will to power encapsulates criteria of judgment by identifying those attributes of situations that make practices possible, a point I elaborate in chapter 4. By locating the ontological conditions that make human practices possible, the concept of will to power also provides criteria for judging statements about the world as more or less adequate to practice. It is in this sense that Nietzsche has a general, and perhaps plausible, theory of truth.

From the perspective of the will to power, then, the cognitive integrity of the world is related to the more general activity of ordering it in practice. This is why Nietzsche can write that "it is highest degrees of performance that awaken belief in the 'truth,' that is to say, the *actuality* [*Wirklichkeit*] of the object."[54] The various aspects of the present world (which factually exist but are meaningless in themselves) become ordered and intelligible, and hence valuable and adequate to practice, to the extent that they become conditions for establishing practices that permit self-interpretations of agency.

Insofar as the present world is ordered in practice, the meaningless truth of the present world is transformed into the "valuable" truth, owing to its appropriation as a condition of self-determination. What has value, in both past and future, are those aspects of the world drawn into the sphere of agency.[55] This is the sense in which Nietzsche writes that "value is the highest quantum of power that a man is able to incorporate. . . . "[56] The notion of truth as adequacy to practice is, then, a *second* sense in which Nietzsche thinks it useful to retain the language of "truth"—one that incorporates the first sense, that having to do with cognitively available facts about the Dionysian world. It is this second sense of truth that departs decisively from both positivism and pragmatism. It departs from positivism because it is now coherence given by the role of claims in enabling practices that endows them with meaning, not correspondence to facts. It is not pragmatism because Nietzsche grants that interpretive coherence may involve suppression of cognitively available facts, and thus the existence of facts does not depend on their utility.

These considerations make sense of Nietzsche's most infamous comments, although it is quite true that many of his formulations provide the impression that the perspectival concept of truth-as-power is little more than a self-refuting relativism. For example, he writes in a note that "every center of force adopts a perspective toward the entire remainder, that is, its own particular valuation, mode of action, and mode of resistance."[57] But one should keep in mind Nietzsche's intention to relate Dionysian truths of experience (truth in the first sense) to truths to which we ascribe value and meaning (truth in the second sense) because they relate experience to self-reflective practices. One has a "perspective" on the world to the degree that one maintains an interest in the intelligibility of the world as a condition of practice. "Perspectival" truth is not the "ugly" truth (as in the first sense), nor is it Nietzsche's own philosophical truth that certain exigencies must be observed in practice as a means to agency (the ontological hypotheses of the will to power—the status of which I investigate in the following chapter). Instead it is the "truth" of the world as it comes to have cognitive integrity *because* one has established a practical relation to it. This is surely what Nietzsche means when he writes, "The degree to which we feel life and power (logic and coherence of experience), gives us our measure of 'being,' 'reality,' not appearance."[58] "The apparent world, therefore, is reduced to a specific mode of action on the world, emanating from a center." [59]

What I am suggesting, then, is that Nietzsche's perspectivism in fact leads to a very demanding theory of truth, or—more accurately —to what he calls his "perspective theory of the affects." [60] In a way, this is surprising only because we equate the relativism that is intrinsic to perspectivism with arbitrariness. But as Alexander Nehamas has cogently argued, given the situational factors that sustain any *particular* interpretation, there are a finite number of interpretations— interpretation will not retain its meaning when extricated from its context. Thus, for example, the meaning of a phrase in a poem depends on its place within the poem as well as on the common experiences of author and audience. One's interpretation of it is relative to a particular linguistic and experiential context: given the context, not just any account would capture its meaning. Perhaps only one would, and for this reason, the meaning of the phrase is relative, while at the same time appropriate, nonarbitrary, and authoritative.

What Nietzsche's theory of truth does, in effect, is to generalize this point by taking into account the kinds of relations that constitute subjectivity, and that would therefore establish the appropriateness of an interpretation in terms of how subjectivity is constituted. In locating these immanent criteria of adequacy, Nietzsche is not, of course, starting out from scratch. Most have in fact been used at some point in the past as the basis of an epistemology. Theories of truth based on coherence and value (most metaphysical correspondence theories), on correspondence between sense data and belief (positivist theories), or on utility (pragmatism) each make one of these criteria into a foundation. In so doing, each reifies it from the totality of relations that sustain human practices. In Nietzsche's perspectivism, however, these criteria come into play in ways that are delimited by their role in sustaining practices.

More specifically, Nietzsche's "perspective theory of the affects" implies that an interpretation must satisfy at least three classes of conditions in order to be regarded as appropriate and authoritative. First, the interpretation must be *intelligible* and *coherent* in terms of grammar, an interpretive tradition, and accumulated knowledge of practical exigencies embedded in culture. This is so even if—as in the case of Christian-moral culture—central tenets of an interpretive tradition are crumbling, for we are nonetheless stuck with pieces of the tradition as resources for thought and expression (see chapter 5). Second, an interpretation must be *legitimate* in terms of historical experience, the "testimony of the senses." It must articulate one's tacit knowledge of the "natural" realm of experience. It must comprehend—albeit sometimes tragically—even the ugly and harmful aspects of experience. Finally, an appropriate and authoritative interpretation must become an element of a practice, and produce effects permitting a self-interpretation of agency—a "feeling of power." [62] In sum, Nietzsche's criteria for distinguishing truths in terms of their adequacy to practice involve *coherence* with respect to interpretation, *legitimacy* with respect to experience, and *practicality* with respect to the self-reflective motives of agency. [63]

"Truths" not satisfying all these criteria Nietzsche counts as errors, deceptions, or factual truths without meaning. In the reading I am suggesting here, these "truths" are inadequate because their criteria of adequacy refer to epistemologies that reify a single criterion of practice into a universal one, and in so doing divorce truth from life. For example, the truths of religion produce the "feeling of power" while repressing the experiences necessary to goal-oriented practices. Likewise, metaphysics constitute values in ways seemingly independent of experience. And positivism fails to account for the activities of the mind, or for the interests that sustain these activities. Each epistemology is incomplete in terms of articulating the conditions under which self-constitution is possible, and in this sense it is potentially irrational and ideological (see chapter 2). At the same time, to the extent that a claim embodies some, but not all, of the criteria immanent to practice, it might be incorporated into a more complete view of what truth entails. This is the sense in which Nietzsche claims that the contemporary problem is to "experiment" with the extent to which "truth can endure incorporation." [64]

With Nietzsche's three layers of epistemological and practical requirements for something to be held as true, one is left with a cautious, hypothetical approach to truth. We do not come to know what something is in itself so much as we encircle the things we are interested in with a series of perspectives. Each illuminates a part of the whole in accordance with its guiding interest: "There is *only* a perspective seeing, *only* a perspective 'knowing'; and the *more* affects we allow to speak about one thing, the *more* eyes, different eyes, we can use to observe one thing, the more complete will our 'concept' of this thing, our 'objectivity,' be."[65] One's concept of a thing is "concretized," to use Hegel's term, by building up perspectives over time. Or, as Adorno has suggested very much in the spirit of Nietzsche's epistemology, one should allow the object of knowledge a fullness and integrity of its own, beyond metaphysical reductions, by developing a "constellation" of perspectives around it, within which one's image of the object comes to crystallize.[66] Nietzsche adds that our "practical" interests in self-constitution are conditions of possibility of "perspectival objectivity." To attempt to know something in a disinterested manner is to discount the ways we involve ourselves in the world, and the way the world supports our involvement. This is why Nietzsche continues the above quotation by remarking that "to eliminate the will altogether, to suspend each and every affect, supposing we were capable of this—what would this mean but to *castrate* the intellect?"[67]

For Nietzsche as for Marx, then, distinguishing between the authority of claims is ultimately a practical problem, since it is in practice that we apply the several conditional perspectives for achieving authority. Only through conception and incorporation of the conditions of practice can the Dionysian truths of experience come to be human truths with meaning and value. This is another reason why overcoming nihilism is not simply an intellectual problem for Nietzsche, but rather a practical problem of transforming experiential truths into human ones by means of practice.[68]

Competing Genealogies: Justifying the Past

With these considerations in mind we can return to Nietzsche's enigmatic but very important statement in *On the Uses and Disadvantages of History for Life* that through critical history we might "gain a past *a posteriori* from which we might spring, as against that from which we do spring," and in this way gain a freedom from the past that determines us.[69] He is not claiming, of course, that the past might literally be altered, but rather that the past assumes a new value and meaning when it becomes a means to constructing the future by being integrated into new modes of practice. Likewise, when Nietzsche says that "in my own way I attempt a justification of history," he means that inheritances can be given new meanings by becoming conditions for new modes of practice.[70]

The reason that Nietzsche believed it possible to justify history retrospectively is because meaning is not tied to history *as such*, but rather constituted by present action on the basis of historical inheritances. This is why he opposed not only religious and metaphysical conceptions of meaning, but also positivist and historicist attempts to discover meaning in historical facts.[71] If meaning and value are not metaphysical, neither are they factual, genetic, or teleological: there can be no historical transmission of meaning in itself, only the transmission of the cultural signs, symbols, and languages as well as the material resources that are means to practice. Meaning is the product of a continuously active integration of historical resources into configurations of power as subjectivity.

For these reasons, meaningful historical reconstruction is always *ex post facto*. All historical writings are, in Foucault's terms, "histories of the present," of which Nietzsche's genealogy of nihilism is an example. This is why Nietzsche can write that "a fact, a work is eloquent in a *new* way for every age and every new type of man. History always enunciates *new* truths."[72] One's sense of identity is partly a question of how one understands the lineages that have constituted one's present. Because one's life is always a complex of lineages, one can reconstruct certain lineages while deemphasizing others, in this way reconstituting some part of one's identity in relation to the past and future. But to do so, in Nietzsche's view, one must often return to an earlier stage of development where "this synthesis of 'meaning' can still be disentangled as well as changed."[73] One's grasp of the way interpretive structures inherited from the past have dictated a range of meanings allows one to alter this determinacy, to shatter the hold the past would have had over the future had there been no critical deconstruction.

Nietzsche's point is especially significant today: many oppressed groups have come to understand that to gain a politically viable identity, they must rewrite their histories, not only to reveal past injustices, but also to bring to light the deeds of their race, gender, or class that have been suppressed or gone unnoticed in dominant versions of history. It is in reconstructing lineages and genealogies that "new truths" become apparent. Through these "new truths," a group can reconstitute its identity, and in this way affect its future.

Yet there are inevitable uncertainties in rewriting one's history in such a way as to justify it, providing it with a meaning *ex post facto*.

In Nietzsche's view, few inheritances are incapable of being justified *in principle*, provided they can be revalued by becoming a means to organizing power as subjectivity. For example, that some aspect of the present has had violent beginnings is no *prima facie* argument against its subsequent justifiability. Nietzsche even goes so far as to claim that "all good things were formerly bad things: from every original sin has emerged an original virtue." [74] In practice, however, the revaluation and justification of the past is more ambiguous. For critical history must proceed from within its historical context. Moreover, revaluation and justification is, in the end, a *practical* problem —a problem of power—whose ultimate success or failure cannot always be known beforehand. One is always in danger of complicity in perpetuating or even intensifying those very aspects of the past one seeks to overcome. Quite necessarily, "what is to come will drag along with it what has passed." [75] "For we are merely the result of previous generations, the resultant of their errors, passions, and mistakes, indeed of their crimes. It is not possible to free oneself completely from this chain. Though we condemn the errors and hold ourselves to be free of them, we have not laid aside the fact that we spring from them." [76] Like Hegel, Nietzsche argues that historical violence might be justified where it has had the effect of producing a greater measure of humaneness, freedom, power, or responsibility. [77] But unlike Hegel, he could not see how to justify past violence absolutely, or with absolute certainty. For Nietzsche, the positive effects of violence are neither logically related to historical violence—as for Hegel—nor do they subsume its totality. Violence, for Nietzsche, is not necessarily *aufgehoben* (that is, abolished and transcended) at the level of the whole. In stark contrast to Hegel—who justifies past violence by seeing Reason as the "rose in the cross of the present" [78]—Nietzsche considers Western history since Plato to have been a "madhouse." [79] His parody of Hegel in *Zarathustra* is piercingly clear on this point: "Everything passes away; therefore everything deserves to pass away. And this too is justice, this is the law of time that it must devour its children. Thus preached madness." [80]

Hegel, in Nietzsche's view, related violence and progress absolutely. Nietzsche neither totally rejects nor totally affirms the relationship. Violence and progress coexist in the present—but in tension. The sublimation of violence into self-consciousness, moral codes, political institutions, and ultimately Reason that Hegel sees in history does not resolve this tension but renders it ambiguous. In his clearest and most beautiful description of this historical ambiguity Nietzsche writes,

> Anyone who manages to experience the history [*Geschichte*] of humanity as a whole as *his own history* will feel in an enormously generalized way all the grief of an invalid who thinks of health, of a lover deprived of his beloved, of the martyr whose ideal is perishing, of the hero on the evening after the battle that has decided nothing but has brought him wounds and the loss of his friend. But if one *could* endure this immense sum of grief of all kinds while yet being the hero who, as the second day of battle breaks, welcomes the dawn and his fortune, being a person whose horizon encompasses thousands of years past and future, being the heir of all the nobility of all past spirit— ... if one could burden one's soul with all of this—the oldest, the newest, losses, hopes, conquests, and all the victories of humanity; if one could finally contain all this in one soul and crowd it into a single feeling— ... This godlike feeling would then be called—"humaneness" [*Menschlichkeit*].[81]

For Nietzsche, the tensions produced within history by violence mean that the justification of history is only a potentiality of competing lineages. Justification is not—as with Hegel—a logical necessity. Nietzsche has more in common with Marx in this respect than with Hegel. If for Hegel the meaning of history is ultimately revealed to consciousness, for Nietzsche and Marx endowing history with meaning is a practical task, achieved through material and interpretive work within history. Only by means of such processes can history relinquish its human possibilities and assume a human form.

The Genealogical Method

Heir to his early conception of critical history, Nietzsche's genealogical approach to history addresses the two problem areas surveyed in the preceding sections: the problem of the authority of a "perspectival" approach to the past and the problem of endowing the past with meaning in relation to present practices. Nietzsche's genealogical method addresses these problems in the following ways. First, genealogy is "perspectival" in that it does not claim universal truth for its results. Nonetheless, the method avoids arbitrariness because it presupposes the criteria of adequacy implicit in Nietzsche's "perspective theory of the affects." The method affirms this epistemology even as it deconstructs teleological, deterministic, and covering law approaches to history. Second, Nietzsche's genealogical method addresses the problem of justifying the past by driving a wedge between historical inheritances and cultural meanings. Nietzsche uses his method to show that while the meanings of cultural entities are relatively arbitrary when viewed in terms of historical lineages, they are relatively determinate as aspects of self-reflective practices. Genealogy also inherits the "critical" functions of critical history: Nietzsche intends genealogy to help individuals gain self-reflective knowledge regarding the conditions of their historical agency. It will do so, Nietzsche believes, especially by severing the relationship between Christian-moral limitations on meaning and future possibilities, a relationship that obtains in part because individuals are unaware of how their actions are determined by cultural reifications. By explaining why specific illusions, ideals, or idols have existed historically, genealogy would show how ideas become reified from practices. By "unmasking" reified ideas, genealogy would bring to light the conditions under which the illusion of interest had been served, and the real interest in power as subjectivity distorted. In this sense, genealogy is a form of ideology critique (see chapter 2), one that provides knowledge about the relationship among interests, ideals, and their conditions of possibility.

With Nietzsche's aims in mind, let us look at the method itself. In itself, Nietzsche's genealogical method is nothing more than a series of criticisms elucidating historical configurations of practice.[82] This apparent modesty of genealogy is not accidental: in Nietzsche's view, the powers of knowledge can only increase through slow, methodical, empirical approaches. He even claims that in modern times "the most valuable insights are *methods*."[83] Of course he is not, like the positivists, suggesting that methods are alternatives to philosophy: the methods themselves should be guided by philosophic insights into the kinds of realities whose existence is assumed in every explanation. Without such grounding, methods would be arbitrary with respect to realities, as they so often are when inspired by positivist approaches to knowledge. Thus it is wrong to claim, as Alexander Nehamas does, for example, that genealogy is "Nietzsche's alternative to ontology."[84] The point, rather, is that ontology can never be a replacement for investigation, observation, experiment, and interpretive reconstruction. The kind of ontology that purports to do so is what Kant called "speculative" or "dogmatic" metaphysics, and this is what Nietzsche, like Kant, opposed (see chapter 4).

The relation Nietzsche thought necessary between method and philosophy appears in his own thought as a complementary relationship between his genealogical method and his philosophy of will to power, with its ontological claims about the nature of practices. This relation is an important key to the structure of Nietzsche's thought as a whole. Genealogy is the methodological explication and complement of the will to power, traversing historically and structurally what the will to power traverses ontologically. The will to power hypothetically stipulates the kinds of relations involved in human practice. Genealogy investigates historical human practices using the relations identified by the will to power as heuristic devices as well as to indicate what would count as adequate explanations, for (as I argue in chapter 4) the will to power underwrites Nietzsche's "perspective theory of the affects." Moreover, by explicating these realities, genealogy leads to the kind of knowledge most appropriate to the problem of nihilism, because it articulates the conditions under which human powers are organized into structures of meaning.

Genealogy entails three distinct, but interdependent, modes of criticism, each of which is necessary for explicating the role that a form of consciousness plays within a mode of power. Together they are sufficient to explain a mode of power, and thus serve Nietzsche's goal of achieving consciousness of the conditions of historical agency. The three kinds of criticism that can be identified in genealogy are (a) *logical* criticism of cultural formations—that is, criticism that focuses on the internal consistency of a system of ideas; (b) *genetic* criticism—that is, criticism that traces the lineage (*Herkunft*) of a cultural entity and focuses on its changing meaning in history; and (c) *functional* criticism—that is, criticism that accounts for the inconsistency and changing meanings of cultural entities in terms of their context of emergence (*Entstehung*) or their function within a historically specific form of life.[85]

The role that the first moment of criticism—the *logical* criticism of systems of ideas—plays in Nietzsche's genealogies is often overlooked in favor of his more striking genetic and functional criticism. He writes in an early note, however, that his task is to "comprehend *the internal coherence and necessity of every true culture.*"[86] Moreover, multiple instances of internal criticism exist in Nietzsche's writings. For example, many of his criticisms of the utilitarian defense of morality proceed on strictly logical grounds. Thus he points out that the utility of altruistic morality for the preservation of all demands that each be willing to give up this utility with regard to himself. Insofar as one upholds the goal of altruism, one contradicts its motives: "The 'neighbor' praises selflessness *because it brings him advantages* ... the motives of this morality stand opposed to its principles. What this morality considers its proof is refuted by its criterion of what is moral." [87] And in the *Genealogy*, to take another example, Nietzsche claims that his point of departure is the failure of both Kant and the Utilitarians to provide a rational foundation for morality.[88] Enough exercises of this sort exist in Nietzsche's thought, especially in his middle-period and unpublished writings, to indicate clearly that he did not believe that systems of ideas could be criticized simply in terms of their genesis and function. Criticizing the internal structure of an interpretation is as important in principle as looking at the relationship of this interpretation to experiences, needs, and interests.

Nietzsche has at least two good reasons for doing so. First, he saw himself as a part of a more general movement of a "*Selbstaufhebung*"— a "self-overcoming"—of Western rationalism, as the "will to truth ... gains self-consciousness." [89] Nietzsche is not convinced that the "truth can endure incorporation [*Einverleibung*]," [90] but to the extent that it might, it would have to retain its internal consistency and coherence, although within a more complete set of criteria for what counts as "truth." For Nietzsche, the problem with criteria of internal consistency is not that they exist, but that these criteria are ultimately practical rather than transcendental. He often notes that logical achievements represent universal conditions of human practice, and that life would perish without them.[91] He therefore does not dispute that internal consistency is an essential aspect of interpretation, so long as its truth status is not reified from "life." Nor does he dispute that his own ideas might rely on certain canons of logical consistency —although he thought that many intelligible insights could only be conveyed through nonlogical modes of expression, like poetry, music, or drama. Nietzsche understood that the only procedure of criticism that could explain ideas by reference to genesis and function without undermining its own (logical) conditions of possibility would be one that either shows (or assumes) that the systems of ideas in question do not satisfy their own criteria of adequacy. This is why criticism that would seek to "incorporate" rationalism would have to be immanent to the cultural text in question.

Nietzsche's second reason for attending to the logical attributes of cultural texts is strictly explanatory. Both systems of ideas and languages display attributes of internal consistency as matters of fact. They involve a historically irreducible "will to truth." When humans act—especially within the Platonic-Christian culture of Nietzsche's interest—they are in varying degrees influenced by the internal consistency of their interpretive schemas. For this reason, the logical attributes of languages and systems of ideas are an irreducible historical reality. To ignore this would be to miss a historical ingredient of willing, an ingredient of special importance in Western cultures.

If Nietzsche can show that a way of thinking has had a historical effect at least partly given by its logical and structural attributes, and yet can show that this way of thinking is contradictory in terms of its own criteria of adequacy, then he has gained the philosophic right to use the same criteria in his own approach. While salvaging these criteria, however, he can also show that logical consistency does not produce complete and self-identical meanings, and must be related to specific forms of practice for their meanings to be established.

Nietzsche's claim that meanings and values are not intrinsic to cultural texts is reinforced by *genetic* criticism, criticism that elucidates the descent (*Herkunft*) of cultural ideals. With the problem of descent one encounters the deliberate irony of genealogy. For here it becomes clear that it is quite difficult, and maybe impossible, to trace the meaning of a cultural artifact. "All concepts in which an entire process is semiotically concentrated elude definition," writes Nietzsche. "Only that which has no history is definable." [92] Cultural ideals, concepts, indeed even material things do not maintain a discrete identity over time. Metaphysical philosophy, Nietzsche argues at the beginning of *Human, All-Too-Human*, has obscured this problem:

For two thousand years, even now in almost all its aspects, philosophy has posed its problem in the following way: how can something emerge out of its opposite? For example, reason from unreason, the living from the dead, logic from the unlogical, disinterested perspective from desirous will, selflessness out of egoism, truth from error? Metaphysical philosophy helps itself over these difficulties insofar as it denies the emergence [*Entstehung*] of one thing out of another and for those more highly valued things presumes a miraculous origin [*Wunder-Ursprung*] from out of the core and essence of the "thing in itself." [93]

Tracing the real "descent and beginnings" (*Herkunft und Anfange*) of "moral, religious, and aesthetic representations and feelings" in the "great and minute aspects of the intercourse of culture and society" presents an irresolvable problem for metaphysical philosophy. The problem cannot be resolved, in Nietzsche's view, without discarding the metaphysical proposition that meaning resides in a correspondence between concepts, ideals, systems of ideas, words, or statements and some metaphysical set of referents.[94] Accordingly, the meaning of cultural formations cannot be decided by constructing a genealogy of concepts alone.

Nietzsche extends his genetic critique to logical reconstructions of history: if cultural "representations and feelings" are historically rooted in their opposites, if ideas do not maintain identical meanings over time, then it is not possible to reconstruct history by tracing the meaning of an idea taken in itself. This is why in the first sections of the *Genealogy* Nietzsche castigates "the English" (that is, the Utilitarians) for attempting to find an "original purpose" to morality.[95] The English, Nietzsche argues, ascribe the present purposes of morality to an original historical situation. In these situations morality is understood to be synonymous with the "useful," an equation "typical" of the English but not of history. To write history in this way is to confuse historical processes with a purely logical attempt to provide rational foundations for morality. This is "unhistorical" because it mistakes a logic of ideas (in this case, the rationale of utilitarian morality) with a history of the emergence of ideas.

Nietzsche is not arguing, of course, that no continuity exists in matters of culture. His point is that cultural continuity resides not in the meaning of cultural entities, but in the relative rigidity of their grammars, interlocking ideas, and ritualized ways of acting, which, taken as a whole, map and delimit a range of meanings without uniquely determining them. In the *Genealogy*, for example, Nietzsche points out that in the meaning of punishment, "one must distinguish two aspects: on the one hand, that which is relatively *enduring*, the custom, the act, the 'drama,' a certain strict sequence of procedures; on the other hand, that in it which is *fluid*, the meaning, the purpose, the expectation associated with the performance of such procedures."[96]

Nietzsche's genetic criticism prepares for his third moment of genealogy, that concerning the context of emergence (*Entstehung*) of cultural ideals. Here Nietzsche takes an explicitly functional approach to cultural entities. Referring to the contradictory descent of cultural ideals, he claims that "the origin of these contradictions need not necessarily go back to a supernatural source of reason: it is sufficient to oppose it to the real genesis of the concepts. This derives from the practical sphere, the sphere of utility; hence the strength of faith it inspires."[97] In order to solidify the ultimate priority of the functional approach over the genetic, Nietzsche employs a methodological distinction between the origins of cultural entities and their subsequent functions at different moments of evolutionary processes:

The cause of the emergence [*Entstehung*] of a thing and its eventual utility, its actual employment and place in a system of purposes, lie worlds apart; whatever exists, having somehow come into being, is taken over, transformed, and redirected by some power superior to it; all events in the organic world are a subduing, a *becoming master*, and all becoming master involves a fresh interpretation, an adaptation through which any previous "meaning" and "purpose" is necessarily obscured or even obliterated. However well one has understood the *utility* of any physiological organ (or of a legal institution, a social custom, a political usage, a form in art or a religious cult), this means nothing regarding its emergence.[98]

This passage does not mean that all cultural entities *reflect* a "superior power," but rather that they become successive *functions* ("utilities") of successive modes of life, and thus also serve as conditions of these modes of life. Because the utility of an entity changes with each new form of life, there is no lineage of utilities. There are only utilities that emerge within a set of interrelated practices.

Thus when Nietzsche considers cultural formations in functional terms he sees them as inexplicable taken in themselves, but still as relatively autonomous conditions of the mode of life of which they are a part. In these terms, cultural texts can be interpreted as a concealing and masking sign language behind which lies a context of experiences, needs, and actions. The text shields, distorts, denies, filters, selects, and unifies, depending on the organization of practices. The text also provides systematic, if always oblique, access to these relations of power. Culture can be "read" as a set of clues that provide entrance to the "practical sphere," the sphere in which the contingencies of existence, interests, and powers are related to modes of interpretation and result in definite forms of life.

Nietzsche poses this kind of problem in the preface to the *Genealogy* when he asserts that he will examine the "conditions" under which "these value judgments good and evil" were devised, and the value that "they themselves possess" as means to self-interpretations of agency under these conditions.[99] The emergence of Christian asceticism—to take a simplified example from the third essay of the *Genealogy*—can be sufficiently explained as the convergence of three classes of interrelated factors, namely, (a) a preexisting Judaic cultural grammar with its own interrelated systems of postulates; (b) a specific set of political power relations that dictated against this-worldly agency for a dispersed "slave" class; and (c) the need for those subject to these experiences to attain a "feeling of power," in spite of their experiences. Christian asceticism functioned to provide that "feeling of power," in the form of a vicarious "will," under these specific cultural and experiential conditions.[100] Nietzsche treats not only ascetic moralities as texts that give access to such contextual factors, but also words and languages, gods and religions, laws, philosophical systems, literary works, drama, music, and the symbolic aspects of power figures like priests, to cite some examples.[101]

The fact that moving through the three moments of genealogy provides sufficient material to understand a cultural entity as a *function* means that the genealogy has provided sufficient material to understand the mode of life in terms of which the cultural entity might be viewed as a function. Thus in its functional moment, genealogy singles out as historical facts the conditions for the possibility of willing posited by the will to power. In this way, it gives historical substance to self-interpretations of agency.

In sum, Nietzsche finds the emergence of meaning to reside in the confluence of a cultural grammar with a sphere of affective powers and interests. In its final reduction, genealogy reveals the fact that it has traversed the conditions for definite organizations of will to power. "Purposes and utilities," claims Nietzsche, "are only *signs* that a will to power has become master of something less powerful and imposed upon it the character of a function...."[102]

The genealogical method, then, follows the pattern of analysis that would have to obtain *if* history is to be seen as the result of human practices. It tells us what kinds of accounts could not have been the case given the textual evidence in light of the demands and constraints of practices. And it tells us that the kind of historical account one gives is intimately related to the problems and concerns of the present. But because genealogy is a defensible enterprise only in relation to these tasks and constraints, its integrity comes to rest on the integrity of the will to power as a characterization of the structure of human practice. It is to this problem that we now turn.

4

The Will to Power

The major issue raised by Nietzsche's account of nihilism is the question of how our activities could have the qualities of agency, given the historical nature of the human condition. Nietzsche's approximation to an answer lies in his concept of will to power. I say "approximation" because, as in so many other areas, Nietzsche leaves it to his readers to reconstruct the meaning of the concept from the way he poses his problems. In this chapter I argue that the concept of will to power serves to address Nietzsche's problems only if one construes it as a *critical ontology of practice*. By characterizing the concept in this way, I mean to suggest that it involves the following attributes. Like Kant, Nietzsche suggests a critical approach: the will to power does not denote the world *in itself*, but rather its "intelligible character."[1] And in a way similar to Heidegger later, Nietzsche's ontological categories characterize the phenomenology of existence. The will to power is a view of the world from "inside" our structures of action.[2] Thus for Nietzsche the "world" means our "being in the world," and the will to power makes this "being" intelligible by hypothetically denoting certain of its attributes. Finally, like Marx, Nietzsche characterizes the priority of "being" in terms of practice— that is, in terms of our material and intellectual metabolism with historical conditions of existence. One might say, then, that Nietzsche's concept of will to power stands halfway between Kant's critical philosophy and Heidegger's phenomenological ontology, while exhibiting a materialism of the sort one finds in Marx.

By construing the will to power in these terms, I mean to rule out several common approaches to the concept. Most common are interpretations of the will to power as a psychological metaphysics denoting a universal motive for power over others or over oneself.[3] Some—like Heidegger—view the concept more generally as a subjective source of creative practice.[4] But precisely because these approaches interpret the will to power metaphysically—that is, as a unified essence, source, or first cause giving rise to phenomena—they must also hold that Nietzsche is naively unaware that his own critique of metaphysics applies also to his concept of will to power. Nietzsche, then, would have failed to understand the demands of his most basic project. Commentators such as Deleuze and Strong who rightly seek alternatives to a metaphysical interpretation of the will to power argue that it characterizes the world as affectivity, force, and *pathos*. Although innovative and certainly more in accord with Nietzsche's project, these views ultimately cannot account for Nietzsche's attributions of organizing capacities to the will to power. Deleuze, for example, finds he must resort to the rather un-Nietzschean and again metaphysical expedient of positing a duality of "active and reactive" forces out of which organization emerges.[5]

The difficulty with these interpretations is not just that they are at odds with the philosophical task Nietzsche thought he was performing with the concept of will to power. They also fail to account for the full range of references he provides for it. On reading Nietzsche, one finds that he varyingly uses the term "will to power" to refer to "the world," to "life," to interpretive activities, to affectibility and *pathos*, to desires for the "feeling of power," and to organizing forces.[6] Any account of the concept of will to power should, of course, accord both with Nietzsche's philosophical project and with his references. As I shall argue, construing the concept as a critical ontology of practice is satisfying in both respects. Equally important, this reading produces a Nietzsche that is interesting for critically postmodern approaches to political thought.

Nonetheless, in taking this approach I also wish to dissociate the concept from certain of Nietzsche's own elaborations of the concept of will to power, specifically, where he does in fact use it in a modernist, metaphysical way. His language of mastery, subduing, exploiting, and commanding often equates subjective capacities with desires to dominate the world, self, and others. Nietzsche often wants to argue that desires for a nonexploitive, egalitarian, and pluralistic society violate the *essence* of life, and therefore violate metaphysical contingencies of life as such.[7]

Now it may be that Nietzsche's ambivalence between a modernist metaphysic of mastery and a critical, postmodernist account of the kind I develop here reflects a philosophical ambivalence on Nietzsche's part. It may be that he was still caught in the modernist debate between those whose most basic concepts express a domination of nature (like Descartes and Hobbes) and their modernist critics who sought a harmony with nature (like Rousseau, at least as Nietzsche understood him).[8] Nietzsche's own position is that the world is neither as susceptible to mastery as some moderns have thought nor as susceptible to harmonization as the modern critics of modernism tried to argue. To the extent that Nietzsche is unable to extricate himself from the language of the modernist debate, we might expect to find an unresolved tension between domination and harmonization within his most basic philosophic concept.[9]

Still, there are reasons to believe that the sources of these ambivalences are not entirely philosophical: Nietzsche usually invokes the will to power as a metaphysics of domination specifically to justify political domination. Whatever ambivalences there are in Nietzsche's *philosophy* of power, they are overlaid, and perhaps overdetermined, by *political* ones. This suggests a different assessment: that the conflicts are not so much between modern and postmodern possibilities within Nietzsche's philosophy (although this is nonetheless possible and probable), as between his postmodern philosophy and his premodern politics. I shall argue in chapter 7 that Nietzsche's premodern assumptions about the nature and limits of political institutions caused him to read a political content back into the concept of will to power that is extraneous to his problematic and philosophy. He is able to do this without noticing because he relies on the ancient practice in political philosophy of equating the organization of the soul (in this case, of willing) with the organization of society. This allows him to use political language (commanding, obeying, exploiting) to make general points about the organization of agency. He is then able to deduce the same social and political effects from his analysis of willing but only because he has used the same terms to cover both kinds of processes.

Nietzsche's procedure suggests that it is necessary, at least for purposes of this chapter, to treat his political terms strictly as metaphors, as well as to suspend any political conclusions one might be inclined to draw from these metaphors, even though Nietzsche himself is quick to do so. Thus in most cases here, I suspend consideration of Nietzsche's overtly political and ideological uses of the concept until chapter 7, and instead offer the more interesting possibility, that is, a reconstruction consistent with Nietzsche's critical postmodernism. The point in doing so, of course, is that this kind of reconstruction is important for problems of critical postmodernism, while Nietzsche's (premodern) politics is not.

The Will to Power as Practice

What does viewing the concept of will to power as a critical ontology of practice involve? First, and most generally, the concept functions within Nietzsche's thinking as an ontological postulate or "hypothesis" (as he sometimes calls it) about the dimensions—experiential, interpretive, and self-reflective—that one must ascribe to the human condition for practices to be intelligible as the practices of agents in a historical world.[10] If the will to power is indeed a critical ontology of practice, then it serves to frame an approach to power rather than to stipulate its essential content—as would a metaphysical concept. It constitutes a conceptual domain of necessary presuppositions rather than describing essential attributes of classes of events. The conceptual domain Nietzsche wishes to constitute, of course, is one adequate to the problem of nihilism. This means viewing human practices as the fundamental problem of philosophy, and moving "behind" traditional philosophical problems. Questions like "How do I act rationally and with good reason?" presuppose questions like "What role does rationality (morality, etc.) play in constituting actions, and how does this make specific forms of life possible?" The first two sections of *Beyond Good and Evil* suggest that Nietzsche might have put his question like this: "Given the historical problem of nihilism, what qualities must we universally ascribe to existence for our activities to be intelligible?"[11] Considered as a whole, Nietzsche's various references to the will to power as a *pathos*, as interpretation, and as a reflexive will turn out to be necessary to the intelligibility of these processes we experience as subjectivity or agency.

Second, the concept of will to power provides Nietzsche with a conception of value that is immanent to historical practice. His approach to this problem is subtle: it involves shifting all past conceptions of agency from the realm of metaphysics to the realm of values, and ascribing a reality to them *as* values—or, in more Nietzschean terms, as self-interpretations possessing value as conditions of willing. He approaches the problem as follows. Pointing out that Western philosophy has gradually reduced all categories of agency to "willing"—the ultimate ground of the soul, the ego, the "I"—Nietzsche reduces willing itself to a series of contingent processes that no longer have a strictly "internal" or subjective character. In this way he removes the last and most fundamental ground of metaphysics, the idea of a unified agent as the underlying originator of actions.[12] In performing this deconstruction, Nietzsche makes a little noticed move that turns out to be essential for his reconstruction of power as agency. He claims that we *do* have experiences of agent unity, of our own subjectivity. These experiences do not reflect an underlying metaphysical agent (like a will or soul), but are self-interpretations based on interactions with the world. Through these interactions, we learn to regard ourselves as originators of causal sequences. As such, experiences of agent unity reflect an underlying continuity of worldly practices and achievements that we learn to associate with an "I." Moreover, this reflexively constituted "I" is also the basis of all possible values. This is why nihilism occurs when cultural or experiential conditions fragment the continuity of practices, the material basis of the self. In Nietzsche's view, then, the agent is both radically contingent *and* has real conditions of possibility. This is why he holds that experiences of agent unity must both be explained as a possibility, and retained as a value.

Rather than simply destroying concepts of agent unity like "willing" or "free-will," then, Nietzsche removes them from the metaphysical realm and places them in the realm of "morals," or the sphere of interpretations that both have value and worldly conditions of possibility but no metaphysical correlates. He writes, for example, that "between ourselves, it is not necessary to get rid of 'the soul' ... and renounce the most ancient and venerable hypotheses. ... [T]he way is open for new versions and refinements of the soul-hypothesis; and such conceptions as 'mortal soul' and 'soul as subjective multiplicity,' and 'soul as social structure of the drives and affects,' want henceforth to have citizens' rights in science."[13] The "soul" as a source of agency remains an experience and a value, and therefore requires explanation. This is what Nietzsche provides by looking at the grounding of agency in practices. In his terse and little-understood formula, "A philosopher should have the right to include willing as such within the sphere of morals—morals being understood as the doctrine of the relations of supremacy under which the phenomenon of 'life' emerges [*entsteht*]." [14] The will to power, in other words, performs in Nietzsche's thought the relatively classical function of equating willing, rationality, and freedom. But it does so in a manner that assumes the full historicity of human practice.

Third, Nietzsche's conception of will to power produces an intrinsically historical approach to human practices. As suggested in the last chapter, explanation of any *particular* kind of agency in Nietzsche's view requires genealogical elaboration of the several levels of human reality posited by the will to power. Thus will to power and genealogy are complementary: genealogy involves investigating how the conditions posited by will to power are organized into historically distinct configurations of power. From these considerations, a definite conception of the historicity of human practice emerges, together with a definite conception of the structure of cultural evolution, points to which I turn at the end of this chapter.

Nietzsche and Kant: The Critique of Speculative Metaphysics

If I am right about Nietzsche's project, then his proposal that the world is will to power presents something of an enigma: If he universally characterizes the "the world" as will to power, then how could the concept *not* be another metaphysic? Is it not simply a *new* metaphysics of agency, one that inevitably carries with it all of the faults of the metaphysical approaches Nietzsche rejects and perhaps others as well?

The concept is, in fact, different than the approaches Nietzsche rejects. But to see this, we need to see not just what Nietzsche *says* about the will to power, but also how the concept *functions* within his thinking. This requires not only that we identify his problematic of nihilism (see chapter 1), but also the kinds of metaphysical thinking that he identifies with nihilism, and therefore would presumably reject in his own philosophy. The context in which Nietzsche introduces the concept of will to power in the second section of *Beyond Good and Evil* is significant in this respect. [15] He introduces the notion toward the end of a sustained and sweeping attack on the universal and transcendental ideas that have formed the conceptual foundations of Western philosophy: the Greeks' ideas of nature, atomism, the spirit, the Christian soul and God, Descartes' ego and the thinking "I," Kant's thing-in-itself and his universal faculties of reason, and finally Schopenhauer's Will. What these ideas have in common, according to Nietzsche, is that each posits a unified, nonempirical quality or substance as the foundation of existence. These concepts served to explain experiences by deriving them from transcendent, universal, and unitary origins. Such metaphysics not only characterize the fundamental attributes of the world, but also do so in moral terms: the notions of God, nature, soul, free-will, and thinking subjectivity serve as bases for judging certain actions to be sinful, unnatural, inhuman, or irrational. When Nietzsche claims that he is moving "beyond good and evil," he is rejecting metaphysical identifications of the world, as well as judgments that follow from them. He does so on both explanatory and moral grounds. With regard to explanation, it is a mistake to think that posited universal categories do more than push explanatory problems into regress.[16] With metaphysical modes of moral evaluation, Nietzsche holds a position that anticipates Heidegger's: Western metaphysics involves a "humanism" that ultimately reduces the world to a reflection of "man" as subject, and thus degrades the fullness of existence. "Supposing," Nietzsche asks, "that not just man is the 'measure of things.'"[17]

In criticizing Western metaphysics, however, Nietzsche is not unprecedented: he is deepening and radicalizing the tradition of critical philosophy that began with Kant. The mistakes Nietzsche identifies in metaphysics are precisely those Kant identified in distinguishing his own "critical philosophy" from speculative metaphysics.[18] It is worth looking at the parallels between Nietzsche and Kant on this issue, because it turns out that Kant's criticisms of speculative metaphysics suggest the sense in which Nietzsche's own universal claims about the world (like the claim that "the world is will to power") are different not just in content but in philosophical status from those he rejected. Kant's critical philosophy is pivotal for Nietzsche in this respect, and it is through comparison that we can see clearly the direction of his project. This is not to say that Nietzsche is not critical of Kant—a point I develop later in this chapter, and return to in chapter 5—but rather that his criticisms proceed on Kantian grounds.[19]

For Kant there are proper and improper uses of universal claims.

The universal claims of absolute (or speculative) metaphysics are improper: they presume to be about some nonempirical and yet substantial reality "behind" experience that gives rise to experience. There are three kinds of transcendental identities or "illusions" that, Kant believes, exhaust the possibilities of speculative metaphysics. The illusions of "speculative psychology" posit a unified thinking subject in its notions of soul, ego, and "I" as foundations of thinking. Those of "speculative cosmology" posit underlying unities in the world such as atoms, causal necessities, points of creation of the universe in time, and so on; each of these ideas requires that the world manifest a simple underlying unity. Finally, the illusions of "speculative theology" posit a supreme being behind the manifold of experience.

The reasons that Kant calls such metaphysical ideas "illusions" is that we could not possibly know about such things, even if they existed. In Kant's view, of course, we cannot do without universal principles as regulative ideas and connectives in our judgments. But we must recognize that these ideas and judgments are simply necessary conditions of our reasoning, as well as of empirical objects in space and time, and not about any other kind of reality. Judgments about causality, for example, are connectives in the structure of our experience that, when we name these as "causes," allow us conceptually to objectify experience. Absolute metaphysics confuses these empirical necessities *of* experience with ontological necessities *beyond* experience.

In the case of speculative (or "rational") psychology, for example, one finds this confusion in the assumption that the empirical experience of subjectivity is the effect of a nonempirical subject or soul. This confuses the unity of the "I think" that is a logical requirement of relations between concepts with the empirical experience of the self. Or to put Kant's argument slightly differently, the necessity for a subject that formally unifies categorical syllogisms is mistakenly held to mean that there are unified thinking subjects "behind" experience. Several mistaken conclusions follow from this "rational science of the soul": (1) "The Soul is *substance*." (2) "As regards its quality, [it is] *simple*." (3) "As regards the different times in which it exists, [it is] numerically identical, that is, [is] *unity* (not plurality)." [20] From these postulates arise the transcendental notion that the soul is immaterial, incorruptible, spiritual, immortal, as well as being the basis of personality and animated life in general.[21] But since none of these conclusions can refer to the empirical experience of subjectivity, Kant concludes that they cannot be about that experience. This is why they are "illusions": they have no *worldly* reality. Reason has no right to such claims, because it has exceeded the realm of possible knowledge.

In rejecting metaphysical concepts of the subject, Nietzsche's reasoning is almost identical:

With regard to the superstitions of logicians, I shall never tire of emphasizing a small terse fact, which these superstitious minds hate to concede—namely, that a thought comes when "it" wishes, and not when "I" wish, so that it is a falsification of the facts of the case to say that the subject "I" is the condition of the predicate "think." *It* thinks; but that this "it" is precisely the famous old "ego" is, to put it mildly, only a supposition, an assertion, and assuredly not an "immediate certainty." After all, one has even gone too far with this "it thinks"—even the "it" contains an *interpretation* of the process, and does not belong to the process itself. One infers here according to the grammatical habit: "Thinking is an activity; every activity requires an agent; consequently—"[22]

Like Kant, Nietzsche is arguing that the mistake of metaphysics is to confuse the formal unity of grammatical subjects with the substantial unity of empirical subjects. We are impelled by the logical structure of grammatical relations, Nietzsche points out, to attach a "logical-metaphysical postulate" of a doer, an agent, to every deed. But it is only a belief—in Kants terms, an illusion of dogmatic metaphysics—that such things exist as unified, substantial entities, and not a fact.[23]

We find similar parallels in Kant's criticism of speculative cosmology in form, if not always in substance. The method of Kant's critique was to show that one can trace the "antinomies" within various metaphysical systems to conflicts between basic cosmological propositions that are themselves unfounded. For example, there is an antinomy between the two cosmological notions that freedom exists and that the world is determined by causal necessities. The antinomy leads to the view that there is an infinite series of causes extending through time, and this produces the idea that there must have been an originating uncaused cause. Kant's method is to show that this kind of antinomy results from mistaking a regulative principle of thinking for one constitutive of experience. In the case of the antinomy between freedom and causality, Kant claimed to have shown that the conflict results from a misunderstanding about the possibility of causality. We actually do experience connections between phenomena, but "transcendental realism changes these modifications of our sensibilities into self-subsistent things, that is, changes *mere representations* into things by themselves." [24] For Kant, all that we can properly conclude is that we organize experience according to the synthetic a priori judgment of causality. Causality is not something that we can know to inhere in the universe. All we can know is that causality is a judgment which, combined with our sensibilities, produces the experience of determined objects.

Nietzsche's criticism of the freedom/causality antinomy of speculative cosmology is quite similar (although, as I shall suggest later in this chapter, crucially different in intention), and explicitly builds on Kant. Nietzsche asks us in *The Gay Science*, for example, to recall "*Kant's* tremendous question mark that he placed after the concept of 'causality'—without, like Hume, doubting its legitimacy altogether. Rather, Kant began cautiously to delimit the realm within which this concept makes sense (and to this day we are not done with this fixing of limits)." [25] And we find Nietzsche criticizing the antinomy of causality and free will along Kantian lines in *Beyond Good and Evil*:

The *causa sui* [self-causation] is the best self-contradiction that has been conceived so far, it is a sort of rape and perversion of logic. . . . The desire for "freedom of the will" in the superlative metaphysical sense, which still holds sway . . . the desire to bear the entire and ultimate responsibility for one's actions oneself . . . involves nothing less than to be precisely this *causa sui* and . . . pull oneself up into existence by the hair, out of the swamps of nothingness. Suppose someone were thus to see through the boorish simplicity of this celebrated concept of "free will" and put it out of his head altogether, I beg of him to carry his "enlightenment" a step further, and also put out of his head the contrary of the monstrous conception of "free will": I mean "unfree will," which amounts to a misuse of cause and effect. One should not wrongly reify "cause" and "effect" as the natural scientists do . . . one should use "cause" and "effect" only as pure concepts, that is to say, as conventional fictions for the purpose of designation and communication—*not* for explanation.[26]

The polarity of free will and causality, Nietzsche claims here, is based on a misunderstanding of the limits of pure reason, a reification of intellectual practices into a metaphysical cosmology. For Nietzsche, the cost of the mistake is that it obscures a more fundamental question—one at which Kant himself does not arrive—the question of how responsibility and freedom are possible as historical modes of activity.

The importance of this kind of comparison is to suggest that Nietzsche, like Kant, had a very definite idea of what metaphysical propositions entail, and why they should not be used "foundationally." Whatever else they might be good for, these propositions should not be used to refer to nonempirical realities that give rise to experience. Nietzsche's position is consistent enough to suggest that, whatever the status of his concept of will to power as a general philosophical proposition, it functions differently from the absolute metaphysics that both Nietzsche and Kant reject.

But if such statements cannot be used metaphysically, is there *any* legitimate use of universal philosophical statements like Nietzsche's claim that "the world is will to power"? Again, the parallel between Nietzsche and Kant is helpful if not pressed too far. For Kant, the existence of certain kinds of universal judgments—for example, synthetic a priori judgments like the existence of cause and effect relations—are conditions of the "objectivity" of experience. Our minds order sense experience in accordance with universal categories. The same ordering that constitutes empirical objects also comprehends and explains them. This is not a problem in Kant's view, as long as we do not confuse these mental judgments with attributes of the world as such.

Although Nietzsche differs with respect to *which* of these ideas and judgments are most useful, he does not object to their use *as such*. Like Kant, what he objects to is their confusion with properties of the world. He sees universal ideas and judgments as pragmatic devices that conceptually objectify our experiences of self and world. Universal claims are not anchored in metaphysical properties of the world, but rather in more or less species-universal pragmatic constraints and possibilities of practices. This is certainly one way of reading Nietzsche's infamous claim that "the falseness of a judgment is for us not necessarily an objection to a judgment; in this respect our new language may sound strangest. The question is to what extent it is life-promoting, life-preserving, species-preserving, perhaps even species cultivating." [27]

Nietzsche's Critique and Radicalization of Kant

Yet Kant would never have written this kind of statement. The reason is that he believed he could show that the Ideas of Reason and his categories of judgment were necessary and logically exhaustive, and therefore universally binding for all rational creatures. As far as Kant was concerned, universality and logical necessity established the authority of objective knowledge within the limits of critical philosophy. Nietzsche, on the other hand, argues that judgments are particular and perspectival, and that their universality is a practical question. We all use "fictions" to interpret the world, but we generally use the *same* fictions only when we have the *same perspective* on the world in space, time, culture, and society. The fictions we use will depend on our situation, our problems, our mode of life, our conditions of existence, our linguistic and cultural history—that is, on the sum total of our historically situated practices. Together, these will determine our "perspective" on the world, a perspective that *may* contain some species-universal elements, but will inevitably contain elements that are historically and culturally specific.

Why does Nietzsche turn away from Kant at this point? The reason is that his problem is different from and more radical than Kant's. Nietzsche retains Kant's critical problematic, but applies it to the problem of conceptualizing historical practices. It is partly because of the nature of Kant's problem that Nietzsche can accuse him of failing to overcome speculative metaphysics in his own thought. His *Critique of Pure Reason* was concerned with the truth of certain kinds of judgments necessary for physical science, say, the judgment that the world is governed by cause and effect relations. These kinds of judgments are synthetic a priori: they are not empirical, since they are already presupposed by empirical statements. Nor are they merely analytic—true by definition. Hence Kant's famous question: "How are synthetic a priori judgments possible?" To answer the question, of course, he argued that the mind imposed certain nontrivial judgments as universally necessary conditions of objectifying experience.

In Nietzsche's view, however, Kant's mode of questioning *already* presupposed a confrontation of mind as (thinking) subject and world as (sensible) object. While Kant was right to focus on the activities of the mind in structuring experience, his problem is not fundamental. Or, better, it *pointed* toward fundamental questions, but could not arrive there because his problems ("Why are scientific judgments possible?" "What is the rational basis of moral judgments?") presupposed the successes of the *activities* of science, and the *activities* of free moral choice, that is, the activities of the thinking subject in a sensible world. With Kant, the "legitimacy of belief in knowledge is always presupposed: just as the legitimacy of the feelings of conscience-judgments is presupposed." [28] In this way Kant also presupposes the activities of the subject as a source of judgments, and makes the integrity of these activities into a formal principal necessary for empirical objects including the self. What to Nietzsche are various dimensions of the subject thus become formal principles rather than problems. In the "I think" that formally attaches to judgments and the (intrinsically unknowable) free will Kant presupposes the fact (that is, the intelligibility of the experience) of scientific thought and moral choice. Thus, Kant cannot ask the crucial question about how agency is possible. Because he cannot address this question, neither can he address a problem like nihilism, since nihilism has to do with the collapse of the very activities he takes for granted. This is *Nietzsche's* problem and *not* Kant's. Kant's is about how science can be true without threatening moral freedom. Nietzsche's is about the more general breakdown of the relation between interpreting and acting that he takes to be at the root of nihilism. This is why his question and project had to be more radical than Kant's, and why he asks questions that go behind Kant's own questions about the possibility of scientific and moral judgments: "Why are such judgments *necessary*?" [29] That is, *what is it about our activities in the world that makes these interpretations an essential part of our activities?* Thus, the proper question is not about the possibility of *judgments*, but about the possibility of *agency*—*viz.*, activity guided by and including such judgments. *Where Kant gives the necessary conditions of synthesizing objects, Nietzsche gives the necessary conditions of unifying agency.*

In Nietzsche's view, Kant makes a wrong turn in the way he asks his questions. By assuming the truths of Newtonian science and Christian morality, Kant assumes the universal necessity of particular kinds of judgments. He already assumes that thought and activity *do* relate, because he assumes the necessity and successes of these judgments. Hence, he also assumes the existence of a rational human agency as manifested in scientific and moral activities that have occurred and continue to occur. It is because Kant did not notice the problem of nihilism with its dissolution of agents that he could take a certain kind of agency for granted. Because of his problem of nihilism, however, Nietzsche cannot. This is why he extends Kant's mode of questioning to the possibility of human agency itself.

In doing so, of course, Nietzsche also makes a radical departure from Kant's fundamentally *epistemological* starting point, in spite of the fact that his epistemological conclusions about the proper use of judgments are similar. Epistemology has to do with how our minds apprehend reality and thus assumes a world of thinking subjects confronting an objectified world of things. In contrast, Nietzsche claims that "when one has grasped that the 'subject' is not something that creates effects, but only a fiction, much follows. It is only after the model of the subject that we have invented the reality of things and projected them into the medley of sensations. . . . [T]he thing-in-itself also disappears, because this is fundamentally the conception of the 'subject-in-itself.' " [30] Nietzsche's radicalizing of Kant involves the question of why thinking subjects exist at all: What must one presuppose about practices so that epistemological issues could in fact be issues? This kind of question is involved in Nietzsche's claim that he is moving away from epistemology and toward a "perspective theory of the affects" (see chapter 3). Thus Nietzsche also moves away from Kant's question about forms of reason and toward his own question about the forms of life within which the activities of thinking are bound up with activities in general.

In doing so, Nietzsche nonetheless builds within and upon crucial aspects of Kant's critical approach. Kant's contribution to epistemology was to point out in a nonidealistic way that the mind is active; there is no perceiving without conceiving. For this reason, Kant's questions always presuppose *mental actions* as a subject matter (as opposed to forms, laws, rules, and the like). Synthetic a priori statements, for example, are always *judgments*; they are activities involving the intelligible ordering of experiential reality. Moreover, an active mind presupposes an active body within a sensuous world. The unity of apperception means that there must be a unity of consciousness for there to be an object of experience as a synthesized manifold. We know such unities because we participate in them in everyday life. The unity of the idea of a line, for example, stems from the unity of the *act* of drawing the line. The conceptual synthesis of the line as well as the experience of the line as a synthesis is based on the unity of the action. Likewise, one might argue that the unity of the synthetic a priori category of cause and effect unifies objects of experience only because we engage necessary connections in time and space.

Nietzsche takes Kant's line of reasoning one step further. The unity of the conceiving subject and the manifold of experience synthesized into an object emerge out of embodied activities. Only on the basis of activity do we begin to articulate subjects and objects as unities. They emerge as conceptual entities out of processes of acting, and the unities and continuities of actions reinforce these conceptualizations. The unity of thinking, Nietzsche argues, is something like a conscious articulation of embodied activities that are constantly taking place:

> There could be no judgments at all if a kind of equalization were not practiced within the sensations: memory is possible only with a continual emphasizing of what is already familiar, experience.—Before judgment occurs, the process of assimilation must already have taken place; thus here, too, there is an intellectual activity that does not enter consciousness, as pain does as a consequence of a wound. Probably an inner event corresponds to each organic function; hence, assimilation, rejection, growth, etc.
>
> Essential: to start from the *body* and employ it as a guide. It is the much richer phenomenon, which allows of clearer observation.[31]

Our embodied activities articulate a kind of order that corresponds to conditions of existence. The activities of thought are further articulations of these, and they manifest one dimension of the way we, as subjects, reproduce our lives. The conditions of existence—some species-universal, others situationally specific—come to enforce a *particular* set of judgments, and these are necessary to sustain "the kind of creatures that we are." For these reasons, then, the perspective of embodied action is both logically and ontologically prior to the articulated subject/object perspective that forms the basis of Kant's questions.

Nietzsche's new question, then, requires a new way of thinking about the activities out of which articulated subjects and objects emerge. The new question is something like this: "What are the conditions for experiencing ourselves as subjects or agents of our activities?" What is "willing" if it is *prior* to a subject who wills? That is, how can one conceptualize willing if the "will" is an effect rather than a cause of willing? Nietzsche's first two sections of *Beyond Good and Evil* carry him into an analysis of willing, and this analysis leads in turn to an introduction of the concept of will to power. The will to power, as I shall argue, is Nietzsche's attempt to characterize the conditions of willing. Again, Nietzsche's perspective here is rooted in his problematic: if nihilism signifies the loss of the capacity to will (agency), then resolving nihilism requires an analysis of the conditions of willing. The will to power characterizes the conditions of agency in the same way that, for Kant, synthetic a priori judgments characterize the conditions of empirical objects. The several kinds of universal attributions of the concept of will to power have the same philosophical status as Kant's synthetic a priori judgments, but they answer a prior question. Because Nietzsche's question is about materially embodied practices, he in effect historicizes Kant's critical philosophy in a way that makes it compatible with the social theories of Marx and Weber. And because Marx's and Weber's theories are about social practices, they in turn presuppose some account of agency such as Nietzsche's.

Reconstruction: The Phenomenology of Agency

These considerations tell us nothing about the content Nietzsche actually gives to his concept of will to power, or why he believes that this particular content should be more appropriate to his problem than some other. Still, his intentions are clear in the fact that he seeks to ask a new question about the practices out of which agents emerge. He addresses his question through an analysis of "willing." What we experience as "willing," he claims, consists in an organized "multiplicity" of conditions.[32] The will is not a unified entity, but rather a dynamic series of "treaty drafts of the will [*Willens-Punktationen*]."[33] The reality of the will or agent exists not as a metaphysical essence but in the self-reflective value and certainty that the individual ascribes to himself as an agent. By dissolving the concept of the will into a conditional and relational entity—one dependent on self-reflective ascription rather than on metaphysical certainty— Nietzsche sets his agenda for the concept of will to power.

Aphorism 19 of *Beyond Good and Evil* provides an outline of the agenda in four points, each of which identifies an "ingredient" or condition of willing. In making the first point, Nietzsche explains that if one were to decompose willing into its constituent aspects, one would find that it involves an experienced bodily encounter with the present world. Nietzsche's language anticipates Heideggerian categories. In willing, he says, there is a "plurality of sensations." These sensations are relational: we experience "the sensation of the state 'away from which' [*von dem weg*], the sensation of the state 'toward which' [*zu dem hin*], and the sensations of this 'from' and 'toward' themselves...."[34] The world is at first relationally and affectively present: it effects us as we act in and through it. Moreover, we experience this presence as a "muscular sensation."[35] For the mature Nietzsche such formulations locate the Dionysian qualities of the world—the "natural" ground of all willing that includes whatever is thrown into our sphere of existence, from within and without, with its own intricate order that becomes a basis for further articulation in practices. Here one finds the first aspect of the will to power, the one Nietzsche sometimes describes as the *pathos* of embodiment.

Second, along with the moment of embodied experience, Nietzsche emphasizes that there is an interpretive moment in every act of will: "Just as sensations (and indeed many kinds of sensations) are to be recognized as ingredients of the will, so, second, should thinking also: in every act of will there is a commanding thought—let us not imagine it possible to sever this thought from the 'willing,' as if any will would then remain over!"[36] Thus the second moment of will to power is *interpretive*: the act of will cannot be understood apart from the interpretive framing of power. Because interpretations are mapped by language and culture, every human act of will partakes of an intersubjective network of meanings. This, as suggested in chapter 2, means that there is no purely individual or subjective source of power as agency.

These two moments of willing together form a "complex of feeling and thinking" in terms of which the third moment of will to power becomes intelligible. This moment of willing Nietzsche calls the "affect of command."[37] Nietzsche's reference to this "affect" as *will* to power suggests that power has itself as an object—that human power is not only interpretive but also *self-reflective*. The power motive consists in a self-reflective desire to be a subject, an agent, a self-determining center of action. So essential is the self-reflective moment of power, the "feeling of growth," the "feeling of increased power," that Nietzsche describes it as the "basic text of *homo natura*."[38] He views action as always a means to the self-experience of agency and never an end in itself. The motive to agency, however, gains a reality as "will" only through the incorporation (*Einverleibung*) and appropriation (*Aneignung*) of the experiential and interpretive worlds. We cannot trace the character of acts of will to an "underlying" motive, because the motive for power has no character in itself. The universal motive to will is rather, for Nietzsche, a general need that depends upon historically situated practices for its characteristic modes of satisfaction.

The confluence of these three moments of willing into the experience of the self as a "will," subject, or agent is the final moment of the will to power. The agent, in Nietzsche's view, is produced by a series of self-reflective moments within practical processes; this is why "willing is above all something complicated." Nietzsche claims that what has in the past been called the "will"—especially the *free will*—is really a unified "feeling of power" resulting from a complex of relations leading to a (self-reflectively) successful action. Willing involves a "command" to oneself to act together with an "obedience" to the conditions of action, conditions that "we know as the sensations of constraint, impulsion, pressure, resistance, and motion, which usually begin immediately after the act of will." [39] Every act of will is conditional: it is contingent on engaging the world and on "obedience" to contingencies of the world. This contingency of the will is hidden by the synthetic concept "I" "to such a degree that he who wills believes sincerely that willing suffices for action." [40] But in actuality, Nietzsche argues, the unified feeling of having a will, of being an "I," is an interpretation of the self that anticipates the success of an action. This suggests that a continuity of directed practices is the basis of plausible self-interpretations of agency. Rather than being the effect of an underlying, unified agent, one's experiences of agent unity depend on a continuity of practices: "Since in the great majority of cases there has been an exercise of the will only when the effect of the command—that is, obedience; that is, action—was to be *expected*, the appearance has translated itself into the feeling, as if there were a *necessity of effect*. In short, he who wills believes with a fair amount of certainty that will and action are somehow one; he ascribes the success, the carrying out of willing, to the will itself, and thereby enjoys the increase of power that accompanies all success." [41] The concreteness of Nietzsche's approach here consists in the fact that his analysis of the will gives it only as much substance as it has power in practice. Although the desire to be an agent motivates an act, one becomes an agent—that is, one attains a unified will—only by actualizing the desire in practice. By claiming that the will is the self-reflective effect of historically situated actions, Nietzsche is shifting the locus of the will from metaphysical certainty to a historically contingent process. The metaphysical concept of the agent now appears as a value and goal, rather than as a metaphysical entity or fact. Its real and valuable core consists in the possibility of a self-reflective interpretation: "'Freedom of the will'—that is the expression for the complex state of delight of the person exercising volition, who commands and at the same time identifies himself with the executor of the order—who, as such, enjoys also the triumph over obstacle, but thinks that it was really his will itself that overcame them." [42] Nietzsche is not saying the will is simply an illusion, but rather it is a self-interpretation that is a value with worldly conditions of possibility.

These are the considerations that allow one to develop a Nietzschean concept of rationality, a possibility I introduced with promissory notes in chapters 2 and 3. Agency is a *rational* self-interpretation to the degree that its worldly conditions of possibility are met in practice. Conversely, if the motive to be an agent fails in successive encounters with the world, then self-interpretations of agency grounded in practice become impossible. An illusory sense of selfhood must develop if the experience of nihilism is to be kept at bay. This failure of congruence is expressed in *irrational* or *ideological* self-interpretations, and involves a false consciousness of one's own conditions of possibility *as* an agent. As I suggested in chapters 1 and 2, this is why Nietzsche traces all illusory or ideological conceptions of the will in religion and metaphysics to situations of failed practice, which he symbolizes with the situation of the slave. In this context, however, we can see that these specific critiques are supported by a more general philosophy of power as agency: the value orientation of the concept of will to power is toward locating practical possibilities of individuality, freedom, and reflexive rationality. Nietzsche intends to remove these ideals from the realm of metaphysics and to show how they can be conceptualized as historical possibilities and goals. This why his philosophy of power points toward a critically postmodern political thought.

The Will to Power as *Pathos*

With this outline of Nietzsche's reconstructive project in mind, we can turn to his formulation of the will to power itself. What I shall suggest is that Nietzsche condenses these three conditions of willing—affectivity, interpretation, and self-reflection—into his concept of will to power, and this is why the concept has seemed confused and difficult. Let us return to the first and most fundamental condition, the *affectivity*, or *pathos* of existence—that is, our sensual embodiment in the world. In Nietzsche's terms, the way we most immediately relate to the world is through our body, through the affectibility of our embodiment. Clues to the fundamental nature of this moment of will to power are provided by Deleuze's and Heidegger's interpretations. Deleuze describes the will to power simply as a "capacity for being affected" and as an "affectibility" in relation to the world.[43] In the same spirit, Heidegger points out that the will to power cannot be construed as a *biological* affect, as so many have done.[44] As Heidegger so nicely puts it, "We do not 'have' a body; rather, we 'are' bodily." [45] Our primal, tacit, Dionysian awareness of the world is of an immediate enveloping flux we experience in relation to our movements, as "away from which," "toward which," and "the sensations of this 'from' and 'toward' themselves." Thus one can understand Nietzsche's claim that the will to power is "not a being, but becoming; but a *pathos*—the most elemental fact from which a becoming and effecting first emerge." [46] The Greek term *pathos* refers to events, experiences, sufferings, emotions, and attributes, and thus summarizes what Nietzsche calls the Dionysian aspects of the world.[47] As *pathos* the will to power signifies the immediate world in which we are at all times thoroughly embodied, a world of living sensuous relations that are the material limits and possibilities of willing.

Nietzsche's descriptions of this first moment of will to power are not always clear. Especially problematic is the constant tension between his apparently biological language—his talk of reducing the world to "physiological" drives, for example—and his phenomenological approach. Nonetheless, Nietzsche's actual analyses are phenomenological and not "physiological," suggesting that one should not interpret his scientistic language literally. Indeed, referring to his physiological language, Nietzsche notes that the fact that he speaks crudely "does not mean that I want to be heard crudely or understood crudely...."[48] His intention to express a phenomenological relation of embodiment as basic to our knowledge of all other things is clear in his introduction of the concept of will to power in *Beyond Good and Evil*. "Suppose nothing else were 'given' as real," he asks us to speculate,

> except our world of desires and passions, and we could not get down, or up, to any other "reality" besides the reality of our drives— ... is it not permitted to make the experiment and ask the question whether this "given" would not be *sufficient* for also understanding on the basis of this kind of thing the so-called mechanistic (or "material") world? I mean, not as a deception, as "mere appearance," a "representation" (in the sense of Berkeley and Schopenhauer) but as holding the same rank of reality as our affect—as a more primitive form of the world of affects in which everything still lies contained in a powerful unity before it undergoes ramifications and developments in the organic process....[49]

Three aspects of this description provide a clue as to the kind of ground Nietzsche is seeking. First, one should note that Nietzsche ascribes to the "so-called mechanistic (or 'material') world" the character of the affects. By "affects" Nietzsche means our drives, instincts, and passions, the experience of which is conditioned by both physiology and environment, but which present themselves to consciousness *experientially* (rather than biologically) as an impelling, sensuous, nonrational order. He carefully points out that he is not— like Berkeley and Schopenhauer—viewing the external world as a mere reflection of inner affects.[50] "Affects" are not simply inner phenomena but relational ones. Their experienced quality of being "inside" presupposes an "outside" in terms of which inner experiences differentiate themselves. Thus Nietzsche understands the external world as necessarily of the *same* order of reality as the affects. Neither internality nor externality is conceivable without the other. The reality of the will to power as affectibility, then, is synonymous with the relationship between internal and external order—that is, with experience.

Second, one should note the meaning of Nietzsche's description of the "so-called mechanistic (or 'material') world" as a "more primitive form of the world of affects in which everything still lies contained in a powerful unity before it undergoes ramifications and developments in the organic process...."[51] The world is presented for us as a "preform" of life, as a powerful Dionysian nature of which we have

a tacit awareness prior to interpretive and material activities—
indeed, prior to cognition, which is itself an organizing activity.
Through interpretive and material activities the affective world is
organized and developed as a means to "growth." In this way it is
articulated in the "organic process" as a discrete and intelligible
reality. All ramifications and developments of the "organic process"
occur as we engage this Dionysian presence of the world. Our practices or "life" within this preform of life humanize the primal unity
of experience, making it the kind of reality within which we might
develop and experience our own subjectivity.

Finally, by emphasizing the nature of the world as *pathos*, Nietzsche
is attempting to correct the defects of idealist metaphysics insofar as
it derives the world from conceptual categories. For Nietzsche, consciousness is a "thin" dimension of existence, one that is relatively
impoverished when compared with the totality of relations and processes that make up "life" without necessarily entering consciousness.[52] The relations between thought, judgment, action, and life
emerge from within such a rich complex of experience—that consciousness could never be the "ground" of existence, no matter what
its ultimate value.

The Will to Power as *Physis*

Notwithstanding Heidegger's helpful comments on Nietzsche's understanding of embodiment, he interprets the will to power as a *physis* of
the subject, a metaphysical source of interpretive practice. His point
in doing so is to show that Nietzsche's concept of will to power is the
last form of metaphysical humanism.[53] Although this interpretation
may correspond to some of Nietzsche's references to the concept, it
does not correspond to most of them, nor to the critically postmodern
nature of his problematic. But there is a sense in which Nietzsche
quite intentionally (and consistently) does use the concept to denote
a *physis*: he claims that the world *in itself* is a field of forces, actions,
and reactions. Here he uses the concept of will to power as a cosmological conception of *totality* (*Gesamtspiel*). By characterizing the world
in its totality as will to power, Nietzsche uses the concept to understand the world as a dynamic interrelation of centers of power. Within
this totality, every "thing" is the sum of its relations with other
"things." "Things" themselves are essentially organized centers of

power that maintain an identity over time. The world is a sum total of actions that each part of the whole sees from its own position within the totality. "Every center of force adopts a perspective toward the entire remainder," Nietzsche explains in a note, "that is, its own particular valuation, mode of action, and mode of resistance. The 'apparent world,' therefore, is reduced to a specific mode of action on the world, emanating from a center. Now there is no other mode of action whatsoever; and the 'world' is only a word for the totality [Gesamtspiel] of these actions. Reality [Realität] consists precisely in this particular action and reaction of every individual part toward the whole...."[54] In much the same way that Hegel views the world as a totality, Nietzsche characterizes it as a concrete network of interdependent relations evolving in time. The world is a "unity in difference," as are all seemingly discrete identities in the world.[55] The determination and meaning of each aspect of the whole is incomplete in isolation from other aspects of the whole. Thus the will to power simultaneously seems to be a systematic, contextualistic, and perspectival view of reality, within which all things are constituted by relations of power, and modeled on the metaphors of practice. For Nietzsche, this is the most adequate way of conceptualizing the world as "viewed from inside, the world defined and determined according to its 'intelligible character.'"[56]

Is this not, however, precisely the kind of speculative cosmology that I have argued that Nietzsche, together with Kant, rejects? It is clearly a cosmological characterization of the world. But again, the issue here is not whether Nietzsche makes universal statements, but rather one of their philosophical status. Nietzsche intends his characterization of the world as a field of countervailing forces to provide the assumption necessary to conceptualize the world of physical necessities. In this way he hopes to allow for the possibility of natural science as an interpretive utility. Still, he also intends to do so critically in the Kantian sense. This is the reason for his careful phraseology in the aphorism quoted above: he asks whether or not the will to power as a characterization of embodiment would also be "sufficient" to explain the "so-called mechanistic (or 'material') world"—the world of material limits and resources we must conceptualize as conditions of acting.[57]

One might reconstruct Nietzsche's move from phenomenology to a (hypothetical) cosmology in the following manner. When we think or speak of the world as *pathos*, we already begin to give a mental structure to the world in such a way that we can explain how it is possible for us to experience the world as *pathos*. When we do this, the will to power begins to serve the function of a *physis* for our thought, that is, a characterization of universal qualities of the world as such. The will to power is not literally a *physis*, but it comes to function for thought *like* a *physis* by characterizing the world that makes our practices possible. What we feel as the *pathos* of experience we abstract as a metaphor for the externalities that are a condition of this experience. But in so doing we have already moved away from the Dionysian immediacy of experience toward a characterization of the world in accordance with its "organic" development through our activities. It is at this point in Nietzsche's derivation of the concept that he suggests that we consider the world *in itself* as will to power, independently of our Dionysian experiences of it. We can derive our understanding of the *physis* of the world from the world as a *pathos* of embodiment because the external world is a necessary condition for the possibility of embodiment. The world as *physis*, however, is already a world acted on interpretively, objectified, and constituted as an object. The point is not to reject the concept of *physis* because it is "only" an interpretation, but rather to understand its status critically by delimiting its realm of applicability. What Nietzsche's position suggests is that we should make this an explicit part of our thought by understanding the *physis* world after the pattern of the world as *pathos*. For this reason we, like Aristotle, must ascribe to the world as *physis* the qualities of "force," "inner direction," and "will" to ground in worldly experience our practical understanding of the necessities of the "so-called mechanistic (or 'material') world."[58] Thus, in the same aphorism quoted above, Nietzsche writes,

The question is in the end whether we really recognize the will as *efficient* [*wirkend*], whether we believe in the causality of the will: if we do—and at bottom our faith in this is nothing less than the faith in causality itself—then we have to make the experiment of positing the causality of the will hypothetically as the only one. "Will," of course, can affect only "will"—and not "matter" (not "nerves," for example). In short, one has to risk the hypothesis whether will does not effect will wherever "effects" are recognized—and whether all mechanical occurrences are not, insofar as force is active in this, will-force, effects of will.[59]

Nietzsche's movement from characterizing the will to power as *pathos* to characterizing the cosmos as will to power indicates that he was attempting to allow for the practical use of the realist claims upon which, say, Newtonian physics depends. The point is not that the will to power as *physis* describes the world better or differently from previous cosmologies, but rather that it provides for cosmological assumptions about force, cause and effect, mechanism, and so on that underwrite (say) Newtonian physics as a practical matter, but does so within a critical perspective.[60] Nietzsche believed that the concept of will to power should encompass the practical advances of the physical sciences without seeing its necessary assumptions about laws, forces, and the like as identical with actual entities.

Yet these advantages do not explain why Nietzsche insists on using the *anthropomorphic* metaphor "will" to characterize the world as such, with its seeming movement back in the direction of a Cartesian matter/spirit dualism. Given Nietzsche's critical concerns, it is likely that he moves in this direction to underscore the metaphorical status of all cosmological language. Once we have granted that our grasp of the world as *physis* is necessarily hypothetical, we can become aware that the *physis* metaphor inheres not in the world as such but in our practices. To use the term "force" as a literal characterization of the physical world in itself, for example, is to forget the origin of the metaphor: "Has a force ever been demonstrated? No, only *effects* translated into a completely foreign language. We are so used, how-ever, to regularity in succession that its oddity no longer seems odd to us."[61] All that we experience is the *pathos* of effects.[62] Nietzsche is adamant to point this out and still to avoid an idealistic collapse of the "so-called mechanistic world" into a mere function of human experience and interpretation. Its independent complexity is a condi-tion of the possibility of human practices. We can conceive of and refer to this independent complexity of the world even if we cannot represent it. Thus, Nietzsche points out, although "we cannot change our means of expression at will, it is possible to understand to what extent they are merely signs. The demand for an adequate mode of expression is senseless."[63] Even though the linguistic and logical aspects of thought limit possible interpretations, we can gain a critical awareness of the necessary distance between language, the world as *pathos*, and the world as *physis*. In addition, we can become aware of our interests in humanizing the world, in making it a meaningful place to live. This is why Nietzsche suggests that we recognize the needs and interests of willing as the sources of all characterizations of the *physis* of the world: "One is obliged to understand all motion, all 'appearance,' all 'laws,' only as symptoms of an inner event and to employ man as an analogy to this end." [64] To employ man as an analogy for all events and movements of the material world means to ascribe an "inner will" to force, while understanding that the terms of expression are rooted in our interested perspectives within the world, and not in the things themselves. [65] In this way, the language of cosmological identities can be used for practical purposes, but with a critical awareness of its limitations.

The Will to Power as Interpretation

Viewing the world as *pathos* and as a totality of force is necessary but not sufficient to account for the conscious, intentional, and self-reflective aspects of willing. For this reason Nietzsche suggests that interpretation is intrinsic to the will to power: "The will to power interprets (—it is a question of interpretation when an organ is constructed): it defines, limits, determines degrees, variations of power. Mere variations of power could not feel themselves to be such: there must be something present that wants to grow and interprets the values of whatever else wants to grow." [66] Power interprets external conditions to transform them into means of growth, and self-reflectively interprets itself to be doing so. Power is not simply *Macht*, but *Wille zur Macht*. Thus, insofar as the concept of will is applied to power, power includes consciousness and self-consciousness, interpretation and self-interpretation. Here, of course, Nietzsche clearly understands power with a human analogy: he characterizes power in terms of the attributes of self-conscious, self-interpreting creatures that have "one more condition" of existence than other kinds of creatures. [67]

Nietzsche does not view these interpretive qualities of power as existing a priori, however. The dualism of *pathos* and interpretation/self-reflection manifest in human power must itself be explained. Interpretation is a quality of power because of the historical facts of culture and language—facts that could have been otherwise, and certainly are for most nonhuman beings. Power is *will* to power, and thus potentially *agency*, for those specific historical forms of life that have evolved consciousness and self-consciousness at an individual level, and culture and language at the level of society.

Because Nietzsche believes interpretation is historically rather than a priori universal he believes this universality itself requires explanation. To do so he regards the historical development of interpretation in functional terms, as a "means" of life to itself.[68] Accordingly, Nietzsche takes a functional approach in many of his comments relating consciousness and self-consciousness to practices. To view the interpretive capacities of humans as a means to power is to understand the role they play in organizing actions, whether for physical survival, communication, or constitution of the self. From the purely functional perspective, Nietzsche points out that human will to power can be contrasted with other kinds of life—say, of lower animals— by its highly conscious character. The actions of animals are more "direct" than those of humans, which are conditioned by a culturally structured consciousness as well as by the experienced world. While the actions of lower animals are already "fit" to particular environments through instinct and rudimentary learning, the success of human actions often requires conscious calculation and more complex, culturally-sustained habits: "Consciousness—beginning quite externally, as a coordination of and becoming-conscious of 'impressions'—at first the furthest distance from the biological center of the individual; but a process that deepens and intensifies itself, and continually draws nearer to that center."[69] From a functional perspective, the faculty of consciousness and the culture it implies can be seen as a "tool" or means of adaptation to situations for which the human is not preadapted.[70] Consciousness presumably evolved because those so endowed were "more fit" in the Darwinian sense that they persisted and reproduced more successfully than those relatively lacking in this capacity. Nietzsche draws on the idea of organism-environment relativity in remarking on the development and evolution of consciousness: "In all becoming-conscious there is expressed a discomfiture of the organism; it has to try something new, nothing is sufficiently adapted for it, there is toil, tension, strain—all this *constitutes* becoming—conscious...."[71] The intellect can be considered (in this functional perspective) to be an "apparatus" or "tool" that organizes impressions of the world as a condition for acting and hence for "growth" and power. From this perspective we can also understand Nietzsche's occasional claim that to act "instinctively" is to act "perfectly"—in contrast to actions that require the additional mediation of consciousness.[72] For the latter case presupposes an "instinctual" weakness relative to the environment. From this point of view, the deepening of consciousness in evolutionary history must be seen as a sign of an "imperfection," an increasing inability of the organism to fulfill its needs in a particular environment.[73] Nietzsche attributes the slave's increase in cunning, calculation, and memory, for example, to his real lack of power and inability to act on instinct in an environment shaped by a master class.[74]

Nietzsche bases his occasional praise of "instinctive" action at the expense of "conscious" action on the idea that instinctive action expresses a successful adaptation of the organism to its environment. For this reason he considers man to be the animal with the most "bungled" instincts, but for the same reason one who is essentially "undetermined."[75] For this reason as well, man is the animal with a capacity for historical agency.

Although Nietzsche often seems to denigrate consciousness, he does so only from the standpoint of "instinctual" adaptation. But he does not view adaptation as such to be of value. Like his contemporary Thomas Huxley, Nietzsche takes care to distinguish what is most "fit" from what is "best": what is maladapted, weak, and rare might be of the greatest value. He regards consciousness itself as a weak and imperfect organ, but one with the capacity to alter the very nature, organization, and goals of power. Ultimately, consciousness has the potential to *perfect* the "body" by projecting prior organizations of the "organic" to higher levels: "Put briefly: perhaps the entire evolution of the spirit is a question of the body; it is the sensible becoming historical that organizes a higher body. The organic is rising to yet higher levels. Our lust for knowledge is a means through which the body desires to perfect itself."[76]

The Will to Power as Self-Reflection

It is not just that consciousness in a more subtle and effective tool for organizing power, but that as consciousness becomes *self*-consciousness, a quantum leap in the organization of power becomes possible. In being conscious and self-conscious, humans increasingly strive less for external goals than for the self-reflective goal of experiencing the self as agent. In Nietzsche's terms, there is a "basic will of the spirit" that strives for the "feeling of delight in being a commander." [77] Power as a motive "involves the complex state of delight of the person exercising volition, who commands and at the same time identifies himself with the executor of the order—who, as such, enjoys also the triumph over obstacles, but thinks within himself that it was really his will that overcame them ... *L'effet c'est moi.*" [78] The motive Nietzsche is describing here is a reflexive one: because humans strive to effect their environments as a means to self-constitution, it is possible for power to be organized as "will." "It seems to me," he writes, "that the feeling of increase, the feeling of becoming stronger is, in itself, quite apart from any usefulness in the struggle, the real *progress*: only from this feeling does there arise the will to struggle." [79] By discounting the external effects of power ("usefulness in the struggle"), Nietzsche focuses on the self-constituting character of the motive for power. From the moment the self-consciousness of power emerges in the evolutionary process, it is possible to characterize human power in terms of "will," and to impute a striving for the self-experience of agency to all beings that have a rudimentary consciousness of the organization of their own power, whether this power is highly organized or frustrated, whether it is the power of a master or a slave.

It is true that statements such as these can be (and usually are) read in quite a different way, namely, as evidence that Nietzsche posits a basic desire for power in the sense of becoming dominant over others. Certainly, as we shall see in chapter 7, this kind of reading fits the language of his politics. But there are problems with this interpretation. It is not, for example, consistent with Nietzsche's problematic of nihilism as a dislocated subjectivity. Nor does it capture his own distinction between external successes of actions (which do not necessarily motivate) and reflexive effects of actions on the self (which do). But there is another difficulty as well—one that intersects Heidegger's charge that the concept of will to power is essentially nihilistic. If one were to interpret Nietzsche's emphasis on will to power as command, mastery, and subduing, then this would suggest that he is elevating the self as agent over all natural and social conditions of existence *in such a way that he reduces other beings—social and natural—to symptoms of the subject's power.* In this case, Heidegger would be right in suggesting that Nietzsche's concept of will to power is ultimately nihilistic, for it would consist in a positing of the existence of the world as an effect of subjectivity.

But if Nietzsche's language of mastery is put in context, we can see that an interpretation such as Heidegger's misses his project. In aphorism 230 of *Beyond Good and Evil*, for example, Nietzsche makes a general claim in the language of mastery and domination. He writes that the "basic will of the spirit" is a will that "ties up, tames, and is domineering and truly masterful." Yet in the same aphorism, he explains that these desires lead to a will to be ignorant of the world, to be deceived, to exclude the world. Humans may be motivated by an "affect of command" over the external world, but it is precisely this, Nietzsche is saying, that leads them to a nihilistic reduction of the world, as well as to an inability to realize the "affect of command" itself. To guard against this will to exclude and deceive, he argues that the "basic text of *homo natura* must again be recognized"—not as something that is apart from nature, but as a center of activity that can only emerge on the basis of recognizing the fullness of the world: "To translate man back into nature; to become master over the many vain and overly enthusiastic interpretations and connotations that have so far been scrawled and painted over that eternal basic text of *homo natura*; to see to it that man henceforth stands before man as even today, hardened in the discipline of science, he stands before the *rest* of nature, with intrepid Oedipus eyes and sealed Odysseus ears, deaf to the siren songs of old metaphysical bird catchers who have been piping at him all too long, 'You are more, you are higher, you are of a different origin!' "[80] Texts such as these point to Nietzsche's view that humans have ignored the conditional nature of their own "mastery," and that they have degraded the world in the process of pursuing mastery. In so doing they have misunderstood the worldly bases of their own agency, individuality, self-determination, and freedom.

These considerations suggest that we should understand Nietzsche's language in such a way that it includes the conditional and reflexive nature of the power motive. For Nietzsche, the power motive is not descriptive of classes of external goals of action—such as political domination over others—understood as the aim of all human acts. Instead, he is interested in the meaning that behaviors have for individuals in terms of their experiences of agent-unity. Stated otherwise, to claim as Nietzsche does that humans are universally motivated by power is not to make a claim about what kinds of acts they will engage in if they only have the chance, but rather to claim that human motives are necessarily self-reflective in nature: humans are fundamentally motivated by a desire to experience the self as autonomous, as a free will.[81] Nietzsche's psychological comments suggest, of course, that this motive may be more or less conscious, and more or less developed.[82] The will to power as autonomy of the self in these senses is, in Nietzsche's view, a universal motive, and thus a universal value of self-reflective beings.[83]

The Will to Power as History

These three dimensions of Nietzsche's concept of will to power— experience, interpretation, and self-reflective motivation—together describe universal dimensions of practice. In so doing, the concept supports and merges with Nietzsche's concept of history generally, and his views on the development of Western culture specifically— something I have presupposed in previous chapters. Nietzsche views human history as both the precondition and the result of practices. He conceives of practices as a confluence of those kinds of historical inheritances demarcated by the will to power—namely, materially structured experience and linguistically structured culture. Practices occur on the ground of, and within the limits of, those kinds of historical realities identified by the concept of will to power. History is the convergence of these structured conditions within practices that are motivated by the individual's need to experience the self as an agent. With Marx, one might say that for Nietzsche human agents make history. But they do not make history just as they please, or under conditions of their own choosing, but under conditions immediately found, given, and transmitted by the past. History consists in practices structured by the conditions under which they occur.

While the analogy to Marx is helpful in suggesting the priority of practices in Nietzsche's concept of history, it cannot be pushed too far. The most obvious difference is that in Nietzsche one does not find the notions of historical progress, purpose, and meaning that motivate Marx's historical reconstructions. For Nietzsche, if historical processes can be said to have goals, they can only reflect the desires of individuals to incorporate the past as a means to the feeling of power. The will to power leads to a conception of history that has its movement and its justification in processes of willing. The only goals of history are local and situated, immanent to the life-worlds of individuals. "Every power," Nietzsche claims, "draws its ultimate consequences at every moment." [84]

The overarching structural logics of history—those given by language, culture, and various material processes—can be conceived as goals or purposes only in the restricted sense that they are necessary means to continuous self-constitution. Thus, Nietzsche writes in the *Genealogy of Morals* that

purposes and utilities are only *signs* that a will to power has become master of something less powerful and imposed upon it the character of a function; and the entire history of a 'thing,' and organ, a custom, can in this way be a continuous sign-chain of ever-new interpretations and adaptations whose causes do not have to be related to one another, but, on the contrary, in some cases succeed and alternate with one another in a purely chance fashion. The "evolution" of a thing, a custom, an organ is thus by no means its *progressus* toward a goal, even less a logical *progressus* by the shortest route and with the smallest expenditure of force—but a succession of more or less profound, more or less mutually independent processes of subduing, plus the resistances they encounter, the attempts at transformation for the purpose of defense and reaction, and the results of successful counteractions. [85]

Let us continue to bracket the political residue in Nietzsche's choice of words (mastery, imposition, subduing) for consideration in chapter 7. If we do so, then we are left with a description of history as a process with an accidental character, making it impossible to ascribe to history any overarching logic, purpose, or goal. For Nietzsche, any teleology in history is only that introduced by centers of power as means of experiencing themselves as such, or as means of reproducing the conditions of these experiences.

Within this limited and local conception of purpose, supraindividual goals might nonetheless be conceived as an aspect of social projects or political institutions. Hence, there is no *necessary* conflict between Nietzsche's conception of individual goals and, say, Marx's conception of class goals, provided one accounts for the mediation between the two. But this conception of teleology is different from one that sees purposes and goals inherent in global history, structures, classes, and political institutions. In Nietzsche's view, these supraindividual conceptions may reflect the local successes of humans in assuring future conditions for reproduction of their own agency. Or, perhaps more often, they may reflect the ideological displacement of local goals onto institutional ones.

Nietzsche views history, then, as a totality of actions with local logics, purposes, and teleologies, but without unified logic, purpose, or teleology as a whole. History is inherently pluralistic, complex, and in large degree random. These qualities of history do not, however, deprive us of our abilities to conceptualize the structure and determination of historical processes. For despite the local reproduction of events, actions, and meanings, history possesses those structural attributes given by language, culture, and material processes. Nietzsche understands the continuity of culture, for example, to be integral to material forms of life. Moreover, history possesses that immanent kind of necessity that he describes by noting that "one and the same event is not another event as well," and that "power draws its ultimate consequences at every moment." [86] This is why, for Nietzsche, the "forces of history are doubtless discernible if one strips off all moral and religious teleology." [87] Nietzsche inverts Hegel much as Marx did. They both attempted to account for the *appearance* of lawful continuity—Marx in matters of material labor, and Nietzsche is matters of culture—by showing how these continuities are reproduced by practices.

A very specific theoretical conception of historical determination does in fact emerge from Nietzsche's concept of will to power, one that deliberately excludes all teleology save those local purposes introduced as conditions of future individual self-constitution. The above quotation on evolution suggests that the growth of an entity takes place in such a way as to be functionally related to local environments. Resistances and incorporation of various aspects of the environment together organize growth, thus giving it a distinctive form over time. The evolutionary formation of a "thing, an organ, a custom," might be understood to occur through continual selective delimitation and articulation of growth.[88] We can see, then, that the concept of will to power produces a conception of history consistent with Nietzsche's genealogical method as described in chapter 3.

The Will to Power and Cultural Evolution

It is now possible to return to the problems of chapter 1, and theoretically reformulate the question raised by Nietzsche's view of nihilism in Western history, namely, the question of how Western culture could have *determined* the modern crisis of nihilism. Or, stated in slightly different terms, how could Western culture have had an ideological effect powerful enough to displace people's self-conceptions of agency? How could an entire culture have become reified from practices? How could it have become a seemingly independent barrier to the formation of power as agency—and hence, a barrier to realizing the capacities presupposed by all of its own fundamental values?

The theoretical structure of Nietzsche's answer follows from his concept of will to power. Since he articulates practices in terms of the concept of will to power, one finds that he also conceives cultural evolution in terms of the kinds of realities spanned by the will to power. Specifically, he views cultural evolution as determined by a convergence of the realities of situated experiences, language structures, self-reflective desires for agency, and physical limitations of action. The mutual delimitation of these realities is sufficient, in Nietzsche's terms, to account for both continuity and crisis in culture. These are the same kinds of realities presupposed by Nietzsche's account of nihilism, and deconstructed/reconstructed by his genealogical method.

The creative ground of cultural evolution consists for Nietzsche in the will to power as *pathos*. The will to power captures the Dionysian "fundamental ground of the world," the historically situated experiential and affective pole of culture. The Dionysian world is a field of emergent possibilities that is richer and fuller than anything that could be transmitted through culture. The *pathos* of experience is prior to agency, and prior to the order of public practices and discourses, as a field of emergent, yet culturally unarticulated, possibilities. The *pathos* of experience is the "spontaneous" ground of novelty, and the organism reflexively processes new experiences, in this way creating new possibilities for meaning. In Nietzsche's words, "there is an essential priority of the spontaneous, aggressive, expansive, form giving forces that give new interpretations and directions, although 'adaptation' [to historical conditions of existence] follows only after this." [89]

The Dionysian world produces kinds of interpretation that might be likened to products of the primary process—to use Freud's term. These interpretations are close to the affective reality of experience, but distant from the exigencies of cultural and linguistic intelligibility as well as from purposeful action. Although such interpretations are unorganized at a social level, this very unintelligibility of the individual imagination provides the material of culture, and the source of change and novelty. It is a field of possibility that—although remaining for the most part inarticulate—is far deeper and richer than either inherited culture or that which can become a part of culture. Interpretative growth stems from inner and outer experience, organized into new meanings by individuals according to the cultural resources available to them.

By identifying meaning shifts in the individual's life-world, Nietzsche can account for cultural change—even transitions to new cultural epochs—without relying on a transindividual teleology, as we saw in chapter 1. Insofar as the reflexive organization of powers is enhanced by this process, historical possibilities of meaning become richer. Nietzsche writes in a note that "every elevation of man brings with it the overcoming of narrower interpretations; ... every strengthening and increase of power opens up new perspectives and this means believing in new horizons—this idea permeates my writings." [90] But such growth is not unlimited in any given case: the exigencies of practice that bear on the field of interpretive possibilities mean that only a few of these possibilities will become *historical* as culture. "Adaptation," as Nietzsche points out, maps "growth," and this combination of growth and adaptation sets the course of evolution. [91]

To what must this growth adapt? If one were to conceive of these possibilities in terms of the will to power, one would find that they are selectively organized by two other conditions of practice—namely, language and the world of limiting forces, both natural and human. Thus, *the will to power conceived as the possibility conditions of practice includes the selective environment of interpretation*, and this is what produces Nietzsche's conception of cultural evolution.

Language, understood broadly as the logically and/or structurally interconnected grammatical field of culture, dictates (and therefore selectively delimits) a range of transindividual intelligibility. Owing to its intersubjective and intergenerational qualities, language determines in the first instance which interpretations might become *historical*. Language is intersubjective because its rulelike structure is maintained and reproduced by social practices. It is intergenerational because it replicates itself through mimesis, from generation to generation, apart from any meaning or utility it might have in practice. These qualities of language specify a range of interpretations—from among all of those reflexively organized out of the Dionysian aspect of life—that will serve as conditions of practice in future generations.

If language constrains what *might* become historical in terms of intersubjective intelligibility, then this intelligibility must itself be seen as subject to further selective pressures according to its use. Presumably from among many possibilities, only those systems of interpretation will be transferred to future generations that can constitute practice under existing historical conditions. This means that those interpretations that become historical must also be "practical" in the two senses that Nietzsche conceives of practicality. First, interpretations, if they do not actively formulate material exigencies of life (as many mystical, mythical, primitive, and religious interpretations do not), must at least not conflict with them to the degree that the individuals embodying the interpretations become extinct. Second, beyond these minimal requirements, interpretations are selectively delimited by having to serve the self-reflective function of constituting individuals as agents. They must, in other words, provide a "feeling of power." In both these cases, the "practical" functions of interpretation will be constrained to a greater or lesser degree according to existing political power relations and levels of material development—Nietzsche, unlike Marx, being more sensitive to political constraints than economic ones.

In sum, in a Nietzschean conception of cultural evolution, cultural formations become historical to the degree that they satisfy the several conditions of willing articulated by the concept of will to power. Cultural formations are historical insofar as they live in each generation as that generation's distinctive interpretive means to practice according to its conditions of life. A cultural formation retains its historical character to the degree that it continues to have utility in forming the wills of individuals vis-à-vis their worlds of experience. Thus a cultural formation must be both *coherent* in relation to a cultural grammar and *legitimate* in relation to the worlds of experience and reflexively motivated action. For a cultural formation to survive and grow, it must continually weave these grammatical, experiential, and reflexive conditions into a unity, in this way permitting the desire for agency to transpose these conditions into a "will" through action and hence to transpose the individual into an agent. In a Nietzschean conception of cultural evolution, then, the direction and form a cultural formation takes in history are determined by the exigencies of practice, broadly construed. Change and crisis can be viewed in terms of the selective relations obtaining between these several conditions of practice, as a mutual delimitation of the possibilities projected by the will to power.

The Structure of Western Cultural Evolution

The foregoing analysis reconstructs the theoretical structure implicit in Nietzsche's critique of Western culture as it follows from his philosophy of power. For this reason it makes sense to return to the issues of chapter 1, and illustrate the way in which Nietzsche's analysis expresses this structure. Recall that Nietzsche's diagnosis of Western culture reveals a crisis of power as human agency, and that the crisis can be seen as a failure of Western culture to meet the minimal requirements of its own expectations and possibilities for power as agency, partly because it masks the nature of agency itself. Western culture, in Nietzsche's view, has come to an impasse in which it cannot simultaneously mediate the demands and constraints of the existence of which it is a part, and which it has partly created.

The theoretical structure implicit in Nietzsche's analysis suggests that not all of these demands and constraints are of the same origin and nature, and this has implications for the solutions he envisages. Some demands and constraints cannot be altered without destroying the possibilities of Western culture; others must be altered in order to realize these possibilities. Some are intrinsic to culture as such; some are specifically Western permutations of these intrinsic demands and constraints; and some are specifically Christian-moral permutations of Western culture.

The distinctive attribute of Western culture is the premium it places upon intelligibility and "truth" against all immediate considerations of practice. Nietzsche supposes that at some prehistorical time the opposite was the case, and that considerations of utility reigned supreme in determining the intellectual content of practice: "Over immense periods of time the intellect produced nothing but errors. A few of these proved to be useful and helped preserve the species: those who hit upon or inherited these had better luck in the struggle for themselves and their progeny."[92] "Productions of the intellect" could become *cultural* characteristics only by becoming embedded in languages coevolving with their utilitarian aspects. For the species, the utility of language depends on its ability to communicate useful "productions of the intellect." As we saw in chapter 2, the resulting pragmatic simplicity in expression would have led to a further narrowing of the field of cultural possibilities.

The pragmatic qualities of language are bound up with its grammatical qualities: communication requires intelligibility and intelligibility requires rule-following. These rules solidify as grammar, and any single grammar selects a range of interpretive relations of which a culture might partake. With regard to the effect of language on the evolution of philosophical systems, for example, Nietzsche explains that "individual philosophical concepts are not anything capricious or autonomously evolving, but grow up in connection and relationship with one another; that however suddenly and arbitrarily they seem to appear in the history of thought, they nevertheless belong just as much to a system as all the members of the fauna of a continent—is betrayed in the end also by the fact that the most diverse philosophers keep filling in a fundamental scheme of philosophies." [93] The "invisible spell" that keeps philosophy "revolving in the same orbit," whether Indian, Greek, or German, stems from the common origin and structure of their languages: "Where there is an affinity of languages, it cannot fail, owing to the common philosophy of grammar—I mean owing to the unconscious domination and guidance by similar grammatical functions—that everything is prepared at the outset for a similar development and sequence of philosophical systems; just as the way seems barred against certain other possibilities of world-interpretation." [94] These selective pressures of language—pressures stemming from its communicative functions and grammatical structures—are common to all human cultures.

Western culture, however, is subject to further constraints, which led first to its *rational* character, and ultimately to its relative autonomy from the practicalities of agent-formation.[95] In a note that could only apply to the evolution of Western culture, Nietzsche claims that there was "originally a chaos of ideas. The ideas that were consistent with one another remained, the greater number perished and are perishing." [96] The view that ideas might be measured against one another for their internal consistency presupposes the kind of interpretation born with the Eleatics: it was here, and "only very late that truth emerged—as the weakest form of knowledge." [97] Once this development occurred, the evolutionary stage was set for a further refinement of what Nietzsche here calls "truth"—that is, a set of internally consistent ideas. This was especially the case, suggests Nietzsche, where preexisting religious and mythological interpretations came to exist side by side with a more subtle "honesty and skepticism": "This subtler honesty and skepticism came into being wherever two contradictory sentences appeared to be applicable to life because both were compatible with the basic errors [that is, the basic concepts of existing religion and mythology], and it was possible to argue about higher or lower degrees of utility for life; also wherever new propositions, though not *useful* for life, were also evidently not harmful to life: in such cases there was room for the expression of an intellectual play impulse, and honesty and skepticism were happy like all play." [98] Nietzsche argues that such cultural "space" for honesty and skepticism became an ingrained cultural need: "The intellectual fight became an occupation, an attraction, a profession, a duty, something dignified—and eventually knowledge and the striving for the true found their place as a need among other needs." [99]

The "need for truth" to which Nietzsche refers here, however, is much broader and also more useful for "life" than the specific *kind* of need for truth that led to European nihilism. The need for truth narrows the range of interpretive possibilities in Western culture, but not so decisively as does that kind of truth born in the Christian-Platonic world view: the need for a metaphysical kind of truth, a hidden "natural" world that is stable and eternal, and counterpoised to the "false" world of experience. How different this is, exclaims Nietzsche, from the rationality of Thucydides, who looks for "*reason in reality*," and who—unlike Plato—possesses "courage in the face of reality." [100] The "need for truth" both predates and—Nietzsche hopes—will postdate the Christian-Platonic period.

The Platonic conception of truth, together, in Nietzsche's words, with the "Platonism for the people" of Christian-moral culture, fatally delimited the range of possible cultural interpretations. The consequence of this particular narrowing is that cultural possibilities for the reification of interpretation and its consequent divorce from practice come to be realized. This narrowing can be explained only in terms of a new kind of selective pressure on interpretation—that of political experience. As I suggested in chapter 1, such experiences dislocate the real bases for the constitution of subjectivity in acting, and have the immediate effect of original nihilism. Only those interpretations that could simultaneously veil such experiences and vicariously reconstitute the "feeling of power" of the oppressed could be transmitted subsequently to new generations. Only an *ideological* set of interpretations, those inappropriate to practice but still providing a self-interpretation of agency, could survive this political delimitation.

The mode of practice born with original nihilism and coexisting with Platonic-Christian demands for "truth" Nietzsche calls "decadence." Decadence describes a disorganized capacity for agency. The capacities that could provide agency are disjoined; they fail to relate to one another in such a way that practices can be oriented toward worldly goals. This disjunction in turn undermines the worldly basis for experiences of agency. Any "feeling of power" attained by the decadent will be a vicarious feeling of power, not grounded in practice. In Nietzsche's formulations, the importance of the emergence of decadence in Western culture is that it reflects a nihilistic situation: *the set of interpretations satisfying all conditions of agent-formation becomes empty.* What remains are interpretations that can satisfy the need for a self-interpretation of agency only by becoming distant from experienced realities. As a result, decadent modes of practice suppress "nature," embodied experience that is an essential condition of power as agency. Similarly, only on the basis of decadent practice can the "will to truth" appear as an "objective," independent, and self-justifying formalism when in fact—according to Nietzsche's concept of will to power—the independence of the will to truth is only apparent, for it both reflects and maintains a decadent mode of practice.

The kind of cultural evolution sustained by the decadent will, however, is also the kind of distancing of interpretation from the present world that introduces into history the potential for a rigorously internal evolution of culture. The slave comes to will a "truth" so distant from capricious circumstance that there emerges the possibility of rigorous measurement of one idea against the next, without the interference of worldly experience. Moreover, because Platonic-Christian truth becomes a sphere in which "feelings of power" are sought, its coherence and self-sufficiency become increasingly important. For this reason, the interpretive sphere becomes increasingly subject to the selective pressures of internal consistency. In Nietzsche's view, this very internal delimitation of rationality shows fundamental elements of the culture system to be mutually exclusive, and this leads to a crisis of rationality. Recall this quotation from the chapter on nihilism: "You see what it was that really triumphed over the Christian god: Christian morality itself, the concept of truthfulness that was understood ever more rigorously, the father confessor's refinement of the Christian conscience translated and sublimated into a scientific conscience, into intellectual cleanliness at any price."[101] The rationalization of Western culture comes to severely limit the range of interpretations, up to the point that those remaining suppress every experiential (or "natural") condition of agency. European nihilism develops when those other-worldly spheres (such as Christianity) that sustain a vicarious sense of agency become implausible, thus exposing the underlying failure of power as agency. This is the point at which the crisis of rationality deepens into a general crisis of cultural legitimacy.

The relation between selective pressures and the structure of nihilism can be summarized in the following way. *Original* nihilism results from selective pressures (social and political experiences) that militate against interpretations that could satisfy *all* conditions of *actual* agent-formation. *European* nihilism, on the other hand, results from the situation in which the internally selective pressures of rationalization gradually eliminate interpretations that could sustain a *decadent* or *vicarious* sense of agency. The peculiar character of nihilism in the history of Western culture, then, is owing to a historical potential for the formation of power as agency being realized only in illusory forms. This was first caused by the violence of social and political experience that produced original nihilism, and later by other-worldly forms of rationalism that resulted from attempts to lend meaning to these experiences. European nihilism exposes the heretofore veiled failure of power, and results in experiences of meaninglessness that were latent in other-worldly rationalism, but held at bay by the metaphysical conceptions of agency that were attached to it.

Shortly after his first announcement of the death of God in *The Gay Science*, Nietzsche describes the increasingly rigorous practices of "truth" in relation to competing conditions of "life," and he speculates on the outcome:

Thus knowledge became a piece of life itself, and hence a continually growing power—until eventually knowledge collided with those primeval basic errors: two lives, two powers, both in the same human being. A thinker is now that being in whom the impulse for truth and those life-preserving errors clash for their first fight, after the impulse for truth has proved to be also a life-preserving power. Compared to the significance of this fight, everything else is a matter of indifference: the ultimate question about the conditions of life has been posed here, and we confront the first attempt to answer this question by experiment. To what extent can truth endure incorporation?—that is the question, that is the experiment.[102]

Any new "incorporation" of truth, in Nietzsche's view, will overcome nihilism just insofar as it acquires a self-understanding of the relation of interpretation to practice. This is what his concept of will to power begins to provide.

Nietzsche and the Metaphysics of Modernist Political Thought

It is perhaps well to pause for reflection here, to ask once again what Nietzsche's thoughts on such questions have to do with problems of political thought. The answer is straightforward, but complex in its implications. Nietzsche's critical, postmodern understanding of power draws into question our modern tradition of political thought. The reason is simply that modernist discourse about politics relies on metaphysical assumptions about agents: they are seen as subjects embodying natural desires and interests (Hobbes, Locke, and Bentham), as bearers of natural rights (Hobbes and Locke), as parties to a social contract (the entire liberal tradition through Kant), and as the epistemological foundation of rational action (Kant). These modernist assumptions are especially pronounced among contemporary liberal thinkers, who still rely on formal conceptions of rational action, abstracted from social and power relations, language, culture, and the other aspects of practice within which agents develop. Those who work within liberal utilitarian traditions (including pluralists, neoclassical economists, and rational actor theorists) very often construct models of instrumental rationality that they treat as universal. Sometimes these models are meant to be normative, sometimes explanatory. In every case they rely on metaphysical constructs of utility maximizing agents, and thus assume what ought to be explained. Those working within the Kantian tradition of liberal thought (such as Rawls and Dworkin) rely on versions of Kant's intrinsically unknowable Idea of a rational subject, which serves to ground a social morality of rights and duties. While their aims and analyses are different from the Utilitarians, they also turn the problem of rational agency into a metaphysical assumption. The agent likewise becomes an abstraction (in this case, a necessary presupposition), divorced from the social and cultural contexts that make agents what they are. Of course liberal thinkers are not always unaware of the problem at some level. Since John Stuart Mill, most liberal political thinkers have intuited the contingency of the individual as a rational agent. These intuitions did not begin to issue in theories until Weber and Freud (who were political liberals), and their theories of agency have been treated with suspicion, misunderstanding, and ignorance by the liberal mainstream.

Marxism ought to be more promising, since its concept of class agency both presupposes and requires a historically oriented and critical conception of individual agency. The mainstream of Marxism, however, has relied on unquestioned assumptions about rational actors no less than in the liberal tradition, especially by attributing to individuals a rational class consciousness. Marxists have often assumed that, under the right conditions, this consciousness will appear and manifest itself in a class agency. Events of the early twentieth century suggested that the assumption was a poor guide for revolutionary movements, and it was only then that, within limited circles, agency came to be seen as a problematic.[103]

Why are these assumptions problems for contemporary political thought? Ultimately, the reason is that the tradition cannot, on the basis of these assumptions, live up to its own ideals. These ideals are certainly not foreign to Nietzsche's own, even though they are conceptualized differently. Most important, they have always included individuality as some form of self-determination, and some kind of ability to influence courses of events in society. Liberal democracies are assumed to be good, for example, because they broadly empower individuals by providing opportunities for political influence. Such empowering implies the existence of capacities for rational choice and action, and therefore the existence of powers of individual agency. In this case, a rationalist defense of liberal democracy involves showing that it enables individuals to make social things happen differently than they otherwise might, as well as enabling them to protect their own agency. For liberal democracy to be morally viable, then, it must presuppose a society made up of selves with the capacity to choose and act.

But one must know what capacities for agency are like if one wants to explain, for example, how social relations could be altered to empower individuals to participate in political processes. One must equally be able to explain how capacities for agency develop if one wants to show why some individuals in society have a relatively greater capacity for freedom of action and self-determination than others. But rather than thinking though the relation between power and agency, modern political thinkers very often combine metaphysical assumptions about the subjective grounds of power (assumptions about desires, interests, rationality, and free will) with sciences purporting to explain the socially structured manifestations of power. One result has been sets of categories that polarize the agent as a subjective source of power, and society as a set of objective constraints.

This marriage of individual agent and political world is artificial, and there are both explanatory and moral costs. The explanatory costs stem from the fact that many notions central to the integrity of political thought—such as interests, individuality, autonomy, freedom, ideology, consensus, and obligation—are often defined in terms of metaphysical actors (often in the form of hypothetical rational actors of one sort or another). As higher level explanations come to depend on these assumptions, it becomes less likely that the assumptions themselves will become the focus of study. But difficulties in assumptions tend to become expansive: structural phenomena such as markets, classes, states, societies, and democratic institutions are conceived as outcomes of idealized agents, and thus also become highly idealized constructs. We know, of course, that social structures rest on, engage, and in important respects define categories of agency: our empirical social sciences always assume this in one way or another. But in this case, political thinkers have been slow to formulate what we already know. There are good reasons: as I suggested in the introduction, to forsake the metaphysics of agency altogether would seem to foresake the moral promises embedded in the metaphysics—a fear that I think Nietzsche shows to be unfounded. The irony of the problem, of course, is that if the conditional and worldly nature of agency cannot be theorized, then neither can the conditions under which agents might develop as free and rational beings.

These considerations suggest the central problem of contemporary political thought: the promise of the modern rationalist tradition is inextricably bound to its difficulties. Its assumptions make it difficult to relate rationalist ideals to historical conditions of possibility, and the promise becomes either ideological (if confused with reality) or utopian (if not). Most political thinkers even today fail to conceptualize human agents as entities constituted within a historical world of language, culture, and power, and who possess resources, interests, and goals only as part of this complex. In the place of what ought to be problems, political philosophers still put metaphysical placeholders. The contingencies of agents cannot be addressed because of the metaphysically foundational roles of the concept of agency itself. For this reason, the connection between knowledge of the political world and rational action—a pillar of the modern rationalist project—remains only dimly articulated. The conflict between the explanatory deficiencies of its assumptions about agency and the moral requirement that these same categories of agency be retained has left the tradition of progressive rationalism to work with the unworkable. It seems to me that this conflict presents the foremost challenge to contemporary political thought.

While many political thinkers within the rationalist tradition implicitly called this assumption about agency into question (Rousseau and Hegel, for example), with Nietzsche the agent becomes an explicit problematic. He is the first to break explicitly and completely with the Cartesianism of modern rationalism, to view the subject as a problem, and to distinguish clearly between the moral ideals of rationalism and its metaphysical foundations.

In what ways do Nietzsche's thoughts on the nature of the agent/ subject/self alter the problems of progressive rationalism? Most fundamentally, of course, they suggest that it is both possible and necessary to dispense with modernist assumptions about agency in favor of a critical postmodernism. If the tradition of political thought were to absorb Nietzsche's suggestions, however, it would have major ramifications for the way political thinkers conceive their problems, and it would do so in all three planes in which they operate—the ontological, the epistemological, and the valuative.

On the ontological plane one would find that agents are no longer metaphysical sources of interests, resources, and actions, or conceived in ways such that questions about the possibility of agency cannot be asked. With Nietzsche, the individual as agent turns out to be a problematic. Individuated power turns out to be a contingent feature of existence, and this phenomenon must itself be explained. Individual power therefore cannot serve as a stable building block for developing a domain of political subject matter. Power turns out to be constituted as agency by practices that emerge out of a fabric of language, culture, and world view in conjunction with the material attributes of the life-world—all supraindividual features of existence. Individuated capacities are, in a sense, the problem—both from explanatory and valuative perspectives. The self-reflective desires of individuals for agency that, in Nietzsche's view, really exist can only be realized through practices that are both enabled and channeled by historically given structures and resources. Because cultural and linguistic phenomena are integral to Nietzsche's understanding of power, his thought is especially interesting with respect to understanding how political ideologies (for example) form individual interests, capacities, and actions under different experiential conditions.

On the epistemological plane, Nietzsche combines a critical formulation of the concept of power with intelligibility and practicality criteria of adequacy. Like Kant, Nietzsche inquires after the conditions of intelligibility of the world, thus sidestepping the correspondence theory of truth. But Nietzsche rejects Kant's transcendental view of reason, and formulates a position closer to Marx and Weber: our good reasons for holding views about things stem from their abilities to secure conditions of agency in practice. The universal "hypothesis" about what these conditions are—will to power—is ultimately rendered reasonable or not by its pragmatic successes in addressing the crisis of individual agency in Western cultures.

Nietzsche's shift in the valuative plane is the most easily misunderstood, given his claim that "there is nothing to life itself that has value, except the degree of power—assuming that life itself is will to power." [104] What this means is that self-experiences of agent-unity—experiences of freedom, volition, control over one's future—are the grounds of value. Stated slightly differently, Nietzsche asserts that highly organized, highly individuated power is the value that sustains other values—such as rationality, moral responsibility, autonomy, and freedom. He judges that some kinds of interpretive phenomena—some truths, some ideals, some moral notions—are means to individuation. Interpretive aspects of practice once thought to possess value in themselves possess value only insofar as they are means to "life" or individuated power. [105] Values like those of Christianity that displace individuation are without value and hence nihilistic. [106]

Thus Nietzsche's "revaluation of values" stems from his removal of the categories of agent-unity that lie behind the ideals of Western culture—especially the notions of autonomy, individuality, and free will—out of the realm of the metaphysically given (where they serve as assumptions divorced from practices) and into the realm of human morals or goals (where they can be conceived as projects). As goals, they can no longer be viewed as having a "natural" existence, and for this reason can become problematics. This does not mean that values have no reality whatsoever, for they can denote plausible self-interpretations under the right circumstances. Value, for Nietzsche as much as for Marx, is a practical matter, and thus a historically contingent achievement with real, historical conditions of possibility.

By shifting the manner in which questions about power and agency are traditionally put, Nietzsche dissolves several polarities that have structured the perennial problems of political thought, probably for the best. There is no ontological polarity between agents and society or between agents and history—since Nietzsche sees individual agency as enabled by social attributes and achieved as history. There is no longer an epistemological polarity between an objective and merely subjective constitution of the subject matter—since Nietzsche's criteria of truth include subjective and objective conditions for the possibility of practice. And there is no longer a valuative polarity between power and morality—for Nietzsche sees morals as one category of the many evaluations that enable or disable power as agency.

If Nietzsche did experiment with dissolving these polarities by asking new questions rather than by reducing them to one term or the other, then his thought should be of major importance to political philosophy. Far from dissolving the subject matter of political philosophy, as, for example, Eric Voegelin claims, Nietzsche suggests new beginnings on the basis of old promises.[107] Still, these new beginnings are clouded by Nietzsche's own politics, which does not suggest these possibilities. But let me anticipate my conclusion in chapter 7. There I shall argue that the political logic of Nietzsche's philosophy of power taken by itself could affirm a postmodern politics: a pluralistic society in which egalitarianism underwrites individuality, and in which politics is an arena allowing agency to be developed and manifested. This is not what Nietzsche's politics *is*. But this is the kind of political identity his philosophy of power *might have*, if one developed it in isolation from his actual politics, since (as I shall argue) his politics is not generated in any important sense by his philosophy of power. Before developing these conclusions, however, it is necessary to show how Nietzsche develops and makes concrete his understanding of practice as will to power.

5

Cultural Criticism: Elements of a New Power

"The uncovering of Christian morality," Nietzsche proclaims in *Ecce Homo*, "is an event without parallel, a real catastrophe. He that is enlightened about that is a *force majeure*, a destiny—he breaks the history of mankind in two. One lives before him, or one lives after him." [1] Does this mean, as commentators often hold, that "Nietzsche did not think, as did Marx and the liberals, that our present condition contains the conditions of its own self-transcendence"? [2] It seems to me that this interpretation overemphasizes the apocalyptic at the expense of the historical. It suggests something that would have been quite unlike Nietzsche: that there could be a future without connection to the past.

It is important in this regard that Nietzsche saw European nihilism as a very specific kind of crisis, a crisis of modern culture producing a crisis of agency. To him it was important that the problem could be precisely identified as a disorganization of power as agency, because this also means that he could see the problem of overcoming the nihilism of modern culture, however ambitious, as something quite specific. Overcoming nihilism would require a culture and society that build on historically acquired capacities, and lead humans to engage historical experience without religious, metaphysical, or other transcendental supports. And, in fact, Nietzsche put enormous labors into questions of cultural transition, questions of how Christian and modernist values might give birth to postmodern ones.

Nietzsche's conceptualization of a new culture falls into two parts. The first part, examined in this chapter, consists in taking stock of our cultural inheritances by distinguishing their self-reflectively rational possibilities from their ideological uses. Like Marx, Nietzsche intended to avoid a utopian view of future possibilities. This meant that he had to find the elements of a new culture contained in the present one. All real possibilities for cultural renewal must emerge from our specific situation in history. Although Nietzsche claims many times in *Zarathustra* that "man is something that must be overcome," he never suggests that postmodern man—his *Übermensch*—would consist of anything that does not in some way exist in present man.[3] "Only a jester thinks that man can also be skipped over."[4] This is why Nietzsche labors to criticize Christian and modern ideals: they can be "revalued" only immanently to the practices they sustain. The major classes of inheritances that could be revalued according to his new understanding of practice are science, morality, nobility, and art. For Nietzsche, although each is implicated in different ways in the cultural crisis, each is necessary to a new culture insofar as it enables the organization of power as agency.

The second part of Nietzsche's effort to conceptualize a new culture is examined in the following chapter. This involved identifying and advocating a stance toward existence that would be compatible both with self-identity and with the historicity of the human condition. Nietzsche's approach here was to teach rather than analyze critically; the most central of his teachings are to be found in his notions of tragic wisdom and the eternal return of the same. The consciousness achieved through these teachings would presumably allow the values of Western culture to function differently than in the past, and this is what would lead to a "revaluation of values."

Nietzsche's view that cultural renewal would be *sufficient* to overcome nihilism, however, requires qualification.[5] In the final chapter I argue that Nietzsche's solutions to the problem of nihilism are necessary but not sufficient because they are primarily cultural and not political. This inadequacy is a result of his failure to understand fully the dynamics of modern societies, a failure that caused him to miss those modern sources of nihilism that are immediately social and political, even though he is sensitive to ancient political causes of nihilism. Because of this gap in Nietzsche's analysis, in this chapter and the following one I follow his logic in seeing cultural renewal as a necessary condition of overcoming nihilism, while postponing the question of sufficiency.

Revaluation and Historical Development

If Nietzsche's view of history is not as apocalyptic, even prophetic, as commentators often make it out to be, what *is* an appropriate image? His phrase for cultural renewal, the "revaluation of values," suggests a process that is grounded in and yet breaks with the past. Perhaps most important, Nietzsche knew that his demands for a nontranscendental view of historical being would require him to locate future possibilities in present historical realities: to posit an absolute break would only be to develop a transcendental idea of the future. And yet his emphasis on cultural transition and crisis implies newness, something that had not been there before.

Although Nietzsche sees past and future as in some sense radically discontinuous, he does not argue for a liberation from the past but rather for a reconstitution of its resources. On the one hand, human potentialities and capacities are products of history, resulting from a slow (although not necessarily continuous) development by social and cultural forces. Certainly his genealogical method presupposes that resources are continuously inherited. On the other hand, breaks occur when inheritances are taken over into new forms of life. In *Human, All-Too-Human*, Nietzsche uses the metaphor of a bell mold to express this relationship:

Culture has emerged like a bell, within which is encased a cruder and more common material: falsehood, violence, the unlimited expansion of all individual egos, of every separate people—all of these are encased by culture. Can it now be lifted off? Has the liquid set? Have the good and useful drives, the habits of the nobler disposition become so certain and so general that the support of metaphysics, the errors of religion, the hardness and violence as powerful bonds between human and human, people and people, are no longer required? No sign from God can help us any longer to answer this question: our own insight must decide.[6]

The crisis of European nihilism indicates that the form of life cast by Christian-moral culture can no longer develop without recasting itself. Nonetheless, cultural crisis makes a full understanding of inherited capacities all the more important: Nietzsche's metaphor of the bell suggests that although nihilism might shatter the outer form of a culture—its self-certainty—its effects still remain impressed on everyday practices. Forms of consciousness can never exhaust cultural formations, since cultural formations consist in a multitude of habitual and ritualized ways of acting, doing, and interrelating, as well as in countless (but perhaps inexplicit) forms of competence and knowledgeability. The crisis of nihilism means that the integrity and meaningful coherence of Christian-moral culture and its modernist shadows are lost. But the form of life cast by Christian-moral culture continues to exist, in spite of its lack of overall coherence, meaning, and value. It exists as the random pieces of the once intact "bell" of the Christian-moral world view, and remains embedded in our capacities, orientations, rituals, and social interactions; in our intellectual habits, rationality, honesty, moral sensibilities, and conscience.

Nietzsche's genealogical insight is that because these fragments have no intrinsic value apart from modes of practice, any might attain new value—value not dependent upon its past functions—by becoming a part of a new form of life. This is why Nietzsche can have Zarathustra proclaim that "I walk among men as among fragments of the future."[7] And the same point is quite clear in Nietzsche's discussions of "our virtues" in *Beyond Good and Evil*: The "historical sense" of nineteenth-century Europeans consists precisely in their new self-consciousness of multiple inheritances: "Our instincts now run back everywhere; we are ourselves a kind of chaos." But this is not necessarily a bad thing in Nietzsche's view: " 'The spirit' sees its advantage in this." Prior cultures, no matter how noble, were rigid in their tastes. But contemporary Europeans can "enjoy Homer again." For them, history comes to provide numerous possibilities of cultural style:

The hybrid European ... needs a costume: he requires history as a storehouse for his costumes ... again and again a new piece of prehistory or a foreign country is tried on, put on, taken off, packed away, and above all *studied*: we are the first age that has truly studied "costumes"—I mean those of moralities, articles of faith, tastes in the arts, and religions.... [We are] prepared like no previous age for a carnival in the grand style, for the laughter and high spirits of the most spiritual revelry, for the transcendental heights of the highest nonsense and Aristophanean derision of the world. Perhaps this is where we shall still discover the realm of our *invention*, that realm in which we, too, can still be original, say as parodists of world history and God's buffoons—our *laughter* may yet have a future.[8]

Within the myriad of our inherited resources, Nietzsche sees nihilism as playing a particular role in providing both the opportunity and the imperative for cultural innovation. Viewed in terms of nihilism, it becomes clear that Nietzsche links continuity, growth, and crisis as closely as Marx links evolution and revolution. This dialectical quality of change is so central to his thought that it finds its way into the preface of *Beyond Good and Evil*: "The fight against Plato or, to speak more clearly and for 'the people,' the fight against the Christian-ecclesiastical pressure of millennia—for Christianity is Platonism for 'the people'—has created in Europe a magnificent tension of the spirit the like of which has never yet been seen on earth: with so tense a bow we can now shoot for the most distant goals. To be sure, European man experiences this tension as need and distress. . . ." Precisely this "distress" of nihilism, Nietzsche believes, will once again force a "revaluation of values," as it did when ancient slaves were forced to find meaning in oppression.

Of the major strains in Western culture that Nietzsche assessed and reformulated, two—science (*Wissenschaft*: explicit knowledge) and morality—come directly from our Christian-Platonic heritage. These consist in interpretive practices as they relate to nature and society. A third inheritance—what Nietzsche calls "nobility"—is specifically *self*-reflective, because it is rooted in self-experiences of agency. Nietzsche views art, a fourth type of inheritance, as a manifestation of power as agency, evidence that organized capacities of agency have always existed, albeit naively. Nietzsche's immanent criticisms of these inheritances are, in a sense, successive genealogical overlays that describe the historical possibility of his *Übermensch*.

Revaluation and Science

One of the two most powerful strains of Western culture is, in Nietzsche's view, its "will to truth"—a strain that culminates in modern science (*Wissenschaft*). Science seemed to Nietzsche to have displaced the Christian-moral world view as the dominant ideal in Western culture—an ideal at once continuous with its legacy and a radical departure from it.[9] Accordingly, his attitude toward modern science at first seems complex and enigmatic: sometimes he praises science and equates it with progress; at other times he identifies it with the forces of nihilism. Not surprisingly, this has resulted in some confusion in the secondary literature.[10]

Much of the confusion over Nietzsche's apparently ambiguous

attitude toward modern science can be dispelled by noting that his approach to science—as in other cases—is an immanent critique in which he seeks to distinguish its self-reflectively rational from its ideological aspects. Nietzsche rejects metaphysical realist and positivist *views* of science.[11] But he affirms the actual experimental *practices* of science. He does so for two reasons. First, by grounding its practices in the material and sensuous world, science is able to produce kinds of knowledge that undermine the Christian-moral world view and its modernist shadows, helping to prepare for a practice-oriented culture. Second, because experimental science involves a methodical and hypothetical approach to the sensuous world, it would itself be involved in any self-reflectively rational practice. Although intrinsically incapable of creating values or goals, science is essential to any new form of life: "We must become *physicists*," writes Nietzsche, "in order to become *creators*."[12] In Nietzsche's view, science is necessary and legitimate when individuals come to understand the products of science as conditioned by specific situations and related to specific interests and practices.

Because those in contemporary society generally lack this understanding, however, the products of science are susceptible to reification and thus to serving ideological functions. In his later writings especially, Nietzsche saw contemporary understandings of science as consisting in mixtures of Christian-Platonic metaphysical realism and positivism. Western perspectives retain the objectivist illusions of the Christian-Platonic universe to the extent that they see science as "discovering truth," that they view such discoveries as good in themselves, and that they assume that science will—together with secular morality—lead to an overall progress for mankind.[13] This self-understanding of the scientist stems not from scientific practices themselves, but from a faith that orients and sustains some aspects of scientific practices while hiding others. Scientists fail to understand their interpretive practices to the extent that they see science as a purely objective process of discovery, one within which the self holds a contemplative relation to sensuous reality.

Nietzsche objects to this kind of understanding of scientific practices not only because it is philosophically untenable in an era of Kantian and post-Kantian epistemology (epistemology focusing on the synthetic, object-constituting aspects of cognitive and linguistic processes), but also because it perpetuates the reification of interpretive activities. When conceptual structures of man's own making are mistaken for natural entities, they often function as ideology. Every "lawful necessity" that is "discovered" has the potential to deprive humans of an arena of action beyond the requirements of actual contingencies. This is especially the case when science is applied to human affairs. The generalizing ("objectivistic") historians of Nietzsche's time who saw themselves as discovering laws of history, for example, mistook historical outcomes of human actions for "objective" processes unrelated to contemporary interests and practices.[14] This kind of mistake perpetuates human powerlessness over history even as it extends human power over nature.[15] Indeed, Nietzsche considers science to be so closely tied to the objectivistic illusions of the Christian-Platonic perspective that it would be quite unlikely that scientific "types" could provide the "new values" that would sustain scientific activities.[16]

Scientific practices, however, have progressive dimensions in spite of the self-understandings of scientific practitioners. Science hastens the destruction of the Christian-Platonic world view simply by interrogating the world of experience. Early modern science inherited the Christian idea that nature is controlled by a *super*natural God, and labored under the idea that God provided nature for man's use. In this sense, early modern science worked within Christian perspectives, and Christianity rationalized the harnessing of nature for man's exploitation. But scientific investigation also demystifies nature, and in so doing undermines the foundations of the Christian-moral perspective. Science is especially subversive when it turns its eye toward humans: "Our attitude toward *ourselves* is hubris, for we experiment with ourselves in a way we would never permit ourselves to experiment with animals and, carried away with curiosity, we cheerfully vivisect our souls."[17] As science turns inward—consistent with the Christian hubris toward nature—it begins to dissect that internal territory of human nature posited and colonized by Christianity as a means to its interpretive hegemony. Science becomes, as Nietzsche puts it, the "nutcracker of the soul."[18] It discovers that the systems of spiritual causalities upon which Christianity had depended are fictions, and replaces them with mechanically causal concepts. Although science cannot provide the functional equivalents of Christian illusions with respect to self-interpretations of agency, it nonetheless shatters the notion that free will, responsibility, guilt, sin, suffering, and redemption are causally related, a notion that provides legitimacy for Christian explanations. In so doing, science can produce the kind of psychological knowledge that will provide for progress beyond Christianity and its modernist successors. "We are gentler and more humane," Nietzsche writes in a note, and "all gentleness and humaneness exists in the fact that we now ascribe much to circumstance and not everything to the person! And that we frequently ascribe value to egoism and no longer consider it to be evil and reprehensible in itself. . . . Thus: our overcoming of the belief in the absolute answerability of the person and the reprehensibleness of the individual constitutes our progress beyond barbarism." [19] Still, Nietzsche also emphasizes that the experimental honesty of modern science was in large degree channeled and motivated by Christian ideals that turn out to be "errors." At the same time, their potential value outlasts the errors themselves; the errors and their effects grow to be mutually exclusive.[20] Nietzsche characterizes the practice of science in terms of its experimental and methodical approach to the sensuous world, and points out that the rudiments of a new understanding of science already exist in its systematic interrogation of experience—in its non-Christian-Platonic acceptance of the "testimony of the senses." [21] These practices are more substantial and better founded than the self-understandings of their practitioners. Thus in one of his late notes he writes that it "is not the victory of science that distinguishes our nineteenth century, but the victory of scientific method over science." [22] Similarly in *The Antichrist* Nietzsche argues that methods are the unique contribution of modern science and distinguish it from other forms of knowledge. "The most valuable insights are discovered last; but the most valuable insights are *methods*. *All* the methods, *all* the presuppositions of our current scientific outlook, were opposed for thousands of years with the most profound contempt." [23] The real value of science is to be found in its "conscientiousness in small things." [24] Nietzsche follows Enlightenment thinkers in being intrigued with the fallibility of metaphysical propositions relative to the results of experiments: "I favor any *skepsis* to which I may reply 'Let us try it!' But I no longer wish to hear anything of all those things and questions that do not permit any experiment. This is the limit to my 'truthfulness'; for there courage has lost its right." [25]

Nietzsche would even have agreed with twentieth-century positivists that science is distinguished by its experimental methods rather than by its results or its metaphysical and moral self-understandings. But, as I suggested in chapter 3, he would have disagreed with the positivist view that experimental activities are presuppositionless, that they can be canonized in an objective set of rules, and that only "facts" can be called "knowledge." Instead, Nietzsche placed a high value on experimental methods because they seemed to be a means for taking the sensuous world seriously. Not until the Renaissance and Galileo's experiments did scholars see the sensible world as a key to gaining knowledge. Modern science began to advance when it rejected the beliefs of the Eleatics and Plato that the senses can only lead to deception. In pointing this out, Nietzsche argues that "we possess science precisely to the extent to which we have decided to *accept* the testimony of the senses—to the extent to which we have decided to sharpen them further, arm them, and have learned to think them through." [26] Science's systematic investigation of the world of experience increases human powers in spite of the residual Christian-Platonic perspectives that have sustained its activity. Nietzsche was thoroughly modern in his view that science is the hallmark of an "accumulative" epoch, "in which the forces and means of power are discovered that the future will one day make use of." [27]

Nietzsche hoped that science-as-method was part of a more general movement in which the nineteenth century was "coming to its senses"—in both the literal and the figurative sense of the phrase:[28] "If anything at all has been achieved, it is a more innocuous relation to the senses, a more joyous, benevolent, Goethean attitude toward sensuality; also a prouder feeling regarding the search for knowledge." [29]

For all Nietzsche's interest in the prospects of modern science, however, he still views it as a "proud possession" that can be no more than a means. Anticipating Max Weber's arguments, he points out that because science is essentially method, it can "never create values." To serve as a condition of a new culture, science "first requires in every respect an ideal of value, a value-creating power, in the *service* of which it could believe in itself." [30] Although science is a necessary condition of a new culture, it also provides an incomplete perspective on the human condition. Science has to do with interpreting the world as a set of objects. A broader perspective—

specifically, that of art—is needed to link this way of interpreting the world to self-reflective practices, these being the bases of new values.

Revaluation and Morality

Secularized morality is the other key modernist ideal inherited from Christian-moral culture. As in the case of science, Nietzsche's criticisms of Christian morality and its modernist successors are immanent: "Our whole activity is only morality turning against its previous form."[31] Nonetheless, although Nietzsche diagnoses the eclipse of Christian morality, it is not clear that he is able to conceptualize the kind of post-Christian morality that might take its place. Nietzsche never rejects the possibility of a post-Christian morality in principle,[32] but he sometimes seems quite prepared to accept the possibility of moral chaos. Such chaos he assumes would eventually settle down—perhaps at high cost—into a hierarchical society in which a few powerful individuals would attain a morality beyond the categorical judgments of "good and evil." Most would be subject to a categorical social morality created and administered by the powerful.[33] If this is Nietzsche's image of a morality "beyond good and evil," then it hardly seems a very satisfying one.[34]

The fact that Nietzsche's politics does not involve a development of a post-Christian morality, however, reflects neither the nature nor importance of his thoughts on morality. Frederick Olafson has suggested that Nietzsche's fundamental contribution to moral theory does not concern the canons and principles of morality—the subject matter of traditional ethical philosophy. Rather, it has to do with viewing humans as evaluative beings: "Nietzsche is the prophet not so much of an ethical as of a 'meta-ethical' revolution."[35] If by "meta-ethical" one simply means that every ethics presupposes an account of how judgments relate to practices, then Olafson's characterization is quite apt. Nietzsche is indeed less interested in distinguishing between reasons for specific judgments than he is in the question, "What is the meaning of the act of evaluation itself?"[36] This question, of course, refers us back to his philosophy of practices, the will to power. Because Nietzsche's concept of will to power reconstructs the concept of agency, it also reconstructs the question of how capacities of agency relate to moral choices. His approach leads to a critique of traditional conceptions of moral agency, and in this way implicitly provides a new ethical orientation.

If Nietzsche is not interested in ethical rules so much as in the conceptions of agency they presuppose, one would think that he would have been well-disposed toward the utilitarian attempt to evaluate practices in terms of their benefits for the self. After all, utilitarianism breaks down the Christian polarity between the demands of the self and what is good, between morality and life. But one finds little praise of utilitarianism in Nietzsche's writings. Part of the reason is that utilitarianism embeds a metaphysics of moral agency in its concept of the "ego," and it is this metaphysics that is expanded into notions of general welfare.[37] Nietzsche's argument is that the utilitarian self is not given as a fact, but must itself be explained as the result of a specific historical organization of power. Utilitarianism in effect takes over and simply reevaluates the Christian "false dogmatism regarding the 'ego': it is taken in the atomistic sense, in a false antithesis to the 'nonego'; at the same time, pried out of becoming, as something that has being."[38] This is why "the 'welfare of the individual' is just as imaginary as the 'welfare of the species': the former is *not* sacrificed to the latter; [the] species viewed from a distance is just as transient as the individual."[39] Nietzsche's point, as we saw in chapter 2, is that the powers, capabilities, and needs of agents become something "individual" through an incorporation of historical experiences, culture, and language. Insofar as moral judgments attribute selfhood to individuals, they as much constitute individuals as they flow from them. What utilitarianism really does, then, is read interests of general welfare ("the happiness of *England*," as Nietzsche puts it) onto the individual.[40] In this way, it usurps the good of the individual into the good of society—precisely the opposite of what its proponents intend.

Nietzsche has similar complaints against Kantian imagery that sees morality as a barrier of practical reason against the amoral and asocial desires of human nature—a point I return to below. Kantian imagery is appropriate to historically specific cases—indeed cases that are mostly prehistorical.[41] But in general, such polarities are historically specific phenomena that themselves require explanation in terms of genealogical explications of the will to power. Indeed, what is most radical and significant about Nietzsche's approach is that he avoids altogether the traditional ontological polarity between external moral regulation and individual desire. The meaning of

Nietzsche's attack on morality, as Georg Simmel so aptly put it, can only be understood in terms of his view that "all social institutions, all giving and receiving by which the individual becomes a social being, are mere preconditions or consequences of his own nature.... [T]he individual's value does not reside wholly in himself: part of it he receives as the reflection of processes and creations in which his own nature has fused with beings and circumstances outside of him." [42]

These intentions become clear when we examine Nietzsche's reasons for attacking Christian morality, essential aspects of which are carried into modernist utilitarian and Kantian ethics. He was not interested in defending the desires and passions of individuals against right action. Rather he was defending what I called in chapter 2 the "third nature" of individuality against social moralities of the sort that deprive the individual of capacities for agency. Put simply, Nietzsche objects to the ideological functions of most social moralities. The commandments and structures of Christian morality, for example, are categorical, universal, nonreflexive, and external to willing. The categorical forms and ideological functions of Christian morality are so tied together that objecting to one entails objecting to the other. While Christian morality holds individuals responsible for their acts, it also subverts the possibility of responsible agency by holding the individual to universal and categorical maxims of behavior that prescribe and proscribe conduct. This is why Nietzsche called Christian morality a "slave" or "herd" morality that "trains the individual to be a function of the herd and ascribe value to himself only as a function." [43] What Christian morality effects is an externally regulated behavior, enforced by promises of salvation and threats of damnation. Although Christian doctrine asserts that individuals are endowed with free will and moral responsibility, it simultaneously denies them an understanding of the worldly conditions of agency, and for this reason undermines the worldly possibility of moral agency. Instead, it uses the doctrines of free will and responsibility to tie the individual's sense of agency to a system of spiritual rewards and punishments. Christianity instills a reflexive examination of one's motives, but it does so in such a way that the self is externalized from, and defined against, worldly experiences. This kind of reflexivity denies the possibility of a worldly self by constructing a transcendental self tied to correct behavior. Foucault's more general insight that these kinds of transcendental identities can serve as means of social control is indebted to Nietzsche's case against Christianity.

The "herd" or ideological functions of Christian morality stem not only from its form, but also from the institutional mechanics of the church. According to Nietzsche, the priestly rulers of the church do not simply minister to the sufferings of their followers. They exploit this suffering in such a way that they gain control over the abilities of sufferers to sustain their self-identifies. The priest entices his followers to interpret their experiences though Christian dogma, and in so doing they become dependent upon his exegesis of the world for their self-interpretations of agency. The structure of the Christian-moral world view is uniquely suited to the kind of interpretive privilege that the priest claims for himself. The reason for this, Nietzsche takes care to point out, is that Christian-moral interpretation—in contrast to earlier magical, mythical, and philosophical modes of thought—removes all criteria of truth from the sensible world of everyday experience, with the exception of experiences of hardship and bad conscience that serve as evidence of guilt and sin. The other-worldly structure of Christianity allows the priest to create the view that all natural events are conditioned by invisible laws, causalities, and forces to which he alone has access.[44] Sensuous and psychological experiences are accounted for in terms of other-worldly and supernatural causes. This kind of explanation, argues Nietzsche, shatters the possibility of constructing appearances as practical kinds of knowledge, such as knowledge of natural necessities that is a minimal interpretive condition of any kind of individual agency, moral or otherwise. "When the natural causes of a deed are no longer 'natural,' but thought of as caused by the conceptual specters of superstition, by 'God,' by 'spirits,' by 'souls,' as if they were merely 'moral' consequences, as reward, punishment, hint, means of education, then the presupposition of knowledge has been destroyed...."[45] The kind of exegesis of the world that reads all "natural" or experienced events in terms of a shadow world of invisible actors and fictitious causes leads to cognitive incapacity to engage reality, and thus deepens whatever de facto, politically maintained incapacity already exists. This, Nietzsche claims, is the Christian priest's "*greatest crime against humanity.*"[46]

The priest's intellectual authority resides not only in his ability to locate causal agents in a nonempirical, metaphysical world but also in his interpretation of suffering and bad conscience as empirical evidence for his exegesis. Since suffering produces a hope for redemption or release (*Erlösung*) from suffering, the priest increases the likelihood that his interpretive authority will be accepted by tying the promise of redemption to acceptance of his exegesis. Failure to accept the exegesis threatens damnation and eternal suffering—the possibility of which is always real to those who suffer. Thus Nietzsche views the priest "type" as an ideologist who employs politically produced sufferings to solidify his interpretive authority and who destroys the rational capacities of those subject to his authority in the process of doing so.[47] This is why he can claim in discussing Pauline Christianity that "with morality it becomes easiest to lead mankind by the nose."[48] As in the case of all ideology, individuals gain a vicarious identity, but only through the systematic destruction of their capacities for self-reflective rationality.

In contrast to the ideological functions of Christian morality, Nietzsche sometimes suggested that a post-Christian morality could be based on the Christian *ideal* of responsibility—what he referred to as "sovereign" individuality. To understand Nietzsche's attempt to conceive a morality beyond the categoricals "good and evil" requires clarification of a difficulty that arises in the English translations of his works. While the English words "morality" and "ethics" generally mean the same thing, modern German philosophical usage since Lessing distinguishes between the strictly exterior and social aspect of morality (*Sittlichkeit*, sometimes inadequately rendered as "mores"), and that aspect which is individual and intentional (*Moralität*). This is why it makes good sense for Nietzsche to call his "sovereign individual" "autonomous and supramoral [*übersittliche*]" while also claiming that "we want to be the heirs of all previous morality [*Moralität*] and *not* begin afresh. Our whole activity is only morality [*Moralität*] turning against its previous form."[49] Since the categorical form of Christian *Sittlichkeit* conflicted with the Christian ideal of responsibility, Nietzsche thought it essential that it overcome and destroy itself (*selbsthebt auf*) in its rule-governed and dogmatic aspects.[50] Nietzsche's post-Christian morality would shed the "outer shell" of Christian morality—what he refers to quite specifically as the "morality of mores" (*die Sittlichkeit der Sitte*),[51] in this way allowing Christian morality to realize its potential for sovereign individuality.

That Nietzsche's approach to Christian morality consisted not simply in a rejection but also in an immanent critique is apparent in the continuity between his ethical individualism and the Kantian movement within moral philosophy.[52] In the *Critique of Practical Reason*, Kant's point was to show that freedom, autonomy, and morality belong to the same complex of practical reason.[53] One of Kant's major innovations in moral philosophy consisted in bridging the abstract polarity between individual action and social morality in Christian and various quasi-utilitarian ethics. Notwithstanding their major differences, Nietzsche continues and even concludes Kant's inversion of morality into the autonomous will, morality itself thus becoming a condition rather than an obstacle to willing.[54] Georg Simmel explains that on the basis of its insight into the social origins of the individual, "ethics (above all, Kantian ethics) has shifted the ground on which to appraise man, from his deeds to his attitude. . . . [Nietzsche] translated the Kantian contrast between the attitude and success of an external action (which already has freed the value of the individual from its social dependence) into the contrast between existence and the effect of man in general. . . . Thus Nietzsche overcame the limitations of a merely social existence, as well as the valuation of man in terms of his sheer effects. . . ."[55] Simmel emphasizes that the claims of individual personhood—what he refers to here as those of "mankind in general" (and what I refer to as the self-reflective need for agency or subjectivity)—go "far beyond any given society" to ground the "various complaints and self-assertions of the individual against society." Such claims are not brought to society from the outside—as in the early liberal defense of the individual—but are a potential of social morality within which a "qualitative *being* of personality" develops, that is, an organization of power as subjectivity.[56] Nietzsche's implied contrast between *Sittlichkeit* and *Moralität* indicates a dialectical progression of morality toward individual responsibility. This Kantian element of Nietzsche's moral ideal appears clearly in a speculation from his middle period that the laws of a future society might be "based on the fundamental idea: 'I bow only before laws I have given to myself both in small and great matters.'"[57]

Nietzsche's critique is based on Kant's failure to realize the immanent potential of his moral philosophy, a failure that could, in Nietzsche's view, be traced to the very nature of Kant's project. Kant's intention was to provide a rational foundation for Christian morality when Christian faith was being seriously eroded by the new sciences of the Enlightenment. Thus it is hardly surprising that Nietzsche ultimately finds Kant's project impossible, and consisting in the last analysis in a continuation of Christian *Sittlichkeit*. In Nietzsche's assessment, this continuity shows up most clearly in Kant's categorical imperative, demanding as it does obedience to universalizable maxims of behavior. He finds in Kant a residue of social oppression refracted into and maintained by Christian morality. "The categorical imperative," he remarks in the *Genealogy*, "smells of cruelty."[58] Kant in effect undermined his ideal of autonomy by defining it in terms of the categorical imperative and so detaching it from situated and reflexive practices. In this way he carried the ideological effects of previous social morality into his attempt to provide a rational basis for individual morality. According to Nietzsche, a workable equation between autonomy and responsibility would require even these last remnants of *Sittlichkeit* to be overcome, "for 'autonomous' and 'moral' [*sittlich*] are mutually exclusive."[59] While Kant holds that action in accordance with the categorical imperative would produce freedom, Nietzsche holds that the capacity for moral responsibility requires freedom from all residues of *Sittlichkeit*, the categorical imperative included.

That Nietzsche would sever all conceptual relations between *Sittlichkeit* and autonomy does not, however, mean that he dissociates them historically. Past beliefs and practices need not have been rational for them to have produced practices subsequently lending themselves to rational action (chapter 3). And so it is with *die Sittlichkeit der Sitte*, the "morality of mores." Because Nietzsche, like Aristotle, Hegel, and Marx, takes human nature to be "cultivated" (*züchtet*) over time, he ascribes importance to the "morality of mores" for cultivating the kind of agent capable of responsible action, "notwithstanding the severity, tyranny, stupidity, and idiocy involved in it."[60] Owing to the "prehistoric labor" of the "morality of mores," it is now possible, Nietzsche thinks, to conceive of a morality that would lend itself to responsible, autonomous, individual practices.

Nietzsche's model of autonomy is his "sovereign individual." In two well-known sections of the *Genealogy*, he describes the sovereign individual as the "ripest fruit" of the "tremendous process" of forging human nature into something "regular, calculable, necessary, even in his own image of himself."[61] Two distinct qualities are present in the sovereign individual: he represents a self-overcoming (*Selbstaufhe-bung*) of the morality of mores into moral responsibility; and he represents the kind of individual who has the capacity to practice this morality by virtue of a fully developed agency, providing the power that gives the "right to make promises." [62] For a morality to be truly responsible, one must have the capacity to anticipate the consequences of one's actions, and in this way to "stand in security" of the future. Nietzsche refers to this capacity as "a real *memory of the will*: so that between the original 'I will,' 'I shall do this,' and the actual discharge of the will, its *act*, a world of strange new things, circumstances, even acts of will may be interposed without breaking this long chain of will." [63] "But how many things this presupposes," he exclaims—namely, that humans in fact be able to anticipate the future, to think in causal terms, to understand necessities, to choose means and ends, and to calculate and compute. As Weber later emphasized in "Politics as a Vocation" and other writings, an ethics of responsibility requires a complementary (scientific) grasp of the world sufficient to understand the antecedents and consequences of action. [64]

Although Nietzsche's conception of an ethics of responsibility sketches certain aspects of a post-Christian morality, it does not by itself specify what a new morality would look like. But Nietzsche's suggestion that his "sovereign individual" represents an ethical incarnation of the will to power does indicate the *parameters* of possible moralities. The grounds of any Nietzschean morality would reside in the way moral interpretations serve as conditions for freedom and autonomy in the Kantian sense, or the organization of power as agency in the terms used here. Thus, even though Nietzsche does not tell us what a post-Christian morality should look like, he does suggest that—as an ethical extension of the concept of will to power—it should serve as a condition of sovereign individuality and have responsible action as its goal. While specific moral canons would no doubt remain relative in the sense that they will be conditions of constituting humans as agents under varying conditions of existence, what is not relative for Nietzsche is the value of subjectivity itself, at least no more so than his "hypothesis" of will to power. The reason is that the value of subjectivity is presupposed both in his problematic of nihilism and in his description of practices as will to power. For this reason, Nietzsche's philosophy of power outlines a post-Christian morality that affirms some kinds of actions while proscribing others.

Nietzsche did not universalize this approach, in part because he held that only a few had the potential for subjectivity in this sense. However, taken by itself, his approach *could* be universalized without violating his critique of Christian morality and its secular successors. If one were to do so, this approach would involve a quasi-Kantian respect for persons as ends in themselves. There is nothing intrinsic to Nietzsche's philosophy of power that would suggest that a society could not, in principle, embody this kind of moral perspective. Nietzsche himself suggests that under some historical conditions and social arrangements, for example, a social morality of reciprocity might effectively increase the power of each individual in a society (see chapter 2).[65] If these possibilities fail to be expressed in Nietzsche's politics, it is not because his analysis of willing militates against morality as such, but rather because he read the necessity of domination from his politics back into his philosophy of power. How and why he did so will be taken up in the final chapter.

Revaluation and Nobility

In turning to the third type of inheritance Nietzsche thought necessary to overcome nihilism—that of "nobility"—one finds that he is no longer concerned with interpretive mediations of the world as an object (science) or social relations (morality) but with *self-reflective* interpretations that permit the formation of the self as an agent. In Nietzsche's view, nobility inheres not in external actions or works but rather in an esteem for the self: "*The noble soul has reverence for itself.*"[66] His term "nobility" denotes good conscience in action together with the feeling of self-certainty that attaches to successful actions. Nietzsche's conception of nobility, in other words, is not the sociological category it first seems. Rather, he understands nobility in psychological and phenomenological terms: nobility refers to a type of self-experience rather than to a sociological typology in much the same way that his categories of mastery and slavery refer to typologies of political experience rather than social or political classes. In principle, nobility might occur anywhere in society.

By using the term "nobility" to denote a type of self-reflective experience, however, Nietzsche does mean to suggest that such experiences typically originated in master classes.[67] The link he draws between psychology and sociology makes sense when one considers his estimation of the importance of social experience in forming different "types" of psychologies. The socially privileged , the "well-born," and the politically powerful can command the resources of their existence and, at the same time, produce cultural evaluations that link social position and moral worth. This is true even during the Christian-moral period, for—as Nietzsche is careful to note—Christian estimations of moral worth have always been flexible enough to coexist with, and often affirm, those who hold political power.[68] Nietzsche does hold that for the most part the social and political conditions for noble self-certainty no longer exist, and that the last congenial political arrangement was prerevolutionary France.[69] Yet, in spite of Nietzsche's evaluation, one might expect that nobility—insofar as it depends both on cultural orientation and on self-experiences of power—might survive its genesis to become a function of a different political configuration of power.

That nobility might outlive aristocracy is not a possibility that Nietzsche seriously considered. In part, the reason he did not is because he believed that, even if noble and slave psychologies are social in origin (that is, there are no "original" psychological types—they are "bred" by social conditions), these psychologies become innate through the biological inheritance of socially acquired characteristics. The political consequences of this discredited theory of evolution I take up in the final chapter. The fact that Nietzsche was wrong about the biology of evolution and not overly interested in social structure is important for the political conclusions that one might draw from his typology of noble and slave psychologies.

Nonetheless, this should not be allowed to obscure the strength of Nietzsche's psychological analysis itself. Like Freud later, he was interested in the *kind* of reflexivity that provides the self with an identity: the crucial difference between noble and slave psychology is that the slave fails to integrate experience of powerlessness, leaving this experience to remain in the memory as an excess, and leading to obsessions with past injuries that poison the ability of the self to function.[70] In contrast, the "robust health" of noble self-experience stems from the capacity to integrate experiences, and thus "forget" the many occassions that, daily, threaten to derail one's identity. Nietzsche explains that "forgetting is no mere *vis inertiae* of the superficial imagination; it is rather an active and in the strictest sense positive faculty of repression [*Positives Hemmungsvermögen*] that is responsible for the fact that what we experience and absorb enters our consciousness as little while we are digesting it (one might call the process "inpsychation" [*Einverseelung*]) as does the thousandfold process involved in physical nourishment—so-called 'incorporation' [*Einverleibung*]."[71] By means of repression, a free space can be created for the ego as an experience of self-identity, the repression making room "for new things, above all, for the nobler functions and functionaries, for regulation, foresight, premeditation (for our organism is an oligarchy)—that is the purpose of active forgetfulness, which is like a doorkeeper, a preserver of psychic order, repose, and etiquette."[72] Nietzsche held, as did Freud, that ego-identity requires repression; that repression serves to exclude both internal and external threats to identity.[73] He also understood that some situations do not permit successful, ego-creating repression. Repression is ego-creating when it leads to and is continually reinforced by experiences of agency in the world. When conditions are otherwise, repression is unsuccessful, and the past poisons the self. "The man in whom this apparatus of repression is damaged and ceases to function properly may be compared (and more than merely compared) with a dyspeptic —he cannot 'have done' with anything."[74] For the slave who is "denied the true reaction, that of deeds," memories of powerlessness and injury turn first into bad conscience and eventually into *ressentiment*.[75]

Not all memory need become poison, however, as it does with the *ressentiment* of the slave. Nietzsche is not arguing that psychological health requires amnesia. Indeed, the sovereign individual is distinguished by his memory, indicating that it is the *kind* of memory that is at issue. Nietzsche calls the memory of the sovereign individual a "memory of the will," suggesting that it is actually based on noble repression. It consists not in memories of injuries that cannot be repaired, but rather in a memory of past self-identities, identities maintained over time in such a way that long-term projects— "promises"—can be carried into the future.[76] We grasp our historicity partly through memory, and like historicity more generally, memory can either be a burden or a resource depending on how it functions in practice. Nietzsche understands slavery to have introduced into Western history the potential for sovereign individuality, for example, but this potential cannot be coupled to self-constituting practices as long as it is detached from noble self-certainty. The self-identities that emerge from slavish Christian morality, in other words, remain ideological until they are coupled with a noble psychology forged out of successful repression.

Revaluation and Art

The final category of inheritances to which Nietzsche gives systematic attention is art. Nietzsche understands art not as a set of artifacts and works, but rather as an archetype of practice; he is interested in the process more than the products. Particular works, genres, styles, and modes are seen by Nietzsche as more or less adequate examples of creative activity. *Art is an arena of activity within which power exemplifies itself as agency.* For this reason Nietzsche also sees art as providing the contemporary world with its most valuable resources against nihilism.

That Nietzsche sees art as an exemplification of agency does not mean, as Heidegger argues, that art is the "essence" of the will to power.[77] Rather, the will to power describes the worldly conditions under which artistic activities could be a manifestation of power as agency. For Nietzsche, art discloses the worldly possibilities of subjectivity, and in this sense art manifests a specific possibility of "life" as it is characterized by will to power. It is important for Nietzsche that artistic practices form a worldly arena of activities within which self-identities emerge. It is through such practices that a reflexive sense of agency can develop precisely because through them one recognizes the effects of creative activities on the world. This is why, in Nietzsche's terms, it is incorrect to see aesthetic practices as stemming from an internal "will" that produces artistic works, as in Heidegger's account. Nietzsche's formulation suggests a priority of practices over self-identity, and this is quite different from metaphysical formulations that see the agent as the underlying source of external effects, a difference that Heidegger misses in Nietzsche.

For Nietzsche, art discloses the worldly conditions out of which a self-reflective sense of agency develops; it is a model of how practices integrate these conditions in ways that sustain subjectivity. The artist takes appearances seriously, not looking "behind" the world for its content, as do metaphysical views of the world. Moreover, he does so within an intersubjectively sustained cultural context.[78] Art can never be an isolated practice because it relies on the discipline and resources of interpretive traditions—whether drawing on rules of composition or on the storehouse of human knowledge. Works of art are simultaneously based on, and alterations of, an intersubjective reality governed by rules of use and composition. The practices of the plastic arts, painting, dance, and music are worldly as well as rule-oriented: they build on necessities that govern the instruments and media of expression. For Nietzsche, artistic practices show the close and proper relationship between necessity and creativity by integrating material and social conditions into something new. Creative activities produce a basis for self-identity. In transforming the social and natural worlds, one both creates and recognizes oneself in the worlds one participates in and transforms. This is why Nietzsche claims that art has the "organic function" of creating value in life.[79] Indeed, Nietzsche sometimes emphasizes the fundamental nature of artistic activity by using metaphors of pregnancy. The highest art is "born." The artist is a "mother type" in the "grand sense"—"one who knows and hears nothing any more except about the pregnancies of the 'spirit.'"[80]

If we are to understand just how fundamental Nietzsche takes art to be in this respect, we must underscore his view that art ultimately encompasses *every* historical manifestation of creative practice and interpretation. The insight that Nietzsche carries from *The Birth of Tragedy* through to his latest works is that humans are always artists in spite of themselves. With respect to moral interpretations, for example, he writes in *Beyond Good and Evil* that man "has invented the good conscience to enjoy his soul for once as *simple*: and the whole of morality is a long undismayed forgery that alone makes it possible to enjoy the sight of the soul. From this point of view much more may belong in the concept of 'art' than is generally believed."[81] Nietzsche views not only morality but also science and philosophy as distinctive modes of the more comprehensive paradigm of activity denoted by art.

It is this point that has, above all, inspired Jacques Derrida's influential interpretation of Nietzsche—an interpretation that is crucially insightful but also flawed in that it ultimately loses Nietzsche's critical dimension.[82] Derrida's insight is that Nietzsche, having rejected the language of metaphysics and having found metaphysics *in* language, allows art *qua* "style" to step into the void of decentered metaphysics. Art in this sense supersedes philosophy, just because philosophy must use language and language involves propositional content. Indeed, Derrida's view of the relation between art and philosophy suggests that one cannot separate the content of Nietzsche's thought from his style of writing, the art of his text, his word-praxis. His texts themselves are not statements *about* the world, but demonstrations of truths that cannot be spoken without violating the nature of the world, what Derrida calls its *differance*—his neo-Hegelian insight that identities are maintained only by distinctions in space and time.

Derrida makes the point by looking at Nietzsche's use of metaphors—specifically, his famous metaphor in the very first sentences of *Beyond Good and Evil*: "Supposing truth is a woman—what then? Are there not grounds for suspicion that all philosophers, insofar as they were dogmatists, have been very inexpert about women?"[83] On Derrida's account, Nietzsche's metaphor is not simply, nor even primarily, an example of his notorious antifeminism. Rather, he intends it as a way of demonstrating what kind of thing "truth" must be. "Woman" becomes a metaphor for the intrinsic relation between truth and style, truth and superficiality.[84] The truth of a man's relation to a woman, Nietzsche held, was precisely in the fact that he can interpret her as a substantial entity only superficially, at a distance. For their part, women know that their substance depends on appearance and style; this is why, in their modesty, they resist intrusive masculinity. The truth that women know is therefore relational— it requires distance in order that the appearance might constitute itself with the integrity of a thing. When desires and practices span this distance while still allowing it to be a distance, appearances can retain their appearance of substance; superficiality can be interpreted as substantial being. But when desires become a will to truth, then the superficial identity of things is violated, its veil of appearances torn apart, and it reveals that "woman" is nothing in herself. She has no essence. The wisdom of "woman" is that she already knows this : she, like truth, is entirely appearance, superficiality, style. "Woman" is therefore Nietzsche's metaphor for the way truth is possible. As Derrida puts it,

The question of the woman suspends the decidable opposition of true and non-true and inaugurates the epochal regime of quotation marks which is to be enforced for every system of philosophical decidability. The hermeneutical project which postulates a true sense of the text is disqualified under this regime. Reading is freed from the horizon of the meaning or truth of being, liberated from the values of the product's production or the present's presence. Whereupon the question of style is immediately unloosed as a question of writing. The question raised by the spurring-operation [that is, Nietzsche's own stylistic use of words as weapons] is more powerful than any content, thesis, or meaning.[85]

On Derrida's account, all meaning is style. This is why Nietzsche's own writing is fundamentally a demonstration of style, play, and intensity; why his aphorisms push beyond themselves, showing more in their style than could possibly be identified in words. In this way, Derrida places art *qua* style at the center of Nietzsche's philosophy, not as a metaphysical essence (Heidegger), but as a way of going beyond the thin identities of language; as a way of forcing the reader to provide a meaning from without, in such a way that the text interacts with the audience. What Derrida suggests is that all interpretation of Nietzsche must be readings of his style. To do more than this would be to use language wrongly, and to miss the new and postmodern nature of his philosophy.

Derrida does as good a job as anyone of showing why Nietzsche writes differently from traditional philosophers, and how his writing often demonstrates what cannot be represented in propositions. But there are limits to Derrida's approach. What Derrida misses is that Nietzsche also gives an account of the world in terms of which texts function as Derrida says they do; a world in which some kinds of truths cannot be formulated in direct propositions that identify essential contents. To hold that Nietzsche's philosophy is exhausted by his style, with its message that there are no metaphysical essences, Derrida must confuse the world with a text—something that Nietzsche himself never does, as I pointed out in chapter 2. For Nietzsche, artistic style is a model of meaningful practice, not a model of the world within which style could have its meaningful qualities. This is why, in his 1886 "Attempt at Self-Criticism" of the *The Birth of Tragedy*, Nietzsche argues that the lasting task of his book was "*to look at science [Wissenschaft] in the perspective of the artist but at art in that of life.*"[86] What is significant here is that *art* is the middle term between *Wissenschaft* (representational-realist metaphysics, in Nietzsche's usage here) and *life*. Derrida takes us only to the middle term. What he fails to see is that Nietzsche does identify a general model of the kind of "life" within which creative practices are possible. He does so with the concept of will to power, and he hypothetically identifies it in philosophical terms. This is why style is only a part of Nietzsche's message, and why art is central to, but not exhaustive of, his philosophy.

That Nietzsche has a conception of "life" that is, in some sense, more complete than "art" is not accidental, or even a residual metaphysical essentialism in his thinking. Rather, Nietzsche wishes to develop immanent criteria of judgment, criteria that allow him to distinguish interpretive activities, and to see them as more or less adequate to life. The point is that Nietzsche's approach to art specifically and to practices generally is *critical*, while Derrida's is not. Nietzsche distinguishes between interpretive activities in terms of the standards implicit in their interests and genres. In this way he avoids reducing one distinctive genre of interpretation, like science, to another, like poetry. Science is not poetry, even though both are interpretation. Moreover, not all interpretations have the same effect; not all increase the organization of power as agency. For this reason, Nietzsche also distinguishes ideological arts—those of illusion and escape—from self-reflectively rational arts—those of expressing worldly engagement.

Art and *Wissenschaft*

To see how Nietzsche makes these distinctions, let us return to his claim in his "Attempt at Self-Criticism" that his "much older, a hundred times more demanding, but by no means colder eye" has not become "a stranger to the task that this audacious book dared to tackle for the first time: *to look at science [Wissenschaft] in the perspective of the artist but at art in that of life.*"[87] The statement is revealing, not least because Nietzsche is treating "science," "art," and "life" as if they were Russian dolls, with the larger perspectives embodying the smaller. The perspective that comes to encompass both science (or knowledge: *Wissenschaft*) and art is "life," or the perspective of practice. It is on the basis of this perspective that Nietzsche rejects the received idea—traceable to Plato—that art and knowledge are fundamentally opposed sorts of activities. He means to show that the polarity of art and knowledge is unnecessary, misleading, and destructive of self-reflective rationality.

It is important in this regard that, in asserting that art is a disclosure of life, Nietzsche is not subscribing to the view—so often attributed to him—that we create a world of myth and illusion, and that our life is sustained only by a world of illusion. Heidegger arrives at this kind of conclusion, and a very similar view is presupposed by Derrida, albiet for quite different purposes. This conclusion, however, requires the mistaken view that the art-knowledge relation in Nietzsche can be cast in terms of a polarity between illusion and truth—one in which Heidegger opts for truth, and Derrida for illusion. This is neither the most defensible nor the most interesting way to construe the problem. Nietzsche's strategy is to cast doubt on the polarity itself, rather than to argue for the primacy of illusion, as Heidegger and others suggest. In Heidegger's case, to structure Nietzsche's argument in terms of this polarity, he must limit the terms "art" and "truth" to their meanings in Nietzsche's earliest works.[88] There Nietzsche attached the term "art" to rapture, appearance, and illusion, while he reserved the term "truth" for the specifically Platonic understanding of a world of essential forms. Still working within Plato's polarity of truth and art, he opts for art, and thus for illusion; the early Nietzsche is indeed an "inverted Platonist." But in his mature works Nietzsche deconstructs the polarity. He understands the "raging discourse" between art and truth, as Heidegger puts it,[89] to be historical rather than necessary, limited to the terms of the problem as understood by Plato and dating from that time.

Instead of distinguishing knowledge and art in terms of truth and illusion, Nietzsche looks at the different ways they formulate the structures and necessities of the life-world. They are not distinguished by their creative aspect (since both are creative), but rather by the fact that they operate at different levels of abstraction, achieve different kinds of articulations, and embody their own rules of interpretive organization. What we usually think of as art is more closely tied to the life-world than is knowledge because art's content always refers back to immediate and expressive articulations of experience. Knowledge, on the other hand, is relatively abstract and general, often using terms that refer to nonsensuous qualities of the universe like, for example, the concept of "force" in physics or, one might add, the concept of "social structure" in social science. In Nietzsche's view, we tend to forget that abstraction from experience to conceptual generalities is a creative and thus a broadly aesthetic process.[90]

Nietzsche's point is also that we misunderstand the knowledge-ability of art. Art is a kind of knowledge in that it makes reference to a world that is "illusion" only in the sense that it escapes explicit, generalizable reference. Nietzsche notes that the "laws" of the life-world, of which the artist possesses a tacit awareness, are so complex as to escape explicit conceptual reference. These laws, "precisely on account of their hardness and determination, defy all formulation through concepts (even the firmest concept is, compared with these laws, not free of fluctuation, multiplicity, and ambiguity)." [91] Nietzsche suggests here that art and knowledge are distinguished by their abilities to represent a tacit awareness of the complexities of the sensuous world. The artist possesses a higher level of tacit awareness of these complexities than could ever be formulated into the explicit concepts and generalizable propositions required by knowledge. Thus the artist requires other modes of expression and communication. Knowledge, on the other hand, requires a process of conceptual explication that necessarily moves away from the complexities of the tacit knowledge of the artist and toward a more general system of abstractions. While this process of conceptual articulation allows our instrumental knowledge of the world to become communicable, manipulable, and cumulative, these very qualities begin to distinguish between the explicit knowledge of the scientist and the tacit knowledge of the artist's practice. This is why Nietzsche considers knowledge to differ from art not in its creative aspect, but rather in the fact that its interpretive work on the world moves away from the sensuous world and toward explicit and systematic but abstract conceptualizations. Still, as Nietzsche first argued in *The Birth of Tragedy*, art remains the more fundamental activity. The complexities of the sensuous world that one finds in works of art form the raw material and creative element of knowledge. Nietzsche seems to regard art as a kind of Dionysian "preform" of explicit knowledge, out of which knowledge is born before being articulated as a conceptual/linguistic universe, and to which it must return time and again if it is to be both creative and "faithful to the earth."

On the other hand, Nietzsche also suggests that art is more like knowledge with respect to its rule-governed and nonarbitrary aspects than is generally supposed. Art is not, as Plato claimed, simply "illusion." To be successful in producing a work, artistic activity must incorporate many of those attributes of knowledge that identify the world in terms of structures, constraints, regularities, and laws. The artist must know or intuit the complex and subtle structures and constraints of the world, for these are the content and the medium of his work. Moreover, art as well as knowledge is lodged within interpretive traditions: the artist loses his ability to create if he does not build on rules of interpretive technique involving relatively rigid languages and rules that transcend individual creativity.[92] Art is not, then, necessarily the immersion in a world of illusion it may seem. When the artist confronts the Dionysian world and "forgets himself" within it, it is on the basis of a subjectivity in the process of articulation. As Nietzsche describes it, "Every artist knows how far from any feeling of letting himself go his 'most natural' state is—the free ordering, placing, disposing, giving form in the moment of 'inspiration'—and how strictly and subtly he obeys a thousand laws precisely then...." [93] Although rapture and illusion may be involved in art, they do not describe the worldly conditions of art, the intuitive control of the artist, the subtleties of interacting with complex contexts, and the knowledgeability embedded in the artist's use of techniques and styles. This is what Plato missed.

Art and Ideology

If Nietzsche rejects the Platonic equation of art and illusion, and if he views art as more fundamental than knowledge—that is, closer to the Dionysian life-world—he is not claiming that cases do not exist in which art *in fact* allies itself with illusion. In these cases, the Platonic equation turns out to be correct—but for the wrong reasons. Historically existing artistic practices, in Nietzsche's view, have rarely been self-conscious, and almost never critical. Because by nature art is affirmative and idealizing, it allies itself with whatever exists, if only by making existence livable in one way or another. We possess art, Nietzsche likes to remind us, "lest we perish of the truth." [94]

Implicit in Nietzsche's discussions is a distinction between strong and weak arts—arts of engagement and arts of illusion. Strong art discloses the agent in his practices, while weak art provides only an imaginary identity of agency. The distinction is based on the degree to which art involves continuous transformations of the world that provide practical bases for self-identity. The strongest arts, such as Greek tragedy, use interpretive alterations of the world to orient creativity in action. These arts are closest to the sensuous world, the world of Dionysus, and use this world as raw material for constructing a coherent and meaningful human world. In contrast, weak arts such as Christian "fictions" and romantic genres must end up as arts of illusion, for they move away from the world of experience to create new and better worlds, but worlds that are disconnected from experiential conditions of practice.[95] What enables Nietzsche to find in strong art a "genuine countermovement" to Christianity is precisely this difference in relations to the experiential world. Rather than negating the world of experience with an illusion or veil, strong art "idealizes" it, striving to "bring out the main features" of the actual world "so that others disappear in the process."[96] Arts that appropriate the world in the course of imposing a human form on it are born of "overfullness," while those that manufacture illusory escapes from engagement are born of "hunger."[97] For Nietzsche, only those arts born of hunger need lead to the Platonic equation of art and illusion. Without the strength to use the present world as a means to self-constitution, the artist produces arts of decadence—arts that perform a therapeutic function by allowing escape from the present world into an imaginary one. Such arts are essentially ascetic: they are arts for an audience, arts for spectators, arts leading to romantic narcosis, and arts produced in worship of gods. These arts are ideological, for they fragment rather than organize power as agency.[98]

Because arts of illusion are, in Nietzsche's view, only a decadent subset of all artistic practices, knowledge, art, and self-constituting practices could grow in a complementary way out of an aesthetic relationship to the world. This complementary relation is expressed in Nietzsche's claim that we want to become "poets of our lives," and in this way we shall "*become those who we are*—human beings who are new, unique, incomparable, who must give themselves laws, who create themselves. To that end we must become the best learners and discoverers of everything that is lawful and necessary in the world: we must become *physicists* in order to become *creators* in this sense."[99] Nietzsche captures the conjunction of art, knowledge, and practice in two vivid images. The first is the image of a "gay science" (*fröhliche Wissenschaft*), which suggests that creativity in knowledge requires both discipline and a joyful aesthetic involvement with the objects of concern. Here "laughter will have formed an alliance with wisdom."[100] The "Provençal concept of a *gaya scienza*," Nietzsche writes in *Ecce Homo*, signifies the "unity of *singer, knight, and free spirit*."[101]

The second image recommends creativity in practice based on a knowledge of necessary things. This is captured in Nietzsche's metaphor for "grand style"—the *architect*. The architect combines power and worldly necessity in creative projects, and for this reason produces the strongest examples of art: "His buildings are supposed to render pride visible, as well as the victory over gravity [*die Schwere*: both physical gravity and seriousness], and the will to power. Architecture is a kind of eloquence of power in forms—now persuading, even flattering, now only commanding. The highest feeling of power and sureness finds expression in *grand style*."[102]

Nietzsche occasionally extends this view of power as art beyond the realm of the individual's aesthetic relations to his life-world and into the intersubjective realm of politics. The tension found in Nietzsche's two models of political culture (chapter 2) also shows up in the political dimension of art. The meaning of the political dimension would, in Nietzsche's terms, depend on how the social world is incorporated into aesthetic activity. He occasionally refers to humans as the "raw material" of politics upon which "artist" masters violently impose an aesthetic form.[103] Indeed, more seriously, he sometimes argues that higher cultures require violence; that wars, "the greatest and most terrible wars" are the only way of revitalizing the "raw energy" that higher culture requires.[104] If this is the case, extending aesthetic notions to social relations quite clearly justifies political oppression and violence, and this may very well have been Nietzsche's intention.

Such references lend credence to Eric Voegelin's view that Nietzsche inappropriately extends creativity into politics without care for social substance, thus losing the intrinsic pluralism of his philosophy.[105] But the issue here is not, as some commentators have argued, a question of this being the effect of aesthetic conceptions of political activity *as such*.[106] His claim that higher culture requires the "energy" of violence is asserted without analysis. The evidence Nietzsche provides is that Greek and Roman culture were associated with war—a point he combines with repeated assertions that war provides spiritual strength.[107] On the other hand, when Nietzsche actually analyses cultural endeavors, culture does not seem to require violence. In fact, quite the opposite is the case: art, for example, can develop its highest

potential only on the basis of a highly developed fabric of communication.[108] The difference depends on how one conceives of the
world of political activity. When Nietzsche is not referring to political
situations, he is unlikely to view humans as "objects" of artistic
activity, but rather as intersubjective, cultural beings, and to see
communicative practices as the basis of aesthetic expressiveness.[109]
Nietzsche did not politicize this conception of the aesthetic because
he held that most people were incapable of living its potential. If he
had, he would have conceived a political sphere intimately connected
to the intersubjective fabric of speech, and leading to a politics
combining individual creativity and social care—a point I further
develop in chapter 7.[110]

Science, morality, nobility, and art, then, are the major categories
of skills, practices, and self-reflective identifications that form the
legacy of Western culture, and out of which a new culture might be
created. Nietzsche can only suggest what outlines a new culture might
actually take. This he does by dramatic portrayal through his figure
of Zarathustra. Any other means of suggestion—say, a blueprint of
a new culture—would violate Nietzsche's insights into the nature of
culture: culture is both the historical precondition and the sedimentation of self-constituting practices. Thus a new culture cannot be
designated in advance: it is simply not that kind of thing. As he puts
it in *Zarathustra*, "There are many ways of overcoming."[111] The
conditions and processes of making a new culture can be described
but its content cannot. If it cannot be blueprinted, neither can it be
legislated: a politically imposed culture violates the very nature of
culture. In this one sees just how incompatible Nietzsche's philosophy
of culture is with the German attempts at cultural engineering from
Bismarck to Hitler. In contrast, Nietzsche points only to what a new
culture ought to accomplish: it ought to guide actions in such a way
that the world constituted by actions permits a plausible interpretation of self-identity. Nietzsche is clear about this criterion of success.
Against disintegration, he writes, "I sought a new center."[112] By this
he means a new individuality based on a reflexive understanding of
practices.

6

The Teachings: Affirming
Historical Being

The problem of a "new center" is framed but not resolved by Nietzsche's genealogical criticism of cultural ideals. The inheritances of Western culture provide resources and possibilities for power to be organized as agency, but they are not sufficient: there still needs to be a way of understanding how the self could understand its own historicity in a world without transcendental identities. The conditions for this kind of self-understanding are the same as in the past: the self must be able to know itself by means of stable, identifiable points of reference. Nietzsche's problem arises from the fact that there are no historical examples of self-identity that are not also self-defeating—self-defeating in that they violate the historical nature of the human condition, and hence the conditional and conditioned nature of agency. Nobility and artistry are naive in this respect, while science and morality presuppose views of the world based on metaphysical conceptions of agency.

Moreover, the very question of a nontranscendental agent/subject/self is different from the question of inherited cultural resources. In order to show that the identification of oneself as an agent is possible in the historical world, Nietzsche must find a conception of the *being* of the self that does not deny the *becoming* or historicity of the human condition. This new conception of being would have to incorporate within itself the Dionysian world—a world characterized by time and change rather than eternity, by flux and becoming rather than stability and being, by sensuous pleasure and pain rather than good and evil. Nietzsche's problem is to show how the historicity of existence could be consistent with self-identity, how it is possible for the self *qua* agent to identify itself as a continuous locus of practices, as a continuous entity in time. In Nietzsche's terms, the question is how the individual can attain a "real memory of the will" that manifests a capacity for originating and following through on projects, "so that between the original 'I will,' 'I shall do this,' and the actual discharge of the will, its *act*, a world of strange new things, circumstance, even acts of will may be interposed without breaking this long chain of will."[1]

Nietzsche only began to frame this problem, and thus only hinted at solutions. He did leave some clues, however, and they can be found in two complementary concepts: the notion of tragic wisdom and the idea of eternal recurrence of the same. With his new conception of tragic wisdom, Nietzsche meant to show that acceptance of the historicity of existence is both possible and desirable. With the idea of eternal recurrence—what he called the "fundamental conception" of *Zarathustra*[2]—he meant to show that self-identity can be consistent with a full awareness of our historicity.

Both doctrines are teachings rather than critical or philosophical analyses. They presuppose cultural criticism, and they presuppose a philosophical view of the historicity of existence and its conditions— that is, they presuppose both genealogy and the will to power. But they function in Nietzsche's thought as imperatives: they suggest states of consciousness that humans must possess in order reflexively to organize their inherited potentials as agency. Nietzsche's teachings suggest that, under the conditions of nineteenth-century Europe, acceptance of the historicity of existence is possible—at least for the few he was addressing. But they also *implore* this acceptance, as a shift in consciousness necessary for organizing power as agency. Together, Nietzsche's two doctrines sketch an attitude toward existence that would allow one to reorder inheritances and determine historical futures. Yet the very qualities of historicity—change, suffering, finitude, and mortality—make this kind of consciousness as difficult as it is necessary.[3] This is why Nietzsche believed he was, in the end, addressing only a select few.

Tragic Wisdom and *Amor Fati*

Looking back on his life in *Ecce Homo*, Nietzsche suggested that his distinctive and lasting innovation in *The Birth of Tragedy* was to suggest the "transposition of the Dionysian into a philosophical *pathos*."

This he wrote, would constitute a *"tragic wisdom."* His conception of a union between tragic art and Socratic knowledge would, then, make him the "first *tragic philosopher.*" [4]

Nietzsche's conception of tragic wisdom involves the following argument. He views the Dionysian world—the "natural" world of experience—as an irreducible aspect of the human condition. Dionysian experience inevitably involves pain, suffering, change, and death, that is, all of the questionable aspects of existence. To reject these elements of experience, however, involves rejecting experience as such. Historically, this kind of rejection has also meant a denial of the value and even the reality of experience—that is, the worldly conditions of agency. But since experiences of the world as a valuable place stem from self-experiences of agency, these denials of experience also undermine the possibility of value. Thus a refusal to accept the painful and changing elements of life leads to nihilism. Any self-reflective rationality must therefore involve a "tragic" acceptance of the Dionysian aspects of the human condition.

With one important difference, Nietzsche's concept of tragic wisdom is based on the Greek conception. He found in Greek tragedy the possibility of a cultural response to existence that affirmed a realm of individual responsibility and action on the basis of insights into the Dionysian aspects of existence. The Greeks, however, had at best a tacit awareness of the tragic elements of existence, an awareness they formulated not philosophically, but *mythically.* Nietzsche wished to transform this tacit, mythical awareness into a *philosophical* stance. In his writings after *The Birth of Tragedy* he understood that the modern world lacks the naiveté that once made mythology possible. The "profound superficiality" of the Greeks, their adoration of appearance and illusion, cannot exist in the same way today because Christian-moral culture developed distinctively intellectual needs for truth. Any new concept of the tragic would therefore have to go beyond the Greek concept to incorporate not only the will to truth developed by the intervening periods of culture, but also the reflexive awareness deepened by the crisis of European nihilism. Such a concept would have to include an explicit, philosophical awareness of the historical qualities of existence, together with a full understanding of the human capacity and necessity to endow existence with meaning through self-constituting practices. Nietzsche summarizes these requirements in his doctrine of *amor fati*—the "love of fate," referring to it as "my formula for greatness in a human being." [5] It is this doctrine that forms the core of his concept of tragic wisdom.

Amor fati is an imperative grounded in the idea that, to achieve his full status as a creator, man must come to know that he is fated to be a historical being, and come to love this fate with a full awareness of both its necessity and desirability. "I want to learn more and more to see as beautiful what is necessary in things; then I shall be one of those who makes things beautiful. *Amor fati*: let that be my love henceforth!" [6] Similarly, one can achieve the full potential of existence only by avoiding all transcendental judgments of existence: "What justifies man is his reality—it will eternally justify him." [7] By affirming fate absolutely, Nietzsche recommends faithfulness to the historicity of the human condition.

Nietzsche's idea that humans should "love fate" is a deliberate assault on traditional conceptions of fate. Even in Greek tragedy, fate had been identified with chance and fortune, that is, with a world beyond man's control. Thus traditionally man has been seen as a creature opposed to fate—a being able to actualize his freedom only by setting himself against and mastering fate. The traditional conception of fate placed man outside history in a way requiring a metaphysical understanding of one's identity as an agent, and a judgment of worldly existence as an obstacle to freedom.

Nietzsche's conception of *amor fati* is sometimes interpreted as if it repeated this traditional understanding, but without a metaphysical affirmation of human freedom. [8] This, however, leads to the mistaken view that Nietzsche's idea affirms the world just as it is. It suggests that humans can do nothing about the way history proceeds, and it suggests that humans ought therefore to sacrifice themselves to the course of history. This is not at all what Nietzsche means the concept to convey. Rather, he wishes to overcome the very terms of the polarity that oppose a metaphysical conception of man to the world. The polarity itself is untenable, leading either to passive acceptance of fate or to the view that the nature of man has no relation to fate. Nietzsche's affirmation of fate is *comprehensive*. It includes not only an affirmation of present circumstance, but also human capacities to think through and act upon circumstance:

The truth is that every man is himself a piece of fate; when he thinks he is striving against fate . . . it is being realized here too; the struggle is imaginary, but so is resignation to fate; all these imaginary ideas are included in fate.

The fear that most people have of the doctrine of determinism of the will is precisely the fear of this Turkish fatalism. They think man will give up weakly and stand before the future with folded hands because he cannot change anything about it; or else he will give free rein to his total caprice because even this cannot make what is once determined still worse. The follies of man are just as much a part of his fate as his cleverness: this fear of the belief in fate is also fate. You yourself, poor frightened man, are the invincible Moira reigning far above the gods; for everything that comes, you are a blessing or a curse, and in any case yours are the bonds in which the strongest man lies. In you the whole of the human world is predetermined; it will not help if you are terrified of yourself.[9]

Amor fati is not, then, affirmation of fate as something apart from what man is, but rather the affirmation of all human powers and their historical conditions of existence. It is not a sacrifice of man to fate, but the self-awareness of the fatality of the human condition with its limits and powers. Involved in this fatality is that man must continually produce and reproduce his life in relation to what exists.[10] This is the sense in which history is, meaningfully, fate. From this fate there is no escape, nor should any who desire "life" seek to escape.

Yet accepting historical being in all of its aspects involves accepting certain of its problematic features: this is why the wisdom of *amor fati* is *tragic*. Nietzsche foresees a revaluation of suffering such that it would not be seen as an "objection" to life but rather as a "seduction" to life.[11] Suffering is not intrinsically objectionable, for without suffering higher human capacities—in both the individual and the species—would never have come into existence.[12] Without barriers to overcome, neither the motive nor the necessity to new and creative ways of thinking and acting could exist. Indeed, Nietzsche's insight into the necessity of suffering parallels Freud's: without a certain level of repression, a child's desires could never be organized into an adult ego.

Freud, however, distinguishes that amount of repression necessary for the development of the self from some greater amount that would result in neurotic illness. Nietzsche is not always so careful. When he speaks of suffering, he often fails to distinguish between kinds, sources, and quantities of suffering, and for that reason comes dangerously close to glorifying suffering as such. True, many of Nietzsche's arguments presuppose such distinctions. For example, Nietzsche claims in the *Genealogy* that punishment does not make men "'better'—one might with justice assert the opposite."[13] But Nietzsche loses his distinctions in his enthusiasm to point out that suffering is ontologically given to life as such. Life simply is suffering, he says. One must resist "all sentimental weakness" and accept that "life itself is *essentially* appropriation, injury, overpowering of what is alien and weaker, suppression, hardness, imposition of one's own forms, incorporation and, at least at its mildest, exploitation."[14] One finds that here, as in other areas, Nietzsche rushes from the insight that every person's life and actions involve a necessary and sometimes desirable amount of suffering to the conclusion that misery, exploitation, and violence in social and political life are inevitable and perhaps desirable—so much so that their reduction ought not to be a goal of politics.[15]

Nonetheless, one need not agree with Nietzsche's conclusions regarding kinds, sources, and levels of suffering—which must be addressed before any *political* conclusions can be drawn—to accept his basic point, namely, that to reject suffering *as such* is to reject life itself. As one examines more closely Nietzsche's analysis of suffering and his opposition to Christian pity, then, one should not allow his failure to attend to these distinctions to discredit his view that *some* kinds and amounts of suffering are simply part of existence, without which humans would not be able to organize their powers as agency.

Nietzsche develops his understanding of suffering primarily in opposition to the Christian rejection of all this-worldly pain and suffering. If life inevitably includes suffering, he reasons, then to reject suffering is to reject life. Yet this is precisely what the Christian-moral world view had done by defining its goal as redemption (*Erlösung*) from worldly suffering. This might have been inevitable in certain *specific* situations like that of the slave. But to reject "life" because it involves suffering would be to reject the worldly bases of agency. This in turn perpetuates powerlessness and nihilism, and thus suffering. Somewhat ironically, the effect of the Christian rejection of suffering would have been to affirm culturally and even to increase suffering.

Christianity increases suffering not only by institutionalizing weakness but also because it emphasizes a communal consciousness of suffering. Christianity forged its community before God out of all who suffer, and in this way transformed the experience of suffering into a link between individuals. Indeed, Nietzsche points out at length in the *Genealogy* that the spectacle of suffering, cruelty, and blood becomes a "seduction" to life when integrated into a system of explanation that endows it with a "meaning"—as happens through the "mysterious machinery of salvation" in Christianity.[16] As the religion of pity (*Mitleid*: literally, suffering with), Christianity developed and exploited a collective consciousness of suffering. In Nietzsche's view, pity—the sharing of suffering—has the psychological effect of multiplying one's experiences of suffering many times over, turning basic experiences of suffering into an obsession.[17] Thus while the Christian need for redemption from suffering is partly real (in the case of the slave), it is also partly the result of a culturally perpetuated weakness, as well as of the sympathetic identifications of pity.

Nietzsche's essential point is that it is detrimental to "life" to make the abolition of suffering the central goal of existence. Such a goal not only leads to an increase in this-worldly suffering; it also undermines self-constituting practices. Suffering is part of individuation, and this is what Nietzsche believes we can learn from Greek tragedy. The hero of the Greek tragedy would take the cruel aspects of existence upon himself as a challenge and turn suffering into a discipline of the will and means to increased power. Nietzsche generalizes the Greek insights into suffering:

The discipline [*Zucht*] of suffering, of *great* suffering—do you not know that only this discipline has created all enhancement of man so far? That tension of the soul in unhappiness that cultivates [*anzüchtet*] its strength, its trembling in the face of great ruin, its inventiveness and courage in enduring, persevering, interpreting, and exploiting suffering, and whatever has been granted it out of profundity, secret, mask, spirit, cunning, greatness—was it not granted to it through suffering, through the discipline of great suffering? In man *creature* and *creator* are united....[18]

A tragic wisdom would turn the same consciousness of suffering exploited by Christianity into a means of organizing power as agency.

Nietzsche believes that a tragic wisdom would restore good conscience to action, selfhood, and responsibility by affirming the fatality of historical being in the comprehensive sense demanded by *amor fati*. This is possible in the contemporary period to the degree that humans are more "natural" in their attitude toward existence, are better able to conceptualize the necessities and actualities of historical being, and are thus able to affirm them as conditions of subjectivity.

The Eternal Return of the Same

Nietzsche intended his concept of tragic wisdom to evoke an awareness of the worldly conditions of individual power. He did not believe, however, that such an awareness would be sufficient for constituting new self-identities. Tragic wisdom involves an acceptance of the historicity of the human condition. But it does so without giving good reason to think that self-reflective experiences of agency are possible *in principle* in a world of becoming, flux, power, suffering, and *pathos*, a world in which all identities stem from interpretations and not from the world itself.

What qualities of reality, then, does Nietzsche believe would allow self-interpretations of identity without falsifying the historicity of the human condition? If anything is clear in his philosophy, it is that humans, whether they like it or not, are doomed to confront the historicity of their being, without mythical, religious, or metaphysical comfort. Although willing may ultimately require an understanding of the self as an identity, this identity cannot be gained through a transcendental projection, nor can it contradict what we know about the historicity of existence. Myths, illusions, and fictions of identity are no longer possible in the modern world.[19] These circumstances outline what Nietzsche thought to be the greatest problem of a historical sensibility. With the idea that all elements of life eternally recur, he thought he had begun to meet the challenge.[20]

The thought of the eternal return of the same (*das ewige Wieder-kunft des Gleiche*) initially seems both simple and quite implausible. Nietzsche's idea is that all experiences and thoughts that have occurred in the past will recur again and again for eternity. History involves endless repetition and endless duration.[21] Nietzsche is attracted to such a notion not least because it would remove misplaced hopes of escape from the present world by denying the very possibility of transcending the past for an existence outside of history, whether projected into an afterlife, into a utopian future, or even into an image of what one might have been, had the past been different. The eternal return is thus the nondualist, nontranscendental thought *par excellence*, one fully consistent with Nietzsche's counsel of *amor fati*.

Despite the apparent simplicity of the thought, its seeming im-plausibility raises a number of difficulties of interpretation. These difficulties stem from Nietzsche's failure to develop the thought ex-plicitly and consistently: references to the thought are often oblique, and not every reference is consistent with other aspects of his thinking. If, for example, Nietzsche meant the eternal recurrence of the same to denote a cosmology of time, it is difficult to see how the thought makes sense. Even so, two hypothetical possibilities exist for such an interpretation. First, in many notes (although *only* in notes) Nietzsche experiments with the notion that the workings of the physical world cause all configurations of force to repeat themselves infinitely through time. But the difficulties with this way of construing the thought are numerous, Nietzsche's experiments notwithstanding. They have been dealt with extensively and conclusively in the secondary literature and warrant no further attention here.[22]

The second possibility for interpreting the eternal return as referring to a cosmological characteristic of historical time is more interesting, and has the virtue of some support in Nietzsche's published texts. Any moment of historical time, in Nietzsche's view of history, encapsulates all of its determinations up to that moment. Moreover, at any point in time the totality of existing moments determines all possible future moments. On the basis of these truisms, one might conclude that owing simply to the attributes of necessity in the universe each moment will occur again, incarnated in the future moments it determines.[23] Suggesting this possibility, Nietzsche has Zarathustra ask, "And are not all things knotted together so firmly that this moment draws after it *all* that is to come?"[24] All moments of the past "return" in the present by virtue of their determination of the present. Hence every moment of the past and present will return in the future.

Nietzsche's comments in *Zarathustra* notwithstanding, this interpretation of the doctrine of eternal return fits badly with other, more explicitly developed aspects of his view of historical determination. To support such a notion of the return of moments, Nietzsche would have had to hold a quasi-Hegelian conception of history, one in which each moment logically entails the whole, and all possibilities of the whole logically entail each of its moments. Nietzsche does of course accept what might be called the "local" implications of Hegel's concept of totality regarding the determination of entities. But he does not believe necessary connections exist between different courses of development in history.[25] Necessary connections between parts and wholes may or may not exist: in the "history of a 'thing' . . . causes do not even have to be related to one another, but, on the contrary, in some cases succeed and alternate with one another in a purely chance fashion."[26] A logic of the whole does not exist. Thus no reason exists to think that any moment of history necessarily encapsulates its possible futures.

One might be inclined to accept the testimony of Nietzsche's notes and his one comment in *Zarathustra* were it not for another and ultimately more plausible interpretation of the doctrine of eternal return. It seems to me Heidegger has picked the right starting point (if only a starting point) in suggesting that Nietzsche attempted to make the eternal return serve as a horizon of "being." This is densely formulated in one of Nietzsche's notes—one he considered to be a "high point" of his thinking—which asserts "that *everything recurs* is the closest *approximation of a world of becoming to a world of being—* . . . ." [27] The eternal return is certainly the only doctrine of "being" Nietzsche ever affirmed, presumably because he thought it the only one consistent with historical existence. Still, Heidegger's notion of the role of the eternal return in Nietzsche's thought is inadequate. He argues that the eternal return and the will to power are complementary metaphysical propositions, claiming that insofar as the will to power has "being," it manifests this being as eternal return. [28] But because, as I argued in chapter 4, Nietzsche's project does not involve metaphysics in this sense, the status of the doctrine remains unclear. A more defensible position is Joan Stambaugh's. She builds on other aspects of Heidegger's suggestion by holding that the eternal return is a doctrine of thought, a teaching of an appropriate attitude toward existence, rather than a metaphysical characterization of the world. [29] While this seems to me a fruitful point of departure, it is still inadequate: Stambaugh construes the problem of self-identity as one of the disintegrating effects of *time* on the self. As I argued in chapter 3, this misses what I have argued to be Nietzsche's central point about the self: that its identity stems from agency, and presupposes a continuity of practices with respect to historical conditions of existence. [30] The achievement of a self-interpretation of agency is a practical as well as a reflexive accomplishment. Like Heidegger, Stambaugh reduces history to the empty abstraction "time," and in this way polarizes historicity and subjectivity.

The point of Nietzsche's doctrine of the eternal return is precisely *not* to polarize historicity and subjectivity, and this is its importance. As in so many other cases, however, Nietzsche only hints at new directions. On considering his published writings together with consistent notes, one finds that he speaks of the eternal return primarily as a thought that creates identity on the basis of active engagement of experiences. To understand why this is important, one needs to remember Nietzsche's project: what he is looking for is a concept of identity that is consistent with history, historicity, and embodiment; a concept that could, for this reason, underwrite a worldly constitution of agency. His concern is with the possibility of an "approximation" to self-identity that does not violate the historicity of existence. The problem with metaphysical concepts of identity is that they repress experience because of its changeable, historical qualities. This disconnects metaphysical concepts of agency (the soul, will, subject, and the like) from the situated, conditional qualities of action, and splits agency from the possibility of changing the world and the self. For this reason, metaphysical concepts of agency are incompatible with the process of self-definition through which agency becomes a worldly possibility.

The doctrine of eternal return constructs a conception of identity that *is* compatible with embodied experience and historicity because it is an identity in process, an identity that is constructed and reconstructed out of experiences by means of engaging the world.[31] Constructing such a conception of identity is important for Nietzsche because of his proposition that personhood and character development depend on action and interaction. For this reason, the eternal return must somehow describe the possibility of identity within this process of engagement, and it must at the same time be open to the difference and newness that accompanies the process. Should the thought of the eternal return succeed in this, it would show that nontranscendental horizons of willing are possible, and thus suggest a conscious and nonnaive self-interpretation of identity.

This possibility follows from some relatively mundane insights into the structure of time consciousness. The doctrine calls attention to the way we experience the identity of the self over time. The thought describes our cognitive situation when we are confronted with experiences of change within duration—that is, our historicity. By noting these experiences and relating them to structures of the life-world, Nietzsche would explain how it is possible to experience the world and self as a recurring set of identities without fundamentally contradicting historical being. Fundamental to historicity is that it does not consist in characterless passage of time, but rather in series of recurring points of familiarity that we experience as recurrences of the "same thing." Historicity is never abstractly linear: it possessess a circular quality that stems from identifying things as "the same." It is because we experience continuity within duration as a series of recurrences that we can know our way around in the world. In this sense recurrences of "the same" establish the experiential grounds for self-interpretations of identity. This aspect of the life-world situation renders many interpretations of identity plausible and practical, in spite of change, flux, and becoming.

As a quality of experience, however, "the same" is not a fixed essence. It is not something that resides in the world apart from our practices within it: this is what is new in Nietzsche's doctrine. "Sameness" is a quality of our relation to the world, our assimilation of it, our interaction with it, and our appropriation of it. "Sameness" is a cognitive stance that we take toward existence, a stance that is replicated and reinforced through its function in willing. In this case, identity is never closed or exclusive; it is never metaphysically guaranteed because it constantly must be constructed and reconstructed.

The effect that the doctrine captures is really quite familiar, and one that we usually take for granted but rarely recognize. We can see this in a very commonplace example. Say you live in a community for a period of time. Changes happen around you. Sometimes you involve yourself in them; sometimes you simply observe them taking place. Usually you integrate them into your habits and life, often without really being aware that you are doing so. In the process, you manage to maintain your identity and the identity of your situation simply by carrying on with everyday life. What is important to notice here is that the identities that you construct are not qualities of either an unchanging self or an unchanging situation, but rather sediments of your interactions with your situation. That this is so is suggested by another kind of possibility. Say you move to a new location after having lived in one place for some time. Then, after a couple of years, you go back for a visit, and find that circumstances have changed in your absence. It is not uncommon to experience the changes in the old place as strange, and even to experience the whole place as strange (that is, nonidentical with what it was in the past)—even if the changes in people and physical surroundings are *less* than those that took place while you lived there. Or perhaps you have another kind of experience: you find the place and its people "just the same." In this case, it is not uncommon to feel a strangeness in any case, to feel as if you are out of place because "I have changed, I am no longer the same person." What is significant in both cases is that the *experience* of change and difference does *not occur in the process of changing itself, but only when everyday relations of engagement are broken off*—here, because of moving and development. In contrast, you experience the identity of yourself through the process of change owing to the continuity of engagement.

This example captures a fundamental aspect of Nietzsche's doctrine (although not necessarily its most striking aspect: see below), and can be reconstructed by looking closely at his references. The full phrase of Nietzsche's doctrine, "the eternal return of the same," suggests that the eternal return refers, at least in the first instance, to this character of our cognitive situation in a changing world. "The same" is a translation of *das Gleiche*, which means the "like" or the "similar," but not the "identical." [32] Nietzsche's choice of words implies that identity is a plausible interpretation of experiences that are recognizably "like" one another. Given the cognitive basis of identities, Nietzsche is not claiming that identical cases *actually* exist and recur. Rather, he suggests that such self-identities and the identities of one's situation can exist because *similar* cases appear and reappear in forms that can be assimilated to categories of identity. That identities remain interpretive phenomena and yet have some ground in experience is suggested by Nietzsche's substitution in the following quotation of the term "identical cases" with quotation marks for his usual expression, "the same." "The *calculability of an event*," he writes, "does not reside in the fact that a rule is adhered to, or that a necessity is obeyed or that a law of causality has been projected by us into every event: it resides in the *recurrence of 'identical cases.'*" [33] That such calculability exists, that "identical cases" recur, means that it is possible for a horizon of familiar things, relations, and identities to form, and for practices to gain a continuity in and through the continuity of one's life-world. The return of *das Gleiche* permits identical interpretive signs and symbols to be used over and over, constituting a realm of the identifiable. We come to know the world as a set of identifiable objectifications through *re*cognition. This provides recognizable points of reference, and makes it possible for the self to identify its location in the world over time and hence to identify itself as a continuous entity, a personality. Nietzsche has Zarathustra make the point this way: "The time is gone when mere accidents could still happen to me; and what could still come to me now that was not mine already? What returns, what finally comes home to me, is my own self and what of myself has long been in strange lands and scattered among all things and accidents."[34] At this point in the drama, Zarathustra has learned to recognize the identity of himself in his past experiences. His insight is that everything that has happened to him makes him who he is, and by affirming everything that he has been, he affirms his own identity.[35] Nietzsche summarizes this point succinctly in an epigram in *Beyond Good and Evil*: "If one has character, one also has one's typical experience, which always comes again."[36]

As we saw in Nietzsche's analysis of "noble" forgetting, the reason that our past can become a resource for the continuity of the self (rather than being simply "accidental") is that we cognitively synthesize experience by repressing and forgetting what we cannot assimilate into categories of being. We repress difference—that is, those aspects of experience that are not recognizable. Nihilism occurs when experience resists cognitive synthesis, either because of the quality of experience or because the culturally structured categories we use to interpret the world are inappropriate to experience. In contrast, nobility, sovereignty, and autonomy presuppose experience that can be synthesized. In this way the eternal return characterizes the qualities of *historicity* that allow self-identities to express the continuity of practices. By noticing that our most important experiences "return," we can approximate the experience of being without sacrificing awareness of the historicity of the human condition. Nietzsche means this to show that nonreligious, nonmetaphysical, and nontranscendental self-interpretations of agency are possible in principle.

The Eternal Return as a Teaching

That the eternal return is a philosophical possibility is important for Nietzsche, because he believes it necessary to transform this possibility into a teaching, a mode of consciousness. He is interested in the eternal return as a mode of awareness, one that is possible for some individuals at some historical junctures. The possibility of this awareness is rooted in the fact that the eternal return is *already* a part of everyone's life-world. The doctrine highlights everyday experiences that *already* have a role in creating self-identities. To become aware of this fact is another matter, however: its immediate effect is to remove transcendental illusions. It *dis*illusions because it destroys transcendental identities. For this reason, the doctrine can be a proximate cause of European nihilism.

The fact that the identities of all knowledge and self-knowledge are based on eternal recurrence is unproblematic *as long as this fact remains concealed*—that is, as long as the eternal return is mistaken for self-identical being. But when the worldly ground of identity is discovered in the thought of the eternal return, it is a discovery "that could change you as you are or perhaps crush you." [37] The thought asserts the utter impossibility of escape from historical being into another world and another set of identities. One is condemned to live with history. This may mean many things, but Nietzsche points out that one is ready for it only when one can bear the thought that "every pain and every joy and every thought and every sigh and everything unutterably small or great in your life will return to you, all in the same succession and sequence—even this spider and this moonlight between the trees, and even this moment and I myself. The eternal hourglass of existence is turned upside down again and again, and you with it, a speck of dust." [38] The truth that the thought captures is that the only ground for self-identity is the repetition of existence. The only ground for being turns out to be the absolute denial of any essence behind existence. The only possibility for experiencing eternity is the absolute affirmation of history. Thus in the moment of discovery, the eternal return becomes an existential imperative: it places the individual face to face with all of the offerings and limits of existence—nothing more and nothing less. Nietzsche's *Zarathustra* describes such a process of discovery.

The meaning the thought of the eternal return has for any individual, however, will always depend on practical possibilities given by historically specific factors, since the identity of the self is a contingent sedimentation of practices. The situation of original nihilism, for example, signifies conditions under which the self as a practical achievement is impossible. In situations like these, no amount of affirmative *thinking* will provide the practical conditions for self-identity. Here, the thought of eternal return would only make the nihilism that already resides in the situation manifest to consciousness. On the other hand, awareness of eternal recurrence without nihilism is possible in an environment that allows a continuity of practices, since these situations allow individuals to interpret the thought of eternal return through a preexisting continuity of practices.

Situational opportunity is not the only factor determining the effects of the thought, however: in the contemporary situation, whether the thought of eternal return serves to complete the organization of power as agency or to deepen nihilism will depend on whether individuals have within themselves the accumulated powers of Western history. As suggested in the last chapter, Nietzsche views the powers of science, sovereign individuality, nobility, and art as cultural conditions of reflexively organized power. But he also thinks that these resources have been selectively inherited: some individuals have less potential for agency than others, and more potential for nihilism. For these persons, the thought of eternal return can only make the nihilism of their situation explicit.

But for those who have assimilated these powers and need only arrive at a self-reflective consciousness of the historicity of being, the thought can serve to organize their capacities to the fullest. From the standpoint of cultural inheritances, the psychological means of achieving self-identity are given especially by the traits of the noble individual and the artist. The thought of eternal return encapsulates the repression and selective illumination of experience already cultivated by the noble individual and the artist, in this way drawing these traits into a self-identity founded on practices. Noble self-certainty is based on healthy repression, while the artist specializes in selective illumination and organization of experience.

Although the repression of difference entailed in the thought of eternal return would seem to repeat the errors of metaphysics, it is a repression of a different sort. While in metaphysics the repression of difference becomes a permanent attribute of thought, the eternal return requires that identities be continually reconstructed out of the resources of the historical world. The experiences incorporated by the eternal return do not permit absolute closure within identity, because history throws difference into the realm of experience again and again, thus requiring that identity be reconstructed continually in practice. The eternal return can become a means to self-interpretations of identity only insofar as the worldly resources of identity are brought into existence in practice: one makes possible a non-nihilistic experience of the eternal return by constructing the kind of world within which one recognizes one's agency. In this sense identity must be willed; when one constructs identities in practice, one has created the experiential basis for a self-interpretation of agency. Nietzsche's most powerful description of the transformation of the eternal return into a mode of willing is found in *Beyond Good and Evil*:

> Whoever has endeavored with some enigmatic longing, as I have, to think pessimism through to its depths and to liberate it from its half-Christian, half-German narrowness and simplicity ... whoever has really, with an Asiatic and supra-Asiatic eye, looked into, down into the most world-denying of all possible ways of thinking—beyond good and evil and no longer, like Buddha and Schopenhauer, under the spell and delusion of morality—may just thereby, without really meaning to do so, have opened his eyes to the opposite ideal: the ideal of the most high-spirited, alive, and world-affirming human being who has not only come to terms with whatever was and is, but who wants to have what was and is repeated into all eternity, shouting insatiably *da capo* [from the beginning]—not only to himself but to the whole play and spectacle—and who makes it necessary because again and again he needs himself—and makes himself necessary. . . .[39]

Would this not be, Nietzsche asks with unforgettable acuity, the *"circulus vitiosus deus"*—the vicious circle made God?[40]

This synthetic time-consciousness, the "circle" in time, is the only postmodern possibility for self-identity, for it is the only perspective that reconciles knowledge and self-knowledge with historical being. One must will the past—the "whole play and spectacle"—because the past is the ground and resource of willing the future. One loves fate because it is the only means to willing. By willing the past, one makes possible a self-identity of the will based on practice, thereby making oneself a necessary recurrence. This is the point at which power can become identical with freedom and autonomy, for only here are past determinations incorporated into self-constituting practice as material for the future. Here, the will's "revenge against time" is overcome, and—as Nietzsche puts it in *Zarathustra*—the will becomes a "liberator."[41]

Nietzsche's critical philosophy gives way at this point to his figure of Zarathustra. Through Zarathustra, Nietzsche provides his audience with a dramatic and speculative reconstruction of a possible transition phase to that new set of self-understandings and practices signified by the *Übermensch*. Interpreting *Zarathustra* would go beyond the present project; nonetheless, any interpretation of the speculative philosophy of *Zarathustra* presupposes an understanding of Nietzsche's critical philosophy of the kind I present here.[42]

7

Nietzsche's Political Thought
and Its Limits

If Nietzsche provides a framework for a critically postmodern political philosophy, it is no more than a preface, an incomplete beginning, a set of pregnant suggestions. We find the preface in his reconstruction of the capacities of agency presupposed by the modern rationalist values of freedom, responsibility, rational autonomy, and individuality. These values presuppose that human powers can be organized as an agency capable of acting in a historical and social world. Nietzsche tells us how, and under what conditions, this is possible. In so doing, he provides an account of the relation between subjectivity and historical practices that could not develop within modern rationalism because of its metaphysical assumptions about humans as agents. By going beyond the assumptions of the tradition, Nietzsche's philosophy could enable many of its progressive values.

But Nietzsche's own political thinking does not reflect this preface. When he politicizes his philosophy of will to power, he describes human agency in the language of exploitation, domination, struggle, mastery over others, and hierarchy. As far as Nietzsche is concerned, these are inevitable aspects of politics and society. He writes, for example, that "'exploitation' does not belong to a corrupt or imperfect and primitive society: it belongs to the *essence* of what lives, as a basic organic function; it is a consequence of the will to power, which is after all the will of life."[1] On the basis of texts such as these, most commentators quite reasonably conclude that Nietzsche's philosophy of power intrinsically celebrates domination, exploitation, and mastery over others. According to this view, Nietzsche does not immanently criticize modern rationalism so much as launch an irrational assault and regress behind it. Nietzsche's own understanding of the political implications of his philosophy is a *prima facie* case against the interpretation of his philosophy of power I have developed here—namely, as a philosophy of human agency that shows how individuality, responsibility, and positive freedom are possible, and as a philosophy that could be developed consistently with the social values of reciprocity, mutual processes of individuation, and equality, assuming one wished to do so.

The conflict between these two Nietzsches is real: both exist and both are authentic. This is to say that the problem is not one of a mistaken reading of what Nietzsche meant. Rather, it is one of explaining how these two Nietzsches can coexist within the same body of thought. My interest in explaining these two aspects is not purely scholastic: I wish to show how one might choose the philosophical Nietzsche while excluding his politics, but do so without eclecticism— that is, without fragmenting the internal necessities of his thinking. In my view, it is important to show this possibility, since the Nietzsche I have elaborated here is intrinsically preferable for those who, like myself, subscribe to many of the political ideals of progressive rationalism while also believing that realizing these ideals requires a postmodern view of the world. But the problem is not just one of political preferences. Nietzsche's own politics, I shall argue, violates the intellectual integrity of his philosophical project. Viewed through his politics, Nietzsche's philosophy becomes crude and uninteresting. Here is an example: when Nietzsche asserts that exploitation is explained by the fact that life is will to power, he violates his own critique of metaphysics. The reason is that this kind of assertion involves the use of the concept as a speculative or dogmatic metaphysic: he "explains" empirical events of exploitation by deducing them from a posited, universal, nonempirical entity of precisely the sort he rejects in other philosophers. Thus, to accept Nietzsche's political reading of the concept of will to power would require rejecting his critique of metaphysical conceptions of agency. Yet to do so would be to misunderstand Nietzsche's importance, since it is here that one finds the most innovative and systematic aspects of his project.

What I am suggesting, then, is that we should not automatically assume what we would be inclined methodologically to assume in any other case—namely, that Nietzsche's philosophy is faithfully reflected in his political judgments. In most cases one is justified in assuming that a thinker's philosophy is accurately reflected in his political judgments. In Nietzsche's case, however, the innovative aspects of his philosophy find little expression in his overt politics. What he does, unsuccessfully, is combine a postmodern philosophy with a premodern politics. In this chapter, I argue that Nietzsche's philosophy *underdetermines* his politics, and in crucial respects is also at odds with it. At the same time, I provide an explanation of this disjunction. Nietzsche, I argue, was often able to provide uniquely incisive criticisms of modern political ideologies. At the same time, he could not account for every political effect he observed, even those of most importance to his problematic of nihilism.

In the last analysis, the reason for Nietzsche's failure here is that he lacked categories of analysis appropriate to contemporary social organizations, especially those organized as markets and bureaucracies. This caused him to incorporate two different kinds of errors into his politics. First, he relied on the classical method of drawing an analogy between soul and city, between organizations of the human will and organizations of society. He subscribed to the organic metaphor for society that was common to political philosophy from Plato through Hobbes, and remains in use among conservatives even today. Nietzsche's reliance on this analogy allowed him to use in his theory of agency terms describing political phenomena (such as exploitation, domination, hierarchy, and command) to describe constituent aspects of action processes. By using this method, he was then able to claim that these qualities manifest themselves as universal aspects of social and political orders. Nietzsche's procedure here is, of course, methodologically suspect, even in his own terms. It is also substantively suspect: since Adam Smith, Marx, Durkheim, Weber, and other theorists of modern social organization we can no longer assume that attributes of action are analogous to those of society. Indeed, on the basis of the analysis of action that Nietzsche actually provides, the connection between action and social organization should have remained an open question. By relying on the classical analogy, Nietzsche prematurely closed the question of how these relations are to be conceived.

Second, Nietzsche's lack of modern categories of social analysis caused him to account for many of the effects of modern social structures (such as exploitation and domination) in metaphysical terms, as well as to account for the massification of modern societies in (unfounded) "physiological" terms, and to account for modern political crises solely in cultural terms. These analyses in turn justified his political ideal of a hierarchical society with a small leadership of aristocrat-philosophers as the most desirable of all possible political organizations in a postmodern world.

Although Nietzsche did not understand modern societies in the way he needed for his problematic, one need not go outside of his thought to find his politics inconsistent with his philosophy. Here, as in other aspects of Nietzsche's thought, I begin with an assumption of internal consistency. In the first several sections of this chapter I shall be concerned with the sense in which the insights of Nietzsche's philosophy are contained in his politics. In the last sections of the chapter I turn to critique, and argue that the continuity between Nietzsche's philosophy and politics obtains if and only if one adds four major assumptions about the limits of politics—assumptions concerning domination in politics, division of labor in society, human nature in cultural evolution, and the causes of modern nihilism.

Following an immanent method of criticism such as this will have a number of important advantages. First, the method preserves the overall coherence of Nietzsche's thought, but it does so by isolating his major assumptions about social and political life. If it turns out that these assumptions were poor ones, then providing better ones will alter the political meaning of his philosophy. If, as I shall argue, this is indeed the case, then this method of criticism will have the effect of liberating the political possibilities of Nietzsche's philosophy from the constraints of his politics on the basis of his own strengths and weaknesses. Insofar as Nietzsche's politics are underdetermined by his philosophy of power, and insofar as they require unfounded assumptions to be added to his philosophy, one is justified in distinguishing the *political implications of his philosophy of power* from his *political philosophy*, and treating them as radically different things. This suggests that in spite of the contributions of Nietzsche as a *philosopher* to contemporary political thought, he lacks a politics adequate to his philosophy. It follows that Nietzsche as a *political* philosopher must be rejected, leaving the politics of his philosophy still to be determined.

Second, the immanent method of criticism allows one to look at Nietzsche's political claims for what they are rather than ignoring them (as many commentators do) or viewing them as metaphorical (as do many others). One need not see a direct line from Nietzsche's thought to its appropriation by the Nazis to see that at least some aspects of his political vision are distinctively fascist.[2] Nietzsche's vision of an aesthetic-cultural and political domination of the spiritually superior few over the "herd," for example, had close parallels in Nazi ideology. Although it is true that Nietzsche's overall world view cannot be made to fit with Nazi ideology, and although it is true that Nazi interpreters had to distort and even invent texts in order to appropriate Nietzsche, these affinities of political form remain.[3] Pacifying Nietzsche's politics is inevitably an unsatisfying and inconclusive way of "saving" his philosophy from the abuses it has encountered. Instead, the questions that need to be asked are how and why Nietzsche extended his philosophy of agency to support a repressive politics. To answer these questions, one needs to ask what Nietzsche's politics are like, how they stem from his criticism of Western culture, and, finally, what assumptions he had to make to support his political conclusions.

Finally, the immanent method of criticism explains our common experience that there are really two Nietzsches, a "gentle" Nietzsche and a "bloody" one. Both strains exist in Nietzsche, and by taking this approach we can see how they are identifiably separate, and yet follow from his attempt to combine a postmodern philosophy with premodern assumptions about the social and political world. In this way, we shall also be able to see why so many different political elaborations of Nietzsche could exist, many of them diametrically opposed to one another—that is, why Nietzsche is more like a Hegel than a Locke in having an impact across the political spectrum.[4]

Characterizing Nietzsche's Politics

In contrast to his philosophy and critique of Western culture, there is little in Nietzsche's *political* philosophy that is novel or radical. Indeed, if Nietzsche's political philosophy is not easily placed, it is not because of its novelty, but because of its sketchy qualities. Still, something of a *prima facie* case can be made for characterizing Nietzsche's political philosophy as a *neoaristocratic conservatism*. On the face of it, Nietzsche's politics has more in common with a conservatism like Burke's or even Hegel's than with any other existing political philosophy. Despite his warning to conservatives that it is neither possible nor desirable to recapture the virtues of past eras,[5] his views on social and political matters are conservative in definitive respects. Like Burke, for example, Nietzsche emphasized that valuable traits of individuals, cultures, and societies grow slowly and organically. Radical changes result in chaos, and for this reason they are not intrinsically desirable even though they may often be unavoidable. Nietzsche also argued that societies can only be held together through evolved social custom and habit (what Burke called "just prejudice"). Rational agreement between individuals is an epiphenomenon of this underlying and arational unity of the cultural practices of a people. Nietzsche believed in ascriptive hierarchies of functions in society rather than in social and economic equality. And he thought that societies should be ruled by superior individuals rather than democratically.

In all these respects Nietzsche's ideas are traditionally conservative. It is true that Nietzsche's ideals of sovereign individuality are more akin to liberal than conservative ideals, but—unlike liberals— he did not think it either possible or desirable to universalize these ideals. Sovereign individuality is necessarily an attribute of the few, and possible only within an aristocratic society. In accordance with this, Nietzsche held that the ends of political community should be the production of a few culturally exceptional individuals rather than a universally satisfactory life. Moreover, he believed that these two possible ends must inevitably be in conflict, the demands of the many (who have neither the inclination nor capacity for cultural excellence) always endangering the cultural privileges of the few.

As a conservative Nietzsche was self-consciously political in the sense of desiring a hierarchical, ascriptive society in the future. Still, it is difficult to associate his politics with any contemporary political movement. For example, he certainly did not intend his politics as a defense of the monopoly capitalism developing in Germany in his day, as Franz Mehring argued (even though it may have had this effect).[6] Nietzsche was not a defender of the bourgeoisie, and—as I shall suggest—had little use for the economic ideals of market societies. It is also clear that his thought could not have led directly to fascism as Lukács and many others have argued (although elements of his politics were undoubtedly consistent with fascism).[7] He was antistatist, anti-*Reich*, and disgusted by anti-Semitism. Where we do find some positive political commitments in Nietzsche is in his nostalgia for the European nobility of a prebourgeois era, which he tended to see as a cultural rather than political or economic class. This tends to support Marc Sautet's contention that his politics expressed the aspirations and concerns of an increasingly marginalized landed aristocracy—the social base of a "romantic anticapitalism," to use Lukács' expression.[8] For these reasons, it seems most accurate to characterize Nietzsche's politics as a neoaristocratic conservatism—a conservatism looking back to the social orders that developed in Europe between the Renaissance and the emergence of bourgeois political orders, and forward to a time when similar cultural aristocracies might be established.

Nihilism and Liberal Democratic Culture

Nietzsche's assessment of the political situation of European cultures combines his neoaristocratic conservatism with an analysis of the political effects of nihilism. On the one hand, he held that Christian-moral culture had instilled political expectations for community, universal rights, and equality. Like other conservatives, he held that such expectations contravened the natural limits of the political universe, leading to a vulgar and trivialized politics.[9] On the other hand, he thought that the contemporary cultural crisis had also determined the possible and probable course of liberal democratic political culture. One finds the continuity between Nietzsche's philosophy and his politics in the intersection of these perspectives.

Any attempt to interpret Nietzsche's criticisms of modern politics generally, and liberal democratic politics specifically, must be highly reconstructive, owing to the sketchy and fragmented nature of his comments. What follows in this section is *one* possible way of reading these comments, but they are so incomplete that it is undoubtedly not the *only* possible way. Many of Nietzsche's criticisms of liberal democracy seem simply to reflect his conservative assumptions, and would be interesting only if these assumptions were well-founded. Other criticisms are more interesting because they extend his analysis of nihilism to political culture.

Still, even in this latter case one needs to proceed with caution. The reason is that Nietzsche views liberal democratic political culture as little more than a secularized development of Christian culture. Nietzsche was either unaware of or chose to ignore essential differences, such as those having to do with the rise of market economies and the development of bureaucratic organizations. While these developments certainly have dimensions related to Christian-moral culture, they are not reducible to them—a problem to which I shall return. Thus while Nietzsche's approach may yield important insights, he cannot be said to be a critic of liberal democracy in any comprehensive sense, even though commentators often construe him in this way.[10] The scope of his criticism should be viewed as being limited to those aspects in which Christian and liberal democratic culture are in fact continuous. Here, the important point is that if one takes these limitations into account, one finds that Nietzsche's views on the continuity of Christian and liberal democratic culture do reveal significant affinities. This suggests that in important respects he was justified in holding that liberal democracy was implicated in the crisis of European nihilism. The value of Nietzsche's criticisms of liberal democracy lies in these affinities, and they can be best appreciated if not overextended.

In what senses did Nietzsche see liberal democratic culture as developing out of Christian culture? Nietzsche seems to relate its *liberal* aspect to Christianity's conception of the individual, and its *democratic* aspect to Christianity's conceptions of community and social justice. The important difference between Christian and liberal democratic culture, Nietzsche seems to think, is only that the latter is an attempt to politicize the ideals of the former. Early liberal thinkers sought the foundations of a new political order in the Christian concept of the individual as an indestructible soul, although they revised the concept to make the individual into a subject of natural rights and inclinations. Democratic ideals, according to Nietzsche, consist primarily in the notion that the Christian promise of community can be realized in this world, combined with the view that (Christian-Platonic) ideals of justice can be politicized. But because liberal democracy relies on ideals that are part of a collapsing culture, it too is implicated in the crisis of nihilism.

Insofar as Nietzsche's criticisms of liberalism here have any plausibility at all, it can be found in his view that liberalism inherits the contradictions of Christian ideology that stem from its metaphysics of the subject. Christianity posited the existence of individual souls as unconditional, nonempirical, and irreducible beings. For this reason, the Christian individual remains nonactive and nonworldly; the self is displaced into a set of metaphysical identities that are divorced from practices. Liberalism inherited this metaphysical conception of the subject, while giving it a different content and putting it to different uses. Like the Christian concept of the individual, for example, the liberal concept is abstract in the sense of being unconditional. Similarly, it lends itself to reification from its material, social, and cultural conditions of possibility. The metaphysical formulation shows up clearly in the thought of liberal individualists beginning with Hobbes and extending at least through Bentham: the individual consists fundamentally of a set of natural inclinations, preferences, and rights that manifest themselves through social organizations (or least *ought* to do so: the concept of nature played both a normative and empirical role for early liberal thinkers). Society also becomes an abstraction: rather than a condition of individuation, society is seen as the result of individuals agreeing to enforce rules in terms of which they can maximize their desires and preferences. Similarly, liberal individuals become political beings by recognizing the need for, and assenting to, sovereign institutions that ensure orderly satisfaction of preexisting needs and desires.

By positing the individual as something that is prior to society in some metaphysical sense—as a locus of natural rights and inclinations, for example—liberal thinkers could justify political arrangements that preserve a private space for the individual. But they did so in an inherently unstable way. Because liberals put a metaphysical placeholder in the space of the individual, they failed to theorize this space. As a result, they justified liberal forms of the state in terms of a historically conditioned effect mistaken for a universal essence. This is why Nietzsche's understanding of nihilism in Western culture as the collapse of the individual *as agent* also implicates the individualistic metaphysics of liberalism. Extrapolating Nietzsche's logic, the criticism would be that in failing to theorize this space, liberalism unwittingly takes over the vacuous private space of the Christian soul, a private space that existed as promise and ideology but not as a reality. Building on this suggestion, one might say that if the private space of the Christian soul had served as an escape from social and political reality, liberalism turns this escape into a political foundation, for it represents the body politic as an aggregate of private spaces, socialized and politicized though contractual relations. Questions about the conditions of individuation become difficult to ask when the individual becomes a metaphysical foundation of society rather than—as in Nietzsche's philosophy—simply a value worthy of being realized. Early liberals confused norm and nature. As a result, even when the fragility of individuation is noticed by liberal thinkers like John Stuart Mill, their insights could not become a part of their social ontology.

Nietzsche's view that liberalism had primarily secularized the Christian concept of the individual (together with the notion of natural rights that attaches to the concept) is suggested by his criticisms of the two strains of liberal morality represented by Bentham and Kant. Nietzsche finds the Christian desire for a passive pleasure in redemption disconnected from worldly activity reproduced in Bentham's apparently un-Christian utilitarian morality with its passive pleasures of consumption.[11] Kant is more interesting, since he attempted to characterize the individual as something more than given desires. For Kant, what is truly individual is the free will of the rational agent—a metaphysical conception of the subject presupposed by moral reasoning. Like other liberal thinkers, Kant's metaphysic of the subject plays a central role in his political philosophy: society is the external form of the categorical imperative, and this in turn expresses the form of activity motivated by the pure will. The categorical imperative is the maxim of reason through which the pure will becomes actual, and society ought to represent the external form of the categorical imperative. Kant's will, however, remains a metaphysic abstracted from worldly practices, an uncritical residue of his critical philosophy (see chapter 4). The lack of substance in Kant's concept of will shows up in his political philosophy: the metaphysics of pure will supports a polarization of empirical individuals who are motivated by amoral desires and a social morality that represents the external form of the pure will. In Kant's view, since individuals are never motivated by a pure will, they ought never to be judges of their own causes. For this reason, the social order that represents the external condition of moral actions—actions motivated by the pure will—must be enforced by the powers of political authorities. Somewhat ironically, then, Kant's conclusion is authoritarian: rebelling against external authorities, no matter how far they may deviate from his ideal, is never justified, for this would threaten a regression to a condition reflecting the amoral desires of empirical individuals, and this would be a war of all against all.[12]

While Nietzsche came to authoritarian conclusions on other

grounds,[13] his critique of Kant is interesting because it exposes the authoritarianism that is often latent in liberal concepts of the individual. Kant's individual can coexist with political authoritarianism only because it is abstracted from social practices and relations, because it is the *inner* freedom of reason that defines what it is to be human. This is why Kant's defense of the individual can degenerate into a defense of inner freedom disconnected from practice.[14] Likewise, when the categorical imperative is extended outward to society as the *sole* guarantor of social relations (which Kant likewise abstracts from history, intersubjectivity, and culture), it can become a defense of political authoritarianism. Nietzsche suggests this kind of critique of Kant in the *Genealogy*. The categorical imperative, he argues, is a metaphysical residue of violent political authority. As such, it "smells of cruelty."[15]

Thus for Nietzsche utilitarianism and Kantianism would seem to represent two sides of the same coin: while Kant's abstraction of the will perpetuated the latent violence of Christian categorical imperatives, Bentham's utilitarianism reflected all of the desires for a satiated happiness without limits—the decadent happiness of *"laisser aller"* that was part of the Christian promise.[16] In both cases, the individual remains an abstraction conceived apart from the worldly activities, practices, and social relations through which individuation becomes a reality.

Regarding the metaphysic of the individual, then, some justification exists for Nietzsche's suggestion that liberalism is a neo-Christian ideology. One might capture Nietzsche's criticism of liberalism by analogy to his more comprehensively developed criticism of Christianity. Like Christian ideology, liberalism demands more of the individual than it can either conceptualize or provide for. Both ascribe responsibility to individuals for their fortunes in the world through the respective notions of sin and merit. And both deny individuals an understanding of the grounds on which they could actualize these ascriptions of responsibility. Both theorize individuality as a manifestation of human nature as such, as if it had no material, social, cultural, or self-reflective conditions of actualization. By disconnecting interior and exterior, they assert the unconditional value of the individual as soul and as a locus of rights, but fail to conceptualize these as historical possibilities. It is true that almost all liberal thinkers empirically recognize and always comment on the conditional nature of individuals. But they fail to articulate these insights theoretically. Because liberalism lacks a theory of power as agency, it also lacks the theory of individuation required by its own individualistic values. This is why the liberal defense of the individual is no guarantee against either politically enforced uniformity or social massification; this is why liberal political thinkers could often affirm social arrangements that undermine the individual as a reality. One sees this in Hobbes' authoritarian Sovereign, in Locke's view that labor activity and its products are the kinds of thing that can and should be alienated from individuals on the market, in Bentham's affirmation of massive poverty produced by capitalism, and in Kant's moral argument for accepting prevailing political authoritarianism. Nietzsche, of course, does not draw these conclusions—his attacks on liberalism are usually no more than crude broadsides. But he *might* have developed his criticisms this way had he been as systematic here as in his critique of Christianity.

Nietzsche reserved most of his criticism of liberal democracy, however, for the democratic ideals that became wedded to liberalism, especially beginning with the French Revolution.[17] He held that the demand for equal rights had been formulated and legitimated within Christianity, insofar as Christianity had bestowed an equal dignity and worth upon each individual as a subject of God regardless of actual circumstance.[18] While the bulk of Nietzsche's opposition to the democratic movements of the nineteenth century can be explained by his opinion that only hierarchical, functionally delineated societies are desirable, here—as in his criticism of liberalism—an element of immanent critique exists from which democratic theory might benefit. To see this, one needs to remember that Nietzsche's thought does contain suggestions of what a positive political equality would involve (see chapter 2), assuming one is interested in this (Nietzsche is not). In order to satisfy Nietzsche's objections to egalitarian ideals, a positive political equality would have to be based on a *de facto* equality of the capacity to act and, inseparable from this, a political culture that sustains rights and duties by adjusting distributions of power in society. Reconstructing this strain in Nietzsche's thought suggests that his criticisms point toward the failure of many democratic ideologies to establish a relation between their ideals and the conditions under which they could be actualized. Without establishing such relations, Nietzsche thought, the ideals would literally demoralize themselves by appearing in retrograde form. Equality, which might be thought of as sustaining conditions of equal strength, becomes an "equality in violating rights" of those who are different,[19] a "certain factual increase in similarity," and a leveling to a universal mediocrity.[20] This inversion would hold true for other ideals of liberal democratic culture as well. Freedom—ideally understood as a capacity for responsible action—can turn into *"laisser aller."*[21] Justice—ideally understood as impartial assessment of competing claims of power—can become an instrument of covetousness or revenge.[22] These considerations suggest that it is possible to give a generous reading of Nietzsche's opposition to liberal democracy, even if such a reading was clearly not his intention. Read generously, his critique calls for distinctions between the ideals of liberal democratic culture and their ideological effects when they are not an integral part of a self-reflective rationality.

Nihilism and the State

Nietzsche's own interest, however, was not in an immanent critique of liberal democracy, but rather in the political impact of European nihilism. His treatment of this issue can be construed in light of the following dilemma: liberal democratic society requires sovereign individuals in order to achieve a society within which individuals can protect themselves via a limited political sphere. But Nietzsche thought that Christian-moral culture had more or less permanently ruined the possibility of sovereign individuality for most people, even though its collapse increased possibilities for a few.[23] The distinctive attributes of sovereign individuality—the capacities of memory and conscience, the senses of duty and obligation—are not, for most people, defining attributes of their self-identities. Rather, these behaviors remain dependent upon "herd" morality, the external commandments of social and religious *Sittlichkeit*. To the degree that sovereign individuals do not exist, liberal democracies remain dependent upon crumbling cultural supports.

The consequences of liberalism's unwitting reliance on a dying culture are not politically benign. They can be understood in terms of Nietzsche's suggestions that a symbiotic relation evolved during the Christian-moral period between the state's construction of political experience and the church's rationalization of this experience.[24]

By gaining its legitimacy through an attachment to Christianity, the state began to take upon itself demands (like those for community) that it could not fulfill without recourse to the Christian form of meaning. While institutionalized Christianity was intact, the state could claim to be the worldly form of community while deflecting the communal experiences that supported the claim back onto the church. With the breakdown of Christian-moral culture, however, the state is left with demands for meaning, but without the kind of culture that had once organized these demands and provided experiences of meaning, even if vicariously. The crisis of legitimacy of the Christian-moral world view (chapters 1 and 4) has a political dimension insofar as the state loses its religious means of legitimation. Because the loss of Christian-moral culture occurs without the formation of a sovereign self, the opportunity exists for the state to provide its own legitimations by manipulating self-identities. In this way, the state assumes a role vacated by the church. Only in the modern period, then, does it become possible for the state to exploit reflexive needs directly by providing a vicarious identity for the self in relation to the community.

In these terms, one can understand Nietzsche's fear that the self might be regressively politicized in the wake of the vacuum left by Christian-moral culture. Although he implicitly shared this fear with liberals, he did not see the possibility of a resolution within the terms of liberal theory. Here again Nietzsche's comments are suggestive: liberals have always opposed the encroachment of institutionalized politics (if not institutionalized economics) into the "private" sphere of the self. They rightly fear totalitarianism in such instances. But liberals tend not to understand why totalitarianism is possible, because they do not understand the historically conditional nature of individual agency.[25] They often make the fatal assumption that the individual provides a natural and unassailable cornerstone of private life, sustained by family, church, and work place. Yet central aspects of this system of identities dissolve in a cultural crisis. Nietzsche thought that for most the cultural crisis would lead to exposure of a "decadent" self, the "private person."[26] The "private person" coincides with what he later called the "last man."[27] The "last man" of the modern period is the result of a political culture that had mediated power relations between individuals through external identities, such as those of God and country. With the loss of external guidance in the modern cultural crisis, the last man's feeling of power is threatened. God is replaced by new kinds of religion, narcotic culture, and identity with national heroes and the state. The existence of "last men" leaves a fertile field for invasion of the self by the state or any other institutionalized power.

Nietzsche's sensitivity to this weakness of liberal democratic societies surely stemmed in part from the fact that liberal culture was never well established in Germany. For this reason, he was able to understand its contingent nature in ways that those in well-established liberal cultures could not. Even in Nietzsche's lifetime, processes of cultural breakdown coexisted with a rising German nationalism, a nationalism expressed in the *Reich* and anti-Semitism. Although Nietzsche welcomed in principle the growth of liberal institutions as a means for curbing state power, he took little comfort in their existence because he saw them as vehicles for the ideals of an increasingly massified society.[28] Thus, reflecting the German situation of his time, Nietzsche emphasized not the pluralism of parliamentary processes but their relative ideological unity. "Parliamentarianism— that is, public permission to choose between five basic public opinions—flatters and wins the favor of all those who would like to *seem* independent and individual, as if they fought for their opinions. . . . Whoever deviates from the five public opinions and stands apart will always have the whole herd against him."[29] "Liberalism," Nietzsche writes elsewhere, is "herd-animalization."[30]

The plausibility of Nietzsche's polemics against the "herd" and its connections to liberal institutions can be found in his view—one already well-developed by de Tocqueville and John Stuart Mill— that parliamentary processes contain the danger of providing merely the formal appearance of pluralism while functioning to legitimate the state as a guarantor of mass values. Should parliament become the tool of the "herd"—and Nietzsche thought this imminent—it would surely use state power to impose "herd" values on everyone. "Liberal institutions," he generalizes, "cease to be liberal as soon as they are attained: later on, there are no worse and no more thorough injurers of freedom than liberal institutions."[31] He voiced similar concerns about leftist movements. Working at first through liberal institutions, the advocates of democracy on the left would wish to politicize "everything" by defining general standards of existence; they would dictate that "everyone should live and work according to such standards." [32] Foreshadowing the objections of later anarchists such as Emma Goldman against statist Marxists, Nietzsche believed that revolutionaries harbor a "reactionary" desire to reassert the power of the state over the individual.[33]

If Nietzsche was concerned about the growth of state power driven by the democratic aspirations of the left, he was equally concerned about the growth of state power fueled by the nationalist right.[34] The attempt of the state to step into the cultural vacuum left by the decay of Christian-moral culture was already occurring in Germany. Through his *Kulturkampf*—his attack on the Catholic Church— Bismarck clearly was attempting to draw the interpretive processes of society into the arena of the state. Nietzsche viewed Bismarck's *Kulturkampf* as a single instance of a more general trend for individual identities to be formed around secular institutions, a trend continuing and deepening the displacement of individual agency that had occurred under Christianity. "If one spends oneself for power," he explains in discussing the decline of German culture,

for great politics, for economics, world trade, parliamentarianism, and military interests—if one spends in *this* direction the quantum of understanding, seriousness, will, and self-overcoming that one represents, then it will be lacking in the direction of culture. Culture and the state—one should not deceive oneself about this—are antagonists. . . . All great ages of culture are ages of political decline: what is great culturally has always been unpolitical, even *antipolitical.* . . . In the history of European culture the rise of the "*Reich*" means one thing above all: *a displacement of the center of gravity* [*eine Verlegung des Schwergewichts*].[35]

Properly understood, Nietzsche's cultural ideal aimed at individual rather than institutional power. This is why even when writing on behalf of a rebirth of culture in Germany (which "matters most") he opposed Bismarck's incipiently fascist *Kulturkampf* and attempt to establish a *Kultur-Staat*. A state-culture—as distinct from a culture that defines a "people"—was for Nietzsche a contradiction in terms.[36]

Nietzsche's fears that the state would move into the contemporary cultural vacuum are stated unequivocally in *Zarathustra*. He warns that the "new idol" (the state) lures the "all-too-many" to view it as a new god. The state attempts to identify itself with the cultural unity of entire peoples: "this lie crawls out of its mouth: 'I, the state, am the people.' " [37] The state hastens the destruction of peoples by usurping their social fabric of customs and rights (*Sitten und Rechten*), and by attempting to replace the lost culture. "'On earth there is nothing greater than I: the ordering finger of God am I'—thus roars the monster."[38] If European nihilism signifies the loss of self-identity for most people, the foremost political expression of nihilism would be an identity of political culture with the state. If connections are to be drawn between nihilism as Nietzsche understood it and the emergence of totalitarianism in the twentieth century—as they so often are—they should be drawn here.

Nietzsche's criticisms of the state provide some insight into the positive political values that are intrinsic to his philosophy. Most strikingly, Nietzsche's criticisms of the state are consistently anti-totalitarian; they suggest the primacy of his concern with the way that different societies empower or subvert individual powers. The value implication, of course, is that societies that sustain individual powers are intrinsically more desirable than those that displace self-identities onto supraindividual institutions such as the state. Nietzsche's comments suggest that all politically sustained hierarchies ("for great politics, for economics, world trade, parliamentarianism, and military interests"[39]) are inconsistent with the intersubjective space of individuation. At least this much is implied in Nietzsche's critique of the state inasmuch as it is a critique on behalf of individuals as agents. Yet these observations only deepen the problem of interpreting Nietzsche's politics: why does Nietzsche fail to follow through on the immanent political logic of his philosophy, especially when he could draw out implications such as these?

Nihilism, Capitalism, and Class Conflict

It is only when one looks at a final arena of Nietzsche's criticism of modern society and politics that the limits of his political thinking begin to emerge. Through these limits one can begin to account for the politics he actually held, as opposed to other possibilities that are consistent with his philosophy of agency—a problem to which I return in later sections of this chapter. Nietzsche opposed not only the increasing tendency for the state to define cultural ideals, but also the increasing tendency for ideals to become economic in nature. Although little interested in the workings of contemporary economies, he resisted their increasing dominion over everyday life. As I have noted, Nietzsche fits quite clearly the pattern that Lukács called "romantic anticapitalism," in spite of Lukács' own assessment.[40] For example, he viewed the capitalist work ethic as self-destructive: what his contemporaries referred to as the "blessing of work," Nietzsche saw as "mechanical activity," resulting in "absolute regularity, punctilious and unthinking obedience, a mode of life fixed once and for all, fully occupied time, a certain permission, indeed training [*Zucht*], for 'impersonality,' for self-forgetfulness, for *incuria sui* [lack of care for the self]."[41] Neither did it escape his attention that the experience of mechanized labor, coupled with contemporary economic ideals, aided and abetted the more general logic of nihilism. Thus Nietzsche set himself against the prevailing "economic optimism": "as if the increasing expenditure of everybody must necessarily involve the increasing welfare of everybody. The opposite seems to me to be the case: the expenditure of everybody amounts to a collective loss: man is diminished—so one no longer knows what *aim* this tremendous process has served."[42]

Nietzsche even registers occasional sympathy for the working classes. He suggests, for example, that Europe's workers possess a good deal more potential as powerful beings than Europe's bourgeoisie, and certainly more than their position in society could ever allow.[43] His concerns for the situation of Europe's laboring classes had narrow limits, however, because he believed class societies to be natural and inevitable. Thus he opposed the "forcible new distributions of property" proposed by socialists.[44] Instead, he could think only in terms of subjecting the working classes to a cultural aristocracy that could provide them with the kinds of vicarious goals lost with the Christian-moral world view.[45]

The conflict between the possibilities of Nietzsche's philosophy and the goals dictated by his views on the limits of social organization produces our common and rather disconcerting experiences that there is both a "gentle" and a "bloody" Nietzsche. Both aspects of Nietzsche have inspired interpretive traditions. His "gentle" aspects belong to his philosophy and critique of culture. They show through in his claim that "I want to proceed as Raphael did and never paint another image of torture. There are enough sublime things so that one does not have to look for the sublime where it dwells in sisterly association with cruelty; and my ambition also could never find satisfaction if I became a sublime assistant at torture."[46] Although

Nietzsche wished to see culture become a means of individuation rather than a means and reflection of oppression, he also believed that without a class of "slaves," no higher culture would be possible. I shall argue that Nietzsche's politics, which contains the "bloody" aspects of his thought, follows in large part from this belief. This belief in turn follows from a number of uncritical assumptions about modern society that I examine in some detail below.

Before turning to these issues, however, it is useful to note a final set of criticisms of liberal democratic political culture that clearly illustrates the clash between Nietzsche's cultural ideals and his belief in the necessity of a class society. Nietzsche discerned the conflict between the economic bases of liberalism and the democratic ideals to which it eventually became wedded. He understood the ideological dilemma of the worker within contemporary societies that promised more than they delivered. He knew that demands for social change are born out of a divergence between expectation and actuality, and thought that liberal democratic societies would become victims of this tension. But owing to his belief in the inevitability of class societies, Nietzsche held that the tensions within liberal democratic societies would have to be resolved—if they still could be—by removing the liberal democratic promise. In a comment on the "labor question," Nietzsche explicitly criticizes liberal democratic society regarding this contradiction from a ruling-class perspective:

I simply cannot see what one proposes to do with the European worker now that one has made a question of him. He is far too well-off not to ask for more and more, not to ask more immodestly. In the end he has numbers on his side. The hope is gone forever that a modest and self-sufficient man ... might here develop as a class. . . . But what was done? Everything to nip in the bud even the preconditions for this: the instincts by virtue of which the worker becomes possible as a class, possible in his own eyes, have been destroyed through and through with the most irresponsible thoughtlessness. The worker was qualified for military service, granted the right to organize and vote: is it any wonder that the worker experiences his own existence as distressing—morally speaking, as an injustice? But what is wanted? ... If one wants an end, one must also want the means: if one wants slaves, then one is a fool if one educates them to be masters.[47]

However penetrating Nietzsche's intuitions are into the fact that liberal democrats consistently call for more equality than a liberal economic system can provide, here we encounter the real limitations of his political thought, limitations that come to appear as conflicts within his ideals. I shall suggest in the next several sections that Nietzsche narrows and even undermines the political possibilities of his philosophy of agency by adding several assumptions that are not essential to it. It is owing to these assumptions that he presents us with the political alternatives of a mediocre and unhuman equality of the "herd," or an inhuman cultural aristocracy. Faced with these alternatives, he chooses the latter.

The Uncritical Assumptions of Nietzsche's Politics

Criticism of Nietzsche's politics cannot concern the question of why he chooses as he does—for the choice follows clearly from the goal of his philosophy and the political alternatives as he sees them. Rather, we need to understand why Nietzsche structures the political alternatives as he does. If Nietzsche conceives of all values in terms of a philosophy of power as agency, then it is axiomatic that the positive goal of politics would be to maintain conditions under which humans can fully develop and exert their powers as agents. Yet he holds this end to be possible only for a few individuals. Insofar as his politics is consistent with his philosophy of power, Nietzsche must hold that natural constraints to politics exist that make it impossible and undesirable to universalize these goals. The best *possible* situation would be a limited realization of these values within a hierarchy of political and economic domination that expresses these constraints. He makes four kinds of arguments that lead to this conclusion. First, he argues that political domination follows from the fact that life is will to power. Second, he argues that material conditions of economic scarcity require a hierarchical division of economic and cultural labor. Third, he argues that an unequal historical constitution of human natures both necessitates and makes desirable a hierarchy of political, cultural, and economic functions. And fourth, he holds that modern politics is overwhelmingly determined by a modern cultural crisis that is irreducibly cultural and not itself the effect of economic or political power relations. These assumptions lead Nietzsche to conclude that a cultural renewal from which a few "higher" individuals benefit ought to be the primary task of future politics.

As I shall argue, the first argument is an unwarranted elaboration of the concept of will to power in Nietzsche's own terms. The other three arguments involve insupportable assumptions about the

political, economic, and biological limits to social and political organization. Together, these assumptions account for the political
elaboration Nietzsche chose to give his philosophy. Without these
assumptions other political elaborations would have been possible.

Nietzsche's Political Elaboration of the Will to Power

Nietzsche's concept of will to power is commonly thought to entail
two kinds of claims about politics. The first is that human nature
includes a will to domination that necessarily expresses itself in political life. The second is that no standards for the conduct of political
life exist except those stemming from the will to domination. Given
these claims, it is not surprising that Nietzsche should be seen as the
ultimate philosopher of *Realpolitik*, one whose philosophy justifies
dominion of the strong over the weak.[48] These impressions are quite
correct in the sense that they express Nietzsche's own view about the
political consequences of the will to power. If Nietzsche does give a
plausible account of the politics of the will to power, then the consequences of accepting his philosophy are serious indeed. Here is the
challenge: Nietzsche *explicitly* claims that *political* exploitation can be
deduced as necessary to any society from the fact that life is *essentially*
will to power. "Even the body within which individuals treat each
other as equals," writes Nietzsche in *Beyond Good and Evil*,

> has to do to other bodies what the individuals within it refrain from doing
> to each other: it will have to be a corporal will to power, it will strive
> to grow, spread, seize, become predominant—not from any morality or
> immorality but because it is *living* and because life simply *is* will to power.
> But there is no point on which the ordinary consciousness of Europeans
> resists instruction as on this: everywhere people are now raving, even under
> scientific guises, about the coming conditions of society in which "the
> exploitative aspect" will be removed—which sounds to me as if they pro-
> mised to invent a way of life that would dispense with all organic functions.
> "Exploitation" does not belong to a corrupt or imperfect and primitive
> society: it belongs to the *essence* of what lives, which is after all the will of life.[49]

There is no mistaking Nietzsche's point: exploitation of one person
by another is ontologically rooted in life as such. Exploitative social
relations can be removed from society only at the expense of "life."
Since "life" is at the root of value, it follows that political exploitation
is both natural and perhaps even desirable.

If Nietzsche seems to want to justify a politics of domination on the basis of the will to power, one must ask whether—within the terms of his philosophical discourse—it is possible for him to do so. While it is quite clear that Nietzsche would *like* to explain political domination in terms of an essential will to domination, it seems to me that Nietzsche is not entitled to his own elaboration of the concept of will to power on three grounds stemming from his philosophy of power itself. The first is methodological, the second substantive, and the third valuative.

The methodological objection concerns the fact that when Nietzsche politically elaborates the concept of will to power, he does so metaphysically rather than critically. To use the concept metaphysically, as Nietzsche does in the above quotation, means to construe it as an essence from which empirical manifestations follow: in this case, political acts of domination are deduced from a posited essence of life. Since Nietzsche's political claims do involve such metaphysical uses of his concept of will to power, his procedure falls prey to the same kinds of criticisms he levels against the metaphysical tradition (see chapter 4).

The reason for troubling to distinguish between the respective methods of Nietzsche's philosophy and politics is, of course, that his metaphysics of domination is not particularly interesting except as an unfortunate historical fact that gave aid and comfort to the Nazis. Beyond this, reconstructing his metaphysics of domination according to what his politics demands is a waste of time: the result would be of little interest for questions of postmodern transitions. The important point here is that the will to power is interesting *only* if it is not just another metaphysic—for if it were, it would be a much less plausible one than the metaphysics of any number of other philosophers in the modern rationalist tradition. If the concept is not another metaphysic, then one would expect it to function differently than a metaphysic in Nietzsche's thinking. In fact, in most cases the concept of will to power does not play the metaphysical role it does in his political applications. Rather than denoting an essence from which events emerge, it denotes the conditions under which *all* human practices are possible, and not just that empirical class of events that involve political domination. If, as I have argued, the concept is *critical* in nature, it cannot be used to specify the substantive content of actions. The will to power can only specify what kinds of explanations of power are intelligible in terms of the possibility conditions of willing, but not the empirical content of specific acts of will. This is a matter for empirical or "genealogical" investigation guided by the universal conditions of practice as denoted by the will to power. Interpreting the will to power as a critical concept in this sense has the virtue of consistency with Nietzsche's overall philosophical project, while his own political elaborations of the concept do not. My argument here is that we can provide an unambiguously critical and postmodern account of Nietzsche's philosophy of power by showing that it is his assumptions about the nature of modern social organization—not about power—that lead to his development of the will to power as a metaphysics of domination at the expense of his philosophical project as a whole.

Still, as I suggested in chapter 4, one might argue a slightly weaker case concerning the conflict between Nietzsche's philosophy and politics, and still arrive at the same conclusions. One might argue that the conflict does indeed penetrate to the core of Nietzsche's philosophy of power, and that his politics merely exploits this conflict. It may be that there is a genuine conflict between modernist and postmodernist language in Nietzsche's concept of will to power that he never successfully resolves. It is possible that he was genuinely torn between a metaphysics of domination and one of affirming "life" because he was still caught in the modernist debate between those whose most basic concepts reflect a domination of nature (like Hobbes and Descartes) and their modernist critics who sought a harmony with nature (like Rousseau, as Nietzsche understood him). From a philosophical perspective, this may simply be a linguistic ambivalence, reflecting his own view that the world is neither as susceptible to mastery as some moderns have thought nor as susceptible to harmonization as the modernist critics of modernism tried to argue. If so, then one might argue (correctly, I think) that Nietzsche allowed his political predispositions to exploit the fact that he could not find language entirely suited to his postmodernist arguments. In this case as well, Nietzsche's politics would turn out to be underdetermined by his philosophy.

Perhaps the most convincing case to this effect is made by Ofelia Schutte.[50] Schutte argues that Nietzsche's philosophy of power includes both "liberating" and "repressive" features, and showing this allows her to account for Nietzsche's politics without doing violence to his philosophy. Still, Schutte's argument is not complete. While she demonstrates these conflicts in Nietzsche's philosophy of power more thoroughly than any commentator to date, she locates the problem in his failure to value the "totality of life." This is no doubt correct, but the question remains as to why Nietzsche should make this kind of "mistake" given his life-affirming philosophy. After all, his politics *systematically* draws on the will to power as a modernist metaphysics of domination—and this cannot be explained solely by looking at conflicts within Nietzsche's philosophy of power itself. Thus, while Schutte follows the traditional method of seeking a unique determination of Nietzsche's politics in his philosophy, I follow a different method by looking for the constraints that Nietzsche's (insupportable) assumptions about society place on his interpretations of the political consequences of his philosophy of power. He understood the political possibilities of contemporary society so narrowly that he systematically exploited the ambivalences in his philosophy of power in a way that it seemed to support a politics of domination.

Before turning directly to these assumptions, why would Nietzsche *not* have been alert to the methodological divergence between his philosophy and politics? As I suggested at the beginning of this chapter, part of the reason is that he systematically conflates "exploitation," "overpowering," "command," and the like as attributes of individual organization of action with attributes of social and political organization, that is, with relations between individuals. Nietzsche consistently uses political metaphors to describe the way that *any* action must be organized. In this way, he follows the well-established practice in political philosophy from Plato through Hobbes of equating the organization of the soul with that of society, and society with soul. For example, in an aphorism on which I relied heavily in chapter 4 for Nietzsche's analysis of willing, we read that, in the process of willing,

the person exercising volition adds the feelings of delight of his successful executive instruments, the useful "underwills" or undersouls—indeed, our body is but a social structure composed of many souls—to his feeling of delight as a commander. *L'effet c'est moi*: what happens here is what happens in every well-constructed commonwealth, namely, the governing class identifies itself with the successes of the commonwealth. In all willing it is absolutely a question of commanding and obeying, on the basis, as already said, of a social structure composed of many "souls." [51]

Nietzsche's equation of society and organism is quite clear here, and its significance is twofold.

First, while there is certainly no problem in using such metaphors for characterizing processes of willing, Nietzsche then uses them in other places to deduce attributes of social organization as if they had some kind of explanatory power outside of his analysis of willing.[52] The same terms are used to cover quite different kinds of processes— but Nietzsche only provides an analysis of one of them, willing. He quite reasonably suggests, for example, that acting involves an organized hierarchy of functions that work together as a whole to form an action. He also notes that actions involve imposing form and order, and that therefore "life" irreducibly involves violence. Again, in itself, the point is quite a reasonable one: creating a house, for example, requires "violence" against trees. An argument involves an intention to "destroy" an opponent's opinions and cause him or her to form new ones. And, as Lenin once observed in justifying violence in revolutions, "You can't make an omelette without breaking eggs." Of course. Both Nietzsche and Lenin, however, use these analogies to cover processes that are in fact quite different. They extend their points about the organization of actions to social organization. They transform the notion that some kinds of violence are intrinsic to any creative process into a political proposition.

Lenin probably knew better, but Nietzsche apparently did not: his analogies have every appearance of being unthinking and naive. But if modern social theory has learned anything, it is that the organization *of* individual actions and that of relations *between* individual actions are two different things, even if they are also interdependent. These kinds of organization are reciprocal, but not identical. Adam Smith, for example, was surely right in noting that individual intentions to maximize satisfaction produce market effects that no one intends. Marx developed a theory of class structure on the same kind of insight: the intentions of capitalists to gain a return from the property they control reproduce class structures in ways they may not even understand, let alone intend. Durkheim noticed that the social functions of actions might be quite different from their individual ones. The point here is not that Smith, Marx, Durkheim, or any number of other modern social thinkers produced adequate ways of thinking about the relationship between the life-world and social organization, but rather that Nietzsche fails even to conceptualize the relationship, let alone see it as a problematic. This is important, because it is precisely his failure to do so that allows him to equate individual and social qualities, and to use the same terms ("exploitation" and the like) to "explain" both.

Second, if one removes the necessity that Nietzsche imposes on social organizations through this analogy, then one can find no other good arguments in his writings to show that the relationship between people in a social organization must be one of domination. This is not to say that no such arguments exist (Max Weber, for example, argues this case at length by examining the imperatives of organizational rationalization), but only that Nietzsche does not make them, and that they do not follow from his actual analysis of agency. Indeed, if one were to draw out many of Nietzsche's suggestions about *how* power is organized as agency, one could just as well make the opposite case. I suggested in chapter 2, for example, that Nietzsche's thinking contains elements that describe and support a positive egalitarianism. In his middle period, a few of his comments indicate that he entertained the possibility that strongly formed individual wills are fully consistent with egalitarian relations between individuals, on the condition that they emerge out of a political culture consisting in mutually agreed upon rights and duties. In chapter 5, I argued that Nietzsche's "sovereign individual" would be consistent with a morality based upon the universality of self-reflective motives, should one choose to elaborate his ideals in this way.

Together, these strains in Nietzsche's thinking suggest that will to power as an organized capacity for action is not inconsistent with social and political equality, simply because the universal motive identified by the concept of will to power is not domination but self-constitution. Under some—even most—historical conditions, the self-constitution of some individuals may turn out to be incompatible with that of others. This would not be a question of the incompatibility of will to power and social and political equality as such, but rather a question of the organization of will to power under the constraints of particular historical circumstances. Thus while it might be absurd, as Nietzsche puts it, "to demand of strength that it should *not* express itself as strength," it is in no way at odds with a highly organized will to power that this be the strength of the sovereign individual. Then "a desire to overcome, a desire to throw down, a desire to become master" might be cultivated as the free will of responsibility.[53] It is true that Nietzsche's historical examples of highly organized will to power often involve political domination—as with Julius Caesar, for example.[54] Nonetheless his future vision of strength is not Caesar, but "Caesar with Christ's soul." [55] Thus one finds that *even* in Nietzsche's terms, individual strength need not imply political domination—assuming one corrects for his metaphysical uses of the will to power and his misleading analogies between individual and social organization.

The same claim can be put in positive terms. Nietzsche thought that the individuality and freedom of some individuals is necessarily incompatible with that of others. But his affirmation of the individual can be elaborated in social and political terms other than those he actually advanced. The possibility of alternative elaborations stems in part from the fact that Nietzsche, like Marx, sees individuality as a social and cultural achievement. In chapter 2, for example, I attempted to show that Nietzsche does not hypostatize the individual against society. Rather he views society as a necessary condition for the formation of individuals—through language, culture, and the "discipline" of life lived with other beings —even though the identities and values of individuals can and should transcend their social origins. Thus even in Nietzsche's own terms aspects of community have value as essential means to self-constitution—a value that, as Georg Simmel pointed out, goes far beyond his political claim that community is valuable to "higher" individuals only as a base upon which they can stand.[56]

These sociological considerations suggest a response to the valuative objection to Nietzsche's concept of will to power. This objection concerns his apparent inability to derive from it any standards of political conduct. According to this argument, even if one could not show that the concept does not postulate a necessary will to domination, it nonetheless fails to provide any criteria for right conduct because of its radically historicist character. By setting himself against metaphysical moral principles, Nietzsche has in effect deprived us of any grounds on which to judge existing regimes. The will to power would thus implicitly provide reasons for leaving prevailing forms of domination as they are.[57]

Nietzsche did, however, regard the concept of will to power as grounds for judgment of value in general. This means that his philosophy affirms some values and not others. These in turn provide grounds for judging social and political arrangements, even if

Nietzsche himself did not elaborate these grounds or perhaps even intend them. That this is so can be seen by surveying the political values emerging from Nietzsche's philosophy of power taken by itself. Power has value for Nietzsche insofar as it is self-reflectively individuated, or organized as subjectivity. Only individuals are the sorts of things that can experience power as value. This is why Nietzsche views "sovereign" individuality—an individuality with the qualities of autonomy and responsibility—as having the capacity for the highest experiences of value.[58] A logically entailed value is the positive freedom of the individual, that is, the individual's capacity for extending a "will" into the future.[59] If Nietzsche had chosen to judge societies on the grounds of his philosophy of power alone, then, he would have done so in terms of their capacities to enable the positive freedom of individuals.

Nietzsche's view of judgment as I presented it in chapter 3 suggests that politicizing a criterion such as this is quite consistent with his philosophy. For Nietzsche, value judgments are intrinsic aspects of self-constituting practices, and relative to them. This does not mean that value judgments are arbitrary, or that it is impossible in a given context to distinguish better and worse judgments. On Nietzsche's account, better judgments about actions will be based upon an ontological hypothesis (the will to power) empirically articulated as knowledge (by means of genealogy). These considerations open up the possibility—again, one not developed or perhaps even intended by Nietzsche—that, when the exigencies of action are *social* in nature, one might quite rationally act on the basis of an ontological hypothesis and knowledge suited to the social world. A consistent development of this possibility would be as follows: a social world consists of a set of beings that gain their self-identities through intersubjectively situated practices—that is, through a constant (if not always conscious) recognition of others through culture, language, and practice. As a whole, these exigencies form an intersubjective fabric that provides a condition of the subjectivity of individuals—that is, of the organization of their powers as agency. Subjectivity thus implies that culture has a value as a condition of one's own agency, as Nietzsche himself makes quite clear (see chapter 2). But culture is not something apart from human actions: it is itself a fabric of value judgments. Valuing culture thus implies valuing the agents that reproduce culture, and this in turn implies valuing individuals as communicative agents. Nietzsche's terms of analysis do not allow for the possibility of subjects without communicative intersubjectivity, and intersubjectivity is not possible without a community of subjects. In this way, Nietzsche's understanding of practice as will to power implies—indeed requires—valuing intersubjectivity as a condition of power as agency. It follows that his philosophy of power could be developed, if one wished to do so, to include criteria involving a respect for others. The concept implicitly values a community of agents and this in turn provides standards for judging political conduct.

I extended these considerations in chapter 4 to show how Nietzsche derives the will to power as an ontological hypothesis to serve as a rational ground for judgments. Of course, any attempt to make the will to power a principle of practical reason in Kant's sense is absent in Nietzsche. Indeed, he often dismisses such principles as pernicious to the possibility of individual, autonomous, responsible action. Still, as I pointed out in chapter 5, if one wished to develop the concept of will to power as a critical ontology of practice, it would involve the claim that *all* humans are motivated by the need for self-experiences of agency. This universal claim is implied not only in the concept of will to power but also in Nietzsche's problematic of nihilism: *only* reflexive beings can experience nihilism, and much of Nietzsche's philosophy is an attempt to conceptualize this reflexivity so that nihilism can be understood and resolved. Moreover, Nietzsche suggests that *all* people have the capacity to experience nihilism, although it is only in European cultures that it has become a crisis (see chapter 1). This single universal—the reflexive need for subjectivity—stands as the possible grounds of a Nietzschean social and political morality.

Interestingly, the implicit value that Nietzsche's philosophy places on individuation within community is reinforced by his view that statements about the world are meaningful only in relation to practice. Because his philosophy of truth is pluralistic, it conflicts with every instance of what we would today call "social engineering," the application of knowledge to persons construed as objects. Of all commentators, only Foucault has appreciated this political implication of Nietzsche's thought—but without developing the insight.[60] For Nietzsche, meaningfulness is a quality that truth claims about the world gain from constituting subjectivity (see chapter 3). Since Nietzsche construes the meaningfulness of claims in terms of their effect in constituting individuals under different conditions of life, one might extend his logic to conclude that truth claims about human matters are not the sorts of claims that could be imposed politically without losing their meaningfulness. In contrast, when truth claims are viewed as neutral discoveries, they enter into practices as a means of manipulating a world of objects. When knowledge of the social world is viewed in this way, humans become subjected to truth claims, rather than being subjects of truth claims. The ontology of the social world that accompanies the view of truth as neutral discovery misses the reflexivity of human objects, and this means that humans are seen as objects of manipulation like any other object in the world. For this reason, the notion that truth about the human world is something that exists apart from reflexive practices, and that it can be discovered and politically applied, is inherently manipulative and latently authoritarian.

Yet such notions are common in Western political philosophies: they are expressed in Plato's *Republic* with its strata of politically empowered philosophers who engineer a *polis* on the basis of their knowledge of the Good. They existed in the political hegemony of the Catholic Church: by claiming to have privileged access to the truth required for salvation, its priests could manipulate the subjectivity of church followers. Such notions exist today in liberal-bureaucratic as well as in fascist and state-socialist regimes that practice social engineering. And they are expressed in the claims of Leninist parties to be vanguards of revolution on the basis of a superior knowledge of history. Each political application of truth claims destroys the intersubjective process of making truth claims upon which subjectivity depends, and thus destroys the individuation that Nietzsche values. Although Nietzsche did not develop his insights in these directions, his refusal to construe truth as something independent of practices leads, as Foucault intuits, to a sensitivity to the relation between conceptions of truth as something that can be discovered and applied in social relations, and politically authoritarian and totalitarian practices. Put in slightly different terms, Nietzsche's conception of truth is inconsistent with the potential totalitarianism stemming from what Hannah Arendt has called politics construed on the model of making—the fabrication of a political sphere through the application of ideas, a model she opposes to the necessarily pluralistic model based on the good of acting itself.[61]

Nietzsche did not develop the pluralistic implications of his philosophy of truth. He followed instead the ancient aristocratic idea that "the best should rule, the best should also want to rule. And where the doctrine is different, the best is *lacking*." [62] By arguing for an aristocracy of philosopher-rulers, Nietzsche reproduced the long-standing connection between a view of truth as something that can be politically applied without losing its quality of being "true" and a view of persons as objects of those applications. In reproducing this connection, however, Nietzsche once again misunderstood the innovative political implications of his philosophy.

Division of Labor: Uncritical Assumptions

The key to understanding Nietzsche's actual political positions is not in his philosophy of power as such, but rather in his misunderstanding of essential features of modern society. This caused him to misconstrue the limits of social and political organization, as well as to distort the causes of modern nihilism. His misunderstandings appear in the form of three assumptions that are sufficient to determine his politics, as well as to explain why he injected into his concept of will to power a metaphysical content fundamentally at odds with his postmodernist project.

The first of these assumptions is that cultures of a sufficient quality to individuate power require an institutionalized division of cultural and economic labor in society. Even if Nietzsche had held that politics should secure the conditions of self-constitution for everyone, he would have seen this ideal as impossibly utopian owing to the constraints of material necessity: human life is possible only through economically productive but dehumanizing labor. Simply securing physical survival, according to Nietzsche, requires that any society must both organize these dehumanizing economic tasks and provide an ideological justification. Nietzsche explains in a note that

the lawgiver (or the instinct of society) selects a number of states of affects through whose operation a regularity in performance is guaranteed (namely, a mechanical performance as a consequence of the regular requirements of those affects and states).

Supposing that these states and affects contain painful ingredients; then a means must be found to overcome these painful ingredients through a value-idea designed to make displeasure seem valuable and therefore pleasurable in a higher sense. Reduced to a formula: "How can something disagreeable become agreeable?" For example, when our obedience, our submission to the law, attains honor through the strength, power, self-overcoming that they entail. As does our consideration for the community, the neighbor, the fatherland, our "humanization," our "altruism," "heroism": That one should like to do disagreeable things—that is the object of ideals.[63]

Since any society is founded upon the performance of a large number of mechanical, monotonous, and distasteful tasks, the first demand of culture is not to be a means of realizing higher human powers but simply to justify the performance of these tasks, and in this way ensure the reproduction of society. This is why Nietzsche claims that "I attempt an *economic* justification of virtue.—The task is to make man as useful as possible and to approximate him, as far as possible, to an infallible machine: to this end he must be equipped with the virtues of the machine. . . ."[64] Thus for Nietzsche the primary social demand of culture is an ideological one. As far as he is concerned, however, this outcome reflects natural constraints on social organization about which nothing can be done.

But because for Nietzsche the end of politics is not to secure mere physical survival but rather to secure a life with the meaning that stems from individuated power, there must be room in a good society for a few individuals to escape the burdens of labor: "A higher culture can come into being only where there are two castes of society: the working caste and the idle caste, capable of true leisure; or, to express it more emphatically, the caste of forced labor and the caste of free labor."[65] That such a higher culture exist is not only valuable in itself, but is also a functional requirement for any society that would maintain an ideological justification of its division of labor. The culture that the few "higher" types would produce as a condition and expression of their individuality must also serve to legitimate a class-divided society; it must be such that it can be consumed as ideology by the laboring classes. As suggested in chapter 2, the Greeks of the tragic age provided Nietzsche with an ideal example of political culture. The political secret of Greek tragic culture, he thought, could be found in the functional balance between its classes of slaves, laborers, and other economic producers and its citizen-warrior aristocracy. Members of the dominant class possessed the capacity to

produce culture that not only justified their existences but also justified vicariously the lives of those subject to their rule.

With respect to these needs, Nietzsche believed modern societies
to be in precisely the same situation as ancient Greek societies. "To
what extent every strengthened species of man hitherto has stood
upon a level of the lower. . . ." [66] This assumption accounts for at least
one kind of limit to politics that led Nietzsche to propose a new
aristocracy of "genuine philosophers" in the place of an apparently
impossible liberal democratic society. The new aristocracy would
rest on the labors of the many. [67] The political life of the few philo-
sopher-aristocrats would be regulated by mutual agreement—as in
the Greek *polis* at its height. These same few would constitute a new
kind of "state" for the many, one that would expropriate the conditions of their individuality that they might be made "useful." "The
essential characteristic of a good and healthy aristocracy," writes
Nietzsche in *Beyond Good and Evil*, "is that it experience itself *not* as a
function (whether of the monarchy or the commonwealth) but as
their meaning and highest justification—that it therefore accepts
with a good conscience the sacrifice of untold human beings who, *for
its own sake*, must be suppressed and diminished to incomplete human
beings, to slaves, to instruments." [68] Such aristocracies, according to
Nietzsche, can justify the subordination of the lower classes because
they can give "meaning"—although not that which flows from
power as agency—to each and every social function in terms of
the ultimate value of its higher types. This is why he takes the position of the conservative critic of culture in viewing Europe's "labor
problem" as one in which liberals, socialists, and democrats, acting
on unfounded optimism, have given unfulfillable expectations to the
working classes. Rather than promising equality for the working
classes, they ought to attend to the cultural problem of assigning
meaning to the worker's station. In the final analysis, concluded
Nietzsche, modern Europe demands such a solution if *any* individuals
are to achieve a "higher state of being." One must conclude that, in
Nietzsche's terms, only for these few would nihilism no longer be a
possibility.

Taking into account Nietzsche's understanding of the economic
limits to politics, then, we should not be surprised that he arrives at
the perverse conclusion that the "mediocritization" of Europe is a
desirable trend. In stark contrast to his desire to be the Raphael of

philosophy, Nietzsche concludes that it is both possible and necessary that the range of capacities of individuals should come to match the kind of enslavement to productive activity required by higher culture. "The dwarfing of man must for a long time count as the only goal, because a broad foundation has first to be created so that a stronger species of man can stand on it."[69] One should note that Nietzsche's political vision differs from the postliberal totalitarianism that he feared only in that his new aristocracy serves a higher culture rather than military or economic ends. In this respect his political ideal is continuous with the aesthetic-cultural ideology of fascism.

Human Nature: Uncritical Assumptions

Even if Nietzsche had attended more critically to his assumptions about the division of cultural and economic labor in society, they would not have been likely to trouble him owing to another assumption concerning the pervasiveness of "weakness" in the modern period. The vast majority in Western cultures were in Nietzsche's estimation incapable of grasping the opportunities for individuated power presented by the dissolution of Christian-moral culture. The majority seemed likely to remain in a "herd" condition, and to continue to have their powers displaced by modern institutions. Indeed, that contemporary culture reflected mass values was an ever-present danger to "higher" types, and for Nietzsche this alone was reason to condemn all institutions open to mass participation— including parliamentary processes, voting, and democratic and socialist movements.[70]

Nietzsche believed that the weakness threatening Western societies had to be seen in "physiological" rather than social and political terms. But because he viewed human nature as something that could be molded by cultural and political forces over time, he could not argue that *innately* higher and lower types exist. However, he could and did hold that at any time *historically evolved* human natures exist that include great inequalities of biological capacity. These inequalities, Nietzsche believed, determined the historically existent range of capacities available for any future politics.

Nietzsche's concept of "race" encapsulates his understanding of the historical development of biological capacities. He does not assume that biological capacity is fixed within a "race," but rather—in a Lamarckian manner—assumes that a "race" evolves by means of physiological transmission of acquired attributes. He attempts to account for the continuity of weakness by assuming that past experiences of powerlessness together with culturally acquired traits become physiological over time, and are transmitted to future generations by physiological mechanisms. The "problem of race," claims Nietzsche, resides in the fact that it "is simply not possible that a human being should *not* have the qualities and preferences of his parents and ancestors in his body, whatever appearances may suggest to the contrary." [71] At most, he continues, one may attempt to deceive "about one's origins, the inherited plebs in one's body and soul." A "plebeian nature" is fixed once acquired, and always passed on as "corrupted blood." Nietzsche seems to think of the "weak"—the majority in the contemporary era—as a "race" in precisely this sense. [72] They are the ones who are "*schlectweggekommen*": they have been "badly wrought" by history. What was once a "political" condition of weakness, Nietzsche asserts in a note, has become a "physiological" condition. [73]

Outside of the fact that Nietzsche's view of race is biologically untenable, it has an unfortunate political implication. Because Nietzsche sees the biological aspects of human nature to be subject to relatively rapid change according to altered conditions of existence, he views the biological capacities of human nature as quite fluid. If human capacities are fluid *biologically*, then in principle it would be possible for all human potential—that is, all potential given by genetically inherited attributes—to be lost to future generations. The unfortunate political implication follows from the biological one: Nietzsche absolutizes the "weak" as a biologically fixed presence at any point in history. Once weakness becomes the attribute of a race or class, Nietzsche sees the potential for strength in this race or class as biologically absent. Thus there is nothing to be done for either those who are *schlectweggekommen* or their progeny. Power cannot be restored to the weak, now or in the future. At best, they might be made "useful" to the strong; at worst, their "self-destruction" is desirable. [74]

I point to Nietzsche's view of biological determination not only to show how it underwrites his politics, but also because I think it is quite unnecessary to the integrity of his philosophy as a whole. Nietzsche's own concept of will to power provides an alternative approach to explaining the historical reproduction of "weakness." Viewed in the perspective of the will to power, one need not see weakness as the result of an alteration of the physiological bases of human nature, but rather as a result of a particular historical organization of culture and experience that merely exploits biological and self-reflective needs in a way that weakens action by dislocating subjectivity.

The Causes of Modern Nihilism: Uncritical Assumptions

That Nietzsche explains the pervasiveness of weakness in the modern period ultimately in terms of a misplaced biological assumption is not accidental. It stems from the fact that he possessed only the most rudimentary notion of modern social and political relations, and therefore lacked other explanations sufficient to the nihilism in modern societies that he both observed and feared. Nietzsche recognized political power relations only in two forms: overt oppression, as in master-slave relations, and in the more ideological form of priestly power. Understanding political power as combination of material force and cultural exclusion is probably adequate for many ancient master/slave societies. Thus one might expect Nietzsche's explanation of the nihilism and passivity of ancient slaves to be adequate, at least on a theoretical plane. Likewise, since Nietzsche possessed an intricate understanding of the cultural organization of power, we might expect his account of the hidden nihilism of Christian societies to be quite good, since culture is a dominant organizing principle in such societies. But he lacked the conceptual apparatus to grasp fully the causes of nihilism and weakness in the modern period—a period in which, at least in Nietzsche's Europe, neither master-slave relations nor Christianity were dominant organizers of social and political life. Thus as Christianity receded and master-slave relations were nowhere to be seen, Nietzsche was forced to account for mass society in terms of a constitutional alteration of human nature by Christianity. Because he lacked the concepts necessary to explain power in modern societies, he assumed that weakness, passivity, mediocrity, and massification could only be explained in "physiological" terms. It followed that any political solution to nihilism would have to flow from the few "higher" types not "ruined" by Christianity. A political solution would have to make cultural renewal its first objective. It could neither afford sentimentality regarding the ruined masses nor allow liberal, democratic, or other "herd" institutions to express their mediocrity against the new flowering of "higher" types made possible by the demise of Christian culture.[75]

As I have suggested, Nietzsche did not have categories that allowed him to understand modern organizers of social and political life such as markets and bureaucracies. In contrast to Marx, he did not understand that relations of political power are reproduced by market mechanisms not requiring overt political oppression. In contrast to Weber, he did not understand the manner in which bureaucratic organizations can attain a subtle power and life of their own, likewise perpetuating individual experiences of powerlessness and producing individual "weakness."

These points are important for how we interpret Nietzsche's own problematic of nihilism: what he missed is that markets and bureaucracies reproduce experiences of powerlessness for many people, even though they are not directly victimized by force. Exactly this kind of experience is the cause of the nihilism of the slave—a nihilism I referred to in chapter 1 as "original nihilism." Because he could not identify modern mechanisms of power, Nietzsche believed that original nihilism no longer existed in Europe, and that European nihilism was a manifestation of inherited weakness combined with cultural collapse. The problem in Nietzsche's assessment is this: if relations of power can be identified that reproduce *experiences of powerlessness in social and political situations*, then he would have failed to understand the actual reasons for the European nihilism *in his own terms*, even though he could both conceptualize and observe the phenomenon itself. If he failed to diagnose correctly the causes of nihilism, then his political solutions will have missed their mark.

If Nietzsche's politics suffers from his failure to grasp the social and political realities of contemporary Western societies, his philosophy of agency is nonetheless quite consistent with theories that do take such realities into account. His concept of will to power suggests that practices must be explained as a conjunction of situated experience, cultural interpretations, and self-reflective needs. This approach serves Nietzsche well in the *Genealogy* where he considers the political relation of master and slave. The power relation itself is transparent, and it is relatively easy to see how it generates specific kinds of experience for the slave. This in turn allows Nietzsche to explain the nihilism of the slave as a political phenomenon within a particular interpretive nexus.

Power relations in contemporary Western societies, however, are rarely so transparent owing to the fact that they work to a large extent through markets and bureaucracies. Because Nietzsche did not understand the dynamics of these kinds of organizations, he assumed that social relations of power no longer generated the kinds of experiences that might cause original nihilism. The fact that overt political tyranny was relatively rare in late-nineteenth-century Europe led him to conclude that modern nihilism and its attending "weakness" would have to be explained in cultural terms, from which he ultimately drew his biological conclusions. But Nietzsche asks too much of his concepts of culture and biology in providing the account of modern nihilism that he does. His analysis misses the way in which modern forms of social organization continue to generate oppressive experiences with the potential to reproduce original nihilism—the nihilism with social and political causes. Economic markets, for example, produce systematic effects on the basis of politically enforced and culturally sanctioned patterns of property ownership. Nietzsche believed, as even Weber did not, that contemporary economic behavior could be accounted for in terms of European culture, which he saw as the sole force behind individual motives to pursue economic ends. Although it is certainly true, as Weber argued, that cultural elements are necessary conditions for explaining economic behavior—especially those assigning meaning to instrumental modes of conduct—they are not sufficient conditions.[76] Culture by itself, for example, does not explain the necessity that the capitalist contract with labor at a rate such that the proceeds of the product are more than the combined costs of labor, materials, and capital. Nor does culture explain the kind of necessity experienced by a worker who must sell his or her labor in order to survive. Yet the experiences and life chances of most individuals in market societies are structured by these kinds of necessities. Even though Nietzsche's problematic requires that he conceptualize these necessities, and even though his analysis of agency would be consistent with them, he nonetheless fails to do so.

The compatibility between Nietzsche's analysis of agency and the conceptions of structural necessities required to complete his analysis can be emphasized by putting the same point in slightly different terms. The willed actions of individuals in contemporary market societies are organized by physical imperatives of nature and cultural orientations in a way that individual actions give rise to systematic social outcomes—of which regularities of exchange, supply and demand, and accumulation of capital are examples. The political aspects of such systematic outcomes reside in the distribution of economic power determined by ownership and management of means of production. This in turn systematically generates classes of experience according to positions individuals occupy in the structure of ownership and control. In terms of the methodological demands of Nietzsche's concept of will to power, economic actions would have to be accounted for in terms of systematically generated experiences together with individuals' interpretive orientations toward them. Thus because these actions are historically specific organizations of culture and experience, they are *conceivable* in terms of the concept of will to power even if Nietzsche does not in fact conceive of them. Similar methodological points hold with regard to Nietzsche's failure to grasp bureaucratic phenomena—the tendency for instrumentally rational modes of conduct to take an institutionalized form and thus become ends in themselves.[77]

Nietzsche knew the symptoms and distinguished between different causes of nihilism, but because he lacked an understanding of modern social organizations he could not always tell which causes were operative. Although nihilism appears in modern Western societies as a universal phenomenon, even in Nietzsche's terms its causes are likely to be dependent upon classes of experience, classes given by the life-situations of individuals in society. European nihilism proper—the nihilism of cultural eclipse—would be more likely to appear among more privileged classes. Original nihilism—the nihilism of social powerlessness—would be more likely to appear among those subject to political and economic relations of domination. Somewhat ironically, even if Nietzsche's new aristocracy would cure the European nihilism of the privileged few, it would deepen original nihilism for most by adding new experiences of powerlessness to those already reproduced by markets and bureaucracies.[78] If Nietzsche's misunderstanding of power relations in modern societies led him to extend his cultural logic far beyond its proper domain of explanation, he did so at the cost of recommending a political solution that would condemn the largest part of society to precisely the nihilism he intended his philosophy to combat.[79]

The effect of Nietzsche's attempt to elaborate modern nihilism as a cultural and biological phenomenon ultimately shows up in his failure to find a political agent for his philosophy. In Nietzsche's view, so pervasive were the effects of Christian-moral culture that the *Übermensch* is merely imaginable for him—but not identifiable—in the aftermath of cultural dissolution. He could not see how the possibilities of self-constituting practice might relate to the situations of actual individuals because he turned the combined effects of a nihilistic culture and experiences of powerlessness into a biological fate.

Although Nietzsche's misunderstanding of the economic and bureaucratic determinants of modern experience is not overwhelmingly important for the philosophical and theoretical nature of his overall undertaking, it does have important implications for the political conclusions one is able to draw from it. Were one to supplement Nietzsche's thought here, one would want to explain the pervasive lack of individuated will to power that he correctly discerned in Western societies not only in terms of culture and cultural eclipse but also in terms of systematically generated classes of political experience. This would then suggest that nihilism is a social and political problem as well as a cultural one, and would in turn suggest social and political solutions. Supplementing Nietzsche's analysis in this way remains consistent with his understanding of the ontology and structure of nihilism, although not with his specific diagnoses.

Conclusion

My argument in this chapter has been that Nietzsche did not give his own philosophy a plausible political identity. He failed to elaborate the broad range of political possibilities that are suggested by his philosophy in large part owing to unexamined assumptions about the nature of modern politics. Some of these assumptions contravene the strictures of his own philosophy. Others are empirically unfounded or inappropriate to modern societies. While Nietzsche certainly incorporated into his political philosophy other kinds of assumptions, identifying these few is sufficient to show that accepting his philosophy entails accepting his political philosophy if and only if one also accepts these assumptions as they come to bear on modern politics. But of course we need not and ought not accept these assumptions since they are not very good ones. If we do not accept them, then we shall have in some sense freed Nietzsche's philosophy from its political straitjacket. We can in this way allow ourselves to accept the most rigorous and inspired aspects of his philosophy—those of his critically postmodern philosophy of power. Precisely this area is underdeveloped in contemporary political thought, suggesting that it is worthwhile to reconstruct Nietzsche's philosophy in those areas in which it achieves rigorous concreteness, and to provide it with a political identity.

If one wished to go further, to supplement Nietzsche's insights with a positive political vision, a vision consistent with his problematic, it would include the values of individuation, communal intersubjectivity, egalitarianism, and pluralism. It would be *individualistic* in that experiences of individual agency—the power of the individual over his or her future—would be the goal of a good polity. Because individuation cannot occur in isolation, this goal implies the complementary value of *communal intersubjectivity*, the space within which humans become individuals. Individuation, in other words, is in many ways a collective achievement. The fabric of intersubjectivity that sustains individuals in turn implies the value of *equality*—not a leveling equality, but a vibrant equality based on an equal respect for persons and the conditions of their personhood. Failure to value equality in this sense leads to exploitative relations that destroy the intersubjective reciprocity upon which a Nietzschean strength ultimately depends. Finally, a good polity would be *pluralistic* precisely because positive equality does not imply sameness, nor does Nietzsche's philosophy permit the kind of interpretive authority that could enforce a sameness.

These four political values are not those Nietzsche affirmed, but they would represent a consistent extension of his philosophy into politics. For this reason, it is a mistake to ask if these values represent the *real* Nietzsche. They represent *one* Nietzsche, the Nietzsche who has something to contribute to the development of critical postmodernism in political thought. Whether this Nietzsche becomes more or less interesting in the future will depend to a large extent on whether the values of his philosophy can gain a political identity in Western societies. This remains an open question: there are countless political problems that would impinge on these ideals, problems that

Nietzsche's philosophy is not equipped to conceptualize and address. Some are organizational questions, such as those having to do with imperatives of scale. Some are economic questions about the technological imperatives of advanced industrial societies. Still others are political questions about strategies of organization. Each of these questions suggests social imperatives that may in fact undermine individuality, reciprocity, equality, and pluralism in social relations. But here we are beyond Nietzsche: while he may have intuited some of these problems and limits, he does not even begin an analysis.

What Nietzsche's philosophy *does* capture is a real movement of cultural change and dissolution—one that has had political implications and will continue to do so in the future. Nietzsche is the philosopher who thought about individuated self-identities, and who placed his hopes in them. The values of self-identity are gradually becoming more important in the politics of Western societies. These are values that shift away from the zero-sum and ecologically insensitive materialistic values of market societies, and toward mutually attainable postmaterial and postmodern values, values oriented toward a meaningful and dignified existence rather than simply toward material comforts and rewards. The political future of Nietzsche's philosophy lies in this transition.

Nietzsche's Works and
Key to Abbreviations

All references to Nietzsche's works consist of an abbreviation for the German title, followed by numbers denoting the section, essay, aphorism, or page, depending upon the arrangement of the specific work. Abbreviations and bibliographic information follow J. Daniel Breazeale's, in his collection of Nietzsche's early notes, *Philosophy and Truth*, pp. lxvii–lxix.

A. Books Published or Prepared for Publication by Nietzsche

GT   *Die Geburt der Tragödie* (*The Birth of Tragedy*), 1872; second slightly altered ed., 1874; third ed., with a new preface, 1886. The number following the title abbreviation denotes the section in which the reference is to be found.

UBa   *Unzeitgemässe Betrachtungen. Erstes Stück: David Strauss, der Bekenner und der Schriftsteller* (*Untimely Meditations. First Part: David Strauss, the Confessor and the Writer*), 1873. The number following the title abbreviation denotes the section in which the reference is to be found.

UBb   ———. *Zweites Stück: Vom Nutzen und Nachteil der Historie für das Leben.* (*Second Part: On the Uses and Disadvantages of History for Life*), 1874. The number following the title abbreviation denotes the section in which the reference is to be found.

UBc   ———. *Drittes Stück: Schopenhauer als Erzieher* (*Third Part: Schopenhauer as Educator*), 1874. The number following

	the title abbreviation denotes the section in which the reference is to be found.
UBd	———. *Viertes Stück: Richard Wagner in Bayreuth (Fourth Part: Richard Wagner in Bayreuth)*, 1876. The number following the title abbreviation denotes the section in which the reference is to be found.
MAMa	*Menschliches, Allzumenschliches. Erster Band (Human, All-Too-Human. Volume One)*, 1878; second ed. with a new preface, 1886. The number following the title abbreviation denotes the aphorism in which the reference is to be found.
MAMb	———. *Zweiter Band. Erste Abteilung: Vermischte Meinungen und Sprüche (Volume Two. First Section: Assorted Opinions and Sayings)*, 1879; second ed. with MAMc and a new preface, 1886. The number following the title abbreviation denotes the aphorism in which the reference is to be found.
MAMc	———. *Zweiter Band. Zweite Abteilung: Der Wanderer und sein Schatten (Volume Two. Second Section: The Wanderer and His Shadow)*, 1880; second ed. with MAMb and a new preface, 1886. The number following the title abbreviation denotes the aphorism in which the reference is to be found.
M	*Morgenröte (Daybreak)*, 1881; second ed. with a new preface, 1887. The number following the title abbreviation denotes the aphorism in which the reference is to be found.
FW	*Die fröhliche Wissenschaft (The Gay Science)*, 1882; second ed. with substantial additions and a new preface, 1886. The number following the title abbreviation denotes the aphorism in which the reference is to be found.
Z	*Also Sprach Zarathustra (Thus Spoke Zarathustra)*, Part One, 1883; Part Two, 1883; Part Three, 1884; Part Four, privately published, 1885. References are cited by the titles of the sections in which they are found.
JGB	*Jenseits von Gut und Böse (Beyond Good and Evil)*, 1886. The number following the title abbreviation denotes the aphorism in which the reference is to be found.

GM	*Zur Genealogie der Moral* (*On the Genealogy of Morals*), 1887. The Roman numeral following the title abbreviation denotes the essay in which the reference is to be found. The number following the Roman numeral denotes the section within the essay in which the reference is to be found.
W	*Der Fall Wagner* (*The Case of Wagner*), 1888. The number following the title abbreviation denotes the section in which the reference is to be found.
GD	*Götzen-Dammerung* (*Twilight of the Idols*), prepared for publication 1888; first ed., 1889. The first number following the title abbreviation denotes the section in which the reference is to be found; the second number, separated by a colon, denotes the aphorism within which the reference is to be found. I have numbered the sections as follows:

Preface	Vorwort (Preface)
1	Sprüche und Pfeile ("Maxims and Arrows")
2	Das Problem des Sokrates ("The Problem of Socrates")
3	Die "Vernunft" in der Philosophie ("'Reason' in Philosophy")
4	Wie die "wahre Welt" endlich zur Fabel wurde ("How the 'True World' Finally Became a Fable")
5	Moral als Widernatur ("Morality as Anti-nature")
6	Die vier grossen Irrtümer ("The Four Great Errors")
7	Die "Verbesserer" der Menschheit ("The 'Improvers' of Mankind")
8	Was den Deutschen abgeht ("What the Germans Lack")
9	Streifzüge eines Unzeitgemässen ("Skirmishes of an Untimely Man")
10	Was ich den Alten verdanke ("What I Owe the Ancients")
11	Der Hammer redet ("The Hammer Speaks")

NCW   *Nietzsche contra Wagner* (*Nietzsche contra Wagner*), prepared for publication, 1888; printed, but withdrawn before publication, 1889; published 1895.

A   *Der Antichrist* (*The Antichrist*), prepared for publication, 1888; first ed., 1895. The number following the title abbreviation denotes the section in which the reference is to be found.

EH   *Ecce Homo* (*Ecce Homo*), prepared for publication, 1888, first ed., 1908. The first number following the title abbreviation denotes the section in which the reference is to be found. The second number, separated by a colon, denotes the aphorism in which the reference is to be found. I have numbered the sections as follows:

Preface	Vorwort (Preface)
1	Warum ich so weise bin ("Why I Am So Wise")
2	Warum ich so klug bin ("Why I Am So Clever")
3	Warum ich so gute Bücher schreibe ("Why I Write Such Good Books")
4	*Die Geburt der Tragödie* (*The Birth of Tragedy*)
5	Die Unzeitgemässen ("The Untimely Ones")
6	*Menschliches, Allzumenschliches* (*Human, All-Too-Human*)
7	*Morgenröte* (*Daybreak*)
8	*Die fröhliche Wissenschaft* (*The Gay Science*)
9	*Also Sprach Zarathustra* (*Thus Spoke Zarathustra*)
10	*Jenseits von Gut und Böse* (*Beyond Good and Evil*)
11	*Genealogie der Moral* (*Genealogy of Morals*)
12	*Götzen-Dammerung* (*Twilight of the Idols*)
13	*Der Fall Wagner* (*The Case of Wagner*)
14	Warum ich ein Schicksal bin ("Why I Am a Destiny")

B. Cited Notes, Collections, and Manuscripts Not Published by Nietzsche

GS   *Der griechische Staat (The Greek State)*, 1871. References cited by manuscript only.

HW   *Homers Wettkampf (Homer's Contest)*, 1872. References cited by manuscript only.

P   *Der letze Philosoph (The Last Philosopher)*, 1872. References cited by manuscript only.

PAK   *Der Philosoph als Arzt der Kultur (The Philosopher as Cultural Physician)*, 1873. References cited by manuscript only.

PtZG   *Die Philosophie im tragischen Zeitalter der Griechen (Philosophy in the Tragic Age of the Greeks)*, 1873. References cited by manuscript only.

WL   *Über Wahrheit und Lüge im aussermoralischen Sinne (On Truth and Lies in the Extramoral Sense)*. References cited by manuscript only.

WM   *Der Wille zur Macht (The Will to Power)*, a collection of notes selected from Nietzsche's notebooks of the 1880s; first published in 1901; second expanded ed. published 1906. The number following the title abbreviation denotes the note in which the reference is to be found.

C. Cited Collected Editions of Nietzsche's Works

GOA   *Nietzsches Werke (Grossoktavausgabe)*, second ed. Leipzig: Alfred Kröner Verlag, 1901–1913. The Roman numeral following the title abbreviation denotes the volume in which the reference is to be found. The number following the Roman numeral indicates the page where the reference is to be found.

Werke   *Werke in drei Bänden*. Edited by Karl Schlecta. Munich: Carl Hanzer, 1954–1956. The Roman numeral following the title abbreviation indicates the volume where the reference is to be found. The number following the Roman numeral indicates the page where the reference is to be found.

WKG   *Werke: Kritische Gesamtausgabe.* Edited by G. Colli and M. Montinari. Berlin: Walter de Gruyter, 1967ff. The first number following the title abbreviation (a Roman numeral followed by an Arabic numeral) denotes the volume in which the reference is to be found. The number following indicates the page where the reference is to be found.

D. English Translations

I have taken translations from GT, FW, Z, JGB, GM, GD, A, and EH from Walter Kaufmann's translations and editions of Nietzsche's works, with occasional minor changes:

Nietzsche, Friedrich. *The Portable Nietzsche.* Edited and translated by Walter Kaufmann. New York: The Viking Press, 1954.

————. *Basic Writings of Nietzsche.* Edited and translated by Walter Kaufmann. New York: Random House, 1966.

————. *The Gay Science.* Translated by Walter Kaufmann. New York: Random House, 1974.

Where they are available, I have taken translations of Nietzsche's *Nachlass*, with occassional minor changes, from

Nietzsche, Friedrich. *The Will to Power.* Edited by Walter Kaufmann. Translated by Walter Kaufmann and R. J. Hollingdale. New York: Random House, 1967.

————. *Philosophy and Truth.* Edited and translated by J. Daniel Breazeale. Atlantic Highlands, NJ: Humanities Press, 1979.

Unless otherwise indicated, translations from all other works, notes, and manuscripts are my own, sometimes based on

Nietzsche, Friedrich. *Complete Works.* Edited by Oscar Levy. New York: Russell and Russell, 1964; first published, 1909–1911.

Notes

Preface

1. Martin Heidegger, *Nietzsche*, vol. 1, "The Will to Power as Art," trans. David Farrell Krell (New York: Harper and Row, 1979), chaps. 2–4.

2. Bernd Magnus, "Nietzsche's Philosophy in 1888: *The Will to Power* and the *Übermensch*," *Journal of the History of Philosophy* 24 (January 1986), pp. 79–98.

Introduction

1. Overtly political approaches to Nietzsche vary by issue. Standard treatments of Nietzsche in light of his use by the Nazis include George Sabine, *A History of Political Theory*, 4th ed. (Hinsdale, IL: Dryden Press, 1973), pp. 810–813, and William Bluhm, *Theories of the Political System* (Englewood Cliffs, NJ: Prentice-Hall, 1978), chap. 14. Many commentators argue that it is not so much Nietzsche's overt politics that accounts for the Nazi abuse of his writings, but his reduction of claims of morality to those of power. See, e.g., Eric Voegelin, "Nietzsche, the Crisis and the War," *The Journal of Politics* 6 (May 1944), pp. 177–212; Leo Strauss, *Natural Right and History* (Chicago: University of Chicago Press, 1953) and "A Note on the Plan of Nietzsche's *Beyond Good and Evil*," *Interpretation* 3 (Winter 1973), pp. 97–113; Werner Dannhauser, "Friedrich Nietzsche," in Leo Strauss and Joseph Cropsey, eds., *History of Political Philosophy* (Chicago: Rand McNally, 1963), pp. 724–745, and *Nietzsche's View of Socrates* (Ithaca: Cornell University Press, 1974), esp. pp. 31, 254–265; Alasdair MacIntyre, *After Virtue* (Notre Dame: University of Notre Dame Press, 1981), esp. chaps. 9, 18; J. P. Stern, *A Study of Nietzsche* (Cambridge: Cambridge University Press, 1979), p. 117; Robert Eden, *Political Leadership and Nihilism* (Gainesville: University of Florida Press, 1984); Walter Sokel, "The Political Uses and Abuses of Nietzsche in Walter Kaufmann's Image of Nietzsche," *Nietzsche-Studien* 12 (1983), pp. 436–442; Bryan Turner, "Nietzsche, Weber, and the Devaluation of Politics," *Sociological Review* 30 (1982), pp. 367–391, esp. pp. 368–372.

For a treatment of Nietzsche through his attitudes toward woman, see Christine Allen, "Nietzsche's Ambivalence about Women," in M. Clark and L. Lange, eds., *The Sexism of Social and Political Theory* (Toronto: University of Toronto Press, 1979), pp. 117–133.

For treatments of Nietzsche through his ideas about class, see Georg Lukács, *The Destruction of Reason*, trans. Peter Palmer (London: The Merlin Press, 1980), chap. 3; Marc Sautet, *Nietzsche et la Commune* (Paris: Le Sycamore, 1981).

2. The best example is Walter Kaufmann, *Nietzsche: Philosopher, Psychologist, Antichrist*, 4th ed. (Princeton: Princeton University Press, 1974). That Nietzsche's political rhetoric can often be

quite plausibly read as metaphors for philosophical points is skillfully demonstrated by Jacques Derrida in *Spurs: Nietzsche's Style*, trans. Barbara Harlow (Chicago: University of Chicago Press, 1979).

3. The best example of this approach is Arthur Danto's *Nietzsche as Philosopher* (New York: Macmillan, 1965).

4. Martin Heidegger, *Nietzsche*, 2 vols. (Pfullingen: Günther Neske Verlag, 1961). *Nietzsche* is translated into four volumes in English. The first section of the first volume (pp. 9–254) is translated as *Nietzsche*, vol. 1, *The Will to Power as Art*. The second section of the first volume (pp. 255–472) is translated as *Nietzsche*, vol. 2, *The Eternal Return*, trans. David Krell (New York: Harper and Row, 1984). The remainder of the first volume (pp. 473–658) and parts of the second volume (pp. 7–29) are translated as *Nietzsche*, vol. 3, *The Will to Power as Knowledge and Metaphysics*, trans. David Krell (Harper and Row, 1986). Pp. 31–256 and pp. 335–398 of the second volume are translated as *Nietzsche*, vol. 4, *Nihilism*, trans. Frank Capuzzi (New York: Harper and Row, 1982). The last section of the second volume is translated as *The End of Philosophy*, trans. Joan Stambaugh (New York: Harper and Row, 1973). The best summary of Heidegger's arguments on Nietzsche and nihilism is his "The Word of Nietzsche: 'God Is Dead'" in *The Question Concerning Technology*, trans. William Lovitt (New York: Harper and Row, 1977).

5. I am thinking here of Jacques Derrida, *Spurs: Nietzsche's Style*, and Paul de Man, *Allegories of Reading* (New Haven: Yale University Press, 1979), pp. 119–131. Perhaps the most plausible version of this approach is Alexander Nehamas, *Nietzsche: Life as Literature* (Cambridge, MA: Harvard University Press, 1985).

6. See especially Michel Foucault, "What Is Enlightenment?" in Paul Rabinow, ed., *The Foucault Reader* (New York: Pantheon Books, 1984), pp. 47–48.

Chapter 1

1. Theodor W. Adorno, *Negative Dialectics*, trans. E. B. Ashton (New York: Seabury Press, 1973), p. 379.

2. Stanley Rosen, *Nihilism: A Philosophical Essay* (New Haven: Yale University Press, 1969). Rosen holds that nihilism is essentially the result of modern man's desire to master nature by claiming all worldly powers for himself. Modern man's overweening pride results in his failure to orient toward the Platonic notion of the "good," seeking instead to reduce the meaning of the powers of thought and speech to historical context. Nietzsche, in Rosen's view, both understood that nihilism characterizes a situation in which "everything is permitted" and was a philosophical nihilist himself, seeking to claim for man all powers of creativity without natural limits. Owing to the hubris of modern man, owing to his failure to know and accept the guidance of Nature, creativity inevitably becomes chaos. See esp. pp. xiii–xiv, 72–76, 136–139.

3. See, Arthur Danto, *Nietzsche as Philosopher*. Cf. Leo Strauss's similar position in "A Note on the Plan of Beyond Good and Evil."

4. For a critique of Danto, see Richard Schacht, "Nietzsche and Nihilism," in Robert Solomon, ed., *Nietzsche* (Garden City, NY: Anchor, 1973), pp. 58–82.

5. Jacques Derrida, *Spurs: Nietzsche's Style*; Paul de Man, *Allegories of Reading*, pp. 119–131.

6. WM 36, 585; GOA XVI: 405.

7. FW 301.

8. FW 301.

9. GOA XVI: 417; cf. FW 346, WM 3, 585.

10. WM 585.

11. WM 3.

12. WM 13.

13. Cf. WM 8, 30, 1020; GOA XVI: 405.

14. WM 18.

15. WM 30.

16. JGB 32.

17. E.g., WM 4, 55, 114.

18. WM 55.

19. WM 55.

20. Although this logic implicitly guides his *Genealogy*, Nietzsche's clearest and most complete formulation is in a manuscript entitled "European Nihilism," dated June 10, 1887—probably written shortly before the *Genealogy*. The manuscript is reproduced as notes 4, 5, 114, and 55 of *The Will to Power*. The editors commissioned by Nietzsche's sister to put together *The Will to Power* rearranged this manuscript, obscuring its original coherence. Put back together, the manuscript sheds light on the underlying structure and intent of the *Genealogy* in relation to the problem of nihilism. See GOA XVI: 497. Walter Kaufmann carefully notes the original progression of these notes in his edition of *The Will to Power*, p. 9. Karl Schlecta's reordering of the notes in *The Will to Power* groups them together, although not in their original progression (*Werke* III: 852–856).

21. WM 4.

22. GM III: 28.

23. See, e.g., GM II: 17, 19.

24. GM III: 1, 28.

25. Gilles Deleuze, *Nietzsche and Philosophy*, trans. Hugh Tomlinson (New York: Columbia University Press, 1983).

26. Cf. Nietzsche's late critique of similar aspects of *The Birth of Tragedy*, EH 4: 1. Deleuze's method is ironic, given his own vehement rejection of Hegel (whom he misunderstands) for the same reasons. For commentary on this issues, see Daniel Breazeale, "The Hegel-Nietzsche Problem," *Nietzsche Studien* 4 (1975), pp. 146–164.

27. GM II: 6; cf. JGB 229. For comparisons of Nietzsche and Foucault on these themes, see Allan Megill, "Foucault, Structuralism, and the Ends of History," *Journal of Modern History* 51 (September 1979), pp. 451–503, and John Rajchman, "Nietzsche, Foucault, and the Anarchism of Power," *Semiotext(e)* 3 (1978), pp. 96–107.

28. GM II: 17.

29. GM II: 17; cf. GM I: 11; II: 5, 6, 18.

30. Cf. GM I: 11; II: 4, 5, 6.

31. GM II.

32. GM II: 3; cf. GM II: 5; M 18, 77, 113; JGB 55, 229.

33. GM II: 17.

34. GM II: 18.

35. GM II: 17.

36. GM III: 28; cf. GM II: 7.

37. E.g., GM III: 13, 28; cf. WM 55.

38. Tracy Strong, *Friedrich Nietzsche and the Politics of Transfiguration* (Berkeley: University of California Press, 1975), pp. 192–197. In *The Birth of Tragedy*, for example, Nietzsche suggests that Greek tragic culture was of this type, having the capacity to reaffirm "the union between man and man" over and against convention, class division, and oppression. GT 1; cf. A 57; GS. See Robert McGinn, "Culture as Prophylactic: Nietzsche's *Birth of Tragedy* as Culture Criticism," *Nietzsche Studien* 4 (1975), pp. 75–138, for a good analysis of the political themes in *The Birth of Tragedy*.

39. GM I: 6.

40. GM I: 5.

41. Michel Haar, "Nietzsche and Metaphysical Language," trans. Cyril and Liliane Welch, in David Allison, ed., *The New Nietzsche* (New York: Dell Publishing, 1977), p. 14.

42. GM III: 13.

43. WM Preface, 4.

44. WM 15: cf. WM 14, 585.

45. Debates about whether or not Nietzsche was himself a nihilist often confuse his positive assessment of nihilism as a psychological stance, which is creative and transitional even if ultimately untenable, with his negative assessment of nihilism as a general philosophical doctrine. For examples of such debates see Richard Schacht, "Nietzsche and Nihilism," and Robert Solomon, "Nietzsche, Nihilism, and Morality," both in Robert Solomon, ed., *Nietzsche*, (Garden City, N.Y.: Doubleday, 1973). See also Arthur Danto, *Nietzsche as Philosopher*, pp. 19–35.

46. FW 353; GM III. Nietzsche's account of the origins of Christianity in FW is different from that in GM. He writes in FW 353 that "Jesus (or Paul), for example, found how small people lived in the Roman provinces—a modest, virtuous, pinched life. He offered an exegesis, he read the highest meaning and value into it—and with this also the courage to despise every other way of life, the quiet Herrnhut fanaticism, the secret, subterranean self-confidence that grows and grows and finally is ready 'to overcome the world' (that is, Rome and the upper classes throughout the Empire)." Nietzsche's comments here correspond to Max Weber's claim that the stratum originally most attracted to Christianity was not the "slave," but a lower stratum of urban artisans and merchants. Cf. Weber's *The Sociology of Religion*, trans. Ephraim

Fischift (Boston: Beacon Press, 1963). In either case, the logic of Nietzsche's explanation remains the same, viz., the focus on the relationship between situationally created/located practices and the needs these practices entail, and the process of endowing these practices with cultural meaning.

47. GM III: 1, 28. The term "mistaken turn" is Heidegger's, although it might have been used by any of those referred to below. See, e.g., Heidegger, *Nietzsche*, vol. 1 (Neske ed.), section V; Bernd Magnus, *Nietzsche's Existential Imperative* (Bloomington: Indiana University Press, 1978), pp. 8–12; Michel Haar, "Metaphysical Language," pp. 12–16; Karl Jaspers, *Nietzsche*, trans. Charles Wallraft and Frederick Schmitz (Chicago: Henry Regnery, 1965), pp. 357–359; George Morgan, *What Nietzsche Means* (New York: Harper and Row, 1965), pp. 162–163.

48. GM I: 10.

49. A 24; cf. GM I: 16.

50. Weber is wrong, however, when he suggests that Nietzsche's concept of *ressentiment* entails the claim that religious ethics in general may be adduced from *ressentiment*. See *From Max Weber*, H. H. Gerth and C. Wright Mills, eds. and trans. (New York: Oxford University Press, 1946), p. 270. *Ressentiment* is specific for Nietzsche, occurring only under certain conditions. But because of the creative aspect of *ressentiment*, the moments of its occurrence have set decisive patterns of religious evaluation. Many other conditions came together, in Nietzsche's view, to form Christianity, most of which cannot be explained in terms of *ressentiment*, such as the concepts of guilt and debt, the psychology of Christ, and the psychology of the ascetic priest. Max Scheler, in his essay *Ressentiment*, trans. William Holdheim (New York: Schocken, 1972), makes the same error. Weber comes crucially close to Nietzsche's real claim, however—as Weber himself suggests—when he argues that a religious evaluation of *suffering* is involved in all other-worldly religions. This is what Weber takes from Nietzsche for his own "Social Psychology of the World Religions," *From Max Weber*, pp. 171–176. Weber uses the concept of *ressentiment* in Nietzsche's specific sense in *The Sociology of Religion*, pp. 110–111.

51. A 15; cf. WM 357; FW 347.

52. A 24; cf. JGB 195.

53. A 24, 27.

54. GM III: 1, 28.

55. EH 4: 1.

56. A 43; cf. WM 30.

57. Cf. A 30, 34.

58. Cf. A 30, 34.

59. A 30, 33, 35.

60. A 30, 34.

61. A 15; cf. A 39.

62. JGB 187, 199; GM III: 18.

63. E.g., WM 1, 427, 437.

64. E.g., EH Preface: 2; GD 3, 4; FW 346; WM 516, 580, 585, 586.

65. Cf. G. W. F. Hegel, *The Logic of Hegel*, trans. William Wallace (London: Oxford University Press, 1931), pp. 158–167.

66. WM 580; cf. 567.

67. Robert Solomon, in "Nietzsche, Nihilism and Morality," considers unconditionality and universality to be the decisive attributes of nihilistic morality for Nietzsche. Solomon's careful survey of Nietzsche's usages of the terms "nihilism" and "morality" is quite helpful. See also George Morgan, *What Nietzsche Means*, pp. 162–163.

68. See esp. Heidegger, *Nietzsche*, vol. 4, *Nihilism*.

69. Heidegger, *Nietzsche*, vol. 4, *Nihilism*, p. 139.

70. See especially *The End of Philosophy*. For a useful criticism of Heidegger on this point, see Bernd Magnus, *Heidegger's Metahistory of Philosophy* (The Hague: Martinus Nijhoff, 1970).

71. Heidegger, *Nietzsche*, vol. 1, *The Will to Power as Art*.

72. This shows up in Heidegger's use of texts. He systematically excludes, for example, the texts that interest Derrida and de Man, those that deconstruct man as "subject." Moreover, he seems uninterested in considering those texts in which Nietzsche attempts to give accounts of subjectivity that parallel his own. See, for example, Heidegger's use of JGB 36 in *Nietzsche*, vol. 4, *Nihilism*, p. 80. Here Heidegger points to Nietzsche's "subjectivistic" formulation of the concept of will, ignoring the remainder of the aphorism that suggests a very different, almost Heideggerian, reformulation of the concept.

73. WM 1.

74. WM 14; no. 3 in the June 10, 1887, MS on nihilism.

75. In Nietzsche's own terms, I shall argue, nihilism of the modern era is actually a mix of original (or political) and European (or cultural) nihilism, since causes of nihilism will differ according to a person's situation in society. The problem is that Nietzsche did not understand how power works through modern organizations (especially markets and bureaucracies), and was therefore unable to identify situations that would produce original nihilism.

76. WM 55; no. 4 in the June 10, 1887, MS on nihilism.

77. WM 2.

78. Heidegger's rendering of Nietzsche's account of nihilism displaces the logic of nihilism into the internal tensions generated by metaphysics: "Nietzsche thought the history of Western metaphysics as the ground of our own history and of its future determinations"; see *Nietzsche* (Neske ed.), vol. 2, p. 42. In order to displace the locus of the historical logic from "psychology" to "metaphysics," Heidegger suggests that Nietzsche's "psychology" is really "anthropology" reflecting the structure of metaphysics; see p. 61.

79. Cf. Nietzsche's references to the "nihilistic will," "the will turning against life," "the instinct for self-destruction"; he even claims that "the nihilistic movement is merely the expression of physiological decadence." A 9; GM Preface: 5, III: 14; WM 38, 55; cf. WM 48–50. Heidegger finds it "strange and incomprehensible" that Nietzsche used biological and scientist language to describe psychology. See *Nietzsche*, vol. 1, *The Will to Power as Art*, p. 113. Heidegger fails to

see the consistently materialistic thrust of Nietzsche's history, and thus fails to understand Nietzsche's view that psychology is structured in relation to material context. Nietzsche's "psychology" is an attribute of the organism and its situation. Aesthetic and symbolic structuring of relations to existence, for example, is a means to the existence of the total organism. Aesthetic relations to the world are an *achievement* of the organism historically—but they are not the "ground" of the organism. Nietzsche used scientist language to emphasize this against the prevailing idealism of German philosophy, not unlike Marx.

80. See Nietzsche's qualification of his own reductionistic language, GM III: 16.

81. Cf. FW 354; JGB 268. The interpretations by Tracy Strong, *Friedrich Nietzsche,* esp. pp. 28–86, and Heinz Röttges, *Nietzsche und die Dialektik der Aufklärung* (Berlin: Walter de Gruyter, 1972), esp. chaps. 3 and 4, are the best on this question. Wolfgang Müller-Lauter, in his *Nietzsche: Seine Philosophie der Gegensätze und die Gegensätze seiner Philosophie* (Berlin: Walter de Gruyter, 1971), is one of the few to attempt to locate the social and political content of Nietzsche's understanding of nihilism. While Müller-Lauter's interpretation is careful on questions of the social origins of decadence, he psychologizes the resulting historical development of nihilism; see esp. pp. 69–76, 81–85. He fails to note the difference in Nietzsche between nihilism that results from an experiential shattering of the will into decadence and the phenomenon of cultural "poisoning," "taming," and "weakening" of the will that Nietzsche saw to occur under Christianity. Thus psychological decadence is originally caused experientially, but it is *perpetuated* culturally. By failing to note this distinction, Müller-Lauter can only account for the modern emergence of nihilism by seeing its historical development as a result of a seemingly preformed and heritable psychology—the "will to nothingness."

82. WM 5; no. 2 in the June 10, 1887, MS on nihilism.

83. WM 2.

84. Cf. FW 109, 110. In this context, "rationalization" has the narrow meaning of internal consistency: although a relatively consistent system, Nietzsche thought Christianity to be irrational and ideological in practice. For example, Christianity uses the analytic conception of causality rigorously enough, but only in terms of nonempirical causes (e.g., sin) and effects (e.g., punishment in an after life). See, e.g., GD 3–6; A 48, 49. On Nietzsche's conception of ideology, see chapter 2.

85. GD 4.

86. FW 357; cf. JGB 54; GOA XIII: 125.

87. GD 9: 5.

88. Cf. FW 122; GT 18, 20; WM 1, 412.

89. GM III: 19–21.

90. WM 5.

91. GOA XVI: 417.

92. See John Wilcox, *Truth and Value in Nietzsche* (Ann Arbor: University of Michigan Press, 1974), esp. pp. 44–50, regarding Nietzsche's "cognitivism." See also Ruediger Grimm, *Nietzsche's Theory of Knowledge* (Berlin: Walter de Gruyter, 1977), pp. 125–168.

93. Cf. WM 118, 120, 403; GD 3: 3, 4.

94. WM 114; no. 3 in the June 10, 1887, MS on nihilism.

95. Cf. GD: 5, 6; A 15.

96. JGB 230; cf. GD 5: 7, 8.

97. GD 3: 3.

98. Cf. WM 125, GM I: 16.

99. Cf. JGB 38, 46, 212.

100. Cf. EH 14: 1, MAMa 473.

101. JGB 208.

102. Tracy Strong, "Friedrich Wilhelm Nietzsche," in David Miller et. al., eds., *The Blackwell Encyclopedia of Political Thought* (Oxford: Basil Blackwell, 1987), p. 358.

103. WM 112. Heidegger rightly places much emphasis on nihilism as a transition point. See, e.g., *Nietzsche* (Neske ed.), vol. 2, pp. 34–35, and "The Word of Nietzsche: 'God Is Dead,'" pp. 70–75. See also Jaspers, *Nietzsche*, pp. 359–62, and Maurice Blanchot, "The Limits of Experience: Nihilism," trans. John Leavey, in David Allison, ed., *The New Nietzsche*, pp. 121–128.

104. GM III: 27.

105. David McLellan, ed., *Karl Marx: Selected Writings* (Oxford: Oxford University Press, 1977), p. 224.

Chapter 2

1. Nietzsche's concept of culture builds upon a German intellectual tradition that understands culture (*Kultur*) primarily as a spiritual environment of customs, morals, and education within which the human animal is formed into a human being. The concept is linked especially to the German terms *Bildung*, meaning formation and education, and *Züchtung*, meaning training, discipline, cultivation, and breeding. Nietzsche's use of the term *Züchtung* follows Hegel's; see, e.g., Hegel's *Philosophy of History*, trans. J. Sibree (New York: Dover, 1956), p. 320. In Nietzsche's use, the terms *Züchtung* and *Bildung* tend to be synonymous—although in his later years he preferred to characterize culture as a means for *Züchtung*, emphasizing the organic and intrinsic functions of culture, rather than *Bildung* with its more liberal and extrinsic connotations. Also in Nietzsche we find the uniquely Germanic opposition of the concepts of *Kultur* and *Zivilization*, the latter denoting material, scientific, and technological progress irrespective of refinement in taste, morals, intellect, and spirituality. The distinction had an established polemical twist by Nietzsche's time. While civilization was seen to be materially progressive, collective, and emanating from a center (presumably, England), Germans often emphasized that culture was a spiritual quality possessed by individuals and peoples, something growing from within their conditions of existence and defining their unique identities. Concerning the German understanding of culture, especially in its polemical contrast to civilization, see The Frankfurt Institute for Social Research, *Aspects of Sociology*, trans. John Viertel (Boston: Beacon, 1972) pp. 89–100.

2. JGB 15; WM 491, 492.

3. GT 25.

4. FW 109.

5. JGB 59.

6. JGB 39; cf. JGB 24, 230; M 40; FW 1.

7. FW, 1886 Preface, 4.

8. M 28; cf. WM 377.

9. JGB 4; cf. WM 430. On the connotations of *Züchtung* see note 1 of this chapter.

10. UBb 6, 10; cf. UBc 3, 5; WM 707.

11. JGB 230; cf. JGB 9; WM 121. Regarding the "danger" of the distinction between theory and practice in this regard see esp. WM 458; cf. M 130; JGB 6, 230; A 39; WM 423.

12. UBa 1; cf. UBb 4.

13. UBc 5.

14. Tracy Strong, *Friedrich Nietzsche*, pp. 24–27; cf. WM 271; UBb 3; A 57.

15. Tracy Strong, "Language and Nihilism," *Theory and Society* 3 (1976), p. 245.

16. WM 522.

17. Cf. JGB 17, 34; FW 354. For good summaries of Nietzsche's thoughts on language, see Tracy Strong, *Friedrich Nietzsche*, chap. 3; Daniel Breazeale, "The Word, the World, and Nietzsche," *Philosophical Forum* 7 (July 1976), pp. 301–320; Arthur Danto, *Nietzsche as Philosopher*, pp. 83–88.

18. GD 3: 5; FW 354.

19. WM 535, 520; cf. WM 522.

20. WM 625; cf. GD 3: 5.

21. See Daniel Breazeale, "The Word, the World, and Nietzsche," p. 313.

22. The significant exceptions are Nietzsche's considerations on dreams, which he likens to rich experience later rationally formulated. See esp. M 119, 312; MAMa 12; FW 54.

23. FW 354. Not surprisingly, Freud was aware of Nietzsche's psychological speculations, and on rare occasions refers to him approvingly. In a late autobiographical reflection, Freud credits Nietzsche and Schopenhauer for having early psychoanalytic insights. Freud read Schopenhauer only late in life, but he writes that he actively "shunned" Nietzsche, "precisely because his hunches and insights correspond in the most astonishing way to the laboriously collected results of psychoanalysis. . . . [Nietzsche's] priority is less important to me than the maintenance of my impartiality"—*Gesammelte Werke* (London: Imago, 1948), vol. 14, p. 86.

24. Michael Polanyi, *Personal Knowledge* (London: Routledge and Kegan Paul, 1958), especially Part Two; cf. FW 244, 354; GD 9: 26.

25. E.g., GD 3: 3; GT 16.

26. FW 354; cf. WL (*Werke* III, 314), and Marx and Engels, *The German Ideology* (Moscow: Progress Publishers, 1976), p. 49: "Language is as old as consciousness, language is practical, real consciousness that exists for other men as well, and only therefore does it also exist for me; language, like consciousness, only arises from need, the necessity of intercourse with other men."

27. JGB 168; cf. JGB 268; FW 354; GD 9: 26; WM 538.

28. Mary Douglas, *How Institutions Think* (Syracuse: Syracuse University Press, 1986), chap. 5.

29. FW 354.

30. JGB 268.

31. FW 354.

32. GM Preface, 1.

33. Tracy Strong makes this comparison in "Language and Nihilism," p. 243. But also see Eric Blondel's essay "Nietzsche: Life as Metaphor," trans. Mairi Macrae, in David Allison, ed., *The New Nietzsche*, pp. 150–175, for an elaboration of the notion of interpretative fetishism.

34. JGB 262; cf. 201.

35. FW 354.

36. GM II: 2; FW 116, 354.

37. WM 403; cf. JGB 262.

38. WM 767.

39. Z, On the Thousand and One Goals.

40. Georg Simmel, *Schopenhauer und Nietzsche* (Leipzig: Duncker und Humbolt, 1907), pp. 208–210.

41. J. P. Stern, *A Study of Nietzsche*, pp. 126–138. See, e.g., GM I: 11; II: 1, 2; M 9, 14.

42. Cf. FW 115; WM 246.

43. FW 143.

44. WM 773.

45. FW 116.

46. These conflicting functions of culture are captured in the distinction between *Kultur* and *Zivilization*. See 1 of this chapter. Nietzsche follows the German tradition in suggesting that *Kultur* ought properly to refer to the means by which the individual is formed (*bildet*) and bred (*züchtet*) into a cultured individuality. Here, cultural horizons work to discipline, improve, and sublimate the "animal" man. Nietzsche uses *Zivilization*, on the other hand, to refer to the situation in which cultural horizons are merely a means to maintain the "herd" against individual differences as well as against the various exigencies of existence. As *Zivilization*, culture functions to poison and stifle the individual, over and beyond the rudimentary "taming" of

the "animal" man required for the emergence of individuals. See, e.g., GD 7: 5; GM I: 11; WM 121, 236, 238. Christianity, for example, made humans more profound, more evil, more capable of love—and in this sense is regarded by Nietzsche as an "improvement" of individuals. But Christianity went far beyond this in stifling the passions and uprooting "nature," in this way precluding the possibility of individuality. The potential for "breeding" that existed here turned into "taming," and became a means for a priesthood to assert the control of the "herd" against emergent individuals. Nietzsche's views here foreshadow Freud's in *Civilization and Its Discontents*, trans. James Strachey (New York: W. W. Norton, 1961), as well as the distinction between "basic" and "surplus" repression made by Herbert Marcuse in *Eros and Civilization* (New York: Random House, 1962), pp. 32–34.

47. In the spirit of Nietzsche, Georg Simmel calls the tension between the individual and collective aspects of a person the "sociological tragedy as such"; see *The Sociology of Georg Simmel*, trans. and ed. Kurt Wolff (Glencoe, IL: The Free Press, 1950), pp. 31–32. Simmel, however, locates the tension not between experiential (individual) and reflective (collective) consciousness as does Nietzsche, but between what is highly conscious and "lowest and most primitive," in a manner reminiscent of the tradition Nietzsche sets himself against.

48. The term "ideology" occurs only twice in Nietzsche's writings, in JGB 44 and WM 351.

49. In the tradition of critical theory that I rely on here, ideologies tend to be viewed in the following terms. First, ideological forms of consciousness conceal essential aspects of social and political reality. Second, the concealing attributes of ideologies are not accidental (that is, ideologies are not simply "errors"), but relate systematically to social, psychological, and cognitive interests within a determinate historical context. Third, because ideologies relate systematically to interests and historical realities, they can be criticized (genealogically deconstructed, in Nietzschean terms—see chapter 3) so as to provide knowledge about these interests and realities.

50. See, e.g., Hans Barth, *Truth and Ideology*, trans. Frederic Lilge (Berkeley: University of California Press, 1976), pp. 129–154, and José Merquoir, *The Veil and the Mask: Essays on Culture and Ideology* (London: Routledge and Kegan Paul, 1979), pp. 7–8. Both argue that Nietzsche's attempt to reduce ideas to reflections of practical power interests is insufficient since it fails to provide the grounds for the truth of Nietzsche's own ideas about ideas. In a slightly more sophisticated version of the same argument, Monika Funke, *Ideologiekritik und ihre Ideologie bei Nietzsche* (Stuttgart: Friedrich Fromman, 1974), asserts that Nietzsche criticizes ideas by relating them to their functions, but fails to understand the ideological thrust of functionalism itself.

51. Jürgen Habermas, "Myth and Enlightenment: Re-Reading *Dialectic of Enlightenment*," trans. Thomas Levin, *New German Critique* 26 (Spring-Summer 1982). Habermas argues here that because Nietzsche reduces "intersubjective validity claims" to the merely subjective claims of taste and power, he is driven to distinguish between claims genetically (that which is more original is "considered to be better"), which then provide "criterion of rank in the social as well as in the logical sense." On Habermas' account, Nietzsche commits the genetic fallacy— that is, holding that the origins of ideas call into question their truth.

52. E.g., WM 129, 216, 282; GM III: 15, 16; A 44; MAMa 472.

53. GM I: entire; A 26, 48, 49.

54. A 43; cf. WM 30.

55. A 49; cf. GD 5: entire, 6: entire.

56. These considerations, as I argue in chapter 5, apply also to modern science. An empirically correct interpretation could be ideological on Nietzsche's view if it is merely a reflective awareness of some state of affairs, and not analyzed in such a way that it relates to willing. If Christianity suppresses the empirical world, contemporary science suppresses the underlying self-constitutive interest in all apparently value-free empirical orientations, and is thus capable of functioning as ideology until related to willing.

57. Sigmund Freud, *The Future of an Illusion*, trans. W. D. Robson-Scott (Garden City, NY: Doubleday and Co., 1961).

58. A 15; cf. FW 357; WM 357.

59. A 15.

60. GM I: 10, 13, 14; cf., FW 205.

61. GT 1, 21. See also note 80 of this chapter.

62. GT 1.

63. GT 18.

64. GT 18; cf. MAMa 439; JGB 257, 258; GS. See chapter 7 for a full account of the assumptions behind Nietzsche's politics.

65. Tracy Strong, in *Friedrich Nietzsche*, pp. 192–195, provides a unique summary of Nietzsche's understanding of Greek political culture in this respect.

66. Cf. GT 18, JGB 211, 257, 258; WM 953–957.

67. A 56.

68. See chapter 4 on the question of Nietzsche's praise of instinct and denegration of conscious action.

69. GT 1.

70. GT 9.

71. WM 809; cf. WM 522.

72. WM 809.

73. Hannah Arendt makes a distinction similar to Nietzsche's between an equality of individuals and a conformist equality of masses in *The Human Condition* (Chicago: University of Chicago Press, 1958), pp. 40–41. Arendt follows Nietzsche in seeking to characterize the political equality of citizens in democratic Athens in terms different from those of modern conceptions of equality.

74. Cf. HW.

75. JGB 259.

76. M 112.

77. M 112.

78. M 112.

79. M 187. See chapter 5 on Nietzsche's critique and appropriation of Kantian morality.

80. It is true, however, that latent elements of Nietzsche's mature perspective on culture as a social phenomena already exist in *The Birth of Tragedy*. Robert McGinn, in "Culture as Prophylactic: Nietzsche's *Birth of Tragedy* as Culture Criticism," pp. 88–96, 124, quite correctly argues that several sociopolitical functions of myth can be found in the early work. Myth (1) preserves the creative aspect of activity; (2) unifies cultural movements by providing common symbolic images; (3) guards against the "aimless wanderings of imagination"; (4) interprets experience; and (5) serves as the legitimating structure of sociopolitical order.

81. This failing and the problems it brings in Nietzsche's later development are rigorously but concisely discussed by Sarah Kofman, in "Metaphor, Symbol, Metamorphosis," trans. David Allison, in David Allison, ed., *The New Nietzsche*, pp. 201–214. Also see Nietzsche's self-criticism in EH 4: 1. The most skillful discussion of the genetic-romantic structure of *The Birth of Tragedy* is Paul De Man's "Genesis and Genealogy in Nietzsche's *The Birth of Tragedy*," *Diacritics* 2 (Winter 1971), pp. 44–53. See Robert McGinn, "Nietzsche's *Birth of Tragedy*," for similar criticisms.

82. WL.

83. Alexander Nehamas, *Nietzsche: Life as Literature*, pp. 90–91.

84. Interpretations relying exclusively on *The Birth of Tragedy* unavoidably see Nietzsche's thought as a simple inversion of the Platonic oppositions of being and appearance, truth and illusion, philosophy and art. See, e.g., George Grant, "Nietzsche and the Ancients: Philosophy and Scholarship," *Dionysus* 3 (December 1979), pp. 5–16.

85. Alexander Nehamas, *Nietzsche: Life as Literature*, p. 98.

86. GM II: 3–7.

87. Alexander Nehamas, *Nietzsche: Life as Literature*, p. 121.

Chapter 3

1. MAMa 2. Most of Nietzsche's commentators fail to appreciate the structure and methodological centrality of Nietzsche's historical approach to knowledge of human affairs. Significant exceptions are Karl Bröse, *Geschichtsphilosophische Strukturen im Werk Nietzsches* (Frankfurt/M: Peter Lang, 1973), esp. Part II; Wolfgang Müller-Lauter, *Nietzsche*, chap. 2; Alfred Schmidt, "Zur Frage der Dialektik in Nietzsches Erkenntnistheorie," in Max Horkheimer, ed., *Zeugnisse — Theodor W. Adorno zum Sechzigsten Geburtstag* (Frankfurt/M: Europäische Verlagsanstalt), pp. 113–132; Michel Foucault, "Nietzsche, Genealogy, History," in *Language, Counter-Memory, Practice*, trans. Donald Bouchard and Sherry Simon (Ithaca: Cornell University Press, 1977), pp. 139–164.

2. WM 1058; cf. FW 357; WM 617. Nietzsche continues this note by suggesting that the concept of eternal return resolves this tension, a point I take up in chapter 6.

3. GD 5: 6; cf. GD 9: 33, 43; M 49; WM 472, 479, 672, 908.

4. Cf. MAMc 61 and my interpretation of *amor fati* in chapter 6.

5. Heidegger, in "Who Is Nietzsche's Zarathustra?" trans. Bernd Magnus, in David Allison, ed., *The New Nietzsche*, pp. 64–79, esp. pp. 70–78, and in *What Is Called Thinking?* trans. J. Glenn Gray (New York: Harper and Row, 1986), pp. 82–110, is followed by his students, Joan Stambaugh, in *Nietzsche's Thought of Eternal Return* (Baltimore: Johns Hopkins University Press, 1972), pp. 8–13, and Hannah Arendt, in *The Life of the Mind*, vol. 2: *Willing* (New York: Harcourt, Brace and World, 1978), pp. 158–172, in relying on Nietzsche's statement in Z, On Redemption, that revenge is "the will's ill will against time and its 'it was.'" Heidegger, Stambaugh, and Arendt each take the statement out of context of the remainder of the passage, in which Nietzsche focuses on the possibility of a reciprocal relation between the past and creative willing.

6. Bernd Magnus, *Nietzsche's Existential Imperative*, pp. 190–195.

7. Cf. UBb 1.

8. The German language distinguishes between *Historie*—the study of the historical past—and *Geschichte*—the experience of living history. The distinction is made, for example, by Karl Jaspers, *Nietzsche*, pp. 236–240, and by George Grant in *Time as History* (Toronto: Canadian Broadcasting Corp., 1969), pp. 3–4. Jaspers, however, fails to do more than articulate the distinction, while Grant uses the term *Geschichte* abstractly to denote the experience of the passage of time. This permits Grant to argue against Nietzsche that we are not equipped to deal with this experience without a Platonic view of the world. More true to Nietzsche on this point are Heinz Röttges, *Die Dialektik der Aufklärung*, p. 73, and Bernard Bueb, *Nietzsches Kritik der praktischen Vernunft* (Stuttgart: Ernst Klett, 1970), pp. 40–49.

9. EH 6: 1.

10. Hayden White, *Metahistory: The Historical Imagination in Nineteenth-Century Europe* (Baltimore: Johns Hopkins University Press, 1973), pp. 331–374.

11. Nietzsche's critical conception of historical method in this early essay has not been elaborated in the secondary literature in spite of its centrality to his philosophy as a whole. The possible exception is Michel Foucault's "Nietzsche, Genealogy, History." Yet Foucault understands Nietzsche's critical history primarily as a critique of the many faces of the Platonism in the contemporary "historical sense." Nietzsche goes further: he sees his approach as preliminary to a historical philosophy of action. For exegeses of this essay that point in critical directions, see Karl Jaspers, *Nietzsche*, pp. 236–239; Tracy Strong, *Friedrich Nietzsche*, pp. 31–34; 236–237; Heinz Röttges, *Die Dialektik der Aufkärung*, pp. 45–50; Wolfgang Müller-Lauter, *Nietzsche*, pp. 36–44; Robert Scharff, "Nietzsche and the 'Use' of History," *Man and World* 7 (February 1974), pp. 67–77.

12. Nietzsche is more explicit about the necessity of these approaches in later work. See Nietzsche's later comments on Hegel in, e.g., M 3, 534; FW 337, 357; JGB 46, 204; WM 1046. On Nietzsche's later attitudes toward "objectivism" in science, see GD 3: 3, A 49, and chapter 5 of this book.

13. UBb 2.

14. UBb 2.

15. UBb 3.

16. UBb 2.

17. UBb 3.

18. UBb 6.

19. See the first of Marx's "Theses on Feuerbach," in *The German Ideology*, p. 615.

20. G. W. F. Hegel, *Philosophy of Right*, trans. T. M. Knox (New York: Oxford University Press, 1967), p. 13.

21. UBb 8.

22. UBb 8.

23. UBb 3.

24. UBb 3.

25. This comparison between Marx and Nietzsche is suggested, although not elaborated, by Henry Kariel, in "Nietzsche's Preface to Constitutionalism," *Journal of Politics* 25 (May 1963), p. 222, and Peter Stern, "Comment on Andrew's 'Theory and Practice in Marx and Nietzsche,'" *Political Theory* 4 (November 1976), p. 507.

26. FW 380; cf. JGB 26; EH 14: entire; WM 14, 218.

27. FW 9; cf. GOA X: 352.

28. Cf. GD 1: 1, 2.

29. FW 34.

30. M 326.

31. Cf. WM 470; GD 1: 26.

32. MAMa 2.

33. MAMa 3.

34. GOA XIV: 223.

35. Cf. FW 110, 111. 35. Nietzsche's reversal of the notion of interest from its traditional meaning as a negative, distorting influence to a condition of possibility of knowledge has a contemporary equivalent in Jürgen Habermas' *Knowledge and Human Interest*, trans. Jeremy Shapiro (Boston: Beacon Press, 1971), notwithstanding Habermas' own interpretation of Nietzsche. See note 46 of this chapter.

36. WM 555; cf. WM 567; M 22.

37. FW 355.

38. FW 355.

39. Cf. M 460.

40. GM I: 1.

41. JGB 39; FW 109.

42. John Wilcox, *Truth and Value in Nietzsche.*

43. WM 487. See also Alexander Nehamas, *Nietzsche: Life as Literature,* p. 53.

44. GD 3: 3; GD 4. I understand the term "positivism" here in the broad sense, that is, as referring to an empiricist account of science such as Hume's, rather than to the positivism of the Vienna Circle. The latter usage would, of course, be anachronistic. Most of Nietzsche's praise of the "hard" and positivistic sciences occurs during his so-called middle period, extending from about 1876 to 1882 (*Human, All-Too-Human* to *The Gay Science*). It would be incorrect, however, to understand Nietzsche's later harsh appraisal of scientists and the scientific attitude to contradict what he earlier saw to be positive aspects of science, as does, e.g., Werner Dannhauser, *Nietzsche's View of Socrates,* pp. 156–157, and Peter Stern, "Comment on Edward Andrew's 'Theory and Practice in Marx and Nietzsche.'" Nietzsche does not "turn to positivism" (Dannhauser, p. 156) during his middle period. Rather, he accepts positivism's experimental method, its relative humility, and its reliance on the senses, while rejecting its self-understanding, motives, and inverted Platonism. Cf. MAMa 1–3; FW 57; GD 3: 3; WM 466, 469; GM III: 25.

45. FW 57, 357. See chapter 4 on Nietzsche's radicalization of Kant.

46. Habermas' analysis of Nietzsche in *Knowledge and Human Interest,* chap. 12, is based on a misreading of this issue. According to Habermas, Nietzsche simultaneously *reduces* knowledge to affective interest (p. 238), *denies* the status of knowledge to all but positivistic knowledge (p. 291–293), and sees all reflective knowledge as mere illusion (p. 299). Because Nietzsche also rejects Kantian skepticism (according to Habermas) he must fall back into the "objectivist" illusion (pp. 290–292, 294), which reduces reflective knowledge to subjective belief. Thus Habermas believes that "perspectivism" describes the relativity of all "reflective" knowledge. Habermas has his own reasons for interpreting Nietzsche in this way. He wishes to show that an intersubjective dimension is necessary for any theory of truth. While I am in sympathy with Habermas' aims, his interpretation of Nietzsche misses the mark. It will suffice to note that because knowledge, for Nietzsche, consists in a relation between culturally and linguistically rooted self-reflection and experience, his concept of psychology contains the reflective dimension that Habermas argues is missing. Habermas misses these aspects of Nietzsche because he relies almost exclusively on work from Nietzsche's transitional period, from the *Untimely Considerations* to *The Gay Science* in which his views on truth and knowledge are less developed. See also Habermas' "Nachwort" in Nietzsche, *Erkenntnistheoretische Schriften,* Blumemberg, Habermas, Heinrich, and Taubes, eds. (Frankfurt/M: Suhrkamp, 1968).

47. Mary Warnock, "Nietzsche's Conception of Truth," in Malcolm Pasley, ed., *Nietzsche: Imagery and Thought* (Berkeley: University of California Press, 1978), pp. 33–63.

48. Alexander Nehamas, *Nietzsche: Life as Literature,* p. 54.

49. JGB 204.

50. JGB 15.

51. *The German Ideology,* p. 618. For a comparison of Marx and Nietzsche on this issue see Edward Andrew, "The Unity of Theory and Practice: The Science of Marx and Nietzsche" in Terence Ball, ed., *Political Theory and Praxis* (Minneapolis: University of Minnesota Press, 1977), pp. 117–137.

52. See, e.g., Karl Marx, "Notes on Adolph Wagner," in Terrell Carver, ed. and trans., *Karl Marx: Texts on Method* (New York: Harper and Row, 1975), pp. 190–191.

53. WM 462.

54. WM 533.

55. WM 583, 674, 715.

56. WM 713.

57. WM 567.

58. WM 485; cf. WM 534.

59. WM 567.

60. WM 462.

61. See Alexander Nehamas' excellent discussion of this point in *Nietzsche: Life as Literature*, pp. 62–70.

62. WM 533.

63. In *Nietzsche: Life as Literature*, Alexander Nehamas focuses on the coherence criterion: a truth is fixed in relation to the text of which it is a part. On my reading of Nietzsche, Nehamas' approach is necessary, but not sufficient.

64. FW 110.

65. GM III: 12.

66. Theodor Adorno, *Negative Dialectics*, pp. 162–163.

67. GM III: 12.

68. WM 605; cf. WM 602; JGB 211.

69. UBb 3.

70. WM 63.

71. This is the major thesis of UBb.

72. WM 974.

73. GM II: 13.

74. GM III: 9; cf. Z, On Redemption; GM II: 11, 12; UBb 7.

75. M 49; cf. MAMa 452.

76. UBb 3; translation based on one by Tracy Strong.

77. Cf. FW 337; M 18; GM II: 2; III: 9.

78. G. W. F. Hegel, *Philosophy of Right*, p. 12.

79. GM II: 22; cf. A 38, 51.

80. Z, On Redemption.

81. FW 337.

82. Interpreters have tended to take Nietzsche's use of the term "genealogy" quite literally, and to assume that it involves only criticism seeking to undermine "noble" ideals by exposing their "base" origins; see, e.g., Judith Shklar, "Subversive Genealogies," *Daedalus* 101 (Winter 1972), pp. 129–154. Others see Nietzsche's method as an attempt to locate value genetically; see, e.g., Jürgen Habermas, "Myth and Enlightenment: Re-Reading *Dialectic of Enlightenment*." These views not only fail to capture Nietzsche's intention and actual procedure—they run counter to it. Of all Nietzsche's interpreters, Foucault has come the closest to capturing the movement and spirit of genealogy, even if he fails to address the question of its philosophical conditions of possibility. See his "Nietzsche, Genealogy, History."

83. WM 469.

84. Alexander Nehamas, *Nietzsche: Life as Literature*, p. 104.

85. In "Nietzsche, Genealogy, History," Michel Foucault draws attention to Nietzsche's systematic distinctions between *Herkunft* and *Entstehung*, and points out that he opposes both to the fruitless search for discrete "origins" (*Ursprung*); see pp. 145–152.

86. P 33.

87. FW 21; cf. GD 7: 5.

88. GM Preface, 3, I: 1–3; cf. WM 530.

89. GM III: 27; FW 110. The context of Nietzsche's use of the term *Selbstaufhebung* suggests that the root verb, *aufheben*, retains the subtleties Hegel capitalized upon—namely, its simultaneous meaning as transcendence, preservation, and abolition.

90. FW 110.

91. WM 454, 498–9, 503, 513, 515, 535; FW 126, 133, 246, 265, 355.

92. GM II: 13.

93. MAMa 1.

94. MAMa 1; cf. M 95; WM 253, 254, 579.

95. GM Preface: 4.

96. GM II: 13. Michel Foucault's *Discipline and Punish*, trans. Alan Sheridan (New York: Pantheon Books, 1977), is in many ways on elaboration of this methodological comment.

97. WM 579, cf. 262.

98. GM II: 12.

99. GM Preface, 3; cf. JGB 196; GD 7: 1; WM 299.

100. This is a condensed summary of several of Nietzsche's points in essays I and III of GM.

101. E.g., FW Preface 2, 43, 83, 104; JGB 20, 48, 246, 289; M 231, 239, GM I: 4, 5, II: 11, 12, III: 11; GT, "Attempt at Self-Criticism," 1.

102. GM II: 12.

Chapter 4

1. JGB 36.

2. JGB 36.

3. Interpretations of the concept of will to power as a motivating psychological substratum are among the most common. Typical are the following: George Lukács in *The Destruction of Reason*, pp. 375–380, accuses Nietzsche of reducing the essence of life to "exploitation" and of achieving a "mythical concreteness" in finding this "essence of the living." Hans Barth, in *Truth and Ideology*, pp. 150–159, objects to Nietzsche's reduction of truth and morality to the desire for power, and concludes that such a reduction presents a problem for the truth status of Nietzsche's own claims. Ludwig Klages, whose book *Die Psychologischen Errungenschaften Nietzsches*, in *Samtliche Werke* (Bonn: Bouvier, 1979), vol. 5, had wide influence in Germany at one time, views the will to power as a biological substratum of psychobiological drives. Carl Jung, in *Two Essays on Analytic Psychology*, trans. R. F. C. Hull (Cleveland: World, 1953), pp. 39–50, interprets the will to power as a conscious desire for power, and hence as a forerunner of ego-psychology. Walter Kaufmann, in his *Nietzsche*, chap. 6, seems to sense the inconsistency between Nietzsche's attempt to explain *all* actions in terms of the concept of will to power while at the same time attempting to use the concept as if it were a motive for *particular* kinds of actions—e.g., those of political domination. Hoping to avoid an understanding of the will to power as a will to domination, Kaufmann views the concept as a drive to "self-mastery." There is a good deal of plausibility to this, as I argue when I characterize the "self-reflective" aspect of the concept. However, Kaufmann's account is neither complete nor careful in identifying the philosophical status of the concept. The result is that he sees the will to power as a metaphysical principle—a "dialectical unity"—from which all appearances can be derived.

4. See esp. Heidegger's *Nietzsche*, vol. 1: *The Will to Power as Art*. Heidegger also argues that the will to power and the doctrine of eternal return have an equal and complementary philosophical status in Nietzsche's philosophy, the former as a concept of "becoming" and the latter as one of "being"; see *The Will to Power as Art*, pp. 18–24. I agree with Heidegger to the extent that one particular organization of will to power as *selfhood* ultimately requires the interpretive *doctrine* of eternal recurrence, placing the concepts in a symbiotic relation if not on the same philosophical plane. The will to power, however, is an *ontological* hypothesis, while the eternal return is a *doctrine* appropriate to the interpretive consolidation of a limited range of experiences. I argue this case in chapter 6. Examples of less subtle, but also less idiosyncratic, interpretations of the will to power as a metaphysics of creativity are J. P. Stern, *A Study of Nietzsche*, pp. 117–123, and Werner Dannhauser, *Nietzsche's View of Socrates*, pp. 31, 254–265. Both argue that the will to power is a kind of creative principle, one leading to the view that the world lacks natural and social limits.

5. Gilles Deleuze, *Nietzsche and Philosophy*. Tracy Strong, in *Friedrich Nietzsche*, p. 234, inadequately concludes that the will to power "is that which gives the forms which are the *pathos* of any life."

6. E.g., JGB 23, 36, 230; WM 635, 643, 647.

7. See, e.g., JGB 259.

8. I thank William Connolly for pointing out this possibility to me.

9. For one development of this argument, see Ofelia Schutte, *Beyond Nihilism: Nietzsche Without Masks* (Chicago: University of Chicago Press, 1984).

10. For interpretations of the will to power as a concept of practice, see, e.g., Alfred Schmidt, "Praxis," in Hermann Krings, Hans Michael Baumgartner, and Christopher Wild, eds., *Handbuch Philosophischer Grundbegriffe*, vol. 2 (München: Kösel Verlag, 1973), pp. 1121–1129, and Wolfgang Müller-Lauter, "Nietzsches Lehre vom Willen zur Macht," *Nietzsche-Studien* 3 (1974), pp. 1–60.

11. Cf. JGB Preface, 4, 10–12, 16–19, 36.

12. JGB 36, WM 17.

13. JGB 12.

14. JGB 19.

15. JGB 36 is the first substantial (that is, argued) introduction to the concept of will to power.

16. JGB 11.

17. JGB 3; cf. JGB 230. See also Heidegger, *Nietzsche*, vol. 4: *Nihilism*.

18. Kant, *Critique of Pure Reason*, second ed., trans. F. Max Müller (Garden City, NY: Doubleday and Co., 1961), I: Second Division, esp. pp. 190–214.

19. This is so in spite of the fact that Nietzsche probably had no firsthand knowledge of Kant, and in spite of the fact that his criticisms of Kant often miss their mark. See Daniel Breazeale's note in *Philosophy and Truth* (Atlantic Highlands, NJ: Humanities Press, 1979), p. 32n, on Nietzsche's knowledge of Kant. See also Nietzsche's misunderstandings of Kant's argument concerning synthetic a priori categories in JGB 11 and WM 530, specifically on the issue of their metaphysical status.

20. *Critique of Pure Reason*, Transcendental Dialectic, Book II, chap. I, p. 218.

21. *Critique of Pure Reason*, Transcendental Dialectic, Book II, chap. I, p. 219.

22. JGB 17; cf. WM 483, WM 485, 487; GD 3: 5.

23. WM 484; cf. GD 3: 5.

24. *Critique of Pure Reason*, The Antinomy of Reason, Section VI, p. 301.

25. FW 357.

26. JGB 21.

27. JGB 4.

28. WM 530.

29. JGB 11; cf. JGB 4.

30. WM 552. Cf. WM 553, where Nietzsche claims that these conclusions are already implied in the way Kant poses his problem of causality.

31. WM 532; cf. WM 544.

32. JGB 19.

33. WM 715; cf. WM 46, 490; JGB 12, 19; FW 127.

34. JGB 19.

35. JGB 19.

36. JGB 19; cf. WM 260, 480, 556.

37. JGB 19; cf. WM 481, 664; FW 360.

38. JGB 230.

39. JGB 19.

40. JGB 19.

41. JGB 19.

42. JGB 19.

43. Gilles Deleuze, "Active and Reactive," trans. Richard Cohen, in David Allison, ed., *The New Nietzsche*, pp. 94–95.

44. Heidegger, *Nietzsche*, vol. 1: *The Will to Power as Art*, p. 23.

45. Heidegger, *Nietzsche*, vol. 1: *The Will to Power as Art*, p. 99; cf. pp. 45–53, 98–106.

46. WM 635.

47. In addition to these meanings, Aristotle uses the term *pathos* to designate power, potentially and change—both with respect to their actuality and potentiality; see F. E. Peters, *Greek Philosophical Terms* (New York: New York University Press, 1967). Nietzsche takes experience in this sense as the fundamental datum from which all conceptions of the world as *physis* are derived.

48. GM III: 16.

49. JGB 36.

50. Cf. JGB 15.

51. JGB 36.

52. FW 333, 354.

53. Heidegger, *Nietzsche*, vol. 1: *The Will to Power as Art*. For general comments on Heidegger's interpretation of Nietzsche, see chapter 1.

54. WM 567; cf. WM 536.

55. Eugen Fink, in *Nietzsches Philosophie* (Stuttgart: Kohlmanner, 1960), refers to the will to power as a "negative ontology of a thing" (p. 162), thus drawing the connection between the ontological and epistemological aspects of the concept of totality, which is absent in Hegel, but suggested by Nietzsche and later developed at length by Theodor Adorno in *Negative Dialectics*. For a good comparison of Nietzsche and Hegel on this issue, see Daniel Breazeale, "The Hegel-Nietzsche Problem." Ruediger Grimm, *Nietzsche's Theory of Knowledge*, pp. 169–170, persuasively puts the case for considering the will to power as a concept of totality. The interpretation of Nietzsche as a working within a neo-Hegelian perspective of totality is now commonplace in the German literature. See, for example, Wolfgang Müller-Lauter, "Nietzsche's Lehre"; Heinz Röttges, *Nietzsche und die Dialektik der Aufklärung*; Heinrich Kutzner, *Nietzsche* (Hildeheim: Gerstenberg, 1978). Kaufmann's comments on Hegel and Nietzsche in his *Nietzsche* pp. 235–246, are helpful in a general way.

56. JGB 36; cf. WM 618–639.

57. JGB 36.

58. JGB 36; cf. WM 619.

59. JGB 36.

60. See, e.g., Nietzsche's comment on Kant to this effect in FW 357.

61. WM 620.

62. WM 545.

63. WM 625.

64. WM 619; cf. WM 569.

65. WM 636; cf. M 453, WM 635.

66. WM 643.

67. FW 1.

68. WM 707.

69. WM 504; cf. JGB 3, 231.

70. Cf. WM 480, 494, 496, 503; FW 111; GOA XIV: 327.

71. WM 440.

72. A 14, 57; WM 440.

73. Cf. GT 13; WM 423.

74. GM I: 10; II: 3.

75. A 14; JGB 62; cf. MAMa 224.

76. WM 676; cf. WM 678.

77. JGB 230.

78. JGB 19.

79. WM 649.

80. JGB 230.

81. Cf. WM 649; JGB 230; GM III: 1.

82. WM 786.

83. Nietzsche's point is corroborated by more recent developmental psychology. Piaget's studies of child development, for example, suggested that a child's sense of agency begins with a rudimentary awareness that its body is distinct from the world. This grows into a greater awareness of the distinctiveness and centrality of the self as the child outgrows magical conceptions of how the self relates to the world. Finally, the child becomes aware of the self as an agent, as a center through which situations can be affected and controlled. Like Piaget, Freud and Lacan claimed that countless activities are motivated by the struggle to gain and situate self-identity in a familiar world, and to distinguish this identity from other beings in the world. Actions are not valued so much for their immediate effects as for their feedback in locating/defining the self. Nietzsche's emphasis on mastery as self-overcoming, self-discipline, and the "feeling of power" anticipates these later psychological insights.

84. JGB 22.

85. GM II: 12.

86. WM 552; JGB 22.

87. GOA XIV: 223.

88. GM II: 12.

89. GM II: 12.

90. WM 616.

91. GM II: 12.

92. FW 110.

93. JGB 20.

94. JGB 20.

95. I use the term "rational" here in Max Weber's sense, as he applies it to early Judaism and Christianity in his *Sociology of Religion*. Weber uses the term here to refer to an other-worldly orientation that is connected both to an intellectual development of other-worldly realms as well as to an ability to judge the phenomenal world in terms of it.

96. WM 508.

97. FW 110.

98. FW 110.

99. FW 110.

100. GD 10: 2.

101. FW 357.

102. FW 110.

103. A critical Marxism has in fact been developing. Marxists responsible for transforming assumptions about class agency into problems include, for example, the early Lukács and, in a more thoroughgoing way, Antonio Gramsci. Likewise, various thinkers associated with the Frankfurt School have attempted to deal with these problems systematically. Work on Freud and on authority in the family in the 1930s, 40s, and 50s, for example, was motivated by this theoretical vacuum in Marxism. See, e.g., Max Horkheimer, "Authority in the Family," in *Critical Theory: Selected Essays*, trans. Matthew J. O'Connell et al. (New York: Herder and Herder, 1972). For a historical account, see Martin Jay, *The Dialectical Imagination: A History of the Frankfurt School and Institute for Social Research, 1923–50* (Boston: Little, Brown and Co., 1973). Much of Jürgen Habermas' work on reconstructing historical materialism has been motivated by similar concerns. See especially his *Theory of Communicative Action*, vol. 1, trans. Thomas McCarthy (Boston: Beacon Press, 1984).

104. WM 55.

105. GM II: 1, 2.

106. GD 5: entire.

107. Eric Voegelin, "Nietzsche, the Crisis, and the War."

Chapter 5

1. EH 14: 8.

2. Tracy Strong, "Friedrich Wilhelm Nietzsche," p. 358.

3. Z, On Old and New Tablets, 4; cf. Z, On War and Warriors, On the Friend, On the Ugliest Man.

4. Z, On Old and New Tablets.

5. See, e.g., GM II: 24.

6. MAMa 245; cf. UBb 3.

7. Z, On Redemption.

8. JGB 223; cf. JGB 224.

9. GM III: 25; Z, On Science.

10. See, e.g., Jürgen Habermas' view of Nietzsche's relation to positivistic science in *Knowledge and Human Interests*, pp. 290–300. For my comments on Habermas, see chapter 3, note 46. For a good summary of Nietzsche's views of contemporary science, see Karl Jaspers, *Nietzsche*, pp. 172–184.

11. See note 44, chapter 3.

12. FW 335.

13. GM III: 25.

14. Cf. UBb 6.

15. Cf. FW 57, 344; GM III: 24, 25.

16. GM III: 25; cf. WM 597, FW 373; Z, On Science.

17. GM III: 9.

18. GM III: 9.

19. GOA XII: 108–109.

20. FW 37; GM III: 25, GD 3: 3.

21. GD 3: 3. Contrast Hannah Arendt's argument in *The Human Condition*, chap. 36, that modern science bypassed experiences of the phenomenal world just as thoroughly as Christian-Platonic idealism. Arendt points out that early modern science quickly developed a reliance on instruments of measurement to get beyond and behind experience to the mathematical laws that were supposed to give rise to experience.

22. WM 466; cf. WM 469.

23. A 13.

24. WM 469; cf. MAMa 3.

25. FW 51.

26. GD 3: 3.

27. WM 597; cf. FW 46, 335.

28. WM 1046.

29. WM 118; cf. WM 117, 120; FW 47, 372. It it worth noting that Nietzsche believed that a general pacification of existence—both socially and otherwise—had made it possible for the nineteenth century to "come to its senses" by reducing the need for the kind of "extreme" rejections of the sensuous world that had occurred at the birth of Christianity. See, e.g., WM 114; M 244, 565; FW 48, 313, 372.

30. GM III: 25; cf. WM 610.

31. GOA XII: 125.

32. See Robert Solomon, "Nietzsche, Nihilism, and Morality."

33. Cf. A 57; WM 127, 130.

34. A rather common assessment of Nietzsche's views on morality is Alasdair MacIntyre's, in *After Virtue*, chaps. 9, 18. MacIntyre argues that Nietzsche represents the eclipse of modern utilitarian and Kantian morality, leaving us with only the ad hoc moralities of powerful

individuals. MacIntyre's assessment is quite consistent with Nietzsche's politics, but not with the sum total of his philosophy. In contrast to MacIntyre, Frederick Olafson suggests that Nietzsche's view that any post-Christian morality would necessarily be the tool of a political elite does not in fact follow from his metaethical considerations on evaluative practices; see *Principles and Persons* (Baltimore: Johns Hopkins University Press, 1967), pp. 53–54.

35. Frederick Olafson, *Principles and Persons*, p. 51.

36. WM 254.

37. Cf. JGB 174, 228.

38. WM 786.

39. WM 552.

40. Cf. JGB 228.

41. GM II: 16.

42. *The Sociology of George Simmel*, p. 62.

43. FW 116.

44. WM 139–141; A 47, 48.

45. A 49; cf. M 58; WM 196.

46. A 49.

47. GM III: 15, 16; A 26; M 79.

48. A 44.

49. GM II: 2; GOA XII: 125; translated by George Morgan.

50. GM III: 27.

51. GM II: 2.

52. Frederick Olafson makes this point in *Principles and Persons*, chap. 3. Cf. Robert Solomon, "Nietzsche, Nihilism, and Morality," pp. 209–219.

53. The autonomy of the will, writes Kant, should be taken as the "sole principle of all moral laws and of the duties conforming to them"—*Critique of Practical Reason*, trans. Thomas Kingsmill Abbot (London: Longman, Green and Co., 1909), p. 122 (Book I, chap. 1, Section 8, Theorem 4).

54. Cf. Frederick Olafson, *Principles and Persons*, chap. 3.

55. *The Sociology of Georg Simmel*, pp. 62–63.

56. *The Sociology of Georg Simmel*, pp. 63–64.

57. M 187.

58. GM II: 6. Theodor Adorno, in *Negative Dialectics*, pp. 252–265, criticizes Kant on precisely the same grounds.

59. GM II: 2; cf. A 10, 11; WM 283; M 339; GM II: 6; FW 335.

60. GM II: 2; cf. JGB 262.

61. GM II: 1, 2.

62. GM II: 1, 2.

63. GM II: 1.

64. Max Weber, "Politics as a Vocation," in *From Max Weber*. See also Weber's "The Meaning of Ethical Neutrality," in *The Methodology of The Social Sciences*, Edward Shils and Henry Finch, trans. and eds. (New York: The Free Press, 1949).

65. Cf. M 112; FW 358; Frederick Olafson, *Principles and Persons*, pp. 53–54.

66. JGB 287.

67. GM I: 4–6, 10, 11.

68. WM 863; cf. WM 129, 216.

69. Cf. GM I: 16; JGB 258.

70. Interestingly, one of the few priestly practices of which Nietzsche approved was confession, precisely because confessing helps one to forget, and forgetting reinforces good conscience. See FW 351.

71. GM II: 1.

72. GM II: 1.

73. These considerations provide Nietzsche with the psychological bases of his doctrine of the eternal return of the same, as I shall argue in the following chapter.

74. GM II: 1.

75. GM I: 10.

76. GM II: 1–3.

77. Heidegger, *Nietzsche*, vol. 1: *The Will to Power as Art*.

78. WM 809.

79. WM 808; cf. WM 794; GD 9: 8, 9.

80. FW 369; GD 9: 22, 23; cf. GD 10: 4, 5.

81. JGB 291.

82. Jacques Derrida, *Spurs: Nietzsche's Styles*.

83. JGB, Preface. Cf. Derrida, *Spurs*, p. 55.

84. FW 60; cf. FW Preface, 4.

85. Derrida, *Spurs*, p. 107.

86. GT Preface, 2.

87. GT Preface, 2.

88. See, e.g., Heidegger, *Nietzsche*, vol. 1: *The Will to Power as Art*, pp. 211–220.

89. Heidegger, *Nietzsche*, vol. 1: *The Will to Power as Art*, pp. 142–150.

90. Nietzsche's insights here are reflected in recent debates within philosophy of science about the roles of aesthetic metaphors in scientific discovery. See, e.g., Judith Wechsler, ed., *On Aesthetics in Science* (Cambridge, MA: MIT Press, 1978).

91. JGB 188.

92. WM 809; cf. WM 522.

93. JGB 188; cf. FW 367.

94. WM 822; cf. JGB 39.

95. Cf. FW 367, 370; GD 9: 11.

96. GD 9: 8, 9.

97. FW 370; GD 9: 11.

98. FW 367, 369, 370.

99. FW 335.

100. FW 1; cf. FW 324, 327, 338, 377, 383.

101. EH 8.

102. GD 9: 11; cf. MAMa 215.

103. Cf. GM II: 17, where Nietzsche refers to early political "masters" as artists giving form to a "raw material of people and semianimals."

104. MAMa 477.

105. Eric Vogelin, "Nietzsche, the Crisis, and the War."

106. Cf. arguments by J. P. Stern, *A Study of Nietzsche*, p. 117, and Walter Sokel, "The Political Uses and Abuses of Nietzsche in Walter Kaufmann's Image of Nietzsche."

107. For a much more honest and careful evaluation of war that is still meticulously "Nietzschean" in its attention to experience and psychological detail, see J. Glenn Gray, *The Warriors* (New York: Harper and Row, 1959).

108. See chapter 2, on Nietzsche's latent model of political culture.

109. E.g., WM 809.

110. Cf. Tracy Strong's favorable comparison of Nietzsche and Hannah Arendt on this point in *Friedrich Nietzsche*, chap. 5.

111. Z, On Old and New Tablets, 4.

112. WM 417.

Chapter 6

1. GM II: 1.

2. EH 9: 1.

3. Another way of describing this dimension of Nietzsche's project is to compare it to Max Weber's "Politics as a Vocation," in *From Max Weber*. The essay was an exhortation to his student audience about the requirements of a political personality in a secular age dominated by depersonalizing bureaucratic organizations. According to Weber, a politician who leaves a mark upon history, who is responsible, and who engages in actions that will change the future requires an attitude that combines realism, passion, and responsibility. Each of these character traits is worldly in a way that requires and manifests a strong and directed personality. Nietzsche sketches the terrain presupposed by Weber's analysis of politics as a vocation.

4. EH 4: 3.

5. EH 2: 10.

6. FW 276.

7. GD 9: 32.

8. George Grant, in *Time as History*, pp. 41–47, interprets Nietzsche's concept of *amor fati* in this way.

9. MAMc 61; Joan Stambaugh, trans., with minor changes.

10. FW 276.

11. WM 852, 853, 1060.

12. Cf. Z, On Old and New Tablets, 22.

13. GM II: 15.

14. JGB 259.

15. JGB 259, MAMa 471.

16. GM II: 7.

17. Cf. JGB 62, 202; Z, On the Pitying.

18. JGB 225.

19. Cf. FW 110; GM III: 27.

20. FW 341 first introduces the thought of the eternal return in conclusion to the original four books of FW. The introduction of the doctrine directly precedes the introduction of Zarathustra in FW 342. Cf. EH 9: 1. Nietzsche claimed that the doctrine of the eternal return was the "fundamental conception" of his *Thus Spoke Zarathustra*, EH 9: 1.

21. Cf. FW 341; EH 4: 3, 9: 1; JGB 56.

22. Thus, for example, I agree with Tracy Strong in *Friedrich Nietzsche*, p. 265, that "whatever the eternal return is, it is not a theory of the cosmos." If Strong's position is correct, as I believe it is, then many of the attempts to understand the thought as a literal proposition about the structure of time are quite unnecessary, as elaborate and interesting as they are. For the best of these interpretations, see Arthur Danto, *Nietzsche as Philosopher*, pp. 200–213, and Bernd Magnus, *Nietzsche's Existential Imperative*, pp. 89–110. These interpretations are supported by Nietzsche's own attempts in this direction in, e.g., WM 1062–64, 1066. Although his attempts to make the eternal return into a literal characterization of the world is by all accounts a failed experiment, we should notice one of his better reasons for pursuing this line of argument. Nietzsche was especially interested in refuting mechanistic views of the world that postulate a future equilibrium or "final state" of the universe; see, e.g., WM 1062, 1064. If he could show that the notions of "final state" and "equilibrium" are incompatible with mechanistic notions of the cosmos, he would have eliminated from mechanics a residue of the Christian hope for a universe at rest and at peace with itself—a hope he equates with death. At the very least, Nietzsche thought he could perhaps show a formal compatibility between the subjective experience of eternal moments of time and the mechanistic notion of the universe as a constantly changing disequilibrium of forces. Here, writes Nietzsche, the "two most extreme modes of thought—the mechanistic and the Platonic—are recognized in the *eternal recurrence*: both as ideals" (WM 1061). But if mechanistic materialism and Platonic idealism are in fact reconciled here, it is at a purely formal level, and in no way counts as a resolution to the relationship between self-identity and mechanistic change. Even if we were to accept the logical possibility of mechanistic recurrence—a logic that others have shown to be faulty—the problem would remain that the time scale of recurrences would likely be such that no single individual could experience a recurrence in the span of a human life.

23. This possibility was suggested to me by David Savan of the Department of Philosophy, University of Toronto.

24. Z, On the Vision and the Riddle.

25. Cf. GM II: 13, and chapter 4.

26. GM II: 12.

27. WM 617.

28. See, e.g., Heidegger, *Nietzsche*, vol. 1: *The Will to Power as Art*, pp. 18–19.

29. *Nietzsche's Thought of Eternal Return*, p. 32.

30. For my comments on Stambaugh on the issue, see chapter 3, note 5.

31. See JGB 56, and my comments on this aphorism below.

32. Joan Stambaugh, in *Nietzsche's Thought of Eternal Return*, p. 31, points this out.

33. WM 551; cf. WM 532.

34. Z, The Wanderer.

35. Alexander Nehamas comes closest to the interpretation I am suggesting here by emphasizing that the eternal return is a doctrine of character. Since *who* one is determined by the uniqueness of one's biography, when one wills the eternal return of the past, one affirms one's self-identity and therefore one's present and future identity; see *Nietzsche: Life as Literature*, esp. pp. 158–159.

36. JGB 70.

37. FW 341.

38. FW 341.

39. JGB 56.

40. JGB 56. Cf. Herbert Marcuse's interpretation of the eternal return in *Eros and Civilization*, pp. 111–112.

41. Z, On Redemption.

42. The relationship between the critical and speculative aspects of Nietzsche's philosophy is quite clear in the relation between Nietzsche's critical works and *Thus Spoke Zarathustra*. With the exception of W, every work after *Zarathustra* ends with an introduction of the figure of Zarathustra. Apparent exceptions to this rule can be explained by looking at the plans of these works. Zarathustra is introduced in FW at the end of Book IV, which was the last book of the 1882 version. Zarathustra appears in the "Aftersong" of JGB, and at the end of the second essay of GM, which completes the formal argument of the work. Nietzsche tentatively conceived of A as part of a larger work (to be called *Umwertung aller Werte*), and thus lacks the unified movement of other published works.

Chapter 7

1. JGB 259.

2. Here I argee with Walter Sokel in "Political Uses and Abuses of Nietzsche in Walter Kaufmann's Image of Nietzsche." See also William Bluhm's careful treatment of this issue in *Theories of the Political System*, chap. 14.

3. I consider the purely *textual* defense of Nietzsche against the Nazi appropriation of his philosophy to be complete and successful, thus warranting no further consideration. Walter Kaufmann's *Nietzsche* must be credited with having performed this service in English-speaking countries. In Germany, Martin Heidegger's and Karl Jasper's work on Nietzsche dating from the mid-1930s can be read as an implicit defense of Nietzsche against the Nazis, although Heidegger's 1930s lectures on Nietzsche were not published until 1961. For early examples of French defenses of Nietzsche, see Georg Bataille, *Sur Nietzsche* (Paris: Gallimard, 1945), and Marius Paul Nicholas, *From Nietzsche Down to Hitler*, trans., E. G. Echlin (Port Washington, NY: Kennikat Press, 1970, first published in France, 1938). For a good summary of the political history of Nietzsche's ideas especially in relation to the Nazis, see John S. Colman, "Nietzsche as Politique et Moraliste," *Journal of the History of Ideas* 27 (October–December 1966), pp. 549–574.

4. See R. Hinton Thomas, *Nietzsche in German Politics and Society, 1890–1914* (Manchester: Manchester University Press, 1983), for a history of Nietzsche's rather wide political influence in pre-World War I Germany. Some examples suggesting that the range of Nietzsche's political influence has gone far beyond the range of his own politics are as follows: Arthur Mitzman, *The Iron Cage* (New York: Alfred A. Knopf, 1970), p. 182, quotes Max Weber as saying that "one can measure the honesty of a contemporary scholar, and above all of a contemporary philosopher, in his posture toward Marx and Nietzsche." Also interesting is an 1892 comment, given both as a Nietzsche scholar and as a leader of the German SPD (Social Democratic Party), by Franz Mehring in a review of Kurt Gisner's *Psychopathia Spiritualis* in *Die Neue Zeit* 10 (1891–1892), pp. 668–669, that Nietzsche might be considered a "moment in the passage to socialism," especially for those with bourgeois class-identities who would find in him the disillusionment of their world. Nietzsche's thought came to figure significantly not only for Mehring but for the young Georg Lukács (who, as Mehring's account predicted, passed from a fascination with Nietzsche to socialism). Nietzsche was also significant for the members of the Frankfurt School, including Theodor Adorno, Max Horkheimer, and Herbert Marcuse, for the anarchists Georges Sorel, Rudolph Rocker, and Emma Goldman, and for the Fabian socialist George Bernard Shaw.

5. GD 9: 43. This text is often cited as proof that Nietzsche distanced himself from conservatism. This is true only insofar as traditional conservatism is both ahistorical and Christian. Modern conservatism, especially in Nietzsche's Germany, could be both historical—in the sense of respecting the evolutionary changes wrought by history—and "spiritual" but non-Christian.

6. Franz Mehring, *Gesammelte Schriften* (Berlin: Dietz, 1960–1966), vol. 13, pp. 159–172.

7. Georg Lukács' attempt in *The Destruction of Reason* to tie Nietzsche directly to the Nazis relies on caricatures of his philosophy, if not his politics.

8. Marc Sautet, *Nietzsche et la Commune.* Cf. JGB 258.

9. See Nietzsche's most extensive considerations on this topic in MAMa, Section 8, "A Look at the State," aphorisms 438–482.

10. For recent characterizations of Nietzsche as an important critic of liberal democracy, see William Bluhm, *Theories of the Political System*, chap. 14; Thomas Pangle, "Nietzsche and Nihilism," *Review of Politics* 45 (January 1983), pp. 45–70; J. P. Stern, *A Study of Nietzsche.*

11. Cf. JGB 228.

12. Kant, *The Metaphysics of Morals*, Part II, esp. Section A, pp. 143–147, in Hans Reiss, ed., *Kant's Political Writings*, trans. H. B. Nisbet (Cambridge: Cambridge University Press, 1970).

13. See, e.g., the conclusion of MAMa 472, and the arguments below.

14. This is quite clear in Kant's defense of intellectual without civil freedom in "What Is Enlightenment?" in Reiss, ed., *Kant's Political Writings*, p. 59.

15. GM II: 6.

16. JGB 228; cf. GD 9: 41, WM 339, 724. John Stuart Mill attempted to derive the Kantian moral effect—that is, universal categorical morality—from a utilitarian history, thereby establishing the classical relationship between happiness and morality lost to both Kant and Bentham. See especially Mill's *Utilitarianism*, chap. 3, in H. B. Acton, ed., *Utilitarianism, On Liberty, and Considerations on Representative Government* (London: J. M. Dent and Sons, 1972). In Nietzsche's view, Mill simply retained the structure of a crumbling Christian morality on the

basis of a decadent utilitarian morality. See especially M 132; WM 30, 925, 926. Nietzsche's criticisms of liberalism point to a complementary duality within liberal thought between religious identities and individualism that has been commented on by Eldon Eisenach in his *Two Worlds of Liberalism* (Chicago: University of Chicago Press, 1981). Eisenach argues that Hobbes, Locke, and J. S. Mill constructed their respective liberalisms on the basis of the complementary abstractions of freedom and reason, on the one hand, and the obedience and duties prescribed by religious life, on the other.

17. JGB 38, 258; GM I: 16.

18. A 43, GD 9: 43.

19. JGB 212.

20. GD 9: 37; cf. M 112.

21. GD 9: 41.

22. MAMa 451; Cf. GD 9: 38; GM II: 2, 11; M 112; Z, On the Tarantulas.

23. Nietzsche's view that the damage of political oppression and Christian ideology was permanent stems from his Lamarckian view of changes in human nature—that is, the view that acquired characteristics are passed physiologically to future generations. See the section entitled "Human Nature: Uncritical Assumptions" below. The contradiction Nietzsche's analysis suggests within liberal democratic societies appears in the history of liberal democratic theory as a contradiction between the view that democracy consists primarily in a majority check on a quasi-independent political process—a view represented by James Mill, Joseph Schumpeter, and Robert Dahl, for example—and the view that democracy also consists in developing the rational capacities of individuals through participation in decision-making processes—represented by Rousseau and John Stuart Mill. For commentary, see C. B. Macpherson, *The Life and Times of Liberal Democracy* (Oxford: Oxford University Press, 1977), and Carole Pateman's two books, *Participation and Democratic Theory* (Cambridge: Cambridge University Press, 1970) and *The Problem of Political Obligation* (Chichester: John Wiley and Sons, 1979).

24. Cf. MAMa 472, WM 211, 282.

25. On this issue, see Herbert Marcuse's "The Struggle against Liberalism in the Totalitarian View of the State," in *Negations*, trans. Jeremy Shapiro (Boston: Beacon, 1968).

26. In *Human, All-Too-Human*, Nietzsche carefully distinguishes the "private person" from the individual. See MAMa 472.

27. Z, Zarathustra's Prologue, 5.

28. Cf. M 183, WM 887, GD 9: 38.

29. FW 174; cf. GD 9: 38; WM 953.

30. GD 9: 38.

31. GD 9: 38.

32. MAMa 438, cf. MAMa 454, M 184.

33. MAMa 473, cf. MAMa 438, 449. See Alice Waxler, *Emma Goldman: An Intimate Life* (New York: Pantheon Books, 1984), p. 50. See also Emma Goldman, *Living My Life* (New York:

Dover, 1970), p. 194, as well as the similar sentiments of Georges Bataille, "Nietzsche in Light of Marxism," Lee Hildreth, trans., *Semiotext(e)* 3 (1978), pp. 114–119.

34. MAMa 475.

35. GD 8: 4.

36. GD 8: 4; cf. Z, On the New Idol. Tracy Strong, in *Friedrich Nietzsche*, pp. 192–201, comments on the positive and active sense of Nietzsche's political vision. He rightly points out that Nietzsche thought the state to be anathema to positive politics insofar as it enforces (and must enforce) a social division of labor. But because a division of labor is necessary in Nietzsche's view, the state is a necessary evil. On Strong's account, the conflict between Nietzsche's political vision and his views on the state is never resolved. In contrast, Karl Jaspers' view that Nietzsche had a positive conception of the state is simply wrong. It is not true, as Jaspers asserts, that to Nietzsche the "state is a power that gives a characteristic stamp to the individual, the people, and the culture." See Jaspers' *Nietzsche*, p. 254. In an early review of Jaspers' book, Max Horkheimer suggests that Jaspers' reading reflected his own German nationalism more than Nietzsche's political thought. See "Bemerkungen zu Jaspers *Nietzsche*," *Zeitschrift für Sozialforschung* 6 (1937), pp. 407–414.

37. Z, On the New Idol.

38. Z, On the New Idol.

39. GD 8: 4.

40. See Michael Löwy, *Georg Lukács: From Romanticism to Bolshevism* (London: New Left Books, 1979), pp. 25–26.

41. GM III: 18; cf. FW 329. See also Karl Löwith's excellent comments on this aspect of Nietzsche's thought in *From Hegel to Nietzsche*, trans. David Green (Garden City, NJ: Doubleday, 1967), esp. pp. 283–285.

42. WM 866; cf. M 175, 179, 186, 203, 204; FW 40; EH 5: 1.

43. WM 764, 784; M 206; GD 9: 40.

44. MAMa 452.

45. Cf. MAMa 457, 462.

46. FW 313.

47. GD 9: 40. The draft for this note is somewhat more explicit about the assumption that economic exploitation is necessary: "If one want slaves—and one needs them!—one must not teach them to be masters"—WKG VIII (2):272; cf. MAMa 452.

48. See, e.g., Georg Lukács, *The Destruction of Reason*, pp. 372–378; J. P. Stern, *Nietzsche* (Glasgow: William Collins Sons, 1978), pp. 82–87, and *A Study of Nietzsche*, pp. 120–122; Alasdair MacIntyre, *After Virtue*, chaps. 9, 18.

49. JGB 259; cf. GM II: 11; EH 14: 4; WM 369, 728, 882.

50. Ofelia Schutte, *Beyond Nihilism*.

51. JGB 19.

52. This conflation is quite clear, e.g., in JGB 259.

53. GM I: 13; cf. GM II: 1–3; JGB 295.

54. GD 9: 38.

55. WM 983, cf. M 112, 187.

56. Cf. WM 888, 890, 898; A 57; JGB 242, 259. For Georg Simmel's comments to this effect, see chapter 5.

57. This argument is put most strongly by Hans Barth in *Truth and Ideology*, pp. 179–94. But also see J. P. Stern, *A Study of Nietzsche*, p. 117, and *Nietzsche*, pp. 84–87, and Ernst Nolte, *The Three Faces of Fascism* (New York: Holt, Reinhart, and Winston, 1966), p. 445. See also Jürgen Habermas, "Myth and Enlightenment: Re-Reading *Dialectic of Enlightenment*."

58. GM II: 1, 2.

59. GM II: 1.

60. See, e.g., Michel Foucault, *Power/Knowledge*, trans. Colin Gordon, Leo Marshall, John Mephan, and Kate Soper (New York: Pantheon Books, 1980), esp. "Truth and Power." Because Foucault rejects the language of truth, however, he is limited to remarking on Nietzsche's insights, and unable to conceive of the nonrepressive understandings of truth that can be drawn out of his philosophy.

61. Hannah Arendt, *The Human Condition*, pp. 192–199.

62. Z, On Old and New Tablets, 21.

63. WM 889. According to GOA XVI: 512, the text reading from the word "entail" on is uncertain. Cf. WM 888.

64. WM 888. This note is together with WM 889 in the original manuscript. Both were revised together in spring-fall 1888. See GOA XVI: 493.

65. MAMa 439. Marion Faber, trans.

66. WM 890; cf. A 57; JGB 242, 259; WM 888, 898.

67. Cf. JGB 212, 258.

68. JGB 258; cf. MAMa 439.

69. WM 890. Cf. MAMa 462.

70. JGB 202, 203, 212.

71. JGB 264; cf. JGB 200, 213.

72. JGB 264.

73. WM 55.

74. WM 55; cf. JGB 264. In attempting to protect Nietzsche from the view that he considered "breeding" and "race" as strictly biological concepts, Walter Kaufmann saves Nietzsche from his abuse by the Nazis only by missing these other issues of political importance; see Kaufmann, *Nietzsche*, pp. 284–306.

75. JGB 262.

76. Max Weber, *The Protestant Ethic and the Spirit of Capitalism*, trans. Talcott Parsons (New York: Scribner's, 1958).

77. On this issue, see my "Max Weber's Liberalism for a Nietzschean World," *American Political Science Review* 82 (March 1988).

78. Ofelia Schutte make a similar point in *Beyond Nihilism*. She argues that Nietzsche's failure to move beyond nihilism is not intrinsic to his philosophy, but rather is owing to his failure to provide a critique of domination.

79. In Max Horkheimer's view, Nietzsche's failure to penetrate bourgeois society led him to glorify an abstract egoism—the will of the *Übermensch*—as the only possible escape from nihilism. "In the last analysis," he writes, "Nietzsche's critique of European nihilism captures the confluence of cultural development since the beginning of Christianity. The nihilism of which Nietzsche wrote is really more narrowly circumscribed than he thought. In truth it signifies the common self-contempt that the individual has for himself owing to the contradiction between bourgeois ideology and the actuality of bourgeois society. It is a kind of self-disdain that is usually connected with the over-arching consciousness of freedom and its strange and peculiar vastness. Because Nietzsche grasped the concept too narrowly and therefore ahistorically, he necessarily erred in thinking that to overcome nihilism would be to overcome society in general, or it would not be overcome at all. . . . [I]n this way Nietzsche intentionally inspired courage for what is still merely the abstract self-consciousness of the ancient slave; but he unintentionally inspired the good conscience of the modern despot in this way as well, which nihilism now also reproduces in the heart. . . . "—from "Egoismus und Freiheitsbewegung," in *Zeitschrift für Sozialforschung* 5 (1936), p. 220n.
    The real issue behind Horkheimer's assessment of Nietzsche—together with the other members of the Frankfurt School influenced by Nietzsche—is whether or not Marx and Nietzsche can be seen as complementary thinkers. Nietzsche is sometimes read as an implicit attack on Marxism, although there is nothing in his writings to suggest that he was even aware of Marx. On the left, Georg Lukács makes this claim in his *Destruction*, p. 313. On the right, Werner Dannhauser, in "Friedrich Nietzsche," p. 743, argues with Nietzsche and against Marxism that "one may summarize" the relation of Marxism to Nietzsche's political philosophy in the following manner: "The Marxist realm of freedom which is to be secured by the revolution is for Nietzsche the realm of the last man, the utter degradation of man." One need not have read too much Marx to know that Nietzsche's tirades against socialism are misplaced. Even less should one look for a criticism of Marxism here, as Dannhauser seems to do. The connections between Nietzsche and Marx are to be found neither in clichés about Marxism nor in Nietzsche's own ill-informed banalities about socialism, but rather in a comparison of their respective philosophies. Others have attended more systematically to the deeper philosophical similarities between Marx and Nietzsche. Some of the more interesting thoughts have come from members of the Frankfurt School, a summary of which can be found in Peter Pütz, "Nietzsche im Lichte der Kritischen Theorie," in *Nietzsche-Studien* 3 (1974), pp. 175–191. Alfred Schmidt's article, "Nietzsches Erkenntnistheorie," also probes in this direction. See also Reinhold Grimm and Jost Hermand, eds., *Karl Marx und Friedrich Nietzsche* (Königstein/Ts.: Athenäum, 1978); Edward Andrew, "The Unity of Theory and Practice"; James Miller, "Nietzsche and Marxism," *Telos* 37 (Fall 1978), pp. 22–41; Georges Bataille, "Nietzsche in Light of Marxism"; Paul Veyne, "Ideology According to Marx and According to Nietzsche," trans. Jeane Ferguson, *Diogenes* 99 (Fall 1977), pp. 80–102; Reinhart Mauer, "Nietzsche und die Kritische Theorie," *Nietzsche-Studien* 10/11 (1981–1982), pp. 34–58.

Bibliography

Adorno, T. W. *Negative Dialectics*. Translated by E. B. Ashton. New York: Seabury, 1973.

Allen, Christine. "Nietzsche's Ambivalence about Women." In *The Sexism of Social and Political Theory*, edited by M. Clark and L. Lange, pp. 117–133. Toronto: University of Toronto Press, 1979.

Andrew, Edward. "The Unity of Theory and Practice: the Science of Marx and Nietzsche." In *Political Theory and Praxis*, edited by Terence Ball, pp. 117–137. Minneapolis: University of Minnesota Press, 1977.

Ansell-Pearson, Keith. "Nietzsche's Overcoming of Kant and Metaphysics: From Tragedy to Nihilism." *Nietzsche-Studien* 16 (1987): 310–339.

Arendt, Hannah. *The Human Condition*. Chicago: University of Chicago Press, 1958.

Arendt, Hannah. *The Life of the Mind*, vol. 2: *Willing*. New York: Harcourt, Brace and World, 1978.

Barth, Hans. *Truth and Ideology*. Translated by Frederic Lilge. Berkeley: University of California Press, 1976.

Bataille, Georges. *Sur Nietzsche*. Paris: Gallimard, 1945.

Bataille, Georges. "Nietzsche in Light of Marxism." Translated by Lee Hildreth. *Semiotext(e)* 3:1 (1978): 109–113.

Bataille, Georges. "Nietzsche and the Fascists." Translated by Lee Hildreth. *Semiotext(e)* 3:1 (1978): 114–119.

Bentham, Jeremy. *An Introduction to the Principles of Morals and Legislation*. Edited by J. H. Burns and H. L. A. Hart. London: Athlone Press, 1970.

Blanchot, Maurice. "The Limits of Experience: Nihilism." Translated by John Leavey. In *The New Nietzsche*, edited by David Allison, pp. 121–128. New York: Dell Publishing Co., 1977.

Blondel, Eric. "Nietzsche: Life as Metaphor." Translated by Mairi Macrae. In *The New Nietzsche*, edited by David Allison, pp. 150–175. New York: Dell Publishing Co., 1977.

Bluhm, William. *Theories of the Political System*, 3rd ed. Engelwood Cliffs, NJ: Prentice-Hall, 1978.

Breazeale, Daniel. "The Hegel-Nietzsche Problem." *Nietzsche-Studien* 4 (1975) : 146–164.

Breazeale, Daniel. "The Word, the World and Nietzsche." *Philosophical Forum* 7 (July 1976) : 301–320.

Breazeale, Daniel. "Introduction" to *Philosophy and Truth*, by Friedrich Nietzsche. Atlantic Highlands, NJ: Humanities Press, 1979.

Bröse, Karl. *Geschichtsphilosophische Strukturen im Werk Nietzsches*. Frankfurt/M: Peter Lang, 1973.

Bueb, Bernard. *Nietzsches Kritik der praktischen Vernunft*. Stuttgart: Ernst Klett, 1970.

Burke, Edmund. *Reflections on Revolution in France*. Edited by C. C. O'Brien. Harmondsworth: Penguin, 1968.

Colman, John S. "Nietzsche as Politique et Moraliste." *Journal of the History of Ideas* 27 (October–December 1966) : 549–574.

Dallmayr, Fred. *Critical Encounters*. Notre Dame: University of Notre Dame Press, 1987.

Dannhauser, Werner, "Friedrich Nietzsche." In *History of Political Philosophy*, edited by Leo Strauss and Joseph Cropsey, pp. 724–745. Chicago: Rand McNally, 1963.

Dannhauser, Werner, *Nietzsche's View of Socrates*. Ithaca: Cornell University Press, 1974.

Danto, Arthur. *Nietzsche as Philosopher*. New York: Macmillan, 1965.

Deleuze, Gilles. "Active and Reactive." Translated by Richard Cohen. In *The New Nietzsche*, edited by David Allison, pp. 80–106. New York: Dell Publishing Co., 1977.

Deleuze, Gilles. *Nietzsche and Philosophy*. Translated by Hugh Tomlinson. New York: Columbia University Press, 1983.

De Man, Paul, "Genesis and Genealogy in Nietzsche's *The Birth of Tragedy*." *Diacritics* 2 : 4 (Winter 1971) : 44–53.

De Man, Paul. *Allegories of Reading*. New Haven: Yale University Press, 1979.

Derrida, Jacques. *Spurs: Nietzsche's Style*. Translated by Barbara Harlow. Chicago: University of Chicago Press, 1979.

Douglas, Mary. *How Institutions Think*. Syracuse: Syracuse University Press, 1986.

Eden, Robert. *Political Leadership and Nihilism*. Gainesville: University of Florida Press, 1984.

Eisenach, Eldon. *Two Worlds of Liberalism*. Chicago: University of Chicago Press, 1981.

Fink, Eugen. *Nietzsches Philosophie*. Stuttgart: Kohlmanner, 1960.

Foucault, Michel. "Nietzsche, Genealogy, History." In *Language, Countermemory, Practice*, translated by Donald Bouchard and Sherry Simon, pp. 139–164. Ithaca: Cornell University Press, 1977.

Bibliography

Foucault, Michel. *Discipline and Punish*. Translated by Alan Sheridan. New York: Pantheon Books, 1977.

Foucault, Michel. *Power/Knowledge*. Translated by Colin Gordon, Leo Marshall, John Mephan, and Kate Soper. New York: Pantheon Books, 1980.

Foucault, Michel. "What is Enlightenment?" In *The Foucault Reader*, edited by Paul Rabinow, pp. 32–50. New York: Pantheon Books, 1984.

Frankfurt Institute for Social Research, *Aspects of Sociology*. Translated by John Verteil. Boston: Beacon Press, 1972.

Freud, Sigmund. *Gesammelte Werke*. Edited by Anna Freud et al. London: Imago Publishing, 1948.

Freud, Sigmund. *Civilization and Its Discontents*. Translated by James Strachey. New York: W. W. Norton, 1961.

Freud, Sigmund. *The Future of an Illusion*. Translated by W. D. Robson-Scott. Garden City, NY: Doubleday and Co., 1961.

Funke, Monika. *Ideologiekritik und ihre Ideologie bei Nietzsche*. Stuttgart: Friedrich Fromann, 1974.

Gendlin, Eugene. *Experiencing and the Creation of Meaning*. New York: The Free Press, 1962.

Goldman, Emma. *Living My Life*. New York: Dover, 1970.

Grant, George. *Time as History*. Toronto: Canadian Broadcasting Corp., 1969.

Grant, George. "Nietzsche and the Ancients: Philosophy and Scholarship." *Dionysus* 3 (December 1979):5–16.

Gray, J. Glenn. *The Warriors*. New York: Harper and Row, 1959.

Grimm, Reinhold, and Hermand, Jost, eds. *Karl Marx und Friedrich Nietzsche*. Königstein/Ts.: Athenäum, 1978.

Grimm, Ruediger. *Nietzsche's Theory of Knowledge*. Berlin: Walter de Gruyter, 1977.

Haar, Michel. "Nietzsche and Metaphysical Language." Translated by Cyril Welch and Liliane Welch. In *The New Nietzsche*, edited by David Allison, pp. 5–36. New York: Dell Publishing Co., 1977.

Habermas, Jürgen. "Nachwort." In *Nietzsche: Erkenntnistheoretische Schriften*, by Friedrich Nietzsche. Edited by Hans Blumenburg et al. Frankfurt/M: Suhrkamp Verlag, 1968.

Habermas, Jürgen. *Knowledge and Human Interest*. Translated by Jeremy Shapiro. Boston: Beacon Press, 1971.

Habermas, Jürgen. "Myth and Englightenment: Re-Reading *Dialectic of Enlightenment*." Translated by Thomas Levin. *New German Critique* 26 (Spring-Summer 1982).

Habermas, Jürgen. *The Theory of Communicative Action*, vol. 1. Translated by Thomas McCarthy. Boston: Beacon Press, 1984.

Hegel, G. W. F. *The Logic of Hegel*. Translated by William Wallace. London: Oxford University Press, 1931.

Hegel, G. W. F. *Philosophy of History*. Translated by J. Sibree. New York: Dover, 1956.

Hegel, G. W. F. *Philosophy of Right*. Translated by T. M. Knox. New York: Oxford University Press, 1967.

Hegel, G. W. F. *The Phenomenology of Spirit*. Translated by A. V. Miller. Oxford: Clarendon Press, 1977.

Heidegger, Martin. *Nietzsche*, 2 vols. Pfullingen: Günther Neske Verlag, 1961.

Heidegger, Martin. *What Is Called Thinking?* Translated by J. Glenn Gray. New York: Harper and Row, 1968.

Heidegger, Martin. *The End of Philosophy*. Translated by Joan Stambaugh. New York: Harper and Row, 1973.

Heidegger, Martin. "The Word of Nietzsche: 'God Is Dead.'" In *The Question Concerning Technology*, translated by William Lovitt. New York: Harper and Row, 1977.

Heidegger, Martin. "Who Is Nietzsche's Zarathustra?" In *The New Nietzsche*, edited by David Allison, pp. 64–79. New York: Dell Publishing Co., 1977.

Heidegger, Martin. *Nietzsche*, vol. 1: *The Will to Power as Art*. Translated by David Krell. New York: Harper and Row, 1979.

Heidegger, Martin. *Nietzsche*, vol. 2: *The Eternal Return*. Translated by David Krell. New York: Harper and Row, 1984.

Heidegger, Martin. *Nietzsche*, vol. 3: *Will to Power as Knowledge and Metaphysics*. Translated by David Krell. Harper and Row, 1986.

Heidegger, Martin. *Nietzsche*, vol. 4: *Nihilism*. Translated by Frank Capuzzi. New York: Harper and Row, 1982.

Horkheimer, Max. "Egoismus and Freiheitsbewegung." *Zeitschrift für Sozialforschung* 5:2 (1936):161–234.

Horkheimer, Max. "Bemerkungen zu Jaspers *Nietzsche*." *Zeitschrift für Sozialforschung* 6:2 (1937):407–414.

Horkheimer, Max. *Critical Theory: Selected Essays*. Translated by Matthew J. O'Connell et al. New York: Herder and Herder, 1972.

Horkheimer, Max, and Adorno, Theodor. *Dialectic of Enlightenment*. Translated by John Cumming. New York: Seabury, 1972.

Husserl, Edmund. *The Crisis of the European Sciences and Transcendental Phenomenology*. Translated by D. Carr. Evanston: Northwestern University Press, 1970.

Jaspers, Karl. *Nietzsche*. Translated by Charles Wallraft and Frederick Schmitz. Chicago: Henry Regnery, 1965.

Jay, Martin. *The Dialectical Imagination: A History of the Frankfurt School and Institute for Social Research, 1923–50*. Boston: Little, Brown and Co., 1973.

Jung, Carl. *Two Essays on Analytic Psychology*. Translated by R. F. C. Hull. Cleveland: World, 1953.

Kant, Immanuel. *Critique of Practical Reason*. Translated by Thomas Kingsmill Abbot. London: Longman, Green and Co., 1909.

Kant, Immanuel. *Critique of Pure Reason*, 2nd ed. Translated by F. Max Müller. Garden City, NY: Doubleday and Co., 1961.

Kant, Immanuel. "The Metaphysics of Morals." Translated by H. B. Nisbet. In *Kant's Political Writings*, edited by Hans Reiss. Cambridge: Cambridge University Press, 1970.

Kant, Immanuel. "What Is Enlightenment?" Translated by H. B. Nisbet. In *Kant's Political Writings*, edited by Hans Reiss. Cambridge: Cambridge University Press, 1970.

Kariel, Henry, "Nietzsche's Preface to Constitutionalism." *Journal of Politics* 25:2 (May 1963):211–225.

Kaufmann, Walter. *Nietzsche: Philosopher, Psychologist, Antichrist*, 4th ed. Princeton: Princeton University Press, 1974.

Klages, Ludwig. *Die Psychologischen Errungenschaften Nietzsches*. In *Samtliche Werke*, vol. 5. Bonn: Bouvier, 1979.

Klossowski, Pierre. "Nietzsche's Experience of the Eternal Return." Translated by Allen Weiss. In *The New Nietzsche*, edited by David Allison, pp. 107–120. New York: Dell Publishing Co., 1977.

Kofman, Sarah. "Metaphor, Symbol, Metamorphosis." Translated by David Allison. In *The New Nietzsche*, edited by David Allison, pp. 201–214. New York: Dell Publishing Co., 1977.

Krell, David. "Heidegger Nietzsche Hegel." *Nietzsche-Studien* 5 (1976):255–262.

Kutzner, Heinrich. *Nietzsche*. Hildeheim: Gerstenberg, 1978.

Lea, F. A. *The Tragic Philosopher: A Study of Friedrich Nietzsche*. London: Methuen and Co., 1957.

Lingus, Alphonso. "The Will to Power." In *The New Nietzsche*, edited by David Allison, pp. 37–63. New York: Dell Publishing Co., 1977.

Löwith, Karl. *From Hegel to Nietzsche*. Translated by David Green. Garden City, NJ: Doubleday, 1967.

Löwy, Michael. *Georg Lukács: From Romanticism to Bolshevism*. London: New Left Books, 1979.

Lukács, Georg. *The Destruction of Reason*. Translated by Peter Palmer. London: The Merlin Press, 1980.

MacIntyre, Alasdair. *After Virtue*. Notre Dame: University of Notre Dame Press, 1981.

Macpherson, C. B. *The Life and Times of Liberal Democracy*. Oxford: Oxford University Press, 1977.

Magnus, Bernd. *Heidegger's Metahistory of Philosophy*. The Hague: Martinus Nijhoff, 1970.

Magnus, Bernd. *Nietzsche's Existential Imperative*. Bloomington: Indiana University Press, 1978.

Magnus, Bernd. "Nietzsche's Philosophy in 1888: *The Will to Power* and the *Übermensch*." *Journal of the History of Philosophy* 24:1 (January 1986):79–98.

Marcuse, Herbert. *Eros and Civilization*. New York: Random House, 1962.

Marcuse, Herbert. "The Struggle against Liberalism in the Totalitarian View of the State." In *Negations*, translated by Jeremy Shapiro. Boston: Beacon, 1968.

Marx, Karl. "Notes on Adolph Wagner." In *Karl Marx: Texts on Method*, edited and translated by Terrell Carver, pp. 190–191. New York: Harper and Row, 1975.

Marx, Karl, and Engels, Frederick. *The Communist Manifesto*. In *Karl Marx: Selected Writings*, edited by David McLellan. Oxford: Oxford University Press, 1977.

Marx, Karl, and Engels, Frederick. *The German Ideology*. Moscow: Progress Publishers, 1976.

Mauer, Reinhart. "Nietzsche und die Kritische Theorie." *Nietzsche-Studien* 10/11 (1981–1982): 34–58.

McGinn, Robert. "Culture as Prophylactic: Nietzsche's *Birth of Tragedy* as Culture Criticism." *Nietzsche Studien* 4 (1975): 75–138.

Megill, Allan. "Foucault, Structuralism, and the Ends of History." *Journal of Modern History* 51 (September 1979): 451–503.

Mehring, Franz. Review of *Psychopathia Spiritualis* by Kurt Gisner. *Die Neue Zeit* 10:2 (1891–1892): 668–669.

Mehring, Franz. *Gesammelte Schriften*. Berlin: Dietz, 1960–1966.

Merquoir, José. *The Veil and the Mask: Essays on Culture and Ideology*. London: Routledge and Kegan Paul, 1979.

Mill, John Stuart. *Utilitarianism*. In *Utilitarianism, On Liberty, and Considerations on Representative Government*, edited by H. B. Action. London: J. M. Dent and Sons, 1972.

Miller, James. "Nietzsche and Marxism." *Telos* 37 (Fall 1978): 22–41.

Mitzman, Arthur. *The Iron Cage*. New York: Alfred A. Knopf, 1970.

Morgan, George. *What Nietzsche Means*. New York: Harper and Row, 1965.

Müller-Lauter, Wolfgang. *Nietzsche: Seine Philosophie der Gegensätze und die Gegensätze seiner Philosophie*. Berlin: Walter de Gruyter, 1971.

Müller-Lauter, Wolfgang. "Nietzsche Lehre vom Willen zur Macht." *Nietzsche-Studien* 3 (1974): 1–60.

Nehamas, Alexander. *Nietzsche: Life as Literature*. Cambridge, MA: Harvard University Press, 1985.

Nicholas, Marius Paul. *From Nietzsche Down to Hitler*. Translated by E. G. Echlin. Port Washington, NY: Kennikat Press, 1970.

Nolte, Ernst. *The Three Faces of Fascism*. New York: Holt, Reinhart, and Winston, 1966.

Olafson, Frederick. *Principles and Persons*. Baltimore: Johns Hopkins University Press, 1967.

Pangle, Thomas. "Nietzsche and Nihilism." *Review of Politics* 45:1 (January 1983): 45–70.

Bibliography

Pateman, Carole. *Participation and Democratic Theory*. Cambridge: Cambridge University Press, 1970.

Pateman, Carole. *The Problem of Political Obligation*. Chichester: John Wiley and Sons, 1979.

Peters, F. E. *Greek Philosophical Terms*. New York: New York University Press, 1967.

Polanyi, Michael. *Personal Knowledge*. London: Routledge and Kegan Paul, 1958.

Pütz, Peter. "Nietzsche im Lichte der Kritischen Theorie." *Nietzsche-Studien* 3 (1974): 175–191.

Rajchman, John. "Nietzsche, Foucault, and the Anarchism of Power." *Semiotext(e)* 3:1 (1978): 96–107.

Rosen, Stanley. *Nihilism: A Philosophical Essay*. New Haven: Yale University Press, 1969.

Röttges, Heinz. *Nietzsche und die Dialektik der Aufklärung*. Berlin: Walter de Gruyter, 1972.

Sabine, George. *A History of Political Theory*, 4th ed. Hinsdale, IL: Dryden Press, 1973.

Sautet, Marc. *Nietzsche et la Commune*. Paris: Le Sycamore, 1981.

Schacht, Richard. "Nietzsche and Nihilism." In *Nietzsche*, edited by Robert Solomon, pp. 58–82. Garden City, NY: Doubleday, 1973.

Schacht, Richard. *Nietzsche*. London: Routledge and Kegan Paul, 1983.

Scharff, Robert. "Nietzsche and the 'Use' of History." *Man and World* 7:1 (February 1974): 67–77.

Scheler, Max. *Ressentiment*. Translated by William Holdheim. New York: Schocken, 1972.

Schmidt, Alfred. "Zur Frage der Dialektik in Nietzsches Erkenntnistheorie." In *Zeugnisse —Theodor W. Adorno zum Sechzigsten Geburtstag*, edited by Max Horkheimer, pp. 113–132. Frankfurt/M: Europäische Verlagsanstalt, 1963.

Schmidt, Alfred. "Praxis." In *Handbuch Philosophischer Grundbegriffe*, edited by Hermann Krings, Hans Michael Baumgartner, and Christopher Wild, vol. 2, pp. 1121–1129. Munich: Kösel Verlag, 1973.

Schutte, Ofelia. *Beyond Nihilism: Nietzsche without Masks*. Chicago: University of Chicago Press, 1984.

Shklar, Judith. "Subversive Genealogies." *Daedalus* 101:1 (Winter 1972): 129–154.

Simmel, Georg. *Schopenhauer und Nietzsche*. Leipzig: Duncker und Humbolt, 1907.

Simmel, Georg. *The Sociology of Georg Simmel*. Translated and edited by Kurt Wolff. Glencoe, IL: The Free Press, 1950.

Sokel, Walter. "The Political Uses and Abuses of Nietzsche in Walter Kaufmann's Image of Nietzsche." *Nietzsche-Studien* 12 (1983): 436–442.

Solomon, Robert. "Nietzsche, Nihilism, and Morality." In *Nietzsche*, edited by Robert Solomon, pp. 202–225. Garden City, NY: Doubleday, 1973.

Bibliography

Stambaugh, Joan. *Nietzsche's Thought of Eternal Return*. Baltimore: Johns Hopkins University Press, 1972.

Stern, J. P. *Nietzsche*. Glasgow: William Collins Sons, 1978.

Stern, J. P. *A Study of Nietzsche*. Cambridge: Cambridge University Press, 1979.

Stern, Peter. "Comment on Andrew's 'Theory and Practice in Marx and Nietzsche.'" *Political Theory* 4:4 (November 1976):506–509.

Strauss, Leo. *Natural Right and History*. Chicago: University of Chicago Press, 1953.

Strauss, Leo. "A Note on the Plan of Nietzsche's *Beyond Good and Evil*." *Interpretation* 3 (Winter 1973):97–113.

Strong, Tracy. *Friedrich Nietzsche and the Politics of Transfiguration*. Berkeley: University of California Press, 1975.

Strong, Tracy. "Language and Nihilism." *Theory and Society* 3 (1976):239–263.

Strong, Tracy. "Friedrich Wilhelm Nietzsche." In *The Blackwell Encyclopedia of Political Thought*, edited by David Miller et al, p. 358. Oxford: Basil Blackwell, 1987.

Thomas, R. Hinton. *Nietzsche in German Politics and Society, 1890–1914*. Manchester: Manchester University Press, 1983.

Turner, Bryan. "Nietzsche, Weber, and the Devaluation of Politics." *Sociological Review* 30 (1982):367–391.

Veyne, Paul. "Ideology According to Marx and According to Nietzsche." Translated by Jeane Ferguson. *Diogenes* 99 (Fall 1977):80–102.

Voegelin, Eric. "Nietzsche, the Crisis and the War." *The Journal of Politics* 6 (May 1944): 177–212.

Warnock, Mary. "Nietzsche's Conception of Truth." In *Nietzsche: Imagery and Thought*, edited by Malcolm Pasley, pp. 33–63. Berkeley: University of California Press, 1978.

Warren, Mark. "Max Weber's Liberalism for a Nietzschean World." *American Political Science Review* 82:1 (March 1988).

Waxler, Alice. *Emma Goldman: An Intimate Life*. New York: Pantheon Books, 1984.

Weber, Max. *From Max Weber*. Edited and translated by H. H. Gerth and C. Wright Mills. New York: Oxford University Press, 1946.

Weber, Max. *The Methodology of the Social Sciences*. Translated and edited by Edward Shils and Henry Finch. New York: The Free Press, 1949.

Weber, Max. *The Protestant Ethic and the Spirit of Capitalism*. Translated by Talcott Parsons. New York: Scribner's, 1958.

Weber, Max. *The Sociology of Religion*. Translated by Ephrain Fischift. Boston: Beacon Press, 1963.

Bibliography

Wechsler, Judith, ed. *On Aesthetics in Science*. Cambridge, MA: MIT Press, 1978.

White, Hayden. *Metahistory: The Historical Imagination in Nineteenth-Century Europe*. Baltimore: Johns Hopkins University Press, 1973.

Wilcox, John. *Truth and Value in Nietzsche*. Ann Arbor: University of Michigan Press, 1974.

Wittgenstein, Ludwig. *Philosophical Investigations*, 3rd ed. Translated by G. E. M. Anscombe. New York: Macmillan, 1968.

Index

incorporation of (*see* Rationalism,
Nietzsche's incorporation of)
and language, 53
and metaphor, 76, 181–183
needs for, 38–40, 147–152
Nietzsche's perspective theory of, 92–99,
102, 156
and nihilism, 13–17, 26, 38–40, 44–45
Platonic conception of, 33, 38–40, 147–152
political uses of, 235–237
positivist theory of, 54, 93–965, 98, 164,
166–167
and power, 90, 95–97, 156–157
pragmatist theory of, 93, 96–97
and value, 95–99, 156–157
will to, 38–40, 45, 105–106, 147–152, 163,
181, 192
Truthfulness, 37, 39, 151, 166
Turner, Bryan, 255

Übermensch, 160, 163, 206, 246, 290
Universal claims, 117–118, 121–122
Utilitarianism, 104–105, 107, 147, 152,
169–170, 173, 216–218
Utilitarians, 105, 107, 152
Utility
of interpretations, 133, 137, 145–150
Nietzsche's genealogical concept of, 108,
146
and pragmatism, 93, 97
social, 56

Value. *See also* Meaning
artistic production of, 179–180
bases in self-constituting practices/power
as agency, 9, 16–17, 30, 109, 114–115,
128–129, 156–157, 175–176, 192, 233–
236
historical determination of, 99–100,
108–110
metaphysical conceptions of, 32–33, 37–39
and truth, 37–39, 93–99
and will to power, 114–116, 233–236
Veyne, Paul, 290
Violence
as a basis of political institutions, 21–22,
36, 77, 231
as a cause of nihilism, 20–29
cultural refraction of, 20–22, 25–29, 31,
35, 41, 151, 217
justification of, 101–102
Voegelin, Eric, 157, 255

War, 22, 43, 70, 188–189, 282
Warnock, Mary, 94–95
Waxler, Alice, 287

Weber, Max, 28, 39, 126, 153, 156, 167,
175, 209, 232, 243–244, 258–259, 277,
283, 286
Wechsler, Judith, 282
White, Hayden, 82
Wilcox, John, 93, 261
Will
free (*see* Free will)
memory of (*see* Memory, of the will)
Schopenhauer's conception of, 10, 75
Will to power
as a basis for value, 114–116, 233–236
as cosmology, 132–136
as a creative/aesthetic principle, 112, 179,
188
and criteria for rational interpretation,
61–63, 90, 95–96, 129
as a critical ontology of practice, 11, 90,
95, 111, 114–116, 123–129, 152, 156, 179,
183, 243–246
and cultural evolution, 143–147, 241–242
and the eternal return, 191, 199, 273
and genealogy, 104, 109–110, 116
as history, 141–143
and human agency/subjectivity, 8–9, 111,
123, 113–116, 123–129, 136–141, 232–
233
as interpretation, 127–129, 136–141
as metaphysics, 33–34, 111–113, 116–117,
121, 132, 199, 207–209, 227–230
and moral agency, 168–169, 175–176,
234–235
as *pathos*, 112, 114, 127, 130–132, 134, 144
as *physis*, 132–136
as a principle of domination, 12, 112–114,
140–141, 207–209, 226–233
as a psychological principle, 111–112
as self-reflection/consciousness, 59,
127–129, 136–141
as totality, 132–133
Will to truth. *See* Truth, will to
Willing. *See also* Will to power
conditions of, 15, 17, 29–32, 64–65,
125–129, 136, 229–232
and the eternal return, 205–206
and history, 141–143
metaphysical conceptions of, 115–116
and moral agency, 170, 173–176
and nihilism, 16, 23, 29–32
and self-identity, 197, 128–129, 200–201,
206
Wittgenstein, Ludwig, 54
Women, 68, 181
Work. *See* Labor
Working classes. *See* Classes, working